MODX Revolution Building the Web Your Way

A Journey Through A Content Management Framework

W. Shawn Wilkerson

MODX Revolution Building the Web Your Way: A Journey Through a Content Management Framework

Published by Sanity Press, a Sanity LLC company (sanitypress.com), Daytona Beach, FL 32117.

Library of Congress Control Number: 2012914262

ISBN-13: 978-0985853204 (Sanity Press)

ISBN-10: 0985853204

Printed in the United States of America

First Printing: August 2012

07 06 05 04   4 3 2 1

Bulk Sales: Sanity Press offers discounts on this book when ordered in quantity for bulk purchases or special sales. For more information, please contact

> Sanity Press
>
> 1-386-322-7999
>
> sales@sanitypress.com

Abbreviated Contents

Contents

Part II: Live Projects

Part III: Administration

Part IV: Development

Appendices

About the Author

W. Shawn Wilkerson has been around most every aspect of the computer and web industries for almost three decades. His client list includes on-line gaming clans, small businesses, ministries and non profits of various sizes, international corporations, and most everything in between.

After two decades in the industry, he returned to school and achieved nine Associate of Science degrees in computer and internet technologies in five years. On the advice of two department chairs and a multitude of professors, he decided to pursue business degrees attached to technology, as the common opinion was the course content in the Computer, Networking, and Internet fields were beneath his skill set and would continue to be so, for quite some time.

In May of 2011, he was awarded a Bachelors in Applied Science in Supervision and Management, which prepares graduates to work for any international corporation on the planet. The BAS also gave insight into the clients perspective, including the uncertainty and fears many of them share when considering the unknown technology universe.

During the Summer of 2012, Shawn began his Masters in Technology Management and expects to graduate in 2014, probably with honors as he has for his ten previous scholastic endeavors.

Over the years, he has programmed in a multitude of languages, beginning in the days of COBOL, RPG, and FORTRAN. Eventually he moved on to C, C++, C##, .net and many others. He finally made the jump to web programming and on a typical day of development, is known to combine as many as six languages into a single application - many of which utilizing reusable code since his move to MODX Revolution in 2004.

He began writing articles for his personal web site (shawnwilkerson.com) and was asked to add it to the official MODX Documentation and eventually joined the official MODX Documentation Team. At the time, he was able to spend quite a few hours in IRC and in the forums helping others work out issues with early versions of MODX Revolution, which didn't go unnoticed.

As a result of his contributions and content on his site and in the official Documentation, a major book publisher contacted him with a concept they were working on for a new line of books. Eventually, this did not work out as the company in two other markets for the publisher, causing them to drop the rest of the projects they had begun under their auspicious - including the three hundred page forerunner of this book.

After spending three decades working with clients and almost two decades working with on-line technologies he has performed every job related to web production from server administration to project management and typically lives in the midst of a few thousand lines of code.

His unique style of writing combines mental imagery and plain common sense.

Dedicated to

Jesus Christ, without whom I would not be alive nor have any purpose.

Victoria Wilkerson, my wife, partner and best friend. No one else could possibly fill your shoes or take the place in my life you have. We have come so very far together and it keeps getting better. There is truly gold and other very rare minerals to be found in your heart and your life. Vickie, my princess, I love you so very much - savf.

My kids: Christina, Joshua, Kymberli, Heather, and Chris. My I continue to discover what you need and better serve you as a father, friend, and mentor - for as long as you will have me.

Monica Wilkerson, my mother, who allowed me to purchase my first computer: TI-99/4A, get on line with CompuServe in the 1980s, and who coaxed me into AFJROTC where I would meet the woman who be more to me than simply a wife.

William L. Wilkerson, my dad and most courageous man I know - never giving up.

Michael Wilkerson, my brother, for ever holding true to the ideal of family. Maybe now he'll understand how there is "so much to say about a computer program."

Jim and Becky Pelletier, life-time friends and Pastors, who continuously pay a very high cost so others can find their place in a very dark and cruel world. Thank you for taking the hit for wounds caused by others in the "ministry" and restoring as many who will come.

Acknowledgments

For building an amazing platform and allowing the rest of us to use it, I would like to formally thank the following individuals who spend countless hours building, expanding, and extending their platform as far as the technology will go:

Ryan Thrash, MODX, LLC CEO

Shaun McCormick, MODX Senior Developer   Jason Coward, MODX Chief Architect

Jay Gilmore, MODX Director of Marketing and Communications

The MODX Community

Preface

As having had decades of opportunity to fulfill many of the roles related to the computer and web industries, I hope to provide a resource which directly benefits site owners, designers, developers, novices and professionals alike – albeit some as a training manual and others as a quick reference. Keeping in step with MODX Revolution thinking, readers of this work can travel as far as they are willing - individually or as a team. The work should prove beneficial to a very wide audience with varying levels of experience, expertise and needs:

- ♦ Individuals who understand the basics of HTML but have little or no prior experience with Content Management Systems, Frameworks, and/or Platforms
- ♦ Those who wish to have a well rounded tool-set, which can grow with them
- ♦ Individuals who build extensive web applications, but would like to be able to build "into" an existing platform and reduce their overall development cycle
- ♦ System Analysts and Team Leaders looking to build a cohesive Web Team

University professors should be able to use this text as a foundation in which to work with students in their capstone, project management, and other web related classes. The structure of the first section is ideal for this purpose and can be conducted by establishing a goal, assigning each of the corresponding chapters to a team member, and selecting a team leader to "manage" the project taking the position to build an entire project as described in the *Quick Start* chapter. More advanced students could oversee many of these "managers" and their teams.

Developers and designers may even decide to provide a copy of this book to each of the members within their various teams as a basis of interaction. *MODX Revolution: Building The Web Your Way* provides a foundation for each person to better understand their own roles, as well as enabling each of them to perceive that role and its significance within the whole project.

MODX Revolution, by its very design, can be implemented to bridge many of the gaps found throughout the web industry. In many situations, these gaps are simply issues of tech-culture and an inability to communicate. While discussing various aspects of MODX Revolution, suggestions, perspectives, and experience may be found, which could serve in making each member more effective as they fulfil their role in the project.

I personally believe, overall efficiency within a web project team can be directly traced to their ability to inter-operate. Not only should each team member be able to expand their own skill-set, they should also be able to effectively interact with the various other members and components of a given project. The ability to coordinate efforts to where one individual or team can build directly towards the needs of the receiving individual or team can prove invaluable.

Purpose for this book

Essentially, there are very few who will read this work, who I have not had the pleasure of having had spent some time in shoes very similar to theirs. Hence, the main purpose of this work is to allow people to take a few steps in my shoes, sharing some of the experience and understanding I have acquired over the years with MODX Revolution.

This book is intended to introduce topics to the reader and also walk with them just far enough to where they can develop and try new things on their own. By no means should this work be considered the final authority, nor can any book be - especially with MODX Revolution which is extensible in every way. I have spent seven years working with this amazing product and simply desire to help others do the same.

My ultimate goal is to facilitate communication and organization while maintaining flexibility and security -- essentially help others be more productive. I am not here to preach or judge anyone, though I do have my own opinions which occasionally are on the strong side, but usually for good reason. Hopefully, I will meekly and gracefully share insight which is considered practical and valuable.

Where I fail to do this, please forgive me.

Audience and Scope

As with all technical works, we could diverge our attention in many different directions, eventually diluting the material into oblivion. I have had to make some assumptions as to the audience and have had to limit the amount of peripheral conversation to those topics which would directly facilitate the utilization and implementation of MODX Revolution.

As to audience, it is assumed that the reader has *some* experience with web site design and is somewhat familiar with (X)HTML and CSS. Previous experience with Content Management Systems is not required, although previous experience with MODX products may provide a reduced learning curve.

The ability to code in PHP is not necessary to implement MODX Revolution for many web project scenarios, but this knowledge or having access to someone who is willing to learn the API and produce very streamline code will strongly assist in the creation of dynamic applications. In those areas where we move into examples utilizing PHP, this assumption extends to having *some* experience with PHP also, specifically versions 5.2 and above. It is my intention to provide content that is easily understood by a wide range of people, even in **Part IV: Development**.

As this work centers around the implementation and interaction of various web technologies, actual instruction concerning (X)HTML, CSS, and PHP will be left to other venues. Having said this, it should be noted the developers of MODX Revolution went to great lengths in their design to ensure usability at just about all experience levels. *MODX Revolution: Building The Web Your Way* shares this goal in allowing the reader to get the information they need, without forcing them into areas they are uncomfortable with -- though we will get into more advanced topics as we go along as discussion in the latter parts will focus on implementation and less on explanation.

Each chapter begins with foundational concepts and may very well grow increasingly more complex as the examples and content is presented. Topics previously discussed and referenced in later chapters, will only be mentioned with regard to the relevant information necessary for the current example leaving the reader to return to the earlier content for more information. Feel free to use the index and table of contents to locate the topic where it is discussed in greater detail.

For those who would like to jump right in and start off running, feel free to jump to **Part II: Live Projects,** taking special note of the *Quick Start: Putting the Pieces Together* chapter, which moves very quickly through the various aspects of MODX Revolution, essentially demonstrating the various steps to quickly get a MODX Revolution project up and running.

Part 1: Foundations contains quite a bit of explanation and numerous examples

regarding each of the topics necessary to become familiar with MODX Revolution. Each chapter presents a single subject, intentionally building in complexity, while incorporating concepts presented in earlier chapters. This section should be considered a reference on utilizing the Manager and a primer on the implementation of the various Elements utilized in web projects.

Part II: Live Projects moves into real world development examples incorporating

jQuery, Ajax, Search Engine optimization, and various other topics for building better projects. In this area, I have endeavored to share concepts garnered from hundreds of projects. The topics presented may occasionally slip into the gray area of personal opinion and experience. Please feel free to treat these topics as introductory and not view them as the "only" methods to accomplish these tasks - especially with SEO.

Part III: Administration introduces the concepts and techniques to effectively

administrate a MODX Revolution project. Access Control Lists and other "difficult" topics are presented in a straightforward manner utilizing very familiar terminology to quickly establish concepts usually considered to be advanced simply due to their assumed complexity.

Part IV: Development takes a "stone tossed across water" view of building dynamic

PHP applications using MODX Revolution as a foundation. The areas of discovery range from the most commonly used methods in the API, to building third-party applications from scratch - including the xPDO schema and extending the generated classes into full applications.

Regardless of your skill level, this book was conceived with the idea of allowing you to begin at your current level of experience and continue as far as you would want to. The examples chosen for this book are intended to relate easily to a large number of readers. I intentionally refrained from using overly technical examples and verbiage so as to relate to a larger audience.

A word concerning Content Management

When choosing a Content Management application, project leaders should consider a few things: the perspective of the developers, the environment within the community, and how well the software matches the mission and vision of the company. Fortunately for us, the MODX developers purposely build applications which do not limit or overly define our interaction, and the MODX community appears to be set on pushing every boundary they can conceive.

Many Content Management Systems, seem to imply anyone is capable of building a web project. While this is true -- to a point, there is always a cost to master a skill and direct benefits which come *only* from doing so. What many web professionals take for granted, may have had an investment of years of college, combined with frustrated hours, days, or even weeks attempting to learn a new concept. This is magnified by MODX Revolution's ability to streamline work flows and package third-party content, which may inadvertently send the message what we do "is easy".

Throughout this work, many streamlined code examples and implementations will be discussed. If web professionals actually value their clients, they will not inadvertently communicate the simplicity of their involvement, skills, or tools. We should also not be unapproachable or exclusive. Project leaders should endeavor to make the client a part of the project, which is almost always mutually beneficial.

All too often, clients will take over their project and attempt to continue their development in-house -- usually in an effort to save cost. "After all, the web people make it look so easy." I have seen multinational corporations, clubs, and non-profits turn their sites over to a volunteer or their IT department only to watch the web site eventually get banned and removed from most of the search engines. The hard lesson for many of them: anyone can throw together a web project only a few understand the "laws" of the World Wide Web which can make the site successful.

MODX Revolution can serve as the foundation for a company to become very successful and profitable, while also providing a platform which allows its users to start where they are and grow into new things. Additionally, it facilitates partnership with clients, by possibly involving them in varying levels of the process, helping clients to clearly understand the value of having experts on board to protect and implement their best interests and represent their business to the masses.

I do not pretend or assume to present the final answer in any of the topics discussed in this book. I am simply presenting techniques and concepts which have proven reliable over time. As you progress through these pages you will undoubtedly find multiple methods presented to accomplish similar tasks. It is my hope, you will be encouraged in discovering even more of them for yourself. Once you have acquired a few of these techniques, your production should greatly increase and continue to do so as more techniques are added to your skill-set.

Welcome to MODX Revolution, settle in and get real comfortable. This is a wonderful place to discover the very edges of the web, your skills, and come together as a very effective team.

P A R T

I

Foundations

The first seven chapters encompass the basic building blocks and principles which can be utilized in any MODX Revolution web site project.

These chapters are intended to be both a reference manual and a practical discussion on each topic.

Real world examples and explanations are used throughout in hopes to clearly communicate each concept.

Introductions

The Manger

Templates

[[$chunks]]

[[*templateVariables]]

[[snippets]]

:filters

1

Introducing MODX Revolution

Early one morning, a teacher sits her young students around a table with the purpose of discussing the various forms of water. The students eagerly await the topic, each eyeing the various colored containers placed before them on the table and the beautiful pictures on the walls. She begins the lesson, by asking the students to describe what they see in the pictures. Various observations are offered by the students: rivers, oceans, rain, snow, thunderstorms, fishing, swimming, boating, sprinklers, showers, snow cones, and everyday ice.

"What do these things have in common?", asks the teacher.

After much discussion, one of the students slips his hand up.

"Joshua, what do you think these pictures have in common?", asks the teacher.

"All of that stuff is wet", said Joshua.

"Kymberli, why do you think that is?", asks the teacher.

"Are we getting snow cones", responded Kymberli.

"Not today, dear. Christina, do you have any ideas why everything is wet?", asks the teacher.

"I just see a bunch of water", replied Christina.

"Exactly. All of these pictures show different ways water appears and is used," concluded the teacher.

Similar to these examples of water, MODX Revolution can be customized to facilitate the individuals using it -- in just about any form they need it to. Of the dozens of products I have used during the last decade, none come close to this flexible, sensible, and powerful platform.

Welcome to MODX Revolution, where you really can build the web your way.

What is MODX Revolution?

The description from the project web site (modx.com): "*MODX Revolution is a Content Management System and platform for building websites and web applications. It is ideal for small and large scale projects alike. MODX is used by both non-programmers and programmers to build web solutions that can be easily managed by end users.*"

MODX Revolution is unique, in its ability to meet a prospective designer / developer where they are, while allowing them limitless means to expand their respective web projects and skill sets in any direction they can fathom. It is definitely not another application which eventually is outgrown and then simply discarded, followed by the senseless drudgery of "starting over". In effect, MODX Revolution was built for developers, of all skill levels, by developers.

To further help define MODX Revolution, I believe it to be the best combination for any web project consisting of three main ingredients:

1. Content management system (CMS)
2. Application platform
3. Sheer ingenuity

To a typical "hobbyist" / "beginner", MODX Revolution provides facilities such as WYSIWYG editors within the Manager and the ability to create simple and / or complex web sites. It also allows the convenience of a CMS, while offering the freedom to explore many of the web technologies being introduced, including HTML 5, CSS3, XHTML 2, and new technologies as they are introduced in the future.

MODX Revolution also serves as an extraordinary platform for many different internet technologies to coexists and operate at levels previously requiring much more effort and time. Once installed, immediate site production can commence, with minimal meetings and phone calls, including the inevitable wait for a response to the last e-mail sent to the client. A company with an established tool set can begin much of the development process - even without client content. Once functionality and project goals are determined, the designers can begin filling in the remaining aspects, even while they are still working on the flow and appearance of the site.

MODX Revolution is not:

♦ Intended as an upgrade to MODX Evolution or versions of MODX before version 2

♦ Limited to being a single user application

♦ Simply a "blog"

♦ Strictly intended for massive corporate sites

♦ A system which continually needs "hacked" for desired functionality

♦ Closed, thereby forcing a single method of execution or work flow

♦ Limited to the original application's developers expectations and thought patterns

♦ Obtrusive, heavy, or bloated

MODX Revolution is:

♦ A standalone product providing a solid Web platform

♦ A single *and* multi-user application

♦ A "blog" (and so much more)

♦ Utilized for corporate web sites

♦ Extendable and flexible

♦ Open, allowing multiple methods to accomplish the same task

♦ Limited only by choice and skill-set

♦ Built upon an open source API allowing complete freedom

♦ Established upon industry standards

♦ A solid foundation for any-sized web project

Astute readers may notice that some items are located in both lists. This is due to the fact that "out of the box" MODX Revolution is completely ready to serve the needs of the web project. For individuals who would like to set up a blog-style web site now, without being confined to such a limited concept, MODX Revolution allows the best of both worlds: a web blog and the necessary framework to extend the site. It can even allow tiers of bloggers within a single web project.

For corporate or community sites, MODX Revolution provides Access Control Lists (ACLs) and the grouping of documents and users, with varying levels of permissions within those groups. It also allows the "administrative" interface to be customized for specific tasks and roles, so that a user is only allowed to interact with content assigned to them by the project leaders. Do not concern yourself too much with this functionality, as understanding these concepts is not required or necessary to use MODX Revolution. The beauty of this amazing product is its ability to provide so much, but require only the skills necessary for the respective project.

MODX Revolution Rule #1: **Focus on utilizing and maximizing your strengths.**

Example MODX Revolution Web Projects

Over the years I have used many of the blog and Content Management Systems available on the web. After a while, it become a test to see how long it would be until I needed to hack the core files to provide functionality required by the client. Eventually, I began using MODX have never had to hack any of the MODX system files, resulting in greater productivity.

Many of our clients want very little to do with the actual design of their sites. In my experience, this is especially the case in smaller organizations and non-profits. These individuals will typically want to send a picture and some verbiage via e-mail or some other method and have it "magically" appear on the web site. The actual details and process are completely of no consequence to them. Others want the ability to control some of their content, while keeping scripts, code, and other content left to the "experts" and away from their own users.

Some projects will simply serve as a static web site which may or may not be periodically updated, while others will require daily updates with new content. I have even had the occasion to have clients wanting to handle the entire project in-house and simply served as the project leader working directly with a board of directors, owner, Chief Technology Officer (CTO) or other specified individual.

As organizations get larger the demand for specific content management applications may include department managers becoming "project leads" for a specific area of a web site utilizing their own web team. Some of their content may be accessible out side of the confines of the department, some of it will also be visible to employees in other departments, while remaining completely invisible to the rest of the visitors to the site.

The ability to assign MODX Revolution permissions throughout a site matching corporate policy may very well become a powerful tool, as indicated during the summer of 2010, when Shaun McCormick (Senior Developer, MODX) released a Microsoft Domain Controller add-on. MODX Revolution serves each of these needs very well.

Over recent years, my company has been asked to develop applications with the following and varied functionality: tracking systems for employees, vacation planning and purchases, Multiple Listing Service (MLS) front end for real estate agents, church / club membership systems, on-line publication as an alternative to spending thousands of dollars using the postal service, gaming clan sites, e-commerce, blogs, and even single page "business cards."

Additionally, we have been instrumental in utilizing MODX Revolution to translate decades of content for various ministries and historical societies into a web based format with the goal of prolonged life and enhanced exposure to their information. As a result, these sites typically proved to be a catalyst of increased donations and recognition to the respective clubs, especially clubs around specific niches, such as the stock car racers before the existence of NASCAR. Many of these types of organizations do not have "new" content. They simply desire to get their "message" to the masses.

In all these instances, an implementation of MODX Revolution has played a very pivotal roll in "revolutionizing" the effectiveness of the respective organization with regards to their intended audience. With close to a decade utilizing MODX, I firmly believe: MODX Revolution can facilitate the realization of any web-based conceptualization. I see it simply standing alone, positioned perfectly for cloud technologies, as well as the integration of new technologies.

What Sets MODX Revolution Apart?

By keeping the "data" away from the design, many are noticing an accelerated production schedule. Each individual assigned to a web project can finally design, develop, and implement their respective parts as a cohesive part of the whole, and not as a series of collisions, where the strongest survives.

Due to this enhanced level of collaboration, specialists can be brought in to handle mission critical applications, without providing them access to sensitive materials or content they are not directly interacting with. These experts can even be given accounts with "expiration dates". This allows new concepts, layouts, and implementations to be tested in the same platform as the "main" site, without downtime or the necessity of a complete site redesign or rebuild.

The freedom MODX Revolution provides is the first "feature" noticed by many coming from other systems. Far too many times in the MODX forums, or in one of the IRC channels has it been typed: "I do not know why I didn't move here before."

For those individuals and organizations having a single person responsible for the implementation of their web applications, MODX Revolution excels in separating the various web project activities, with the layout of the Manager, which is divided into different sections allowing a logical break from one "hat" to another. This helps facilitate work flow, keeping the items not currently being worked on, accessible but not dominating the attention or the view-port.

For those of us, who have requirements not directly provided by the Manger, the capability to create our own Custom Manager Interface has been provided. The default MODX Revolution Manager can be completely "removed" for a given user group and a "new" Manager interface created centered around a specific aspect of the project. An example of this could be a "User Manager" only having access to users, whereas a developer working with a credit card gateway API may not need access to any of the visitor areas of the site.

From the drop-down menus and user interface contained within the Manager to the actual core classes which define the entire platform, every aspect is completely capable of being customized and extended. MODX Revolution is one of the first products, which is intentionally meant to be "created" in the users image, or simply used as installed.

One of the most significant and unique characteristics of MODX Revolution is the very heart, soul and purpose of the MODX project leaders. Each of these amazing people, sincerely welcome and even encourage the community to push MODX Revolution as far as it can be. They will even jump in and help, when they have the time, to help any way they can, even though they now hope the community will take the lead in these endeavors. For my company, MODX Revolution simply enables us to build the web our way and so can you.

Simple File Structure

The MODX Revolution file structure is very simple. We will discuss the actual implementation of these directories in applicable chapters. In overview, the following should by remembered:

◆ **assets** contains content which is presented to site visitors via their browsers and may not appear until created

◆ **connectors** are typically JavaScript and PHP "interfaces" to the core class files

◆ **core** is the heart and soul of MODX Revolution -- these files should never need to be edited outside of contributing back to the project

◆ **manager** is where most of our design and development interaction with MODX Revolution will occur

Communication Facilitation

For well over a decade, I have worked with numerous ministries, small businesses, and international corporations and believe I have garnered some insight which may prove beneficial to each of the "hats" being worn in a project. For simplicity sake, I have taken the liberty to group the typical roles involved in web site development into two very generic groups: designers and developers. There are other peripheral disciplines which facilitate these main groups, such as photographers, marketing (design), server administration, SEO experts (developer), We shall simply focus on the main two groupings. Please understand these stereotypical representations are oversimplifications at best, as each "house" will have their own definitions.

Developers typically speak and think vastly different from designers, but make no mistake, developers are indeed artists. In a nutshell a developer tends to be a linear (bullet-point) thinker, which should be expected, as they are those who are assigned the task of working with markup languages and coding the "framework" of the content. Their work is typically structured and even rigid, while remaining flexible. Essentially, they execute a flow chart, work flow and / or outline following through its logic until it is "flawless." The work of an effective developer is considered an art form and can even have its own "signature".

Developers may feel as if they are working on one thing at a time and tend to see entire projects as a single thing with a single purpose. They also typically concern themselves with function and the transmittal of information – how it is used is usually of little consequence. Developers typically need to know the desired end result as early as possible and may occasionally look backwards from that result to a place to begin their task.

On the other side of the coin are the designers (including project leaders and site owners), who may very well be more abstract in their thinking, being much more concerned with the user interface and overall presentation of the site. Designers are typically tasked with communication and how people "feel" about something -- the emotional impact, as it were. More often than not designers are presented with "feeling" questions by clients. For them, a simple explanation on the direct benefit of a feature on the user experience is usually what ranks high on the priority list. Seldom, do these conversations stray into "how it works".

Very few people have the ability to wear both hats, but both viewpoints flowing in a cohesive theme is mandatory for a successful web application. At the onset it is best to understand the significant differences in these two mind sets. MODX Revolution provides ample opportunity for these individuals to work relatively close together – and to do so very successfully.

In some instances the design mind-set is apparent with the ability MODX Revolution provides to reuse code throughout a site to provide a consistent feel and flow. In others, project costs can easily be reduced as developers are enabled to off-load some of their requirements onto MODX Revolution and simply return a required response. This frees developers to build new applications much faster and designers to produce more concise presentations.

Streamlined Workflow

Of its many strengths, one in particular, serves well to bridge the gap between designers, developers, and project leaders, namely the Manager. As the very heart of everything MODX Revolution, the Manager lays out the web site graphically, so abstract thinkers can view and communicate the feel and flow they are needing. Simultaneously, the Manager, allows a developer to simply provide an expected result from their code without consideration for where it fits in the site, or even how it is to be used. Designers can simply relate a specific need to the developers or project leaders. The developer, in turn, can provide a solution and communication is facilitated as the project is being correctly transmitted as both parties need to understand it-- which is the way they perceive it.

Designers may appreciate that MODX Revolution is released without default content, Templates, or style sheets. In fact, MODX Revolution does not produce any (X)HTML or CSS on its own, and is "web-standards" neutral, in that it does not require, or even concern itself with how you design, or even what you use to design. It will even allow you to completely design "wrong", as it simply processes the content created or accessed by the project team. MODX Revolution also allows for the utmost demanding designs to be implemented at high levels of precision, thereby enabling designers to harness the strengths of a given web technology, without having to be concerned with one section of a site crippling or interfering with another.

Designers can easily create Templates with associated CSS files allowing entire sections of a web site to be "laid out" within minutes - not requiring each and every page to be approved for presentation, especially when they are using the same Template. By utilizing MODX Revolution, designers can easily remove repetitive design components into a separate single Element and be able to concentrate on the content which makes each page unique on the project.

The included MODX browser located in the Element tree should also prove invaluable for quickly adding or changing images, pdf, swf and other files in a given project, thereby limiting access to the file system. Additionally, FTP. SCP and other related technologies can be utilized to transfer static files to the site as well.

Developers should appreciate the facilities offered within MODX Revolution which intentionally empower them to code to their hearts content. Any technology compatible with PHP and HTML is readily accessible: JavaScript, PHP, XML, JSON – many directly via the Application Programming Interface (API). jQuery and other libraries can be utilized without regard to libraries already forced into usage by the CMS itself. Finally, a platform has emerged which allows experts in each discipline to craft their art in a way they see fit.

No longer, are developers forced to compromise their skill-sets, to the limited foresight content management software. No longer, will developers find themselves having to recreate the same application from one web project to another, as if they are "re inventing" the wheel. No longer, are developers forced to code a specific way, and within a given set of parameters.

MODX Revolution allows developers to directly work towards the goals of the project instead of being expected to spend excessive time "hacking" the product software to get it satisfactory. In many projects outside of the MODX family, substantial effort is exerted to "force" the CMS product to satisfy the needs of a large group or people. One of the "rules" concerning MODX Revolution is to *never* alter the core files. The associated belief held in the MODX community is: you should never have to.

Finally, the time has come where we can simply build applications without consideration for having to build a security framework, create or implement a methodology for handling documents, establish user account definitions, implement permissions or even have to come to a consensus of the way a project is to be laid out.

Collaboration can be extremely effective when executed correctly. One of the largest issues, which readily cause frustration, missed milestones, and budget overruns, is simply one of ineffective communication and redundant workflow. MODX Revolution removes many of these issues from the production experience by providing the common ground needed to work. We can work as autonomously or as corroboratively as the project demands or as our skill-sets require.

Project Resources

Community Web Sites	Project Leaders Personal Sites
Main project: modx.com	Ryan Thrash, CEO: thrash.me
Documentation: rtfm.modx.com	Shaun McCormick, Sr. Developer: splittingred.com
Forums: modx.com/forums	Jason Coward, Chief Architect: jasoncoward.com
API: api.modx.com	Jay Gilmore: jaygilmore.ca/
Bugtracker: tracker.modx.com	

Github https://github.com/modxcms/revolution

Sample Community Member Sites

bobsguides.com	codingpad.maryspad.com	sepiariver.ca
butter.com.hk	devtrench.com	shawnwilkerson.com
cmslesstraveled.com	gregorysmart.com	sottwell.com
cmstricks.com	modxrules.com	

Disclaimer: This list is simply provided for reference. At the time of this writing, these sites were active and some of the more prevalent MODX sites within the community. Additionally, many of them have been featured on the official MODX community web site, modx.com, as resources which should facilitate MODX Revolution implementation.

My Current Endeavours

I am actively involved as the sole developer of a social networking site built on top of MODX Revolution which will compete directly with major players on the web in their classifications. The first generation of this application took two years to develop when built under a very early version of MODX. Once I switched the project to MODX Revolution, I decided to restart the project learning the API on the way.

In less than two months, I was able to match much of the previous development. I was also able to start the base site with 80,000 "pages" represented in only four Resources. This base will probably grow to upwards to 100,000 "pages" with our needing to only use a dozen resources to manage all of the "load".

During the last few years, I have moved each of my projects from static (X)HTML and previous versions of MODX to MODX Revolution. Immediately we began to notice a huge drop in the amount of PHP code required in many of our older applications to as little as 10% of the original implementation. In many of these conversions we were able to retain all of functionally, and in many cases vastly increase functionality while still ending up with a much smaller code base. I consistently experience a huge reduction in PHP code under MODX Revolution – which translates to faster production and increased profits.

I also have a large amount of projects catering to non-profits and small businesses. Utilizing MODX Revolution, my company works with a wide array of these clients, finding cost-effective solutions which can be easily implemented while allowing protection to their data. The primary issue with these clients is the need to provide features which will satisfy site visitors, while also keeping the cost within their budget.

One of our largest endeavors, was to establish a member system for site users which not only utilizes MODX, but also closely integrated with the MODX user. MODX Revolution has allowed me to take this concept way beyond the initial concepts. Eventually, this project can grow into a global distributed network involving thousands of sites, while keeping data secure.

Personally, I have spent the last two years working with the project developers in bug tracking and in the official project documentation. I felt it necessary to dive head long into the depths of MODX Revolution and provide documentation for others to follow my steps at a quicker pace than I was capable of, due to the lack of documentation, hence my originally being asked to write this book by a major book publisher.

There was little or no documentation when I started using MODX Revolution and my goal has been to help people implement and understand MODX Revolution. This book is a result of that pursuit.

In Summary

For many of you, much of this chapter contained terminology which may not have been familiar. Please feel free to take a moment to look through the various appendixes, especially the one on *MODX Revolution Terminology*. As you progress through these pages, content contained within the appendices may very well assist filling in necessary areas of information.

This chapter attempted to take a "satellite in orbit view" of this amazing product, as I intentionally tried to get you thinking outside the box. This is simply not another Content Management System. It can be found to be so much more.

For many users, the central issue with MODX Revolution quickly becomes an issue of *how we want* to progress in a project, instead of *what are we allowed to do*. Web applications utilizing the various tools provided within MODX Revolution, quickly take on art forms of their own as project leaders learn to craft projects to maximize their overall effectiveness, rather than feeling like every move is simply their working against the application software itself.

This flexibility comes from the very foundation of MODX Revolution. To my knowledge, this product is the only content management platform available, which was specifically designed from its inception as an extension to a database wrapper and therein created to work very closely with data, in various native forms.

As of yet, I have not found an application I could not build with MODX Revolution. It can easily handle any project from a single page "static" application to immense sites with tens of thousands of pages requiring continuous access to databases and other sources of information. The only question requiring an answer, *is how far do you want to take it?*

This is where MODX Revolution comes into its own: freedom.

I sincerely welcome you to MODX Revolution.

2

Discovering The Heart of MODX Revolution: The Manager

Beneath every web application built using MODX Revolution, abides a faithful servant. Trustworthy in every regard, this silent facilitator eagerly awaits the commands and needs of the project leaders. Simply known as The Manager, this servant exists to do one very important task: **provide the basis to maximize every project entrusted into it's very capable hands**. Similar in function to the human body's circulatory system, the Manager transports the various components to their respective places within the "body" of the web site, while also combining them into a single organism.

To better understand MODX Revolution's Manager, we shall first take a glimpse at some of the older versions, so people making the move to the newer MODX product will be able to visualize the differences. Some of the basic familiarity remains, but there is so much more to be found under the hood.

The Evolution of MODX Managers

The MODX family has been in development since 2004 and began after philosophical differences caused the MODX founders to split from the Etomite project. Since that time, many changes have transpired with the MODX Project, including the release of a second product written from the ground up to be extensible and completely customized. Before we get ahead of ourselves, let's take a short stroll down memory lane.

MODX .0.9.6.3 was very similar to the earliest MODX Managers. and came bundled with MooTools and default web site content. For those moving from Evolution to Revolution the basic layout theory is left unchanged, with the screen divided into three main areas, having much in common with the newest MODX products, albeit without MooTools.

MODX 1.0.0.0 began the implementation of new terminology found throughout MODX Revolution. The paths between two products be-

gan around the advent of this product. For MODX products prior to Revolution, users were presented with multiple tiers of menus, each presenting various options to the user. An issue I had with these versions of MODX was that each tier represented multiple layers of site interaction. For example the "Site" menu opened a sub-tier of options containing various site-wide administrative functions. Similar functions were also found within the same

tier as the original "Site" menu and again in the tabs located within the right panel. I felt as if too much of the view port was dedicated to functions which could be streamlined into a more succinct and functional presentation.

Even with these "issues", the Manager found within these older versions of MODX was thought by many to be better than any competing product. The ability to approach the web project through this intuitive graphical user interface was refreshing and allowed much simpler work flows than previously seen in only but a few Content Management Systems.

For example, to add a new document, a user would simply select the "New Resource" menu and be presented with a very simple form including a WYSIWYG editor, and options defining the placement and details of a given Resource.

Alternately, by right clicking on a preexisting Resource in the left Resource tree, the user would be presented with a context menu providing direct access to any associated function directly relating to that specific Resource. This provided the ability to immediately place a Resource as a subordinate of any other Resource within the site – with very little effort.

This functionality would eventually be seen as the beginning of something much larger and would soon be transformed again. MODX Revolution would take this functionality and apply it in very innovative ways: allowing user specific customization.

Considerations

For those who are joining a web project designed and implemented with MODX Revolution, there are a few things to understand before moving forward. Unlike many other Content Management Systems and Frameworks, MODX Revolution enables site administrators to provide access to only those Components, Elements, and Resources deemed necessary for an individual or group of individuals.

The entire Manager is capable of being edited, replaced, themed, restricted, and even moved. Various display items may not even be created for the interface for a specific user or group, while it is for others. Additionally, there is also no simple workaround or hack available or even possible, as far as the author is aware, to circumvent the security mechanisms built into MODX Revolution - assuming the project's security implementation is sound.

In regard to this high level of customization, it may be advisable to install a copy of MODX Revolution on a localized, dedicated, or shared server where the reader is the actual site administrator. The examples provided within this chapter, and by extension this book, assume the reader has complete access to each of the Elements discussed by the various topics. A default installation of the Revolution Manager, as well as the default location within the site context: namely domain.com/manager is expected. In any case, a fully operational install of MODX Revolution is required to maximize the effectiveness of this material.

An additional thought before we move forward: after successfully installing MODX Revolution a link is provided offering the ability to log into the Manager. The installer provides an option to delete the setup directory and should typically be selected as to avoid various security issues or malicious site destruction by an individual re-installing a clean copy of MODX Revolution over the top of the version currently installed – possibly destroying the data within the database. The utilization of an FTP client, ssh shell, or even a web browser based application, such as the one included with MODX Revolution and in many control panels, will also suffice. The Traditional download versions, are preconfigured to simply remove the setup folder by default.

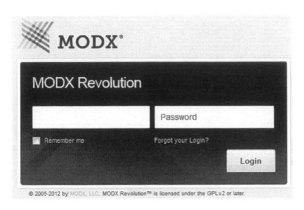

Upon clicking this link or visiting domain.com/ manager we are taunted with the defender of the "Holy Grail" of Content Management Systems: the MODX Revolution Manager. Successful authentication will afford us with opportunity rarely experienced by any mortal in the web world: freedom.

As a side note, the developers utilize this "light" web page to also load much of the JavaScript required by the Manager, thereby reducing the initial load time when it is initially accessed by caching the necessary files to the web browser and MODX Revolution's internal mechanism.

Welcome Screen

The official "Welcome Screen" is displayed the first time the Manager is accessed and is also available by simply visiting http://misc. modx.com/revolution/welcome.22.html. This short document provides a quick summary overview of various topics which are typically of interest to those who have not previously installed MODX Revolution. While reading the default welcome screen is surely helpful, it may also introduce unfamiliar concepts and terminology, which Appendix A: MODX Revolution Terminology should help with.

☞ TIP: WELCOME SCREEN TAKE AWAY CONCEPT

Users interact with much of the Manager content by right-clicking or double left-clicking.

The argument could be made, as this screen appears only once and to the first user to login to the manager, this user is the site administrator, but this may not necessarily be the case. For our purposes we will simply assume the first person to log into the MODX Revolution Manager, is actually the site administrator, as it will be on most implementations, unless an alternative solution, such as externally injecting users into the database, has occurred.

The MODX Revolution Manager

In MODX Revolution, the Manager has been completely rewritten, streamlined, and also simplified. The initial screen is known as the user's Dashboard, providing instant access to all areas of the site, its settings, user information, and quick views of current active users, recent additions / edits of documentation, MODX related news and security notifications. Users making the transition from other MODX products should find the layout familiar enough to facilitate an immediate awareness of the general location of key functions. A brief overview appears below:

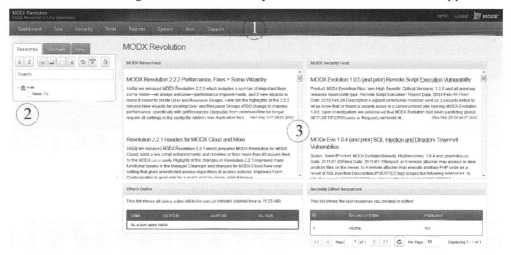

1. **"Global Menu"** available from within all areas of the Manager and comprises the "administrative" function of the web project. Production web sites with multiple users may need to implement Access Control Lists to limit user accessibility.

2. **"Site Component and Resource Trees"** provides direct access to the various items associated with actual web site content. The Home page, Base Template and access to the default Media Source should be available.

3. **"Display Area"** is the largest portion of the screen and where the vast majority of interaction with the Manager takes place. The default installation contains five Widgets, typically catering to site administrators.

⊤ *Note: THIS SCREEN IS COMPLETELY CUSTOMIZABLE*

Alternate Dashboards may be implemented for User Groups containing Widgets to directly address and facilitate Manager user when they log in.

Exploring the Menu

Our tour will begin with the Global Menu area located at the top of the screen. During this chapter, we will briefly take a look at each menu option and describe its basic functionality. The remaining two areas, Site Component and Resource Trees and Display Area, are utilized extensively throughout the remainder pages of this book.

Dashboard

This button simply returns the user to the "landing page" presented to them during their log in providing access to all aspects of the web project they have been given permission to. As we shall see in Chapter 14, Dashboards can become a powerful tool to limit the access to sensitive components of the web project. Suffice to say, Widgets can come from third-party components, custom built PHP (Snippets, in-line code, or external files) and (X)HTML.

Site Menu

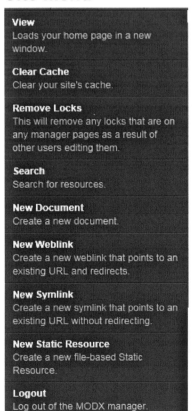

The Site Menu provides functionality with a focus on the top or root level of the project. All of the interaction provided by this menu typically interacts with the entire site or adds new content to the top level of it.

View opens a new tab or web browser window opened at the home page of the web site which is typically found in the "web" Context. This is quite handy when working with content which alters or replaces the content on the "home" page or to browse a fresh copy of the site in a new browser tab during site updates.

Clear Cache empties the cache content from the /core/ cache directory. Essentially, this option removes all of the cached site content from the directories found within the /core/ cache folder and resets the cache index, but has no effect on browser cache or other web server caching mechanisms.

This may very well become one of the most used buttons in the Manager menus by any site administrator. Occasionally, updates to web site content "refuse" to show up or produce the desired action to the site visitor. At other times, it may be necessary to simply empty the cache to ensure that a new feature is working as expected. When something is not working the way you would expect it to, the first suggestion often presented in the forums and IRC is to clear the cache. Doing so as a first response to unexpected behavior, may very well save time waiting on a response to a bug report or a request made in the MODX community forums.

MODX Revolution 2.0.3 introduced a cache busting mechanism which relieves many of the issues surrounding product upgrades, which simply adds the current Revolution version number to the Manager's JavaScript calls. Later versions no longer require clearing the cache and flushing permissions as a prerequisite for performing upgrades to MODX Revolution.

☞ CONSIDER THE CACHE FIRST

When in doubt clear the site cache, before doing anything else. Additionally, try another web browser to see if the issue is reproduced, as the browser cache might be the culprit. Lastly, the suspected offending Element may need to be called uncached.

Remove Locks allows items left in a "dirty" state to be set "clean" allowing future edits. Occasionally, technology and human error enter the situation and documents are left stuck in the middle of an edit: network connections get interrupted, internet routers time out, computers may get infected with viruses, forced operating system updates and other technology related events may very well interrupt the edit in progress. There are also human related events such as closing the browser by accident. Additionally, the resource itself might currently be in the middle of an edit by another user. Remove Locks allows for a document to be unlocked and edited by the administrator. Also, please note: the ability of a cat to simultaneously stand on the Alt and F4 keys is probably not an act of God, but your experience may be otherwise.

Search defaults to a complete listing of all the resources, within a given MODX Revolution installation and allows extremely accurate searches of site content.

The result set is dynamic and allows: sorting by clicking on the column titles, the exclusion of columns by choosing the Columns sub menu within any column drop-down list and can be filtered by simply adding check marks to the Published and other check boxes. This should quickly reduce the list of Resources to a much smaller number. Of particular interest to many site administrators may be the Unpublished and Deleted options, which provide a very quick overview of documents currently in either of these stages within the site structure.

This information may be subject to Access Control List permissions assigned to a user. MODX Revolution allows permission configurations where a user may be able to create a document but not publish it, while others might delete documents but not purge them. This layer of protection allows the administrator to make the final decision concerning these documents. Additionally, the ability to search Resources for key words in the title, long title and content is also provided. As MODX Revolution is capable of running multiple autonomous sites from within a single installation, take note of the significance of an installation verses a single site.

The **New Document**, **Weblink**, **Symlink**, and **Static Resource** options allow the creation of the primary types of Resources site visitors will interact with and defaults their placement to the root of the site.

◆ Document: a single web page within the site

◆ Weblink: typically to an external site, but also internal links

◆ Symlink: allows content to be displayed in multiple pages

◆ Static Resource: a link to a file typically on the file system

Many Manger users will opt for the ability to right-click within the Resource Tree to place the new content directly where they are needing it, but can always drag it into position later.

Logout essentially destroys the $_SESSION data stored on the web server, and the associated cookie information stored in the cache of the web browser attached. Revolution cookies connect the current logged-in user to a $_SESSION which is located in the session table of the MODX Revolution database. This is identical to the Logout button in the top right corner of the screen.

Components Menu

Various MODX **Add-ons**, also known as **Extras**, may optionally provide a Manager interface for working with their specific content, which is placed under the Component Menu. The availability of this Manager based interface is solely up to the author of the Component and is not mandatory whatsoever. Many Elements do not require it, and as such **this menu may not become available** until after the installation of one which does. Some sites may never have this menu.

An example of this functionality is found in the Quip snippet, which allows site visitors to comment on Articles or other site content. A Manager interface is supplied which allows for the moderation, removal, or deletion of visitor comments. Sites may implement a moderator role, providing access to the Quip interface within the Manager or the administrator may choose to monitor these directly. Very few Snippets currently require a Manager interface.

Security Menu

Manage Users
Add, update, and assign permissions to users.

Access Controls
Manage user groups, roles, and access policies.

Resource Groups
Manage the groups resources belong to.

Form Customization
Customize manager forms by security permissions.

Flush Permissions
Flush all permissions and reload the cache.

Flush All Sessions
Flush all sessions and logout all users.

For many web projects, security is of the utmost concern. Fortunately, MODX Revolution has a fully-functional, multiple-tier security framework which allows the creation of document and user groups with varying levels of permissions within those groups. It also allows user-specific rules to be implemented.

These abilities set MODX Revolution in a class apart from many of the other Content Management Systems currently in production. MODX Revolution natively provides this high level of user definition from its very core, where others kludge user groups or rely on a user contribution to add the functionality to the system.

MODX Revolution has site security built it into the foundation of the core, and has from its beginning.

Manage Users allows direct interaction with user accounts either individually or in a batch. As with all areas of the Manager, user management can be assigned and limited to only those individuals requiring access, such as the Human Resources department or a tech support group. All aspects of each user's account can be managed through this interface, including user groups, user-specific settings, and even extended information not natively provided within MODX Revolution. Extreme caution should be exercised whenever user management is considered and especially during its implementation (HIPAA for example).

Here you can choose which user you wish to edit.

New User	Bulk Actions ▾			Search	
☐ **ID**	**NAME**	**FULL NAME**	**EMAIL**	**ACTIVE**	**BLOCKED**
☐ 1	wshawn	Default Admin User	shawn@sanityllc.com	Yes	No

◁ ◁	Page 1 of 1 ▷ ▷	C	Per Page: 20	Displaying 1 - 1 of 1

The initial install of MODX Revolution, only creates the Administrators account. Accessing this menu will produce an interface similar to the one above. Notice the Search feature in the upper right corner which makes it possible to locate a specific user by entering part of their name, full name, or e-mail address into box provided. Simply hit enter / return on the keyboard to filter the list. As with many of the lists in the Manager, this list is also sortable by any column presented.

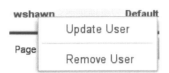

In situations where a user is violating site policy or simply becoming a problem, the Active and Blocked columns can be used directly to make any user inactive or to block them from the site altogether by simply right-clicking and choosing the appropriate setting. It will instantly be saved without requiring any further interaction. Changes can be made to multiple users simultaneously using the check boxes.

⊤ FIRST SECURITY CONCERN: CHOSE THE SITE ADMINISTRATORS NAME WISELY.

For added security, please use an imaginative name for the Site Administrator and avoid using common "administrator" names, such as: administrator, admin, root, su, boss, guest, user, webmaster, domain name, the primary user's name, etc.

For those individuals who used an administrators name which may be easily guessed, simply right-click on any of the columns associated with the account and select "Update User" to make changes. In response, MODX Revolution presents a screen with four tabs and approximately two dozen user specific geographic and demographic fields of information, which can be manually entered through this interface or captured during registration of other users.

Only the Username, Password, Active (check box), Full Name, and E-mail address is created for the administrator during the MODX Revolution installation.

Access Controls provide grouping, positional roles, and access policies. The combination

of these three components can be utilized to create a very expansive and complex set of permissions and access levels mirroring the business rules, corporate structures, or even allowing for high levels of collaboration. Additionally, simple "member only" areas can be created within minutes using the Policy Templates introduced in MODX Revolution 2.0.6-pl and the Access Wizards introduced in version 2.2.2-pl.

As with many access control systems, two default user groups have already been created for use within the site. The administrator account has full access to everything and can even create other administrators, as well as users at any access level. Administrators can also create new Access Control Lists (ACLs) as required by the project. **They will have to ensure they have access in the various control lists,** as new lists are created without users -- not even Administrators.

At the other end of the "food chain" is the anonymous user which has read-only status for any content typically not attached to an Access Policy. These users should never see or have access to the Manager application and are typically confined to the public side of the site.

Right-clicking a specific group produces a context menu to add users to the group, create a user group beneath the current selected group, and provides the ability to update the current user group. Note: users can also be added to groups from the Access Permissions tab, when updating the user's account within the Manage Users menu.

The first two of these options will produce simple popups requesting information. The final option, Update User Group, will send the user to a page dedicated to managing all facets of the user group. Please take caution when editing these groups. It is possible to lock the administrator out of a site or the Manager and also give the anonymous user the abilities of an administrator - edit duplicates of the default instead.

Resource Groups are comprised of "documents," though Weblinks, Static Resources, and Symlinks can also be added to these groups. There are many reasons for grouping documents, but they usually center around access permissions of some sort. An example of this is the creation of "member-only" pages or providing limited access to special areas within the web project, such as a photographer offering a specific client access to the photographs of only their event. The usage of Resource Groups is usually defined by necessity or project requirements.

Form Customization allows site administrators the freedom to change the actual presentation of various user-entry forms presented to Manager users. Often these changes will be associated with the creation and eventual update of Resources.

MODX Revolution 2.0.5pl and 2.0.6pl introduced hundreds of feature requests and updates. During these releases, the Form Customization process was greatly streamlined and simplified with the introduction of Form Customization Profiles.

Once a profile exists, it can be edited, duplicated, deactivated, or removed via a simple right-click on the name or description of the respective profile. Additionally, each of these profiles can be applied to a User Group, which allows administrators to customize the graphical user interface of the various components of the Manager based on Group Membership. For a simple web project this may appear to be overkill, but for corporate web sites with multiple departments responsible for a given Resource, this ability can make things extremely simple to implement.

For example, site administrators can attach the appropriate functionality to a set of components the respective group requires, while removing or write-protecting all components which are not theirs.

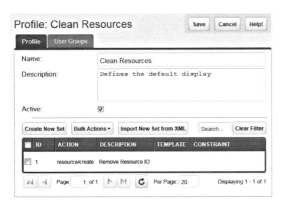

To illustrate this ability, I am going to alter the default appearance of the Create / Edit Resource Forms by removing fields which will not be used on the project. To accomplish this, I need to establish a Profile which will house the global Form Customizations being added to the site.

I also could have created this profile to deal with a specific User Group and simply named the profile after the group user level or a task designation: HR_Manager or HR_Interview.

Once a profile has been created, right-click the profile name or description and select Edit from the drop down menu.

Click the Create New Set button to create a new Action. At the minimum an Action and Description should be provided. A brief summary of each of the fields follows:

♦ Action: either Update or Create Resource

♦ Description: informative summary of rule purpose

♦ Template: restricts the rule to a specific template

♦ Constraint Field: activate rule based on listed field

♦ Constraint: is the value to test for in the field above

Upon saving our new rule, we are returned to the main Form Customization page, where we can choose to right-click and edit the rules applying any changes we may want. In the following example link_attributes (in the main-right set) and page id (unnecessary in Revo 2.2.2-pl) are set to invisible, while replacing the pagetitle and longtitle with more descriptive labels. Upon saving the Set, we can duplicate and simply change the action to Create to handle new Resources.

To configure the visibility of an item, simply utilize the provided check marks. To change the values contained in the Label and Default Value Columns, just double left-click the respective column and provide the desired text. There are two additional tabs available: a list of available Form Customization Regions, and any Template Variable which is available to this set - those unattached from any Templates and those given access to the Template designated. Note: on many of our projects we utilize an Autotag Template Variable for meta keywords and place it in the modx-resource-content Region. This area can also be used for additional Content areas.

Even though we have barely scratched the surface of Form Customization, we have covered the basic techniques which will allow very complex implementations. Feel free to experiment, and pay attention to the context clues as you move through the various options available for Form Customization.

Flush Permissions simply clears and resets the current logged in user permissions (the individual clicking the button). This can be very handy when working with groups and Access Control Lists, as new groups and permissions are established, the user can simply flush their permissions and MODX will update them with the new groups and ACLs which now apply. This can also work in the reverse: once an area is established and functioning as intended, a web master may be asked to remove themselves from that group. Essentially, Flush Permissions keeps the current user in sync with the security changes happening within a given site.

Flush All Sessions forces all users to log out, without their permission or interaction. Any pages currently being edited or other activity on the site will be interrupted at their current stage or status. This affects all users, including site administrators. Flushing all sessions removes the $_SESSION information and clears the MODX_session table in the database. Any change to site security may very well include this operation as a final step.

ᛏ *SECURITY DURING SITE UPGRADES*

As a prerequisite to upgrades of MODX Revolution prior to version 2.0.4-pl, it was necessary to clear the site cache (under the "Site" menu), and to "Flush all Sessions". This is no longer required as this has become the default action of the setup script and does not need the interaction of the site administrators.

Tools Menu

MODX Revolution offers Manager Users the ability to import files from the file-system into the web project. It also allows simple importing of "traditional" web site pages for those individuals finally making the transition to their first content management system or those who desire to import content from another site. For consistency across Elements, default properties can be created and added to any number of Chunks, Plugins, Snippets, Templates, and Template Variables used within a web project providing a simple means to establish a base set variables.

New to MODX Revolution 2.2.0-pl are Media Sources which allow site administrators to use most any internet provider as a source for media contents within the site. Many social networking platforms and cloud companies provide APIs which can be used to create Media Source Drivers, which should be available for installation via Package Management as they are developed in the community.

Import Resources utilizes files previously stored on the site's file system to create static links to those available Resources or as the source to import specified content from within them. The desired result can be selected by a Manager User while establishing the parameters for this tool to operate: **modStaticResource** are links to specific files on the file system, whereas **modDocument** imports the document and places a segment of content into the database and thereby no longer requires the original static file to remain on the file system.

Enter the base file path containing the files to import.	/home/williamw/public_html/assets/static
Select a modResource class for import:	modStaticResource
Specify a comma-delimited list of file extensions to import.	txt
Enter the root HTML element to import:	body
Parent Document:	0

The default directory for importing resources is core/import. In the example, I attempted to provide a path within the web space. Some sites may require this content to originate outside of web browsing space. In its current rendition, this tool would probably best serve as a means to automatically get a list of Resources within a certain area to be manually entered. Additionally, by adjusting the root element as the basis of import, users can limit the amount of content to that of a specific div tag or other area of the document. It is advisable to test settings on a single static file to achieve maximum results.

On occasion, we may choose to import various types of content into an unpublished Parent Document ID and gradually work our way through each Resource moving each into a permanent position after being edited. This helps keep site visitors from being inundated with a bunch of content which looks horrible and probably has broken href and img links.

In the past, we have also this tool as a means to insert the text output from cron scripts via restricted scripts to designated clients. This was an early method we used to provide access to nightly reports for our Resellers to monitor the amount of e-mails sent out of their accounts, the number of spam messages we blocked from the inboxes of their clients, site usage statistics, etc., proving to be a very effective way to transparently import the scripts already in use by clients while placing their content seamlessly in our new site.

This tool can provide a valuable Resource to quickly access file system based content and produce static or dynamic pages depending on implementation. Manager users will probably enjoy the simplicity provided by this tool to import file-based content. Regardless of the technic utilized, this tool allows us to limit the amount of human resources invested in moving static content from one format to another allowing us to get back to being productive.

Media Sources encapsulates files stored on the file system or with a third-party, web-based service provider accessed with the installation of a Media Source Driver, typically associated with cloud provisioning and with an Application Programming Interface (API). I suspect over the coming months we will see many of these drivers appearing in Package Management, requiring little more than an account at a vendor and the acquisition of keys to be supplied to the driver.

A fresh installation of MODX Revolution has a single Media Source and two Media Source Drivers. The Filesystem Media Source allows *all* Manager users complete access to *all* of the files on the site's file system. This could prove problematic for many web projects, as three of the directories have the potential for security issues, data destruction, or simply a non functioning web site - which client's tend to frown upon.

Media Sources greatly simplifies the process of restricting access to sensitive areas of files associated with the site. This has resulted in the deprecation of File System Settings used in Revo versions prior to 2.2.0.

I would strongly suggest changing the Access Permissions available to the default Filesystem Media Source:

♦ Right-click on it and select Update
♦ Click on the Access Permissions
♦ Change the User Group to Administrator
♦ Change the Minimum Role to the Super User
♦ Change the Policy to Media Source Admin

This immediately restricts the File tree from being usable by anyone other than Site Administrators. Typically, I would advise against editing any Component provided in a MODX Revolution installation, but in this instance I am willing to violate my rule to keep any "accidents" from happening. Additionally, this will establish a base template to create very specific Media Sources, while simultaneously forcing it to the Site Administrator, which should serve well to remind us to change the settings to the applicable group, user role, and policy.

After saving the changes, I would next recommend duplicating the Filesystem Media Source and creating one with access limited to only the assets/ directory of the web project, thereby keeping everyone out of the critical areas of the file system which could comprise site security and integrity.

We will revisit Media Sources in later chapters, but at this point in our journey we are taking a tour of the MODX Revolution Manager, not necessarily getting into application or site security.

Media Sources will play a huge role in MODX 3.0 when it is released. In the future we will see very elaborate and effective implementations built on MODX Revolution web sites, because Media Sources provide a gateway to the World Wide Web and all it has to offer - including future technologies.

Import HTML allows site administrators to import content from other sites via static files located within the file system. Simply upload the directory tree of the site to the core/import directory, select the HTML parent element to import, and the location for the content to appear within the current site. This tool specifically is designed to work with (X)HTML content, hence its name and is very effective in retrieving the primary section of content specific to a given page.

For those who are fortunate enough to be importing content with a dedicated content wrapper, the process is expedited by using the <div id="content"> as the parent. In any case, an expectation should exist, which requires the editing of imported content to some extent.

Additionally, it may prove advantageous to create an unpublished Resource within the document tree to use as a temporary home for the imported content. Each of the child documents will inherit the Template of the parent Resource by default. This will expedite the process as each imported document can already have the desired Template assigned, simply by having the temporary parent document use the Template the new content will use. After each page has been successfully tested for use within the site, it can easily be moved to its permanent home and set as published.

Property Sets allow for the grouping of properties, which can be used on a per element basis and / or across various elements within the site. By definition, a property, is a value passed to an element which is in turn utilized by that Element to provide output. Simply stated, a property is a value assigned to a variable used by an Element.

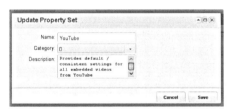

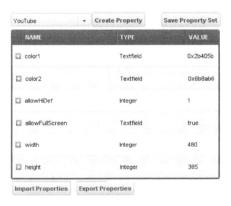

For example, Many web sites have embedded videos from one of the many video sharing sites found on the Web. Our goal is to create a consistent interface throughout our site. To do so we can add properties to a "YouTube" Property Set which define the width, height, color, and other attributes of the embedded videos. In essence, the only attribute left undefined is the actual video id number.

By using a Property Set, we can provide the basis of a consistent presentation throughout the site. As with most of the items in the Manager, simply right-click to edit or to find context menus. Also, make sure the Property Set is saved before leaving the screen or the options will be lost.

The ability to export and import these settings allows for easy transfer between sites. Please note: **All import operations will overwrite any preexisting settings having the same name**. This MODX Revolution tool examples one simple method which can be used in creating a very effective tool set.

Reports Menu

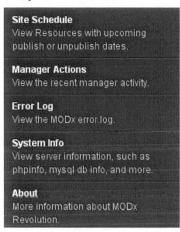

Site Schedule
View Resources with upcoming publish or unpublish dates.

Manager Actions
View the recent manager activity.

Error Log
View the MODx error.log.

System Info
View server information, such as phpinfo, mysql db info, and more.

About
More information about MODx Revolution.

This section provides access to information regarding the various activities, events and issues associated with a given web site project. Site administrators, and other designated individuals, can monitor the many activities of Manager users, as well as site content. This may be one of the first places accessed to discover the basis of problems with a MODX Revolution web site.

Note: many of these areas should probably be considered for protection from many Manager users as some of them may inadvertently provide access to sensitive information. Other areas may simply be made read-only or completely inaccessible to non administrative users. These permissions can be established using MODX Revolution's ACLs.

Site Schedule tracks the Publish and Unpublished dates of content throughout the site which have been created utilizing these optional settings, located on the Page Settings Tab of any Resource. The purpose of content scheduling is define a window of opportunity for the content to be visible to site visitors.

This can best be understood, by thinking about a "Black Friday" sales advertisement for the day after Thanksgiving. These marketing campaigns are typically decided on months in advance, allowing the web team to implement the ads during the same time frame. In an academic scenario, Professors providing a quiz or final exam within a designated time could simply create the exam, schedule it and let the site do the grading. Ministries having guests or events could work up an advertisement campaign in advance, providing full information within the space.

Once the "event" begins, one Resource could end and another scheduled to take its place offering additional information, essentially creating a very fluid transfer from one "advertisement" to another. This could allow a "Featured Speaker" announcement containing event details to be seemingly replaced with "Get the DVD" or some other after event content. The added benefit of being implemented months or years in advance can become a powerful ally for a design team.

Fortunately for us, MODX Revolution provides this "all-seeing" tool to help us track all scheduled Resources within the project. Otherwise, this could be a very daunting task to track and monitor each of promotions created by the Marketing team.

Imagine an environment, where multiple product teams are constantly at work introducing new products and the associated site and media content. Now extend this idea into a global scenario with teams located around the globe.

This tool could save plenty of grief from the lives of site administrators and company owners.

Manager Actions tracks the activity of each Manager user by listing each of their actions, the object of interaction, and an associated time stamp. This report is populated by the content contained within the MODX_manager_log database table.

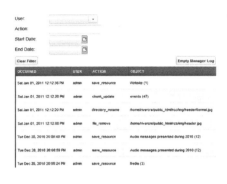

As more people become involved with the actual production and the various components of the web site, it becomes proportionately necessary to monitor and track the actual activities of a given individual. In situations such as a defacement or other undesired activity, it could prove beneficial to see which Manager activities were directly related. MODX Revolution is considered to be a very secure platform, but every application has a wide open security gap: people. In future versions of MODX Revolution, these unsavory activities should be able to "roll back" to a previous state as Resource versioning becomes implemented.

As with many functions of the Manager, filters can be applied to the Manager Log presentation to "drill" down to the content we are actually needing to see: a specific user, the action taken, and / or the associated dates. By applying additional options to our filter we can quickly discover when and how an event took place, as well as the individual associated with that action. This is definitely one of those areas we may want to exclude the majority of Manager users from being able to access.

Error Log provides direct access to the error implementation of the logging facility found within xPDO, and is stored in core/cache/logs/error.log. This information is saved as a text file on the file-system to ensure access in the very rare situations things go terribly wrong and access to the Manager and the database is not possible.

Under normal circumstances, MODX Revolution gracefully attempts to process and present a web page to the site visitor, even in the midst of errors. In the event of abnormal execution, errors are sent to the the main MODX Revolution error reporting mechanism which stores each occurrence within the error.log file. These errors are typically associated with PHP snippets and general MODX Revolution activity. This log may contain information concerning installs, upgrades, and the actual execution of PHP snippets installed within the site. Occasionally, it may also contain sensitive information which should not be publicly accessible.

Even though these MODX Revolution errors are contained within its cache folder, they may not be "cleared" when the site cache is cleared. Additionally, it should be noted that each of these files can get very large depending on the number of visits to the site, as well as the number of \ Resources in which the error appears. Periodically, these files should be checked and cleared to reduce the amount of storage required for those files.

In some situations it may prove advantageous to create a cron job which will append the content of the file to a master log and then remove this file on a scheduled interval. This may require root access to the web server itself.

It has been my experience, the vast majority of errors typically relate to a configuration issue with php.ini, which is referenced upon every PHP file being loaded and the execution of PHP Snippets. I would definitely recommend the Error Log Report to be accessed after any MODX Revolution installation to ensure there are no server errors already invading the Revo error log.

⊤ OTHER SOURCES OF ERRORS

There are other possible sources for errors which can be associated with a web site. The web server software itself may produce errors, in some situations those errors are stored in a single file at the root of the site, possibly named error_log. These files may also be created in the very directory the error occurred in. The actual location can be determined via the web server and php.ini configurations. The MODX Revolution Error log should probably be considered as exclusive to Revo itself, and not by any other error logging mechanisms.

System info provides information concerning core operations of the web site and contains direct access to system configuration values, database storage requirements, and a running log of content edited within the web site. This menu should also probably be considered for limited access.

The System info tab is divided into multiple sections, each containing a specific collection of information. The top section contains a link to phpinfo() which shows the current PHP configuration as defined in the php.ini file. Typically, users will use this file to ascertain the availability of a specific module or library extension to PHP. Other sections contain information concerning software version types and software specific configurations – such as the server's database server related information.

The Database tables tab provides a quick overview of the MODX Revolution database quickly revealing the number of records contained within each table, the data size of each respective table, and the size of each table's index. As information is stored within the database (i.e. Resources, Elements, and users being added to the site) these numbers should increase.

The Recent documents tab contains a running history of edits to Resources contained within the site. It simply displays the document's identification number, title, the user name of the last editor, and the last edit date. Eventually, this page may become more complex, move, or even replaced with an enhanced interface, as versioning and other scheduled enhancements are introduced within MODX Revolution.

System Menu

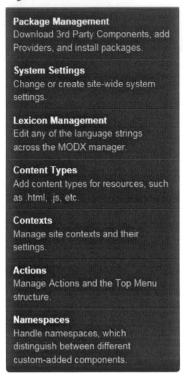

Package Management
Download 3rd Party Components, add Providers, and install packages.

System Settings
Change or create site-wide system settings.

Lexicon Management
Edit any of the language strings across the MODX manager.

Content Types
Add content types for resources, such as .html, .js, etc.

Contexts
Manage site contexts and their settings.

Actions
Manage Actions and the Top Menu structure.

Namespaces
Handle namespaces, which distinguish between different custom-added components.

Every web site has a heart and soul, a uniqueness all its own. If the Manager is truly the heart of MODX Revolution, then the System Menu is the viewport into the underlying system of that heart. From changing the way the system looks to modifying the methods used to present the web site content to the users, this menu handles much of the structure for many Revolution Sites.

Package Management is the gateway to many prepackaged elements which can simplify, extend, or otherwise enhance the web site project.

The vast majority of MODX Revolution users utilize a combination of three methods to extend their web projects with add-ons. The most direct and demanding of these methods requires the user or someone working within the project to program a PHP program which is then copied into the site in the form of a Snippet. Others, simply visit web sites containing MODX Revolution Snippets, github.com, or the repository located at modx.com and download a Snippet to include within their web sites. Using any of these methods, may require the user to manually upload the contents to the specified directory and to create a new Snippet which may also require additional configuration. Many of these types of files are simple stand-alone Snippets which were written to accomplish a singular task, usually very specific to the respective project.

Package Management is the simplest method to add functionality to a web project. With over a hundred options to select from, many users will find much of what is needed to complete or enhance their project located within the Package Management interface.

For our purposes we are going to walk through the installation of Wayfinder, a highly adaptive, customizable, and templated menu system used on web sites numbering in the tens-of-thousands around the globe. I have yet to find an implementation I could not fit Wayfinder directly into, it is an excellent example of great software. To install it, simply repeat the steps as indicated in the following:

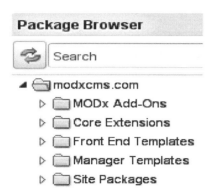

Package Browser

Search

▲ 🗐 modxcms.com
  ▷ 🗀 MODx Add-Ons
  ▷ 🗀 Core Extensions
  ▷ 🗀 Front End Templates
  ▷ 🗀 Manager Templates
  ▷ 🗀 Site Packages

1. Select "Download Extras" from the Package Management Screen

2. Using the Package browser, either begin typing Wayfinder in the Search box (hitting enter) or select the arrow next to MODX Add-Ons and then Navigation. Additionally, you may have noticed that Wayfinder is one of the most popular downloads and it is usually listed in the display area on the Package Browser start-up page.

3. Regardless of the method used, you should be presented with something very similar to:

Name	Version	Author	Released	Downloads
Wayfinder View Details	2.3.3-pl	splittingred	Oct 31, 2011	109,007

4. Clicking the green plus sign provides a summary description, whereas the Details button provides more information. Begin by reading these to understand the capabilities of the software. Note: many addons have documentation located at: `http://rtfm.MODX.com/display/ADDON/Home`.

5. Simply click the "Download" Button to retrieve the package and place it into the core/packages folder. If the download fails, ensure cURL is installed on the server.

6. Select "Finished". The package should be downloaded, but not installed. This is primarily to allow for many packages to be retrieved from the Package browser.

Name	Version	Release	Installed	Provider
Wayfinder Install Check For Updates Remove View Details	2.3.3	pl	Not Installed	modx.com

7. Select "Install" to complete the install process.

Repeat this process as necessary to install any of the add-ons in the MODX Revolution Repository. Note: some packages require additional steps, as required configuration settings are collected during the initial install such as an e-mail address to send notices to.

Upgrading Packages

When a package is first installed, the most recent version is automatically presented for download. Eventually, updates to add new features, fix bugs, or for any other imaginable reason may occur. Fortunately for us, this process is extremely straight-forward. By simply clicking the Yes link presented when an update is available, a Package can typically be upgraded within a few moments by following the on-screen prompts.

NAME	VERSION	RELEASE	INSTALLED	UPDATES AVAILABLE	PROVIDER	
wayfinder	2.1.1	rc1	Jul 27, 2010	Yes	modxcms.com	✖ Uninstall

Removing Packages

To uninstall Packages, simply click on the Uninstall Button. Three levels of removal are possible: uninstall, reinstall, or complete removal. Select the option which is most appropriate and continue from there. Much of the process is automated.

Name	Version	Release	Installed	Provider
Wayfinder	2.3.3	pl	Installed on May 28, 2012 01:02 PM	modx.com
Uninstall Reinstall Check For Updates Remove View Details				

Package Management Considerations

Additionally, web design houses may develop their own set of tools and establish their own repository by using the Add Provider option of the Provider tab on the main Package Management screen. By default, MODX Revolution ships with the ability to download packages solely from the "official" repository. It is also viable to look at PackMan to build your own packages.

Any additional repositories added by site developers should only be utilized from trusted sources. Please remember that Packages installed within the Package Manager will have direct access to the site and the underlying database tables. As a precautionary level of protection, it may prove beneficial to have a developer read through any code being placed into a site to ensure it is not violating security or privacy standards - Github is a great source of MODX Revolution packages.

For illustration, simply think of all of the cute little applications available on Facebook which have complete access to all the user's account information and the myriad of lawsuits and security warnings in the news. Similarly, it really is not that difficult to establish a remote MySQL connection and copy all of a web project's data to another web server via a Snippet once it has been installed by an individual with the appropriate security privileges, i.e. the site owner or administrator.

Fortunately, there are procedures in place, which help safeguard Packages offered within the Manager, but please remember this is only in place for the official repository. In the future additional repositories may very well go online. When in doubt, it would be best to make sure any Package being considered for installation to be subjected to community review and code evaluation. MODX LLC should only be expected to officially support the server hosting its own repository, and not the packages contained in the repository. They are definitely not responsible for any third-party repository.

All support issues should be directed to the respective add-on project leaders, individual package authors, community forums, github project site, and official documentation sites. Please expend all avenues of MODX community based support, and leave the MODX developers to focus on the MODX LLC Projects, such as MODX 3.0.

MODX Revolution Rule #2: **Add all you want, but keep only what you need.**

System Settings is the centralized "brain" behind the Manager, as the majority of settings are defined here and stored in the MODX_system_settings table of the MODX Revolution database. Initially, there are approximately 200 settings available. Fortunately for us, very few of these need to be altered to get a site project moving - and most of those are done for us by the MODX Revolution installer and setup scripts.

We would suggest only changing those fields requiring adjustment for the site to function. If the intent and purpose of a setting is not clear, please feel free to ask in the MODX forums, the #MODX IRC channel. Additionally, please check the official documentation for more information before making changes.

Many of the system settings directly affect the entire site, while others are limited to only the Snippet or other Element which initially created them. Site Administrators can even create their own settings for just about anything they would need to accomplish. Feel free to keep backups of the MODX Revolution database structure and experiment on a development test server before implementing changes on a live production server. It may also be a good idea to keep track of the previous values before the changes were made so they can be replaced if necessary. The end of the world may not be hastened if the MODX Revolution Settings end up afoul of desired specifications, but it can cause some frustrating moments until a resolution can be implemented.

Currently, all settings can be changed and subsequently located by either browsing the list or using the search box. Many of the entries contain a description which can be accessed via the green plus sign, located next to the name. The process to modify any of these settings is very straight forward.

Let us take a look at the steps to change the site name:

1. Type "name" in the Search box and hit the Enter Key (without the quotes)
2. Locate Site Name in the Name column (Revo 2.2.2-pl returns nine settings)
3. Using the left mouse button, double-click MODX Revolution in the Value column
4. Change the Name and press the Enter Key
5. The system is automatically updated with your change

Lexicon Management allows users to customize all language strings used within the Manager and many of the components which have created their own Lexicon entries. Additional languages are available for use within MODX Revolution. As with many Open Source projects, there is always a need for translators to create lexicons for their native language. For those craving a challenge: Klingon, Khuzdul, Elvish, Ancient, Pirate, and other language translations would be nice additions to MODX Revolution.

Content Types define the specific types of files utilized within the site. MODX Revolution includes many of the standard World Wide Web file formats. This example illustrates how to add the Adobe PDF format for use as a static resource within MODX Revolution. Most any MIME type can be added utilizing this method. For additional content types, the Apache project has an extensive list available by visiting their site found at : `http://svn.apache.org/repos/asf/httpd/httpd/trunk/docs/conf/mime.types`.

Contexts allow a site to be divided into "sections" based on any number of criteria. Some project leaders choose to implement a different Context for each language used within the site: English, French, Spanish, etc. Each section becomes its own "web site" with the ability of sharing Resources, Elements, and data throughout the site. Others choose to run multiple web sites from a single installation of MODX Revolution, with each site having its own users, content, and domain name. Additional examples might include creating a "store front" for customers, while creating a "business" site for employees, operating sub domains within a single MODX Revolution site, creating a member-only area where the entire face of the web site changes to reflect membership status or grouping, providing an Adobe Flash site and a non-Flash version. The possibilities and reasons to use Contexts are endless.

Actions allow the customization of Manager menus and associated actions on a per site basis. The changes initiated within this interface take affect immediately, but require a page refresh for all of the contents to be redrawn in their new locations. The most significant usage of the Actions menu would be to create and implement custom Manager pages.

The System Menu pictured at the beginning of this section, is from MODX Revolution 2.1pl. Astute readers may find that the menu structure in their specific version to differ to some extent from this menu, or any menu pictured in this chapter. Using Actions, the entire menu structure utilized in the Manager is easily and completely capable of being customized. Menu items can be reordered, moved, duplicated, or removed from any menu. Essentially, allowing project leaders to create the menu in any way necessary for the project to be successful.

Namespaces allow developers to group and isolate their Packages from other PHP Snippets, Components, MODX Revolution, and their respective System Settings. This helps eliminate any possibility of variable collision where one Snippet overwrites or alters another Snippet's values. For example, the Wayfinder Snippet, we installed previously, utilizes Namespaces, which also allow for easier configuration and implementation, as various sections of the Manager are dedicated entirely to it and are defined by the transport Vehicle.

User menu

This menu simply provides the current Manager user access to their own profile and any private messages which may have been sent to them from the system or other users. Interacting with other user accounts can be done by using Manage Users found under the Security menu.

Support menu

The first line of defense for many MODX Revolution Manager users, providing links directly to MODX resources: the community forums, official documentation, and the bug tracker. After multiple years of using MODX Revolution and assisting others with their installations I have found the following Support procedure to typically work the best:

1. Clear the site cache and see if issue persists
2. Try using another web browser
3. Try using another computer / operating system
4. Search the bug tracker: `http://tracker.modx.com/`
5. Search the forums: `http://forums.modx.com/`
6. Google an answer
7. Ask in IRC chat
8. Post a message in the MODX Forums
9. Get a cup of coffee or other beverage
10. Finish said beverage while taking a break
11. Rethink the situation
12. Check forum / IRC for response
13. Repeat any step as necessary (without violating conduct rules)
14. Once a solution has been found and implemented return to IRC and Forums
15. Post solution so others will understand the solution
16. Help the next person who has the same or similar issue
17. Hire me: `http://www.sanityllc.com/`

By following these steps, the site administrator will typically find themselves in a very favorable position to get the information they need, so they can move on to the next stage of their project. This will also allow them to access venues where one of the MODX Revolution developers or gurus to provide quick assistance.

Please do not make any attempt to skip any of these steps in an effort to get immediate attention from the MODX Revolution developers unless you are under a paid service contract with them. The project itself has enough work to keep them busy. It is better than probable, someone within the community can help you, and you never know who may be paying attention and able to quickly help out.

I have been known to pull a person into private chat in the #MODX channel to discuss their issue, only to be presented with the user name and password to the site. Within a few minutes I can usually get the issue resolved. *Please be careful who you hand your administrative access to.*

In Summary

The heart of MODX Revolution is the very extensive and capable Manager. We have seen how this amazing "control-center" provides direct access to the file system, web site Components, Resources, Elements, users, permissions, and third-party software. We have also taken a glance at the freedom offered to site administrators to customize the interface in almost any conceivable method and configuration. The Manager makes short work of editing user accounts, interacting with third-party software, and clearing the cache. During this chapter we have been introduced to many other Manager features and occasionally tipping our toes into the cool waters of Access Control Lists, site security, and administration.

Additionally, we have also learned that much of the functionality of the Manager, is usually as simple as a double-click of the left mouse button or a single right-click ([CTRL] - click on some Mac Products) to gain access to context menus. When all else fails, help is available on many of the pages and also via the support menu.

Lastly, as an added treat for those who made it this far, we would like to mention the little arrow between the Resource Tree and the main display area. This collapses the tree to give users more room to work. This process can also be easily reversed by clicking the companion arrow, which will appear once the Element tree is collapsed.

We have covered quite a bit of territory in this chapter and as a result we are now ready to begin actually using MODX Revolution.

Congratulations! Now on to the fun!

3

Creating Project Templates

Often entire areas of cities are modeled around a general theme or ethnic group. In some of these, housing sub-divisions are erected using modular homes or cookie cutter homes. The buildings appear to be similar, but each home is actually defined by its occupants and has its own unique characteristics. Essentially, this is the purpose of Templates: to provide a consistent presentation, while allowing content to have freedom of expression.

Concerning Templates

Many modern web sites have been moved to the XHTML 1.x transitional or strict types, in hopes of being easily upgraded as new technologies are introduced. Currently, standards are rapidly moving towards HTML5 and XHTML5, so the temptation to begin implementing areas of the site using these technologies may be expected by clients. For now we will be using XHTML 1 and eventually HTML5 in later chapters. Designers essentially establish a basic foundation and set of boundaries for the site when choosing which Document Type Definition (DTD) to use.

MODX Revolution is standards neutral and as such, is not concerned as to the method utilized by designers to create web content – it simply puts the pieces together. Additionally, MODX Revolution does not create or produce any HTML or any other web language, in and of itself, it is only parsing content referenced through the various Elements and Components added to the respective web site project via the Manager. This affords designers the freedom to utilize any structured markup language currently available, as well as those still in conceptual states - even targeting different technologies towards specific areas of the project Who knows, someone out there may still require HTML3, which can easily be accomplished with a dedicated Template.

For the cutting edge designers, many modern document type definitions strongly encourage the separation of content from presentation. MODX Revolution Templates enable us to take this one step further, by facilitating the separation of page structure, content, *and* associated styling.

MODX Revolution Templates

MODX Revolution allows any text to be used as a Template and does not require that text to actually mean anything. A web page of complete gibberish can be created by designers, parsed, and displayed for the world to see. There are of course two "very minor" issues which may be of concern to some site administrators and their respective clients: 1) search engines typically ignore gibberish and 2) people usually do not enjoy watching their web browser crash. If having a web site actually visited by search engines or humans is of any significance to the success of the web site project, we would suggest using industry standard (X)HTML to design the page Templates.

Any generation of HTML and XHTML will work within MODX Revolution, though it is the author's professional opinion that most modern web sites should use XHTML-1.0-Transitional / Strict as the bare minimum. As we are discussing the utilization of a Content Management Framework, there are extremely few reasons to use page frames, and as such we typically avoid frames at all costs. It has also been our experience, Google and other search engines typically do not value frames very highly and in some instances, will ban a site using them from their search index. The examples within this book should adhere to XHTML-1.0-Strict standards or better.

Template Inheritance

MODX Revolution defaults to allowing any Template to be used in any location within a web project. That being said, it should be explained that when a new page is created it will inherit the same Template as the parent document for the new Resource. At the top (root) of the site this infers, the default Template, as defined in the System Settings (under the System menu), will be assigned to all pages created at that level, unless a new Template is manually assigned during the creation of the individual resource. Assuming a parent document is assigned a new Template such as "blueSkies", via the drop down menu available for that purpose when a resource is created or edited, then its children will also have "blueSkies" as their default Template.

This feature of MODX Revolution functions the way many web projects are built – everything within a directory utilizing the same presentation mechanism. Bearing this in mind, from the outset, could actually reduce the overall production time of a web site. It is by no means an enjoyable experience to manually edit dozens of child resources to change their respective Templates, even if someone were able to do an update query via MySQL based on the `parent`.

The main point here is to plan ahead. It may not be entirely unreasonable to duplicate Templates and use copies of the original in each directory or area of a web site. It is indeed possible, a few months / years down the line, the project lead decides to have each directory themed differently, which could prove difficult to implement after the web site has "gone live." Flexibility often needs to be directly proportionate to the project's complexity and/or client size. Finding an efficient implementation of this flexibility can be a high-wire act – even on good days. Something as simple as the names utilized to refer to a specific Template or other Element can greatly hinder or facilitate a web project.

Naming Conventions

The acceptable *programming* practices associated with MODX Revolution requires the use of naming conventions which provide direct insight into function and purpose. Using this concept across all portions of our web project, even outside of actual programming, should prove highly effective to expedite its progress. By using colorful and descriptive names, non technical and technical users alike can more easily understand how things fit together within the web project.

MODX Revolution allows an optional description for many of the items created within the Manager, do so generously. Also, names and descriptions can be changed at any time.

The second major step for designers is typically to choose a name to refer to a Template. Previously we suggested a Template named "blueSkies". This may appear to be generic, but it could simply indicate the Template implements a blue theme based on sky imagery. Within the context of a specific web project it may be all that is needed. By understanding the purpose of "blueSkies", it should become apparent "greenForests" is a green theme centered around forest imagery.

For corporate web projects naming conventions should be considered even more critical. As sections of web projects are dedicated to divisions and their structures, it may become necessary to actually use the 50 character maximum length, as defined within the MODX_site_Templates table of the database. Often names such as hr_intake, hr_interview, hr_request, reps_order, reps_expenses, and reps_commissions are used to divide the Templates by department and function. This immediately aides in the site design, in that the valid use of a specific Template at a given location is simply indicated by its name. The Human Relations department can enjoy the simple prefix of hr_, whereas all content related to sales representatives can use reps_.

Ministries and non / not for profit organizations are usually more complex. Take membership for example. A church can have recognized members within their organization who regularly meet and interact. In terms of a web site, members can be from anywhere and not even directly related to the ministry itself. By implementing different Templates and naming them after the prospective groups, such as src_ for Sunrise Church and web_ for the members of a web site it should help differentiate between the two groups. Imagine if these two member groups were mixed or reversed. Internal church data could be accessed, as well as possibly creating other privacy issues.

It should be noted, that MODX Revolution includes facilities to handle groups of users as well as documents which directly relate to many of these issues. By creating names which communicate purpose and function, it provides an additional tool to verify the correct implementation of a component within the web site.

MODX Revolution Rule #3: **Choose names indicating function and purpose.**

Creating a Template

The process of creating a Template, for use within a MODX Revolution project, is typically straight-forward. For (X)HTML and CSS gurus this process can take just a few short minutes. Others may take much more time to get their first Template together. Many will revise and adjust a Template until they have it functioning as they have envisioned. Over time, an astute designer will have a hand full of Templates available as a starting point for most sites. Additionally, with experience and a broader understanding of MODX Revolution, these Templates should become more streamlined and standardized in their actual implementation.

Any typical text editor can be used to create Templates – free or commercial. Some will even choose to utilize the Templates included within their hosting package. Others may search the web for hours to find that perfect Template. For users of Adobe Dreamweaver, the process to convert the preexisting Templates to fully-functional MODX Revolution versions is extremely easy. A simple understanding of what is required to get a page working is all that is necessary.

As with many Content Management Systems, MODX Revolution utilizes standard (X)HTML Templates with formatted tags placed in key positions which are dynamically replaced with content and thereby result in a page presentation. Using these tags, designers are provided with immediate access to MODX Revolution configuration settings, resource settings, and user information for utilization within a web page. MODX Revolution provides hundreds of these keywords with the vast majority being optional. To best illustrate Templates, it may be best to look at a working example.

The default install of MODX Revolution provides a minimal Template which will serve nicely to introduce us to two of the types of document tags utilized within Templates and HTML [[$chunks]]. Hopefully, this section of anti-dramatic web page code is very familiar with the expected exclusion of the tags specific to MODX Revolution. As with many Content Manage Systems, much of the content is defined elsewhere and combined into a single tag.

Listing 03.01: default MODX Revolution Template

```
<html>
   <head>
        <title>[[++site_name]] - [[*pagetitle]]</title>
        <base href="[[++site_url]]" />
   </head>
   <body>
        [[*content]]
   </body>
</html>
```

Resource Tags

Recall that a document in MODX Revolution is called a Resource. This naming convention was selected based on the internationally accepted and standardized Uniform Resource Identifier (URI) nomenclature which specifies: *"a string of characters can be used to identify a resource via its location (URL) and its name (URN)"*. This should help clarify why documents, Static Resources and Weblinks are all referred to as Resources, as each of these can be accessed via the address bar of a web browser.

The default Template code introduces us to the resource tags: [[*pagetitle]] and [[*content]]. These particular tags are always associated with the current document being displayed in the web browser and originate as a new Resource is created from within the Manager. These values are stored in the MODX_site_content table allowing many of the column (field) names in this table to be directly accessed via the *field_name formatting demonstrated above. For simplicity, each respective field is consistently named within the Manager, the database, and as Resource tags.

It should be noted, that many of the fields are optional and may return empty if the field is, in fact, empty or comprised of a NULL value. Other fields are reportedly used for internal MODX Revolution functions and may not have a corresponding Resource tag, but are still available programmatically. For the time being, having access to the [[*pagetitle]] and [[*content]] will provide the majority of page content within most sites. The minimum Resource tag required to make a web page functional within MODX Revolution is the [[*content]] tag. All other resource tags are optional, though some are highly beneficial.

System Settings Tags

MODX Revolution is capable of running multiple domains, sites, and other derivatives within a single instance. It should be noted that the primary difference between System Tags and Resource Tags is an issue of scope.

System Tags are uniformly the same across an entire Context (defined in Appendix A), with each Context capable of having it's own set of System Tags as it overrides the base System Settings. Resource Tags are always related to that Resource – regardless of which Context it is found in.

In the last chapter, we were introduced to the concept of System Settings noting that the default installation of MODX Revolution has approximately 150 System Settings. We demonstrated a method to change the name of a web project and indicated that the new name is stored as a variable in the MODX_system_settings table of the database. Many of these settings can be directly accessed following the naming convention demonstrated with [[++site_name]], as all Systems Settings are prefixed with ++.

An additional difference between the System Setting Tag and the Resource Tag, is that none of the System Tags need to be included within a document for it to function. Both [[++site_name]] and [[++site_url]] could simply be replaced with straight text: Shawn's Website and http://www.shawnwilkerson.com/ respectively.

(X)HTML Tags

The majority of the default Template is straight W3C - brand HTML, which is typical of many of the Templates implemented within MODX Revolution Sites. Any HTML or (X)HTML tag specified by the W3C is usable, *keeping in mind that not all web browsers are created equally*. Periodic testing of Templates with test content should be mandatory, as well as validation testing. Web sites such as http://browsershots.org/ are great for letting designers see what a client sees. The W3C provides an on-line validation system, which can be found by visiting http://validator.w3.org/. There are also a host of other sites, in addition to similar functionality of many IDEs, which will validate and analyze the final page as well. It should be noted: the default Template should be edited, as it does not validate in its present form.

All Templates should implement the <base href> declaration, either with <base href="[[++site_url]]" />, <base href="http://domain.com" />, or <base href="/" />.

Storing Templates in the Manager

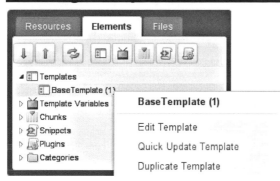

The default mechanism for working with Templates is located within the MODX Revolution Manager. To access this feature we first need to log into the website by visiting yourDomain.com/manager. Once inside the Manager, access the Elements tab located in the center of the Site Component and Resource Trees (left side of the display area).

Next we open the Templates tree by clicking the arrow next to the Templates option. In a default install, this should scroll down and provide an interface similar to the one indicated. By right-clicking the "BaseTemplate" option, we are presented with a context menu providing each of the options available regarding Templates. Go ahead and left-click "Edit" in the context menu or "BaseTemplate" in the Element Tree which will take us immediately to an Editor where we can view the default Template. This can also be accomplished by simply left clicking the name itself.

Text Editors

By default, MODX Revolution includes a plain text editor, as shown when viewing the "BaseTemplate." Initially, I would recommend leaving the default Template untouched, until you master creating MODX Revolution Templates. Optionally, the CodeMirror Package can be installed via the Package Manager in the System Menu, which provides some basic functionality.

If you prefer an editor on your computer and find yourself limited to notepad or some other simplified editor, visit the MODX Development Environment information page, located at http://rtfm.MODX.com/display/revolution21/Setting+up+a+Development+Environment to find a list of editors tested and used by the members of the MODX community.

Syntax highlighting is the main feature of interest here, but additional features like code completion, code suggestion, verification etc., are also nice. The more features the better, especially if they can be turned or off, as it makes reading and editing code much easier during those 18+ hour days. Please keep in mind, it may be wise to create a local backup of the default Template, as well as any other Templates created for web projects.

For future reference, the Template name is used within the Manager for display purposes only. The identification number displayed next to the Template name in the Element tree, is the only reference stored in the MODX_site_content table in the database. This means a Template can be renamed as much as desired without interrupting the web site or inadvertently breaking pages due to a naming mismatch.

Example XHTML 1.0 Strict Template

To get started we will begin by creating a new, somewhat typical, MODX Revolution Template for use on our site. We will be needing access to the Manager, so feel free to keep a Manager tab open in your web browser. Select Elements to move into the Element tree, right-click Templates and select Create a New Template and enter the following, saving it when finished:

Listing 03.02: RevoBook Template

```
<?xml version="1.0" encoding="UTF-8" ?>
<!DOCTYPE html PUBLIC "-//W3C//DTD XHTML 1.0 Strict//EN" "http://
www.w3.org/TR/xhtml1/DTD/xhtml1-strict.dtd">
<html xmlns="http://www.w3.org/1999/xhtml">
  <head>
        <meta http-equiv="Content-Type" content="text/html;
              charset=utf-8" />
        <title>[[++site_name]]'s [[*longtitle]]</title>
        <base href="[[++site_url]]" />
        <link rel="canonical" href="[[~[[*id]]]]"/>
        <meta name="author" content="W. Shawn Wilkerson" />
        <meta name="copyright" content="Copyright ©2010 W. Shawn
                              Wilkerson, All Rights Reserved" />
        <meta name="date" content="[[*publishedon]]" />
        <meta name="description" content="[[*description]] by W.
                              Shawn Wilkerson" />
        <meta name="keywords" content="word1, word2, word3" />
        <link type="text/css" rel="stylesheet" href="revo.css" />
  </head>
  <body>
   <div id="header">
   </div>
   <div id="container">
       <div id="mainContent">
           [[*content]]
       </div>
       <br class="clearfloat" />
       <div id="footer">
       </div>
   </div>
   </body>
</html>
```

Listing 03.03: RevoBook HTML5 Template

```
<!DOCTYPE html>
<html>
<head>
    <base href="[[++site_url]]"/>
    <meta charset="utf-8"/>
    <title>[[*pagetitle]]</title>
    <meta name="author" content="W. Shawn Wilkerson" />
    <meta name="revised" content="W. Wilkerson, [[*publishedon]]"/>
    <link type="text/css" rel="stylesheet" href="revo5.css" />
    <link rel="canonical" href="[[~[[*id]]]]"/>
    <!--[if IE]>
    <script src="//html5shiv.googlecode.com/svn/trunk/html5.js">
    </script>
    <![endif]-->
</head>
<body>
<header>
    <nav>
        [[- global navigation - this is to be a MODX Revo Comment ]]
    </nav>
    <div id="header_middle">

    </div>
</header>
<section class="main_content">
    <div id="container_wide">
            [[*content]]
    </div>
</section>
<br class="clear">
<footer>
      [[ - global footer element will go here]]
</footer>
</body>
</html>
```

W3C Validation

Before we do anything with this Template, we should probably take a minute to validate it. Using the left mouse button, click on the Resources tab, and then on Home. We are now going to change the Template for the Home page to use RevoBook instead of BaseTemplate. Simply use the drop down bar to Select the new Template. If it does not appear, there is a very distinct possibility the Template was not saved and the creation process will need to be repeated. Once the new Template is in place, save the document and select View.

Before panic sets in, remember that we have not began creating web pages or content and the default "Home" is indeed empty, hence, the bland, white, empty page. Copy the URL from the web browser address bar and use the W3C validator by visiting http://validator.w3.org/. Note: HTML5 validators are still a work in process. The page should correctly validate to XHTML Strict and provide a real friendly green "Passed" rating. Without any errors or warnings in our Template, this is a good starting point to begin working on the rest of the site.

Anyone who wants to live on the edge can simply type their name or whatever comes to mind in the content area of the Home Resource, save the document and then View the page. You should now have content appearing on the front of the web site. If you want to go all the way and leave nothing for the return trip, validate the web page with the new content and see if you continue to achieve the coveted green "Passed" recognition from the W3C. At this stage it may very well be prudent to print out the RevoBook Template and the source code from the preview of the "Home" page. Take interest in the changes between the various [[*resource]] and [[++system]] tags used in the RevoBook Template and the final page parsed by MODX Revolution. It also might be useful to use landscape page-layout and a color printer, if your editor supports this functionality.

In the web projects at my company, the use of any on-line based Rich Text Editors is strictly frowned upon – at least as far as designers and developers are concerned. Clients are another matter. There are three main reasons for this: 1) Any updates, overwrites, deletions, and other activities to sites are currently permanent. Once an Element is saved there is no going back. 2) If another Manager user (or ourselves) accesses and destroys our work of genius, we would have to resort to pulling it from a database backup – assuming there is one. 3) Rich Text Editors have a tendency to "fix" correct code. Note: versioning is in future plans for MODX Revolution.

To solve many of these issues before they turn into a perfect storm, we have established a company policy which requires all additions to the web site to be stored on a local system and backed up to a local server, before being put into MODX Revolution. There are many different methods used to have a local version of a web site. We would simply suggest: `type_name-date.ext` (template_Main-201104020.xhtml) or building sub-directories matching those used on the site or even using a directory to match the type of element being worked on (`templates\name-date.ext`). For us, each individual item is stored with a date after the name and before the extension and a combination of these solutions. Feel free to develop your own to suit your needs.

We also have another question which may eventually need to be answered, namely which Template is going to serve as the default Template of the site. Currently, the BaseTemplate is the default Template site wide. This can be remedied in a couple of ways:

1. Duplicate the default Template and rename the copy to something like MODX Default, followed by subsequently over writing the current BaseTemplate with our chosen default Template, and optionally renaming the Template as needed

2. Change the default Template setting in the System | Settings interface by using the drop-down menu.

Template Storage Alternatives

While slightly outside of the purview of this chapter, we should take a moment to mention a non-standard method of storing live Templates on a server.

Templates available via Package Management

We should probably mention, a number of Templates are conveniently available via Package Management located in the System menu. Click on Download Extras and select the Front-End Templates option near the bottom of the list. Be careful to honor the licenses attached to any MODX Revolution Addon.

Using Media Sources: Filesystem

Introduced in MODX Revolution 2.2 was the ability to store Elements using technologies and APIs from all over the web. Each medium can be defined in Media Sources and subsequently utilized through each Elements creation process. In regards to Templates, simply select the Is Static checkbox, and use the Static File (MODX Browser) to locate the file. This allows us to bypass using the Manager for subsequent modifications to the Template, as they can be simply uploaded via the IDE software, FTP, SFTP, SCP, etc.

You could also utilize your own cloud space to store and share Templates and other Elements.

Summary

MODX Revolution Templates can easily be imported via the Manager and provide a consistent presentation, while allowing content to have freedom of expression. Users may design web content using any available W3C standard, as well as any Document Type Definition (DTD) recognizable by web browsers. Multiple W3C standards can even be used within the same site. It is very important each Template utilizes the `<base href=" " />` tag.

Child documents will inherit the Template used by their parents, with the top level pages using the default Template for the site (or as defined via the context the Template is to be used in). By default, Templates can be utilized by any resource located anywhere within a web project and only need the `[[*content]]` tag to function. Many of the hundreds of MODX Revolution system and resource settings are available can greatly enhance and simplify the web design process, while predominantly remaining optional.

The names utilized to create Templates and the other components within a web project should speak to the function and purpose of the given item. Many of the MODX Revolution tags are so well named, that supporting documentation is seldom needed to ascertain their role within a web site. This habit should be developed and extensively exercised throughout the entire project.

Lastly, during this chapter we have been exposed to the vast majority of issues and topics related to Templates, while simultaneously weaving other topics into the discussion. In the process we managed to sneak something past many of you. Back in our RevoBook Templates, we stacked multiple Revolution tags together to create a variable which is changed on every page. This variable simply creates a link to the current page and is parsed from the inside out. First MODX Revolution gets the current document id, and then it creates a full path to it using the documents name: `[[~[[*id]]]]`.

This implementation represents a small sampling of the complexity which can be implemented with MODX Revolution using just its tags. Hopefully, this may be reason enough to explore these tags and to discover the power waiting to be found within MODX Revolution.

4

[[$Chunks]]:Simplifying Web Projects Using (X)HTML

"No one should ever find out our secret ingredient!", exclaimed the grandmother.

"But its only grape jelly," replied the little girl.

In kitchens around the globe, recipe cards are kept hidden under lock and key for the sole purpose of keeping the family secret. In many cases, these secrets are only handed down by word of mouth. So much effort is given to dissuade people from discovering "the truth." How many people have grape jelly in their kitchen? Is it really that hard to buy?

HTML [[$Chunks]] are very much like grape jelly. Many MODX Revolution Manager users have access to them. In some cases, they actually have access to the very same ones. The way the Chunk is implemented can be every bit as important as to the purpose it serves.

As common as these Chunks are, there are those who use them in very artful and complex ways to become very effective tools within their arsenal, to quickly implement solutions across a variety of web projects – without having to reinvent their recipe each time.

Very similar to a kitchen scenario, it is not the identity of ingredient which matters, but how it is used. In this chapter, various common implementations will be explored, hopefully establishing the necessary understanding to facilitate Manager users in creating complex and unique functionality.

The key to Chunks is not what they are, but how they are implemented.

Introducing (X)HTML [[$Chunks]]

The entire concept around using "Chunks" of HTML code is not new or even exclusive to MODX Revolution or even previous MODX products. Many Content Management Systems, blog software, and template engines (like Smarty) use blocks of (X)HTML to accomplish tasks and have done so for years.

Typically, each Chunk performs a single purpose and is similar in function to the "old-school" PHP and server-side includes which many have used for hit counters and global menu systems, which simply inject a section of HTML into a page to perform a task.

The significance of Chunks can best be seen in their inherent high level of re-usability, which can simplify and streamline web projects by establishing relationships or commonality between documents. Additionally, Chunks can provide a bridging mechanism between developers and the design team, which greatly enhances project communication and clarifies expectations.

By splitting larger sections of (X)HTML code into individual pieces, we are afforded the ability to decide which sections of our page will be cached. This directly benefits us as we are able to retrieve our cached content while allowing dynamic content to be created on the fly – effectively allowing us the best of both worlds.. There are even simple methods which can be implemented which will allow a chunk to only be seen on a specific page.

Additionally, we can also control the permissions available to various groups or individuals (edit, view, delete, no access) to any of our Chunks. By implementing MODX Revolution's Access Control Lists we can determine which individuals within the project can actually have "write" access to a Chunk. or simply turn off write access once a section is finalized.

Creating a Chunk

The vast majority of Chunks are probably created by manual entry and require little more than basic (X)HTML knowledge to implement. MODX Revolution, Chunks can be created in four primary ways: Package Management as part of the installation process of a MODX Revolution Package, during Snippet execution, file upload, and key entry.

Most any text editor could be used to produce the actual source code for the Chunk. Some people will simply opt to hand code it directly into a new Chunk Element without using an outside editor, while others will utilize software on a computer.

For my company, it has proven wise on many occasions to create the Chunks locally, and then copy them into the Chunk on the site. Having a local copy will help in situations when the Chunk Element has been accidentally overwritten or removed from the Manager. Additionally, it can readily be copied from one project to another with little effort – especially if we have established a set of Chunks for use on web sites.

By repeating each of the following steps, we can quickly create each of the Chunks used within our Streamlined Template in the next section.

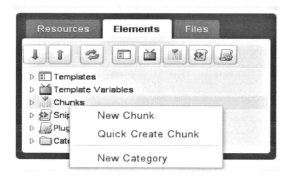

1. Create a block of (X)HTML code
2. Test the code
3. Log into the Manager
4. Access the Elements tab
5. Right-click on Chunks
6. Select New Chunk
7. Paste the contents into the Chunk
8. Save the Chunk

[[$siteHeader]]

Here we have completed all of the steps necessary to create our [[$siteHeader]] Chunk, which contains the information which will remain consistent throughout our site. Some of the actual content has been removed to assist readability. As there is much debate on the necessity of using specific meta tags, research and follow recommended current web standards.

Also, note the use of the CodeMirror Package to provide syntax highlighting.

[[$jQuery]]

To reduce the bandwidth on our sites, we can create another Chunk to load jQuery from Google's Content Delivery Network. By placing this code in a Chunk we can upgrade the library site wide when bug fixes or in the event of new releases.

By using a Chunk, we can isolate a Template to a dedicated version of jQuery, in the off chance an upgrade to jQuery breaks a component, until we can update it. We could also have named the Chunk jQuery-1.5.2 and indicated which version of jQuery we were using, or even have multiple versions available to the web project. The following is all that we need to load the jQuery library:

Listing 04.01: jQuery Chunk which loads the library

```
<script type="text/javascript" src="http://ajax.googleapis.com/ajax/
libs/jquery/1.5.2/jquery.min.js"></script>
```

[[$siteFooter]]

Many web sites have a single site footer displayed throughout the entire site. We shall implement a similar site footer which will also illustrate some interesting MODX Revolution concepts.

Listing 04.02: our site footer displayed on every page

```
<div id="cpyrght">
    &copy;[[*copyRight]] <a href="mailto:shawn@shawnwilkerson.
com?subject=[[++site_name]]  [[*longtitle]]">W. Shawn Wilkerson</a>.
All Rights Reserved.
</div>
<div id="siteDesign"><a href="[[~25]]">Site Considerations</a> |
    <a href="[[~92]]">Privacy/Legal</a> |
    <a href="[[~138]]">Site Map</a> |
    <a href="[[~7]]">Contact</a><br />
</div>
```

The `mailto:shawn@shawnwilkerson.com?subject=[[++site_name]]  [[*longtitle]]` link incorporates the name of the web site, as well as the long title of the current page into the subject line of any e-mail being sent as a result of clicking on that link. Don't worry – my e-mail never appears as plain text.

The `<a href="[[~92]]">Privacy/ Legal</a>` informs MODX Revolution to create a link to the resource indicated by the ID number. There are also links to Resources 25, 138, and 7. By linking to the ID number of the resource, we are afforded the opportunity to move documents anywhere in the site and not break their links, as MODX Revolution creates the URI links on the fly, we just have to supply the text for the link. These additional links allow us to link to pages we don't want to appear in the global navigation, while making them available on every page.

Additional uses of the footer, might be to include Google Analytics, additional JavaScript required within the current page, or optional "jump to" menus to direct visitors to specific content. The possibilities are completely up the design and skill set available to the project.

[[$jQueryBeautyofCode]]

Just before the bottom of the page, we call this Chunk to load all of the JavaScript necessary to utilize the various forms of syntax highlighting found throughout the site. Most recommendations concerning the usage of JavaScript, is to place it at the very end of the page to allow the content to be displayed while waiting on the scripts to be downloaded transparently in the background, instead of the other way around which tends to bore people into leaving.

Typically, we only load the base library we build on, namely jQuery, in the header of the page. Optionally, we will load other libraries as necessary, such as jQuery UI, jQuery Tools, or any of the other major tool sets we will require within the page. Essentially, we attempt to load class files first, and specific runtime parameters later in the page.

Listing 04.03: loading the jQuery Beauty of Code JavaScript

```
<script type="text/javascript" src="js/shCore.js"></script>
<script type="text/javascript" src="js/shBrushBash.js"></script>
<script type="text/javascript" src="js/shBrushCss.js"></script>
<script type="text/javascript" src="js/shBrushJScript.js"></script>
<script type="text/javascript" src="js/shBrushPhp.js"></script>
<script type="text/javascript" src="js/shBrushPlain.js"></script>
<script type="text/javascript" src="js/shBrushSql.js"></script>
<script type="text/javascript" src="js/shBrushXml.js"></script>
<script type="text/javascript">SyntaxHighlighter.all();</script>
```

Please be aware there are more efficient methods to load the following JavaScript, and we would typically only call this Chunk on pages which would use it. *Please see Part 2 of the book for implementation and optimization details.*

Chunks within Chunks

MODX Revolution allows unlimited nesting of Chunks within Chunks, as indicated in the Appendix dedicated to the *Document Parser and the Caching Mechanism*. There are many reasons to implement nested Chunks. For example, when we are building jQueryTools implementations, we will typically have a master for each implementation which, imports those components which serve the purpose of that particular application.

In this scenario, it would be easy to combine everything we need inside a single Chunk named [[$jQueryVideo]] which streamed hours of video. The rule of thumb is to always facilitate communication. Alternately, we could have combined the Chunks in the header of our template, if we did not need to communicate the presence of jQuery, or simply had a [[$header]] Chunk which contained:

> *Listing 04.04: calling Chunks from within another Chunk*

- -

```
[[$siteHeader]]
[[$jQuery]]
```

- -

Using Chunks to Streamline Templates

On my personal web site, shawnwilkerson.com, I have ten templates in use. As I constantly have to update different libraries and other features, I found it suitable to reduce the templates down to the bare minimum to allow them to be considered an actual content-less web page.

In the past I have went even further, to where only the area surrounding the [[*content]] was in the template and everything else was in Chunks. This works very well, but may not clearly communicate function or purpose to the other designers working on the project.

Ten templates may seem excessive, until we take into consideration, I had a MODX Revolution book to write, as well as a variety of things I am currently implementing and converting to MODX Revolution.

On my company web site, SanityLLC.com I have gone the other direction where I have created a single Template which can actually serve multiple presentations. There is no real "right" or "wrong" way to do things with MODX Revolution. It is simply a matter of choice or as mandated by the overall project purpose. By implementing the techniques in the rest of this chapter, it should quickly become apparent why Chunks are so very helpful.

The following is an example of a web site template currently in use:

Listing 04.05: base MODX Revolution Template

```
<?xml version="1.0" encoding="UTF-8" ?>
<!DOCTYPE html PUBLIC "-//W3C//DTD XHTML 1.0 Strict//EN" "http://
www.w3.org/TR/xhtml1/DTD/xhtml1-strict.dtd">
<html xmlns="http://www.w3.org/1999/xhtml">
    <head>
        [[$siteHeader]]
        [[$jQuery]]
    </head>
    <body class="MODX">
        <div id="header">
            [[$globalNav]]
        </div>
        <div id="container">
            <div id="mainContent">
                <h1>[[*pagetitle]]</h1>
                [[*content]]
            </div>
            <br class="clearfloat" />
            <div id="footer">
                [[$siteFooter]]
            </div>
        </div>
        [[$jQueryBeautyofCode]]
    </body>
</html>
```

The above template does not leave much to the imagination. It is concise, clear, and utilizes naming convention which directly indicates function and purpose. Without further explanation, many people who understand plain English should clearly understand what is actually going on within this template and begin to have a mental image of the page content, though not the layout. Note: If a web design staff (and client) all share another native language then the feasibility of using names relevant to that language should prevail.

Taking a closer look at this Template, there are two resource tags and also calls to the Chunks previously discussed, excluding [[$globalNav]] discussed near the end of this chapter. Because we chose to use a full Template, it provides greater understanding to those individuals working on the site. We can also reduce the possibility of syntax errors, by limiting our Template to only structure and allowing each Element parsed into the page to encapsulate its own content.

There are other ways of separating a Template, but after years of working with MODX products I have established a policy to where Templates directly reflect page structure. Chunks, Snippets, and other Elements provide the content. In essence, I separate structure, design, and content into three distinct components. The following section demonstrates, why I used so many Chunks.

Showing the Pieces Together

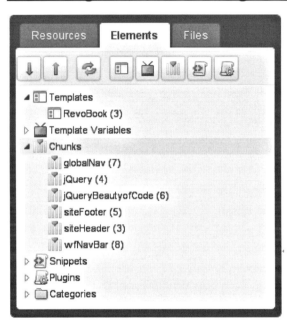

Until now we have spent quite a bit of time making the individual pieces of (X)HTML we are planning to implement on our site.

MODX Revolution will take each of these Elements, and combine them into a single document. Some people may want to know why they have to go to all of this trouble. In a word: you don't. These techniques simply offer insight into the utilization of Chunks, provide re-usability of code, and facilitate readability.

After creating all of the Chunks, our Elements tree has now expanded to show our six Chunks and the Template we created during the last chapter. Once MODX Revolution Parses the page it takes our 24 lines of template and creates 65 lines of code. Keep in mind this is before we have begun to input the actual page content:

Listing 04.06: the Template combined with Chunk output

```
<?xml version="1.0" encoding="UTF-8" ?>
<!DOCTYPE html PUBLIC "-//W3C//DTD XHTML 1.0 Strict//EN" "http://
www.w3.org/TR/xhtml1/DTD/xhtml1-strict.dtd">
<html xmlns="http://www.w3.org/1999/xhtml">
<head>
    <meta name="google-site-verification" content="get your own key
from google"/>
    <meta http-equiv="PICS-Label" content='(PICS-1.1 "http://www.
classify.org/safesurf/" l r (SS~~000 1))'/>
    <meta http-equiv="Content-Type" content="text/html;
```

```
charset=utf-8"/>
    <meta http-equiv="Content-Script-Type" content="text/
javascript"/>
    <meta http-equiv="Content-Style-Type" content="text/css"/>
    <title>MODX Revolution's </title>
    <base href="http://shawnwilkerson.com/"/>
    <link rel="canonical" href="http://shawnwilkerson.com/index.
php?id=1"/>
    <meta name="author" content="W. Shawn Wilkerson"/>
    <meta name="copyright" content="Copyright ©0 W. Shawn Wilkerson,
All Rights Reserved"/>
    <meta name="date" content="0"/>
    <meta name="description" content=" by MODX Revolution"/>
    <meta name="keywords" content="shawn,wilkerson,christian,root
s"/>
    <script type="text/javascript" src="http://ajax.googleapis.com/
ajax/libs/jquery/1.4.2/jquery.min.js"></script>
</head>
<body class="MODX">
<div id="header">
    <div id="mainnav">
        <ul>
            <li class="first active"><a href="http://shawnwilkerson.
com/" title="MODX Revolution Home">Home</a></li>
            <li class="sep">|</li>
        </ul>
    </div>
</div>
<div id="container">
    <div id="mainContent">
        <h1>Home</h1>
    </div>
    <br class="clearfloat"/>
    <div id="footer">
        <div id="cpyrght">&copy; 2009 <a
                href="mailto:shawn@shawnwilkerson.
com?subject=[[++site_name]]  [[*longtitle]]">W.
                Shawn Wilkerson</a>. All Rights Reserved.
        </div>
        <div id="siteDesign">
            <a href="site-considerations.html"">Site
Considerations</a> |
            <a href="legal.html">Privacy / Legal</a> |
            <a href="site-map.html">Site Map</a> |
```

```
                <a href="contact/">Contact</a>
            </div>
        </div>
    </div>
<script type="text/javascript" src="js/syntaxHighlighter3-0-83/
shCore.js"></script>
<script type="text/javascript" src="js/syntaxHighlighter3-0-83/
shBrushBash.js"></script>
<script type="text/javascript" src="js/syntaxHighlighter3-0-83/
shBrushCss.js"></script>
<script type="text/javascript" src="js/syntaxHighlighter3-0-83/
shBrushJScript.js"></script>
<script type="text/javascript" src="js/syntaxHighlighter3-0-83/
shBrushPhp.js"></script>
<script type="text/javascript" src="js/syntaxHighlighter3-0-83/
shBrushPlain.js"></script>
<script type="text/javascript" src="js/syntaxHighlighter3-0-83/
shBrushSql.js"></script>
<script type="text/javascript" src="js/syntaxHighlighter3-0-83/
shBrushXml.js"></script>
<script type="text/javascript">SyntaxHighlighter.all();</script>
</body>
</html>
```

- -

Increasing Readability

As you may have noticed, our very simple (X)HTML code Template can become quite complex very quickly, even before we have included any content within the page. The base (X)HTML code used to produce the page at this point, may already require people working on the site to have more than basic understanding of (X)HTML.

Hopefully this example will help demonstrate one of the key benefits of using Chunks - simple streamlining. Even if an expert User Interface coder is the only individual working on the (X)HTML content on a given web project, we would still suggest breaking the page into enough pieces to expedite maintenance and site updates.

An immediate additional benefit of these Chunks, may become apparent if and when subsequent Templates are added to the site. Much of the code is already finished and simple CSS changes could be used to change the presentation to match the new layout - without having to start over, or piece it together.

Using Chunks With Placeholders

For the first time we are able to directly interact with Chunks in a way which previously required the coding of a PHP Snippet. MODX Revolution provides the ability to send properties to many of the types of Elements utilized within web sites. This allows unique abilities with Chunks which were not possible in previous MODX products.

The following example utilizes a pre HTML5 version of the embed code provided by Youtube as a foundation, as such it is not (X)HTML compliant. In this Chunk, I took the liberty to exaggerate the code and replace some of the parameters with Placeholders for the purpose of providing a consistent presentation:

Listing 04.07: [[$youTubeVideos]] Chunk using Chunk Parameters

```
<object width="[[+width]]" height="[[+height]]"><param name="movie"
value="http://www.youtube.com/v/[[+videoID]]
                    &hl=en_US
                    &fs=[[+allowFullScreen]]
                    &rel=0
                    &color1=[[+color1]]
                    &color2=[[+color2]]
                    &hd=[[+allowHiDef]]"></param>
    <param name="allowFullScreen" value="true"></param>
    <param name="allowscriptaccess" value="always"></param>
    <embed src="http://www.youtube.com/v/[[+videoID]]
            &hl=en_US
            &fs=[[+allowFullScreen]]
            &rel=0
            &color1=[[+color1]]
            &color2=[[+color2]]
            &hd=[[+allowHiDef]]"
        type="application/x-shockwave-flash"
        allowscriptaccess="always"
        allowfullscreen="true"
        width="[[+width]]"
        height="[[+height]]"></embed></object>
```

Any value can be passed to a Chunk (or any MODX Revolution Element) as a parameter, including: System Settings, Resource Settings, results from Snippet executions, and / or a combination of the various Elements provided for use with MODX Revolution.

This simply requires the use of a placeholder as demonstrated in the [[$youTubeVideos]] Chunk above. By matching the placeholder [[+name]] with the parameter &name=`value` MODX Revolution should respond with [[+name]] being replaced with whatever value was sent to the Chunk at runtime. This can allow us to create Chunks to act as templates which can be much cleaner than using the third-party provided embed code, allowing for easier site updates and edits. More importantly it allows is the ability to establish a consistent look and feel of a content type:

Listing 04.08: [[$youTubeVideos]] Chunk call replacing YouTube's Embed Code

```
[[$youTubeVideos?videoID=`0sdMvRuGH9E`
    &color=`0x2b405b`
    &color2=`0x6b8ab6`
    &allowHidDef=`1`
    &allFullScreen=`1`
    &width=`480`
    &height=`385`]]
```

Using Chunks with Property Sets

Alternately, by creating a Chunk and attaching the YouTube Property Set discussed in chapter 2, we can provide a consistent embedded video interface across our entire site, by simply providing the videoID from YouTube of each desired video.

This method allows the Property Set to feed the correct values to our Chunk, requiring only a video ID to be provided where we want the video displayed. Not only does this keep the page source clean for editing it also allows presentation changes to be implemented site-wide with minimal effort. By utilizing Property Sets we can greatly simplify our code and limit the content to only the information required to the specific video.

Listing 04.09: [[$youTubeVideos]] using a Property Set

```
[[$youTubeVideos@YouTube?videoID=`0sdMvRuGH9E`]]
```

Overriding a Property Set

Our YouTube Property Set defined quite a few parameters for us, which is great to establish a consistent presentation. It also helps reduce the number of parameters required in our Chunk call and reduces huge amounts of isolated code which may eventually require editing to match a site's theme or vendor changes.

To implement a case-by-case override, we simply add the necessary parameters after the Property Set. Each parameter we pass directly to the Chunk will override the Property Set values of the same name requiring only a slight change to our previous call:

Listing 04.10: [[$youTubeVideos]] with Property Set and parameter overrides

- -

```
[[$youTubeVideos@YouTube?videoID=`0sdMvRuGH9E`&width=`640`
                                        &height=`513`]]
```

- -

Chunks Used With Snippets

The PHP coding standard for "MODX requires that no (X)HTML be echo'ed or inline in a Snippet. MODX also recommends externalizing any HTML in PHP code in Chunks" – http://rtfm.MODX.com/display/revolution21/Code+Standards. At first this may appear to be a very high expectation, but it can actually help divide the workload among the individuals responsible for each of the various aspects.

By removing the (X)HTML from the PHP code, developers are able to focus on coding, while designers are left to concentrate on presentation, instead of expecting developers to function as designers, or vice-versa. Various implementations are used to accomplish this standard centering around two main methods:

1. Creating a Chunk which contains all the instructions to call a Snippet so that correct formatting is provided via file-based Chunks kept within the Snippet's installation directory tree.

2. Creating a template Chunk, which is then accessed by the Snippet directly to produce output which is then sent to the page. This method is utilized by the star_rating, Breadcrumbs, Login and other Snippets.

The Wayfinder Snippet demonstrates both of these options. We can call the Snippet as is, [[Wayfinder?startId=`0`]] and it will utilize its own default templates or we can apply templates which we have defined within Chunks. To illustrate how a Snippet call with parameters can be combined with a Chunk template, we will take a closer look at the [[$globalNav]] Chunk utilized in our site template.

[[$globalNav]]

To provide consistent navigation for the entire site, we decide on our needs and communicate it via a cached Snippet call. We only wish to customize the individual menu rows, while retaining the default Wayfinder formatting. This is then included in all of our templates.

Listing 04.11: establishing global navigation

```
<div id="mainnav">[[Wayfinder?startId=`0`&level=`1`&sortBy=`menuindex
          `&rowTpl=`wfNavBar`&excludeDocs=`7,25,207`]]
</div>
```

[[$wfNavBar]]

In [[$globalNav]] we instructed Wayfinder to use the [[$wfNavBar]] Chunk as our row template. Before we actually use the [[$globalNav]] Chunk, we will need to create a new chunk and add the following content for Wayfinder to use to produce the output of each menu item it is sending to our page:

Listing 04.12: Wayfinder template Chunk used for the global navigation

```
<li [[+wf.id]] [[+wf.classes]]> <a href="[[+wf.link]]"
title="[[++site_name]] [[+wf.title]]" [[+wf.attributes]]>[[+wf.
linktext]]</a>[[+wf.wrapper]]</li><li class="sep">|</li>
```

Example [[$globalNav]] Output

Listing 04.13: global navigation menu created by the Wayfinder Snippet

---

```
<div id="mainnav">
   <ul>
         <li class="first"><a href="http://www.shawnwilkerson.com/"
            title="Home">Home</a></li>
         <li class="sep">|</li>
         <li><a href="christian/" title="christian
roots">Christian</a></li>
         <li class="sep">|</li>
         <li><a href="camera/" title="camera">Camera</a></li>
         <li class="sep">|</li>
         <li><a href="computer/" title="computer">Computers</a></li>
         <li class="sep">|</li>
         <li><a href="credentials/" title="credentials">Credentials<
/a></li>
         <li class="sep">|</li>
         <li class="active"><a href="MODX-revolution/"
            title="MODX revolution">MODX Revolution</a></li>
         <li class="sep">|</li>
         <li class="last"><a href="xpdo/"
            title="xPDO ORB PDO Database">xPDO Database</a></li>
         <li class="sep">|</li>
   </ul>
</div>
```

As Wayfinder completes its task, it loops through the list of links which satisfy the requirements transmitted through the [[$globalNav]] parameters, and wraps each of them with the contents of [[$wfNavBar]]. Some sites can have multiple Chunks serving as menu templates. We tend to name each of these Chunks prefixed with wf to indicate their association with Wayfinder.

As a design team works with MODX Revolution and creates an array of menu styles, these can later be simply copied from one site to another with little or no configuration required on subsequent sites. This in itself should demonstrate how using Chunks within MODX Revolution can prove to be profitable – so don't forget to donate to the project!

Test Implementations with Duplicate Elements

We would also like to mention it is typically best to duplicate elements for the purpose of editing and testing.

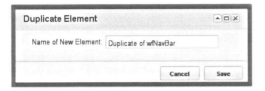

This helps us in multiple levels:

1. The Element being worked on is not "live" and therefore viewable to visitors
2. The working Element is not accidentally deleted or overwritten
3. Working on duplicates, is a habit clothed in safety

To duplicate a Chunk, simply right-click on any existing Chunk, select duplicate from the context menu. This will present a pop-up windows which asks for a new name. Element names and descriptions can be changed at anytime. Keep in mind, any name changes will require those names to be updated in any Resources and Elements which use them.

MODX Revolution Rule #4: **All Element parameters require the use of the backtick `.**

Summary

We have covered quite a bit of territory since leaving grandma's kitchen. We have learned that Chunks are simple blocks of (X)HTML code designed to accomplish a single task. Even at the most basic level of implementation, MODX Revolution Chunks can be very effective in streamlining and simplifying a web project.

MODX Revolution provides a highly functional caching mechanism. Deciding when and what to cache should always be considered as a part of the design process. Issues arise when dynamic content is cached as it can very easily begin to perform outside of expectations.

We have also been introduced to implementations of Chunks which will allow a very high level of cooperation between developers and designers. By simply communicating needs and expectations, designers can interact with developers in very productive relationships.

Chunks can be woven into symbiotic relationships with Snippets and Templates. The ability to transfer these unique interactions from one site to another, should result in reduced production and increased profits. The value of reusable, dedicated content can prove a powerful ally. The initial investment may be large in discovering signature techniques, but should soon pay for itself as subsequent projects take minutes to implement – instead of hours or days.

5

[[*templateVariables]]: Building Interactive Interfaces

Buffet lines are a wonderful thing. For some, the mere thought of being able to eat as much as they would like is all the motivation needed to get them moving in the direction of the car. Others may appreciate the simplicity and freedom of creating their own meal from so many options at a fixed price, which comes in quite handy when a group or the family is involved.

What most people fail to consider, is someone else made all of the choices for them. Sure, a choice was made when the restaurant was selected, but the menu items are the only options offered. This is a simple fact of modern life and where "presentation is everything" really comes into its own.

Understanding the difference of choice versus option is the very basis of implementing MODX Revolution Template Variables. For Manager users to achieve maximum efficiency, they need to have a combination of the best choices *and* options available to them. For site visitors, we want to provide only the options we want them to have without inadvertently communicating a sense of their being limited. **Note: early MODX Revolution versions combined the Input and Output types on the same tab, some of these are shown in this chapter to consolidate the presentation. Please utilize the respective tab in Revolution 2.1.0 and above.**

What is a Template Variable?

Within the MODX Revolution database, a table (MODX_site_content) exists completely dedicated to the resources contained within a web project and provides approximately three dozen fields or attributes for us to use in defining and interacting with each page. For many web sites this is quite adequate, as they do not depend on user interaction or collection of additional data. Other projects may require the implementation of simplistic methods to achieve visually pleasing and interactive content, while retaining the benefits of dynamic and streamlined content. Essentially, Template Variables are user-definable extensions to a web Resource and typically relate to its content. To help visualize the purposed of Template Variables, please consider the concept of implementing an e-commerce application.

I recall working with early versions of osCommerce where countless hours and contributions (hacks) had to be applied to modify various products to correctly represent client catalogs. Typically, these hacks would be "fragile" or not work together easily. Quite a bit of effort had to be invested to ensure a current hack did not break those currently in use within the site. Occasionally, entire sets of these hacks had to be combined to force the software to provide a satisfactory presentation to the user. At the very least, this process was time consuming. Thankfully, this is not the case for MODX Revolution.

Template Variables are one of the answers developed for the purpose of providing a simple method of extending MODX Revolution Resources beyond the default fields contained within the database. In a stroke of genius, the developers decided to attach this ability to Templates, directly allowing each Resource using any given Template to share the extended attribute. Additionally, this allows the same attribute to be shared across Templates, thereby extending a greater number of Resources on the application. *By attaching Template Variables to a specific Template, each Resource utilizing that Template is transparently extended.*

Throughout a typical web project, implementation needs are refined, the user interface is streamlined and typically work flow is simplified. During this process, Template Variables can easily be adjusted, removed, and added as deemed necessary allowing for a straightforward work flow to be implemented. The correct definition and presentation of a given resource, can greatly increase clear communication of its purpose. Ideally, by defining these variables earlier in the web project, scope creep (missed deadlines) and other undesirable activities should become increasingly avoidable.

Creating Template Variables

All MODX Revolution Template Variables can be easily created via the Manager, once a user has logged in by:

1. Accessing the Element Tab of the Resource Menu
2. Right-clicking on the Template Variable Tree Node
3. Selecting New Template Variable

In keeping with our goal to clearly communicate function, we should first pick a name which indicates the purpose of our TV. For example, by using either authorBirthDate or authorDOB as a Template Variable name, we could clearly communicate this variable is used to store the date of birth for an author. Some people may even go further with something like: tvAuthorBirthDate or authorBirthdateTV. The additional "tv" will help distinguish it from a identically formatted Resource Setting: [[*pagetitle]], [[*tv]]. Simply create a standardized naming convention and stick to it to facilitate communication. Also keep in mind all names used within MODX Revolution are case-sensitive: "name" does not necessarily equal "Name".

New Template Variable

General Information	Properties	Input Options	Output Options

Variable Name:

Caption:

Description:

Category:

Lock variable for editing:

Sort Order: 0

Clear Cache on Save:

from Revo 2.1.0

Continue creating the Template Variable by adding a caption which is shown to the Manager user as the name of the TV. Even though we should be choosing names which clearly define function, we should also take the extra few seconds required to complete the description field, as we may need to be reminded several months later what we were thinking when we actually created the Template Variable. Additionally, there is always the possibility we will not be the only person using, implementing or editing a TV.

As an added incentive, the description and caption are displayed to Manager users **when viewing the Template Variable or any other tab during Resource creation and update** providing them with immediate information on what they should be doing with the TV – or why it is present. The more communication provided during the development process the better.

Eventually, a Template Variable will be tested and found trustworthy. Site administrators may choose to "lock" it to keep it from being inadvertently changed at a later date – keeping in mind it can be unlocked later by those with permission to do so. For added functionality, the order TVs are displayed to Manager users can be established utilizing the Sort order field. I typically use 10, 20, 30... leaving room for possible future insertions. This process will be repeated for each Template Variable used within a web project.

Place Holder Template Variables

Up to this point we have simply created a TV without actually defining its properties. For many projects this may very well be an acceptable method of establishing individual key elements while interviewing a client. If the client provides a list of page-specific author data, we could simply create "placeholder" Template Variables, using the client's expectations as the description.

For example, a client may like to have the author's birth date, but wants it displayed in YYYY/MM/DD format. We could easily use "Client wants YYYY/MM/DD output" as our description. When the TV is actually defined we can change the description to read, "Provides YYYY/MM/DD formatted date of birth."

Attaching the TV to a Template

Once we are ready to use our Template Variable, we can attach it to as many Templates as we would like. Simply click on the Template Access tab and place a check mark in the access column associated with the respective Template. Any TV can be added or removed from any Template at any time. Please note: if it is added to a Template already in use by Resources, they may need to be individually edited and saved to attach the TV and its value filled in where applicable.

As of MODX Revolution 2.2.2, the information from a TV is left indefinitely in the table for a Resource even if the Template Variable has been removed from the Resource or its Template. Be forewarned: **removal of the Template Variable itself, will also irreversibly remove all associative data** from the MODX_site_tmplvar_contentvalues database table.

For some situations where interaction with data is not required by Manager users, such as setting a page specific revision date, it is not without reason to simply create a Hidden Template Variable allowing project-wide access, saving Manager Users from performing unnecessary steps.

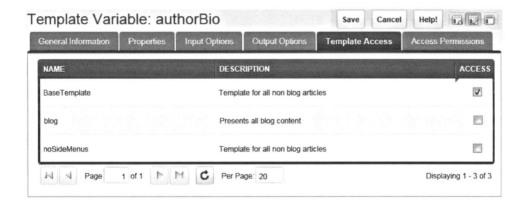

Understanding Input and Output

Template Variables have two faces to them: the one seen in the Manager and its associated public appearance. The side utilized in conjunction with Resources within the Manager is typically considered the "Input." Essentially, this is the type of display offered to Manager users who are able to create and / or edit Resources. Template Variables provide simplified and efficient data collection mechanisms to the individual Resource. As we shall soon see, things can get really interesting when the output of one TV is used as input for another Element.

Output Types can be a bit more complex. The easy answer would be they are the result from the Template Variable which are typically seen on the front side of the web site. While this is true, the output of a Template Variable can be used within MODX Revolution Snippets, Chunks, and even within another TV. It is completely possible to create complex chains of multiple implementations of each. Though sounding very complex, this is usually very straight forward and easier than you may know. It simply becomes an issue of what information to collect, how best to do so, and how it should be presented to the site visitor.

The primary function of Template Variables is to provide effective data collection directly related to a given Resource and store that information within the database. The actual output of that data, to web site visitors, should be considered completely optional, as we are under no obligation to insert a Template Variable tag within our Templates, page content, or Chunks. In fact, in some situations we would not want any information stored within [[*templateVariable]] to ever see the light of day within a visitors web browser or other internet software.

Carefully think through the choice of Template Variable Type. Each step of the work flow process is represented in the creation of a TV. Deciding the best implementation to obtain data during Resource creation is largely relevant to the overall success of the web project. Additionally, understanding how TV data is actually stored in the database could also come in handy and typically is achieved in one of two forms: data (string), and data1||data2 (delimited "array"). Lastly, visualize how the output will be utilized throughout the project. In some instances it may be easier to chose a "text" or "default" output type with the intention of manipulating the TV after it is processed with a Snippet or MODX Revolution's Filters.

For the security conscious, MODX Revolution will first adhere to Access Control Lists before it actually produces the content of each Template Variable. As some of the Template Variables we will be looking at have the ability to directly link, or access files on the file system, MODX Revolution will not only validate the Manager user attempting to use the TV, but also the site visitor who may be afforded the opportunity to view the output. In short, Template Variables cannot be easily manipulated to give access to uses they do not have, but caution should be utilized when allowing users access to the file system to link to content being displayed.

Selecting The Type of Template Variable Input

Once we have named the TV, established the caption to be shown to Manager Users, provided an adequate description and optionally selected the order in which it is to be displayed to Manager users, we now get to choose from approximately twenty types of input. The emphasis on Manager users should be noted, as the input for Template Variables is provided solely within the Manager. As pages are being added or edited within a web project, additional information contained within TVs can easily by added and updated as necessary. As far as visitors to the web site are concerned, any data collected in a Template Variable is simply seen as part of the web page. All TV output is optional and may never even be seen on the "public" side of the site.

As there are many ways to approach the decision on how to receive our input, it may be prudent to view it from the user perspective, while simultaneously deciding what we need from them.

Experience may also indicate, the necessity of our understanding the Manager User's skill level. Additionally, we should keep in mind that any value placed into the TV "can and will be used against you in a court of law" if it becomes viewable to the public.

Essentially, this is where we choose the options we allow our Manager users to have access to. It is generally best to remove as much freedom as possible, while not hindering users from accomplishing their task. Case in point, if providing Manager users a drop down box or a set of radio buttons will allow them to accomplish the function then it is safest to use those as we have already decided upon the appropriate values for input.

Planning the collection of data through its presentation within a site is typically very similar to those used to create mock-ups for clients. Simply visualize each step of the process and implement the web equivalent.

⊤ TIP: LIMITED PROTECTION

There is also the added protection of allowing Manager users to utilize TVs to input the relevant information, but excluding it from the Template and page output. This helps keep sensitive information confined to the Manager.

Template Variable Input Types as of 2.2.2

Auto-Tag	Number
Check Box	Radio Options
Date	Resource List
Email	Rich Text
File	Tag
Hidden	Text
Image	Text Area
List Box (Multiple Selections Possible)	URL
List Box (Single Selections Only)	

These Template Variable types were removed from earlier MODX Revolution versions: Drop-Down List Menu, HTML Area, Text Area (Mini), and Text Box.

Template Variable Examples

To help demonstrate real-world implementation of Template Variables, we will be looking at various aspects to provide information concerning classical authors. A few years ago my wife, Victoria Wilkerson (`victoriawilkerson.com`) decided she wanted to catalog biographical and other information pertaining to authors as their classical works were transferred into the public domain.

As she spent months building this area of her site, in her "spare" time, it became painfully obvious there had to be simpler methods of implementation, which did not require the same information to be entered multiple times. Issues such as sorting by birth dates, genres, and number of works would each require duplicating data unless a better solution presented itself. I suggested she utilize MODX Revolution's Template Variables to address many of these issues and the rest is history. The following pages should provide a fair amount of understanding, in the usage of each of these TVs. Practice indeed makes perfect. Experiment and see what you can do with each of these tools. **Some images are from earlier Revo versions for consolidation.**

MODX Revolution Rule #5: **Do not over think the task. Take the simplest route.**

Auto-tag

A current trend with many web sites is to provide a "Tag Cloud" which combines all the tags utilized within the site in a single display. Here we create such an implementation by utilizing the Auto-Tag type of Template Variable, which allows any tag previously associated with our "tag Cloud" to readily be made available to our current Resource.

By default, each of our Resources will not have any values set for its tags. After creating our first Auto-Tag Template Variable and assigning a value to it in a Resource, it will be listed in any subsequently created Resource utilizing the same Template with the TV assigned to it. To begin, the area beneath our text box may be empty, requiring us to add our own by entering new tags separated by a comma: poem, suspense, 18th century.

Once tags are utilized by another Resource, a list of those tags will be presented. By left-clicking on any of these tags we can easily add them to the current Resource. The first click adds the "MODX" tag to the Resource, as indicated by the green background. A second click on the same tag, currently highlighted with green, will remove it ("revolution") from this Resource and changes the tag to an underlined link. We can add a new tag ("TV") to our list by simply creating it after supplying a comma. If the underlined word has been removed from all Resources, it will be removed from the "tag cloud" list, otherwise it will remain available.

This list is dynamically built throughout the entire site as new tags are introduced to our Auto-tag Template Variable. As new Resources are added to the site, a combination of old and new tags can be utilized to describe the new content. Over time fewer new tags may be needed to describe the content being added in new Resources to the site, as we may previously have utilized them. This simple system could transparently "link" these various Resources via their tags. Additionally, Revolution Snippets such as tagLister and getResources can utilize these tags to provide targeted user interfaces for site visitors.

Initially our web project will not have any tags associate with any of our content. It may prove beneficial to define categories or groups of tags at this point to better serve the site visitor – at least to the best of our ability. As the site is developed and content added, general themes found within a given page can be defined, and over time groupings may develop which will be serviced by our tags.

In some situations, a separate Auto-Tag TV may be required for each group, whereas others may prove more optional or mutually beneficial. For example, my site has MODX Revolution, xPDO, Computers, as well as other sections. Each of these may require a dedicated "tag cloud," whereas MODX Revolution and xPDO might be able to share a set of tags in the same tag cloud. By assigning a Template Variable to designated Templates, the values can be shard across templates or limited to specific one.

One method utilized to simplify navigation within each section within a web project, would be to create sub sections. The complexity of clearly communicating any further divisions can easily get exponentially more difficult with each subsequent layer. To combat this issue, a dedicated Auto-tag Template variable can be created for each template to use throughout the site. Additionally, by limiting the "scope" of a Auto-tag TV to a specific section we could:

♦ Simplify topical navigation – users can choose to browse the site by selecting tags which closely relate to an area of interest

♦ Provide cross-topic inclusion – allows a topic to be "posted" in multiple areas based on nothing more than the tags which have been attached to it, instead of using a Symlink

♦ Provide a basis for driving visitors through sections of a site

♦ Replace sections of "formal" navigation by allowing the content to "categorize" the various Resources within a given web project

♦ Provide a basis to link related content

Functionally, "tagged" documents allow a visitor to filter the pages of a given web site based on a keyword. For example, if a web site is dedicated to discussing authors of classical works, an article on a given author might include genre, type of work, etc., Template Variables. By selecting the tag, the user will only be presented with the articles which also share the same tag, such as showing only content which contains poetry or works in the suspense genre. These could be further limited to works by that author or include all authors depending on the implementation.

Ŧ *Tip: Use lower case for tags*

As a rule of thumb, my personal preference is to typically keep all tags presented in lower case and may prevent the inadvertent broken link, as modx does not equal MODX. The tagLister Snippet provides a parameter to treat these as the same value: &toLower=`1`.

Check Box

Whether the project requires areas to be separated by visitor, gender, or some other predetermined value, the Check Box Template Variable can provide a simple method to directly attach content to a targeted audience. It can also be utilized to provide a means of tracking site updates, allowing a Manger user to mark Resources as completed. Used in conjunction with ACLs, these TVs can even be used by management to "sign-off" on new content.

Check Box Template Variables follow the HTML convention where a value exists only when the box is checked. This is not truly a Boolean value, but can be programmatically treated as such by testing for the value to be present. For each Resource associated with the Template to which the check box TV is assigned, the value will either exist (checked) or it will not (left unchecked).

Has legal signed off on this bio? ✓ Verified
Only approved bios will be visible.

In our classic author scenario, we may want to have some sort of validation attached to the biography we are posting with each author. In corporate, educational, and government environments it may even be necessary to have the legal department ascertain if the content contains any statements which could be deemed as libel or discriminatory. In the majority of situations, any statements concerning other entities should be validated – with or without the use of a Check Box Template Variable.

I would suggest adding a default false value of 0 (zero), especially in situations where Check Box Template Variables are added to Templates with preexisting Resources. This is mainly to avoid confusion, if the default appearance suggests the Template Variable has been checked.

Date

By default MODX Revolution provides plenty of document-specific dates, namely: pub_date, unpub_date, createdon, editedon, deletedon, and publishedon. MODX Revolution developers also have a versioning system in the roadmap, which may provide additional system dates attached to Resources. While these date fields help define much of the activity of each Resource, they do not facilitate content specific dates to be stored, which may be considered a critical requirement for many applications.

Date Template Variables allows content related dates to be stored within a given Resource. In our classical authors scenario, we would like to extend each author's Resource with their birth date, the date of their death, and the date of their first known publication. Depending on implementation, this could allow us to provide a basis of interactive content for our site visitors.

Once we have decided what date values we want stored with each Resource, we will probably need to choose which type of output we want. If we choose to have a "Date" format for our output, we can use many of the native PHP formats listed at the PHP website: http://www.php. net/manual/en/function.date.php, which will provide a consistent display wherever the template variable is displayed. We could also choose "Text" as our output type allowing us to format the string on the fly using MODX Revolution's filters: [[*tvName:strtotime:date=` %Y`]], thereby leaving the design to the designers.

One of the main benefits of implementing a Date Template Variable with our Resources is we do not have to concern ourselves with translating date formats. MODX Revolution utilizes Ext JS, which provides a very nice date picker. One of the nicest features of this date picker, is the ability to click on the month / year at the top and be provided with a simple interface to select any month from any year – without an excessive amount of scrolling or clicking. We can also simply change months by using the right and left arrow links on the same line as the month /year. For those individuals who prefer the keyboard over using the mouse, dates can be entered manually following the YYYY-MM-DD nomenclature. The Date TV provides context help if the format is not correct which facilitates data integrity.

Data Restrictions: MODX Revolution allows dates to be restricted by removing dates and days of the week, limiting the range of dates and hours of the day which can be selected, establishing the day to begin each week, and by allowing Manager users to determine the number of minutes between time values in the picker. There is plenty of in-page documentation to fine-tune any date Template Variable to a very specific implementation definition.

Email

In today's global connectivity, an e-mail address is considered to be a primary means to contact someone. Many people have multiple e-mail addresses: work related, some for personal use, others for privacy, etc. In our classic author scenario, we need a simple way to include an e-mail address in a Resource that facilitates a consistent presentation, and identifies only the address associated with the respective author.

As classical authors have probably deceased, we may want to provide an **e-mail** address which will allow our visitors the ability to access the official society or group which handles the legal aspects of the writer's works. Typically, there is one overriding entity positioned for such a task. Alternately, we could also supply the e-mail address for our own "e-curator" for that Resource. MODX Revolution's E-mail Template Variable allows easy implementation of Resource related e-mail addresses.

Once the Email Template Variable has been created, attached to our Template, and saved we will be rewarded with a straightforward text field extension to any of our Resources using that Template. Any number of e-mail type template variables can be utilized to store pertinent e-mail address(es) whether or not they will ever appear to the site visitor.

In the midst of our research we may have been entrusted with a "private" e-mail account which we do not want to lose, but also did not want to make public. We can simply assign the Template Variable to the Template for data collection, but not include the variable on the front end content. We might even consider naming the private e-mail TV, something like: `author_NotForFrontEnd-address`. Additionally, we could apply an ACL to the TV allowing it only Manager access.

File

Many web projects provide direct access to files for site visitors. The issue typically experienced by site administrators is broken or ineffectual links to those files. MODX Revolution's **File** Template Variable provides an implementation which succinctly resolves these issues.

In our classical authors scenario, we may want to allow our visitors to download a PDF file of the page, author biography, or some other content. We would first choose a variable name, caption, and description for our Manager Users. Then a decision needs to be made on the output type of our **File** Template Variable. Many of the available output types would simply return the name of the file chosen by our Manager Users as plain text. For our purposes, we want this to be an actual link, so we have chosen the URL output type.

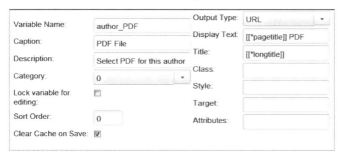

As far as the link text displayed to our site visitors, we opted to have the Template Variable populate itself with the title of the page the visitors is actually viewing followed by 'PDF', as our pages will be titled after the author for which they are developed.

I could have chosen more generic terminology such as "Download PDF" for the Display Text, but personally believe it provides a more "finished" look, when each Resource appears to be completely autonomous and dedicated to its specific topic. This technique could also provide more weight within the page for our topic, when considering search engine optimization.

Tip: This technique could also be utilized if an image was being linked, but the project did not require that image to actually appear within the page itself. This would allow visitors direct access to the file via a link, without the actual image appearing.

As many people are visual and have grown accustomed to using graphic user interfaces, MODX Revolution also provides access to the MODX Browser. By left-clicking the down arrow, Manager users are presented with a GUI, allowing the browsing of approved files due to the Base Path and Allowed File Extensions settings.

Now we have to set the boundaries for this Template Variable, as we may not want Manager users snooping around our file system, configuration files, shopping cart files, database configurations, secret projects in development, etc.

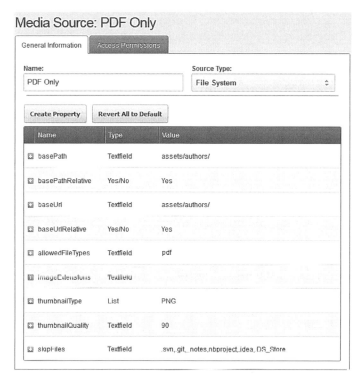

Create a new Media Source:

1. Open Tools | Media Source
2. Create A New Media Source
3. Click Save
4. Right-click the new Source
5. Select Update

In this example, I decided to allow access to only the /assets/authors directory. Manager users using this Template Variable will only be able to select files and directories under the folder indicated here. They will not be able to move up or jump out of the folder to another one on the same level.

This allows us to place all of the Adobe PDF files in the same directory or to create sub folders by author name.

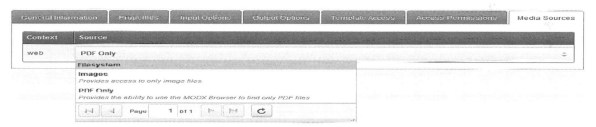

Return to the Template Variable and change the TV Media Source Tab, by double-clicking the "Filesystem" setting in the web context and saving the Template Variable.

Once the settings are as shown above, Manager users will only have access to the designated file extensions and folders via the MODX Browser.

This is definitely much less work than copy and pasting paths and file names!

Hidden

Anyone having implemented or written a form mail script understands the basic reasoning behind the necessity of utilizing hidden fields: provide additional information without user involvement, and the collection of environmental / user data. **Hidden** MODX Revolution Template Variables typically do not appear on any of the Resource Tabs during creation or updating providing pseudo read-only fields to a Template and thereby to a Resource.

These "hidden" fields are not intended to be entirely read only, as anyone bestowed with the corresponding Manager permissions can access the Template Variable – edit or even remove it. Other Manager users, simply may be unaware of their existence or purpose.

Historically, there are only a few reasons to implement "hidden" variables. One of the widest implementations has been to track the current user or specific elements of the environment. As far as MODX Revolution is concerned, there is always the possibility of simply wanting to include additional information to the Resource while not introducing more content to Manager Users to cipher through. Here we create [[*copyRight]] which is placed into our site-wide footer chunk to display a simple copyright notice based on the creation date of the current Resource.

Essentially, we utilize the creation date of each page by applying a MODX Revolution Filter to discover the year the content was actually created. By making this a hidden implementation, we keep the Manager cleaner for our users and clearly communicate this content is indeed a variable – which can change from one page to the next.

Alternately, I could have simply placed the "Default Value" contents of our [[*copyRight]] Template Variable within my page Template or Chunk and called it a day, but I typically choose to reserve my Templates and Chunks for static structural content only. Either method is acceptable and only needs to be tempered by company policy and / or your personal philosophy.

Image

Select author's image [doyle/sir-arthu]
Inserts image into page

Pictures can greatly enhance an article or concept. MODX Revolution provides the ability to allow Manager users the ability to add an image to each page as an extension to the actual page properties.

Image Template Variables function much like their File Template Variable siblings with Manager users being provided the ability to "browse" the site to attached the appropriate **image** to the page.

The purpose of the Image Template Variable is to facilitate the insertion of an image at a specific location within the Template. In the case of our Classical Authors, I would like to have the respective author's image appear in the right column. To do so, I simply add [[*authorPic]] to the main Template. If a value for the Image TV has been set for the Resource, the image will appear in the Template, otherwise it won't.

The Template Variable could be placed anywhere, including an HTML Element style directive, a Chunk, or even the page content area as entered by a Manager user. One of the advantages of using a TV to establish an image in a page, is the ability to ensure proper linking, naming, and other required information - without having to rely on the associated communication and user skill sets. **We simply set the input and output types to image.**

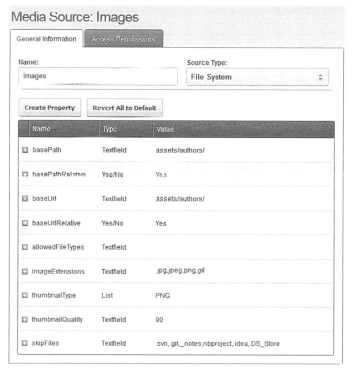

We will also need to create a Media Source which limits Manager users to accessing only a limited directory tree and only image file types.

Fortunately for us, this is the default response, when a new Media Source is create using Filesystem as the source type.

As discussed in the File Template Variable directions, it is a simple matter of adding our path to the Media Source and then saving it.

Return to the Image Template Variable and change the Filesystem to **Images** as the base of our Media Source.

You can have as many of these Media Sources as you need, simply name them accordingly for clarity.

Listbox

MODX Revolution provides equivalents to both HTML listbox types: **single and multiple select**. The ability to select multiple options is the primary difference between the single select and multiple select Listbox TVs. The other difference is on how the data is stored in the database. Single selection list boxes store their data as straight text: `united_states`, whereas multiple selection list boxes store their data as a double-pipe delimited field: `briton||france`.

To utilize a **Listbox**, simply separate each of the name pairs with double "pipe" symbols, typically located just above the Enter key on the keyboard, using the Display Text{equals}{equals}Value syntax. For our purposes we have: `Briton==briton||France==france||United States==united_states`. This facilitates data entry, while eliminating possibility for typographical errors by Manager users - if it was entered correctly here.

Listboxes can take up quite a bit of room in the Manager which might be beneficial in drawing attention to them, but also might be an issue if there are quite a few Template Variables involved. Users typically either do not like to scroll or simply might fail to do so.

Many of the output types could be used to produce content for site visitors. To keep things simple we simply choose to **return a text** equivalent of the string in the database. In this instance we would want to produce an iconic representation of the nationality of the author: `assets/images/[[*author_nationality]].png`. Remember to pay attention to the entire flow of the TV.

The multi-selection choice illustrated above could prove problematic if we had `united_states.jpg` on the file system and not `britonunited_states.jpg`. For displaying the flag indicating our authors nationality, the Single-Select option should probably be used, as people typically are not born in multiple countries simultaneously. In this instance, we could also simply remove the erroneous value by clicking the x associated with it.

Number

This input type simply allows Manager users to enter integer / decimal values into a TV. Primary benefit would be to limit the type of text to that which would indicate numeric values. Examples of use: quantity, rating, size, weight, and other quantifiable units of measure. In our classical authors scenario we may want to catalog the **number** of works in a given genre which have been attributed to the author: 63 Tragedies, 12 Poems, etc. The output type would be left as default.

Radio Option

For many applications, radio buttons provide an effective method of obtaining user input through a limited list of options and their values separated by double pipe symbols. As with the other "form" type interfaces, MODX Revolution rendition of radio buttons mimic the HTML equivalents. This affords us the added ability to reset values without having to reload the entire page, with the use of the green reset icon which appears when the mouse is over the Template Variable in the Resource.

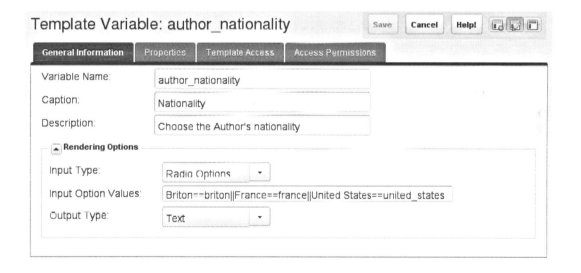

An advantage to using radio buttons over Listbox Template Variables is as simple as calculating the reduction of screen real estate required for the implementation. This is facilitated by the Columns setting on the Input Tab, which allows the definition of the number of columns to be used for presenting the TV.

Resource List

Wikipedia and other sites allow simple linking to other pages contained within the web site. The **Resource List** Template variables provides Manager users similar functionality, to link to other Resources within the given MODX Site providing the bases of a direct linking system.

On our site we have multiple sections with classical authors. We selected the parent Resources of each of those sections to limit the choices available in the drop down list located in the Template Variable tab of attached Resources. If no values are entered in the Parents field, Manager users should be able to select any document within the site assuming they have permission to access it.

We selected a URL for our output type. If the value of the URL is an integer (resource ID) MODX Revolution will replace the Resource List Template Variable with a fully qualified link to the page. Sites which have implemented Search Engine Optimized Friendly URLs will enjoy the seamless creation of a link which honors their FURL settings.

Additional settings are available to further fine-tune the implementation -- start with the defaults.

Rich Text Editor

MODX Revolution provides a facility to implement an on-line, in-browser text editor, but has a prerequisite requirement of a visit to the Package Manager to install a Rich Text Editor, as it does not ship with any rich text editors in its core files. After its installation, TinyMCE could be rendered as a fully functional editor or with restricted features as Site Administrators are afforded the ability to specify functionality, depending on site settings.

MODX Revolution will utilize default values as far as size and the (X)HTML element name and id parameters, when sent to front end. These values can be modified by changing the appropriate settings in the TV. Typically, this TV is used to collect data from within the Manager.

If a Rich Text Editor is not installed, a simple box will be created for the user to enter their (X) HTML – formatted text. Please consider the skill level of the site users when implementing this TV. Also, test the RTE software to make sure it is compatible with your site: HTML5, etc.

When used as an output type and provides code similar to the following:

Listing 05.01: sample output when Text Area is assigned as output type

- -

```
<div class="MODX_RichTextWidget">
    <textarea id="tvauthor_summary" name="tvauthor_summary"
style="width:500px; height:300px;">
    ... your content here ...
    </textarea>
</div>
```

- -

Tag

Tag
Tag this author

`tag||tag2||tag3`

Many sites have begun to implement page tags to help visitors associate key words with a given page or content area of the web page. By creating a **Tag** Template Variable, Manager users are immediately afforded the ability to tag any page within the site using a Tag TV. This allows any content to be categorically related and "linked" and provides the original author the opportunity to directly attach the topical themes they have in mind.

Take note: each tag needs to be separated by double-pipe symbols, and will probably need a Snippet installed which can implement the tags for the site visitor to interact with. The **tagLister** Package provides much of the functionality desired for this purpose, as shown in the *Power Blogging* chapter. The interesting aspect of Tag Template Variables, is the varied methods by which the output can be implemented in addition to simple blogging implementations, tags can also serve as individual link separated by commas and straight text contained within the page.

On one of our web projects, we were asked to create page effects based on the page tags. This was accomplished by selecting HTML tag as the output type and using li as the tag name. We then attached jQuery to the <li> tags created by our TV. This type of functionality, allows for a very wide array of JavaScript libraries and applications to be implemented.

On another site we created site maps based on keywords. By selecting the URL output type we created http://domain.com/tag references, using getResources to create a list of Resources using that tag. This facilitated our ability to present lists of Resources which contained that specific tag. Some people might be thinking this is a cool way to create SEO doorway/gateway pages. Please keep in mind, many search engines will ban a site they catch creating gateway pages. We were simply grouping Resources by topic.

For sites which have an open and free system of tagging, where users are encouraged to tag and create at will, the Tag Template Variable will allow Manager users to implement a tagging "free-for-all." For sites desiring to utilize as few tags as possible, I would suggest using the Auto Tag Template Variable type previously discussed in this chapter.

Text

Of all the available types of Template Variables, the Text type is the one my company implements the most, as we can easily convert and format each occurrence on the fly with MODX Revolution Filters. For example we may we choose to take the various pieces of client contact information and convert them into Text Template Variables. This affords us the ability to establish a consistent presentation, while also enabling us to simply change addresses or other information site wide, without extensive editing - should the need arise.

Developers could see this as a simple $var=string. A TV may begin its service as straight text and may look something like [[*productCodeName]]. If that TV is used to reference an item which is soon to be launched, we can instantly translate each of those references to active links by changing the output type to a URL.

We typically use TVs when it comes to proper nouns, which are going to be repeated more than once in a given site. Far too often, we get the request to link an article or audio file to the authors web site. On the surface, this may seem a simple task until dozens of links are involved – scattered through hundreds of pages. Another implementation could translate product code names to real names or allow developers to float links to new versions, without ever having to replace the original [[*productCodeName]] Template Variable placed in the page.

In our author's scenario, we could use a [[*author]] Text TV to provide a link from each of their works back to the main author page. This may seem unnecessary until we consider the implementation of tagging within a site, which may very well get a user to a page "outside" of normal navigation and possible point to a target page without an easy trail back to the author.

Textarea

Textarea fields provides approximately 9 vertical lines of text, which will scroll as necessary to accommodate more text. As with their, (X)HTML counterparts, these fields simply provide a logical container to retrieve content. Pay close attention on the data input and its eventual output.

Recently, I introduced a set of HTML5 Templates for use within my company, which allows for four "content" areas in each page. I pulled this off by create three additional Textarea Template Variables each named according to the zone of the page they were being used on. Some of you may be thinking this was brilliant. Thank you. Others are wondering what the significance is.

Essentially, my implementation will only include the section in the output that actually has content in it. This also allowed for simple creation of left / right columns and a very simple method for Manager users to choose between primary or alternate backgrounds colors.

Every project is unique its needs should dictate the presentation decided upon. Project leaders may want to consider the psychological expense of users being required to scroll – they tend to "feel" worked. If implemented correctly, these fields can greatly streamline work flow.

URL (Uniform Resource Locator)

Most every resource on the web has some sort of URI attached. MODX Revolution's **URL** TV allows Manager users to directly link a Resource on a project with content found elsewhere on the web.

As many of the classical authors have had Wikipedia articles created for them, we can utilize a URL Template Variable to store the address with the Resource of each author. This makes it incredibly easy to create links to any web sources we would like to.

Once the URL TV type is created, Manager users will be presented with a box allowing them to select the protocol and enter the link. Fortunately, the developers of MODX Revolution had the foresight to automatically remove the protocol from the text box, so as to facilitate data entry. Essentially, the full link: `http://en.wikipedia.org/wiki/MODX` becomes `en.wikipedia.org/wiki/MODX` when the resource is saved to the database.

Each of the four primary protocols associated with the internet have been provided via a drop-down box. By selecting the desired protocol and completing the style, class, title, and display text information in the URL TV definition we can create very effective links to web resources.

Forcing the Use of Template Variables

Some implementations may require additional Resource related information to be added to it in the form of Template Variables. In some scenarios this information is considered mission critical. Fortunately, MODX Revolution includes an Allow Blank setting, which prohibits the Resource from being saved if the Template Variable has not been completed.

Simply, change the setting on the Input Tab of the Template Variable to no, thus forcing the attention of the Manager user to the value requiring their attention. Care should be taken to ensure relevant information has added, by choosing a Template Variable input type which would minimize the user's ability to simply bypass the field with a period or other meaningless content.

Output Template Variables

Throughout this chapter we have provided examples of how Template Variables will appear to Manager users. The output is what we typically are "paid" for and what the client values. Our task is to select the best method of input so as to provide the basis of flexibility for our clients.

Output types are for the site visitor presentation and will only contain the *result* of the input. Changing the output of a TV will change the way it is presented on the front of the web site, but will typically not alter the data collected from the Manager user. To illustrate this, a URL to Wikipedia can be offered as an actual clickable link or as a basis to build a button link.

Assuming, I were to have a client with a massive amount of legal templates and it was decided to move them all to a Content Distribution Network. A little forethought may have had simply the filename being store, while the base URL itself was kept elsewhere. I could easily change the value to point to our "cloud" storage and not have to edit a single Resource to reflect the changes.

Thinking through the possible implementations of a TV should occur during the beginning stages of a web project. Fortunately, many TVs can simply return text, which are the most flexible Template Variable output to work with. We will briefly take a look at a few of the output types which differ somewhat from the input types previously discussed.

Delimiter

Simply provides output in a delimited state. An example might include creating meta keywords for the page header by using double-pipe separated Tag input with a comma being used as the output delimiter. Additionally, we could implement a Snippet call and pass a list of options to the Snippet: `[[someSnippet?includeDocs=`[[*authors_works]]`]]`. This could also be used in conjunction with JavaScript calls or other items within the page which can accept a delimited list.

HTML Tag

This will take any double-pipe delimited list and return each item in its own HTML Tag. This example would take `{one||two}` input from a Tag TV and create the following:

<li id="tagCloud0" class="tag">one</li>
<li id="tagCloud1" class="tag">two</li>

As many JavaScript libraries tend to extensively utilize the list item HTML element, this could prove beneficial to feed some of the many tag cloud implementations seen around the web. Experiment and see what you can come up with.

Rich Text

Some versions of TinyMCE installed via the Package Manager, may have issues being displayed outside of the Manager. We can apply our own version of a Rich Text Editor for our visitors by attaching them one of our choosing to the class or id utilized by MODX Revolution: `<div class="MODX_RichTextWidget"></div>` (for example). There are plenty of theses resources available, many of which are not near as heavy as TinyMCE.

Custom Forms

Many of us may find ourselves in the position to where we need to customize the form used to enter the information for each Resource. By using the Form Customization (FC in MODX speak) located under the Security menu in the Manager, very extravagant presentations for Manager users to work in can be implemented.

In our classical authors scenario, we appropriately named every Template Variable with a prefix of author. We could have also grouped all of our author Snippets, Chunks, Templates, and Template Variables in an "author" category. In either case it is possible to apply a constraint so the customizations would only be applied to the Resources directly related to our authors. One method of doing this would be to apply a constraint to work only on the Resources using the template named "Author."

In chapter 2, I discussed the basics of this process. Form Customization is a massive topic, with far reaching implications. In one instance, a developer was able to completely replace the Manager with a flip book Adobe Flash / JavaScript interface. Currently the best information available on Form Customization can be found by visiting the MODX Documentation site: `http://rtfm.MODX.com/display/revolution20/Customizing+the+Manager`.

Database considerations

The definitions of each Template Variables is stored in `MODX_site_tmplvars` table in the database. The "data" for any of the Resources using the TV is stored in `MODX_site_tmplvar_content`. This allows each these template extensions to be applied to multiple Resources simultaneously. Each Resource simply needs to be updated to set the appropriate value for that page. If the implementation is planned out at the beginning of the site development, each of these values can be established during the initial Resource creation, reducing time and effort later.

On the plus side of the utilization of Template Variables, is the knowledge each Resource combined with these two database tables, can have virtually unlimited extension possibilities and customization declarations. Used in tandem with the `MODX_site_content` table, MODX Revolution provides a very streamlined and flexible method to very exacting demands.

On the negative side of Template Variable implementation, we should be aware once a value is assigned to a Template Variable and stored in the database, we should consider it semi-permanent. While this is a good perspective to have, if a Template Variable is deleted from the site, the associated values will also be removed from the database. On the other hand, if the Template Variable is simply removed from a Template, the values may very well remain in the database indefinitely. Depending on the needs of the project this could be a positive or negative consideration. As of this writing the following methods are some of those used to reliably alter these values:

- ♦ Each corresponding Resource will need to be manually edited
- ♦ An UPDATE query is performed using the TV and Resource IDs in the WHERE
- ♦ A Snippet can be created to programmatically remove / alter the desired values

Summary

With Template Variables assigned to Templates, and Templates assigned to Resources a very straightforward method of design can be established from the conceptual stages of the web project. Developers can easily visualize the entire work flow process for each individual TV during their conception and adjust each accordingly during implementation.

By choosing the type of input Manager users will be presented with, project leaders can provide the options necessary to satisfy data-entry integrity, while avoiding typographical and syntactical errors. This should also expedite project development as most of the "questions" should already be answered in the interface.

Once information is gathered, it is important to understand how it is to be used. In some instances, it will only be stored in the database and never directly presented. In others the output type may need to be "default" or text, so that other Template Variables can use the output as input. Starting with text or the default output type should clearly show what is stored in the database, on a per Resource (page) basis. In any case, project leaders can decide the format of information on both ends, giving them the much needed control missing from many Content Management Systems.

The MODX Revolution Template Variable Buffet is open for business. Every item on the menu is there to be sampled, explored, and experimented with. The are no signs on this buffet which limit sharing, how much you take, or even the minimum age to partake. The good news – this buffet is provided free - no hacks, kludges, or modifications are required!

Have fun – Template Variables can be some of the best components in your tool set.

6

[[Snippets]], Plug-ins and Widgets: Adding PHP Dynamic Content

Pizza.

Such a simple word, and yet with the power to invoke mental imagery, stir emotional desires, and cause physiological responses. For many, pizza is a "people" food – friends appear, parties happen, and fun is usually quick to follow. Not many of us understand the perfect temperature and method to cook pizza or even how to combine the ingredients. The simple universal truth remains the same: looking for good pizza is always subjective.

MODX Revolution Snippets have much in common with pizza. Simply take a look at the Package Manger (our "menu") and see the vast array of specialty items available. In many instances, someone went before us, selected ingredients, and created a product to be used. We simply read the "menu" of Package descriptions and hopefully locate one that meets our needs. If we find it, we can move on with our project and focus our efforts to the specific needs of our clients, instead of mundane tasks such as creating navigation systems.

Excellent cooks and experienced coders have one thing in common – they are artists and their work is an art form. Fortunately for us, the MODX Revolution developers provide us with a very wide selection of brushes and tools to use in our craft. In a stroke of genius, they have allowed us to feel the textures of each ingredient, understand the nuances of each flavor, and the freedom to put them together in very imaginative and creative ways.

Snippets provide direct access to the very core of this amazing system allowing us to create extensions to MODX Revolution or integral components targeted to a specific need. This is where we can begin to explore the depths of the power found within MODX Revolution. This is where we can really spread our wings and fly.

Snippets

MODX Revolution Snippets are simply Elements written using PHP code. If there is a way to write it in PHP, there is typically a way to make it work within the confines of a MODX Revolution web project. The possibilities of innovative web applications are staggering and limited only by the skill-sets of the web project developers and sub-contractors.

To be used, a Snippet has to be included within the page content at some point. This could be in the Template, an (X)HTML Chunk, the actual content, or even from another Snippet. Essentially, Snippets can be implemented by anyone with permissions to do so, at any point during the development and design of the web project.

Snippets are the primary method many developers utilize to customize a web project to extremely exacting specifications and are dynamic by their nature, simply because they can be executed on every page load, user change, or a myriad of other possibilities.. They are also one of the portals used to take a web project "to the next level." A well written Snippet can easily become the foundation of a variety of user interface implementations wrapped in AJAX or simply pulling content from a database table. Essentially, Snippets can potentially accomplish anything PHP allows them to.

This has immense advantages to developers:

- Security has already been implemented in the framework
- The core of MODX Revolution was designed to be extensible
- Snippets can be utilized on multiple sites, thereby increasing the benefits of the time spent in development exponentially
- Direct access to a wide variety of database management systems (DBMS) can be implemented via the xPDO object-relational bridge
- End-users can be provided with a simple and consistent method of implementation
- Snippets can offer precise control over dynamic content
- Implementations can offer administrations, or UI designes runtime configurations reducing the amount of communication required for implementations

This can greatly reduce the time required for project development and decrease the overall amount of code necessary – meaning easier support and updates. Once Snippets become part of the developers / company's tool-set, designers will probably understand how to implement subsequent installations with little interaction from developers. This frees both groups to be increasingly productive – rather than wait on responses.

MODX Revolution has two main types of PHP Elements: Snippets and Plugins. In addition to being installed via Package Management, Snippets and Plug-ins can also be developed in-house and then added manually to a web project, subsequently Packaged for distribution.

Why is it called a Snippet?

Many authors encourage members of the community to join in and help out with their project. In fact, many of the most popular Snippets have been released by the developers of MODX Revolution with the desire for people to eventually take them over and continue their development and support. This basis of development gets more eyes, hands, and ideas into a project making it a richer product which has been extensively tested and implemented - directly translating into lower cost and fewer man hours on a given web project when a well-tested Snippet is used instead of starting from scratch. Some of these projects may involve a single file or a collection of them depending solely on the overall purpose.

Many of these PHP applications can become huge in their own right, as they perform multiple functions and serve as a foundation for users and data to interact. Snippets are just the opposite and by their very definition serve as only a piece of the presentation and typically fulfill only a specific purpose each time it is utilized within the web project. Additionally, many authors choose to minimize the amount of code presented within the Snippet itself to only the code necessary for the Snippet to be implemented. Everything else is summarily tucked into underlying PHP class files away from Manager users. There are multiple reasons for doing this: code re-usability, clarity of communication, security, and the reduction of the footprint in the database to name only a few.

Quality is the single measures of Snippet and translates to how well the needs of the project are met. Over the coming pages we will be looking at some of the expectations and expectations suggested by the MODX Project. In short, Snippets can stand alone or operate as part of a cohesive unit, but should typically be centered on a single task.

The Dangerous Side to Snippets

Snippets have an inherent ability would should be mentioned. They have direct access to the very core of MODX Revolution, including: database, file system, private user data, and other potentially sensitive information. Everything accessible to MODX Revolution may very well be accessed via a simple Snippet. This is typically untrue of Chunks, Templates, Template Variables, etc., because they have a limited scope and typically contain simple text and not PHP commands.

Project leaders should be very cautious and aware of exactly who has the ability to add Snippets to their MODX Revolution project. Concern for what site visitors see, or what data is exposed to the public side of a web site is only one part of the problem. Snippets can run transparently in the background accomplishing any of a myriad of methods to transfer data from one place to another.

MODX Revolution has built in methods to send e-mail. It also has a very powerful foundation in xPDO which could potentially be utilized to create duplicate data to another database. These and other issues are not isolated to MODX Revolution. Most any Content Management System in use can be abused in these manners. The simplest protection is to limit Manager access to only those individuals which need it, and also to limit that access to only those areas required for each user.

Verify Snippet Functionality and Output

Once something appears on a page and is seen by the public, it can not easily be taken back. For some of us, things tend to work out in such a way, Google or some other search engine will index the site just at the moment which may prove the most problematic. This could have massive ramifications as the description added to the search link could have millions of potential clients looking at something we would prefer they hadn't. It is much better to be 100% certain of what is going on, than to take someone's word for it or to move forward based upon an assumption.

In some situations one developer may be asked to implement and work on a Snippet another developer created, as a second set of eyes could prove very beneficial. One of the reasons for this is to ensure a given Snippet does not wander far from its intended purpose. It doesn't take a genius to implement database access, it simply requires opportunity. With all of this in the forefront of our thoughts, let us move on to Snippets.

Package Example: Wayfinder

Over the years, I have seen quite a few comments by individuals creating their own menu system for use within MODX Revolution. Upon reading these comments, I typically have the same thought go through my mind: "Why in the world are they needing to do that?"

One of the most popular Snippets available for download via Package Management is the Wayfinder Snippet, which predates MODX Evolution – and has been completely rewritten for MODX Revolution. This Snippet is an excellent example of a Community based Snippet and also one of the most innovative navigation systems available for any Content Management Product.

For those who would appreciate some "hands-on" training with this Snippet, this is your opportunity, as much of this chapter uses the Wayfinder Package to discuss many of the considerations surrounding the implementation of Snippets. Please ensure Wayfinder is installed in the web project by logging into the Manager, switching to the Elements tab, and opening the Snippets section. If Wayfinder is already listed, feel free to skip these installation steps. Otherwise, Package installation is extensively detailed in the *Discovering The Heart of MODX Revolution: The Manager* chapter. If necessary, install Wayfinder, by referring to that chapter or by following these abbreviated instructions:

1. Using the Package browser, select the arrow next to MODX Add-Ons
2. Scroll down and open the Navigation group
3. Select Wayfinder and then click the "Download" Button
4. Select "Finished" to leave the download screen
5. Select Wayfinder's "Install" Button to complete the install process

All packages available in the MODX Revolution repository are installed utilizing these basic steps. Some of which, may include (X)HTML Chunks, additional Snippets, or other Elements which can be used together in conjunction with the main library. Be sure to visit the primary add-on documentation site: http://rtfm.MODX.com/display/ADDON/Home for more information on individual packages.

Exploring the Directory Structure

Once installation of any MODX Revolution Package has successfully completed, the base files can be found in the core/components/package_name directory of the web project. Occasionally, a Snippet will need additional JavaScript, image, CSS or other support files, which may be found in the assets/components/package_name directory.

Wayfinder is quite a bit older than many of the other MODX Revolution Snippets, and as such, it has had the opportunity to receive plenty of attention during its years of service. For developers beginning to create MODX Revolution Snippets, this is a great Package to learn from, as it utilizes many of the core functions Snippets typically implement.

As one of the "largest" MODX Revolution Snippets, Wayfinder includes dozens of files in the package. Don't overly concern yourself with the number of files, as this Package contains more files than others do. For those individuals desiring to create their own Snippets, Wayfinder's directory structure is typical of many MODX Revolution Snippets, and an excellent example to learn from. Fortunately for us, we can learn much from the last two PHP files and the default.config.php.

The wayfinder.Snippet.php file is the only actual PHP Snippet in this Package stored in the database and found in the Element menu. Its associated wayfinder.class.php file does much of the "heavy lifting" or real work when the Snippet is called, but is simply loaded from the file system by the Wayfinder Snippet as needed. The default.config.php file contains the base set of configuration settings which can be overridden with Property Sets or via the Snippet call itself. Lastly, the docs directory contains various information concerning the Wayfinder Snippet and its history. The license.txt file should be read in all Packages to ensure license compliance.

The Wayfinder Snippet

There are some who may be thinking, "Whoa! Wait a minute. I'm not a coder!" That's the beauty of MODX Revolution: you can go as far as you would like to, but with all frameworks, there is the possibility of a little "job responsibility" overlap. We are going to take a few minutes to introduce some concepts which should help implement any Snippet.

Listing 06.01: Wayfinder Snippet

- -

```php
<?php
/**
 * Wayfinder Snippet to build site navigation menus
 *
 * Totally refactored from original DropMenu nav builder to make
 * it easier to create custom navigation by using chunks as output
 * templates. By using templates, many of the paramaters are no
 * longer needed for flexible output including tables, unordered- or
 * ordered-lists (ULs or OLs), definition lists (DLs) or in any other
 * format you desire.
 * @version 2.1.1-beta5
 * @author Garry Nutting (collabpad.com)
 * @author Kyle Jaebker (muddydogpaws.com)
 * @author Ryan Thrash (MODX.com)
 * @author Shaun McCormick (MODX.com)
 * @author Jason Coward (MODX.com)
 * @example [[Wayfinder? &startId=`0`]]
 *
 */
$wayfinder_base = $modx->getOption('wayfinder.core_path',
$scriptProperties, $modx->getOption('core_path') . 'components/
wayfinder/');
/* include a custom config file if specified */
if (isset($scriptProperties['config'])) {
    $scriptProperties['config'] = str_replace('../', '',
$scriptProperties['config']);
    $scriptProperties['config'] = $wayfinder_base . 'configs/' .
$scriptProperties['config'] . '.config.php';
} else {
    $scriptProperties['config'] = $wayfinder_base . 'configs/default.
config.php';
}
if (file_exists($scriptProperties['config'])) {
    include_once $scriptProperties['config'];
}
/* include wayfinder class */
include_once $wayfinder_base . 'wayfinder.class.php';
if (!$modx->loadClass('Wayfinder', $wayfinder_base, true, true)) {
    return 'error: Wayfinder class not found';
}
$wf = new Wayfinder($MODX, $scriptProperties);
```

```
/* get user class definitions
 * TODO: eventually move these into config parameters */
$wf->_css = array(
    'first' => isset($firstClass) ? $firstClass : '',
    'last' => isset($lastClass) ? $lastClass : 'last',
    'here' => isset($hereClass) ? $hereClass : 'active',
    'parent' => isset($parentClass) ? $parentClass : '',
    'row' => isset($rowClass) ? $rowClass : '',
    'outer' => isset($outerClass) ? $outerClass : '',
    'inner' => isset($innerClass) ? $innerClass : '',
    'level' => isset($levelClass) ? $levelClass : '',
    'self' => isset($selfClass) ? $selfClass : '',
    'weblink' => isset($webLinkClass) ? $webLinkClass : ''
);
/* get user templates
 * TODO: eventually move these into config parameters */
$wf->_templates = array(
    'outerTpl' => isset($outerTpl) ? $outerTpl : '',
    'rowTpl' => isset($rowTpl) ? $rowTpl : '',
    'parentRowTpl' => isset($parentRowTpl) ? $parentRowTpl : '',
    'parentRowHereTpl' => isset($parentRowHereTpl) ?
$parentRowHereTpl : '',
    'hereTpl' => isset($hereTpl) ? $hereTpl : '',
    'innerTpl' => isset($innerTpl) ? $innerTpl : '',
    'innerRowTpl' => isset($innerRowTpl) ? $innerRowTpl : '',
    'innerHereTpl' => isset($innerHereTpl) ? $innerHereTpl : '',
    'activeParentRowTpl' => isset($activeParentRowTpl) ?
$activeParentRowTpl : '',
    'categoryFoldersTpl' => isset($categoryFoldersTpl) ?
$categoryFoldersTpl : '',
    'startItemTpl' => isset($startItemTpl) ? $startItemTpl : ''
);
/* process Wayfinder */
$output = $wf->run();
if ($wf->_config['debug']) {
    $output .= $wf->renderDebugOutput();
}
/* output results */
if ($wf->_config['ph']) {
    $modx->setPlaceholder($wf->_config['ph'], $output);
} else {
    return $output;}
```

- -

When the Code is All The Documentation We Have

In obedience to some unwritten and undocumented phenomenon, developers tend to have an aversion to writing documentation, which may cause designers to actually need to read the code or the comments within the Snippet to acquire the necessary information to implement it within a web project. This may very well be the case for in-house or younger Snippets which are still under continuous initial stages of development, but may also occur with very powerful and useful Snippets. In some instances, we could simply install another Package and provide similar functionality and move forward with the project, while in others we may be forced to use what we have been given.

As a contributor to the official documentation for MODX Revolution, I fully understand how beneficial clear and concise documentation can be. Most of what the documentation team has learned, comes from three places: reading the code, using trial and error, and discussions (in IRC and in the forums). These same methods can help those who are discovering MODX Revolution or one of its many Packages – even the gurus are known to ask questions.

The process of implementing a Snippet with poor documentation can be prove frustrating. Hopefully, this brief glimpse at a well documented Snippet will provide necessary insight on working with Packages requiring more effort. Just keep in mind that the majority of the Packages offered for MODX Revolution are free and the authors are under no further obligation than they accept for themselves. This leaves plenty of room for each of us to take an active role.

Hopefully, the next few paragraphs will serve as a simplified crash course on possible means to implement Snippets, even if they may not have any documentation we can find. Being able to read the code to get a section of the project started, may prove invaluable when time is critical.

Deciphering Snippet Activity

The first item we should notice is the description of the Snippet. This quickly establishes the intended implementation: *Wayfinder Snippet to build site navigation menus*. Additional information is provided to indicate the flexibility of Wayfinder. Immediately following, is a list of people involved in the development and subsequent support of Wayfinder. Kyle Jaebker originated the Snippet and over time others contributed to its success. Two of the primary MODX developers are listed, as well as the MODX CEO, Ryan Thrash.

After this list of names is where things get interesting. The vast majority of the Wayfinder Snippet is doing little else than establishing its own path, setting up parameters, and instantiating a class. For non programmers, it is simply getting all of its piece together. This Snippet is, in effect, gathering the parameters attached to the Snippet's call, feeding them to a class file: wayfinder.class.php, and presenting the results to the site visitor via the page, on which the Snippet was placed.

Finding the Required Parameters

Each Snippet will most likely be very different, as everyone has their own style of coding and Snippets typically have different purposes – and thereby parameters. There is also the issue of lagging documentation where new features have been added, mentioned in the changelog.txt file, but have not been fully documented yet. In these instances, it may be best to immediately post a question in the MODX forum dedicated to the Snippet – especially if we think we have it figured out and have a working sample. The MODX community thrives on communication and sharing concepts – everyone wins.

When it comes to working with installed MODX Revolution packages, designers and project leaders need to know what parameters are available to implement the Snippet. At the bare minimum, we simply need to know where to start looking for these parameters when we do not have informative documentation, support, or other means to discover the possible implementation variables available for use within the Snippet.

In this older version of the Wayfinder Snippet, we are only provided with two sets (known as PHP arrays) of settings: $wf->_css, and $wf->_templates. As indicated in the TODO comment, these may eventually be moved to an external configuration file, thereby reducing this Snippet to a few dozen lines – most of which mere comments. If these configuration settings are moved, then we would have to rely on reading the code directly, documentation, or possibly spend quite a bit of time in the discussion forums hashing out implementation. We may also have to plan to go through each of the files in a local copy of the Package to discern all that we can.

According to the Wayfinder Snippet, the CSS array allows for the following Cascading Style Sheet parameters to be set when the Snippet is executed: firstClass, lastClass, hereClass, parentClass, rowClass, and so on. The template array allows the following parameters: outerTpl, rowTpl, parentRowTpl, parentRowHereTpl, hereTpl, innerTpl, and so on. Essentially, we can look at each of the isset($variable) to see what Wayfinder is looking for. We simply remove the dollar sign ("$") and the rest is usually a parameter to be used.

Even though we are given a couple sets of Wayfinder parameters, there are many more configuration options available, which are not presented within this segment of code. For the time being this could give us a decent start and get things functional. To move further, we would have to begin looking through the wayfinder.class.php, file and see if there are any other parameters we could implement.

Developers should intentionally document their work or find someone capable and willing to interpret their project into documentation for the masses to use. More than a few Open Source projects, have had the community develop its documentation, which proves most anyone can help, even by asking questions and sharing what they have learned with others.

There is always a chance that a Package has limited or no documentation, and in some cases it may simply be written in another language than that of the user. Everyone can help.

When A Snippet Exists For Evolution And Revolution

Wayfinder has plenty of documentation, support, forums, examples, and users to provide much of the information any web project could want to implement. In fact, this Snippet could even be considered one of the best supported Packages provided for MODX due the extensive community activity and number of developers. One of the MODX community members, *kongondo,* even went as far as to write a 140 page book for Wayfinder implementations in MODX Evolution.

⊤ Not All Snippets are created equal

MODX Revolution is based on xPDO and utilizes a completely different API than was used on previous MODX products. Developers and project leaders will need to ensure any Snippets being utilized adhere to the product-specific API.

Fortunately for us, much of documentation attributed to previous Wayfinder products remains relevant, as the authors opted to keep the parameters consistent between the various MODX Wayfinder versions. This makes life easier on potential users and developers of the Snippet. It also allows the time invested in MODX Evolution Wayfinder implementations to reap further benefit when moved to MODX Revolution implementations. This ability should serve as a great example for MODX Revolution developers.

Ideally, we should look for the MODX Revolution content when seeking out documentation. Sometimes, this is simple as looking for the double brackets ("[[ ]]") in example Snippet calls. Using MODX Evolution examples will probably fail due to syntactical and functional changes – though the key concepts translate easy enough between the versions. If needed, simply start by changing the bracket structure to double brackets, and continue from there. More often than not, this will be all that is needed to import a MODX Evolution Wayfinder example into a MODX Revolution project. We simply need to make sure our implementations adhere to the MODX Revolution platform, while .

⊤ Wayfinder resources:

Documentation: `http://rtfm.MODX.com/display/ADDON/Wayfinder`
Forum: `http://forums.modx.com/board/68/wayfinder`
140 Page E-Book: `http://forums.modx.com/thread/40293/new-wayfinder-e-book`

Snippet Calls

There are only a few things to understand about Snippet implementation and ignoring them can easily eat up hours of time and cause frustration. Before asking for help check each of these aspects for a gratifying and successful Snippet experience.

Syntax and Caching Implications

A cached Snippet call will appear similarly to `[[SnippetName]]` and is used with static content which is expected to rarely or never change. An example of using a cached Snippet may appear in a global navigation menu, as the main sections may never change once established.

Most Snippets should begin life with an uncached Snippet call. This varies only slightly from the cached version: `[[!SnippetName]]`, by preceding the Snippet name with an exclamation point. Uncached calls should be used on dynamic content which will possibly or definitely change.

The complaints most often affiliated with caching may include: unexpected Snippet output and issues with page content not updating during page loads or reflecting changes in the data source (database, rss feeds, etc.). Clearing the site cache is the most common resolution to many of the issues people have with Snippets. See the The Document Parser And Cache Mechanism appendix for more information.

Use Backticks (`) For Parameters

The functionality of many MODX Revolution Elements can be modified when they are called. Snippets requiring parameters should utilize the following notation: `[[!SnippetName?parameter=`value`&parameter2=`value?`]]`. Attempting to provide parameters without following this format can end with empty white pages, errors, or confusing Snippet results.

For (X)HTML purists, who prefer to use & in place of &, feel free to do so, but understand Element calls are "instructions" for MODX Revolution and as such, are never intended to be seen via web browsers. There are exceptions to the rule, such as an implementation mistake being made or the deliberate posting of code, such as the examples on my site which have had key characters dynamically replaced to prevent MODX Revolution from parsing them.

All MODX Revolution Elements (Snippets, Chunks, Template Variables, etc.) share the common backtick rule, in regards to parameter passage.

The location of the backtick on the standard keyboard is on the same key as the tilde (~), to the left of the "1", above the "Tab" and beneath the "Esc" keys.

Wayfinder Implementation Samples

With dozens of parameters and virtually unlimited methods of innovative implementations available, we will have to constrain ourselves to examples which are intended to get a web project "live" as quickly as possible. Just be aware, it is completely possible to have Wayfinder implementations combined with jQuery, AJAX, and other technologies to create very elaborate user interfaces.

Global Horizontal Navigation Bar

To establish a simple "top-level" navigation bar for our Templates, we first create a Chunk to store our Snippet call. Simply, right-click the Chunk option in the Element tree and select New Chunk. This will allow us to update the entire site across multiple Templates by editing the globalNav Chunk.

We then place the following code within the Chunk:

Listing 06.02: globalNav Chunk

- -

```
<div id="mainnav">[[Wayfinder?startId=`0`&level=`1`&sortBy=`menuindex
`&rowTpl=`wfNavBar`&excludeDocs=`7,25,207`]]</div>
```

- -

- ◆ [[Wayfinder]] is the base Element of the Snippet call – many Snippets only require their name and little else
- ◆ startID=`0` denotes where the menu should originate – currently the site root
- ◆ level=`1` specifies the number of document levels we want the menu to display
- ◆ sortBy=`menuindex` allows us to manually create the sort order by specifying the Menu Index on each Resource page in the Manager – can also be any of the other document fields such as pagetitle, menutitle, longtitle
- ◆ rowTpl=`wfNavBar` indicates the (X)HTML Chunk name to use as a "template" for each "row" or item of our menu
- ◆ excludeDocs=`7,25,207` tells Wayfinder to not include my resume, and a couple other documents to the global menu – this can be a single Resource ID or a comma separated list

Essentially, this informs Wayfinder to get only the documents within one level of the Resource specified in startID sorted by their menu index and wrap each of them in the template specified in the rowTpl parameter. Additionally, Wayfinder has been instructed to exclude three of these Resources from the menu it is creating for us. To direct how our menu is returned to us we have instructed Wayfinder to use the wfNarBar Chunk as the "template" for each row, containing the following code:

Listing 06.03: wfNavBar Chunk used as template for Wayfinder Row

- -

```
<li [[+wf.id]] [[+wf.classes]]><a href="[[+wf.link]]"
title="[[++site_name]] [[+wf.title]]" [[+wf.attributes]]>[[+wf.
linktext]]</a>[[+wf.wrapper]]</li><li class="sep">|</li>
```

- -

As you may recall, one of the setting groups we could see within the Snippet in the last section was for CSS items. We could have specified our own, but Wayfinder already has default values we can build on. By including some very minor cascading style sheet definitions in our main site css file, we can create a horizontal navigation bar.

Additional CSS may be applied based on the needs of the web project, for a simple Horizontal Navigation bar, this provides a basis which can be easily built upon.

To practically apply CSS to Wayfinder it might be necessary to allow Wayfinder to create the menu and then view the code it creates, taking note of the ID and class settings of each of the respective elements in the resulting menu.

Once these are known, CSS can be applied to Wayfinder's default values or dedicated MODX Revolution Chunk "templates" can be created with the desired id / class parameters attached to each element.

```css
#mainnav {
    padding-top: 10px;
    width: auto;
}
#mainnav ul {
    height: 35px;
    margin: 0 auto;
    padding: 0;
    list-style-type: none;
}
#mainnav ul li {
    display: inline;
}
#mainnav ul li a {
    font-size: 12px;
    text-decoration: none;
    padding: 0 10px 0 10px;
}
#mainnav ul li.sep {
    color: #ddd;
    height: 8px;
    vertical-align: middle;
}
```

Vertical Navigation

Wayfinder makes the creation of menus to be extremely easy in many instances. For our vertical menu, we are going to implement an alphabetical listing of documents based on page titles and simply rely on Wayfinder's default settings to streamline our efforts, as shown in the following:

Listing 06.04: establishing a simple vertical menu

```
[[Wayfinder?startId=`5`&level=`1`&sortBy=`pagetitle`]]
```

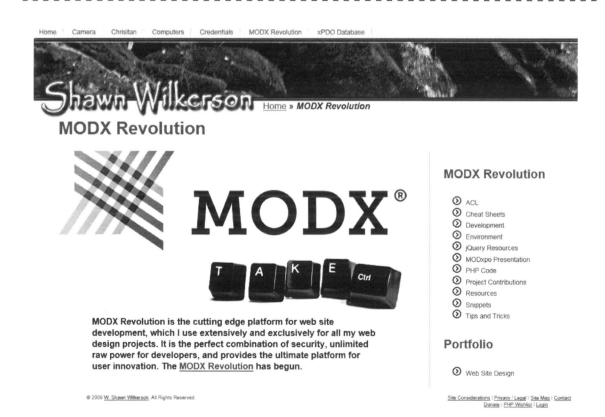

Before I converted the site to Articles, the MODX Revolution area of my web site contained a horizontal global navigation menu and a category specific menu as a result of using two Wayfinder Snippet Calls. The concept is to keep people focused within a topic displayed under the header image as long as they are interested in that area, while simultaneously allowing users to travel to other sections of the site, if they so desire, by using the menu located in the top left.

As with the horizontal navigation bar, much of the layout and structure is defined utilizing Cascading Style Sheets. This provides less code in each page, as well as providing a consistent presentation across the project, while giving designers a single Snippet to interact with.

Building a Wiki-type Layout

User interfaces can be created with Wayfinder which can provide presentations seen in other products or sites on the web. By taking advantage of Wayfinder's extensive templating capability, we can easily replace quite a few of the navigation Snippets which were offered for previous MODX versions, as well as some of those being offered for Revolution.

In this instance we are going to provide similar functionality of the ListChildOrSibs Snippet, which I contributed multiple enhancements during the years I used MODX Evolution. This Snippet provides presentations, somewhat similar to the content links found on Wikipedia and other Wiki-type sites. We shall begin with our Wayfinder call, followed by explanations of the parameters previously not discussed:

Listing 06.05: replacing other Snippets with Wayfinder

```
[[Wayfinder?startId=`31`
    &level=`1`
    &titleOfLinks=`menutitle`
    &textOfLinks=`description`
    &rowTpl=`wfListChildOrSibs`
    &sortBy=`menutitle`
    &showSubDocCount=`true`
    &displayStart=`false`
    &startItemTpl=`wfStartItemWithHeaders`]]
```

- ♦ titleOfLinks=`menutitle` provides Wayfinder with the menu title of each Resource – this could be used to establish the title="some test here" in the href tag
- ♦ textofLinks=`description` provides the Resource description for Wayfinder to use
- ♦ showDocCount=`true` tells Wayfinder to count the documents it found for retrieval for display to the user. We could also have limited the number of menu items
- ♦ displayStart=`false` allows us to call a container without adding it to the list of links, which in this example is the current document - we want all the siblings of this page
- ♦ startItemTpl tells Wayfinder which Chunk to use as its "template" if we decide to display the start link via displayStart=`true`, included in the call for eventual activation once we have created sufficient content under the current page

Project Contributions

Author:

Using Friendly URLs ⌧ activating Friendly URLs (furls)
Using Resource Symlinks ⌧ placing the same content into multiple resources
Extending modUser ⌧ create your own extended modUser class for handling your users

Contributed to:

Installation section ⌧ MODx Revolution Development Environments
Input and Output Filters ⌧ Example section
Moving Your Site to a New Server ⌧ Changed the order, added Writable and Ownership sections
Troubleshooting Installation ⌧ note on corrupted manager in the "Flaky" section

Community:

MODx Bug Tracker ⌧ link may require login
MODx Forums ⌧ may require log in

We need to have links to click on, as well as descriptions of each of those links, so we have implemented Wayfinder to make sure we have access to the various components necessary to create our presentation.

In the following templates pay close attention to how the titleOfLinks parameter is used to create the links to be clicked and textOfLinks to provide the various link descriptions.

Listing 06.06: wfListChildOrSibs Chunk

```
<li [[+wf.id]] [[+wf.classes]]> <a href="[[+wf.link]]" title="[[+wf.
title]] by [[++site_name]]" [[+wf.attributes]]>[[+wf.title]]</a>:
[[+wf.linktext]] [[+wf.wrapper]]</li>
```

Listing 06.07: wfStartItemWithHeaders

```
<h3>[[+wf.title]]</h3><span class="docCounts fltRight">([[+wf.
subitemcount]] entries)</span>
<strong><a href="[[+wf.link]]" title="[[++site_name]] [[+wf.title]]"
[[+wf.attributes]]>[[+wf.linktext]]</a> </strong>[[+wf.wrapper]]
```

These two small (X)HTML Chunks are all that is needed for Wayfinder to replace the entire ListChildOrSibs Snippet. By implementing Wayfinder's placeholders, we can create solid presentations as well as navigation systems - **as long as we remember to to place the appropriate text in the Resource page in the Manager**. Direct benefits are as simple as having less content to install into each web project, reduced learning curves, and increased productivity. The ability to create and utilize a single Snippet to perform multiple similar functions can be the basis of a very solid toolset.

With Wayfinder being implemented, Manager users may already understand the purpose of what they are doing and can focus on presentation instead of implementation, simply because it can be installed on every MODX Revolution project. After a particular user interface presentation has been hashed out on a site, further discussions can simply refer to the implementation currently in action or to screen captures associated with the various components on our in-house web server.

This small amount of code demonstrates the power housed within many MODX Revolution Snippets. In this example, we simply need to add new Resources to the site without another thought to the Global Navigation, Vertical navigation or the Wiki-type presentation, as Wayfinder will automatically adjust the menus and presentation as documents are published.

Additionally, this amazing Snippet also recognizes the authentication privileges and other ACL settings established within the MODX Revolution project, so implementations can focus on the task itself, instead of getting mired in each of the security issues a project may require, leaving those decisions and implementations to those in position to handle them.

Wayfinder is a very straightforward Package requiring very little interaction once installed. It gladly handles much of the guess work and coding typically associated with site navigation, whether as a part of the page Template, as a result of a Chunk, or in the page contents itself.

Included Navigation Configurations

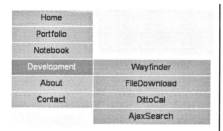

The Wayfinder installation also contains approximately a dozen predefined navigation menu configurations. To use any of these:

1. Create an `assets/components/wayfinder` directory at the top of the site, if it doesn't already exist

2. Copy the `core/components/wayfinder/examples` folder to `assets/components/wayfinder/examples`

3. The last step is to simply call Wayfinder with the configuration name and a starting Resource ID to build the menu from:

Listing 06.08: implementing a menu style included with Wayfinder

```
[[Wayfinder?config=`cssplay-flyout`&startId=`0`]]
```

For more information and specific requirements, please take a look at the individual configuration files located within each example directory. To view working examples visit the original authors website: muddydogpaws.com, keeping in mind Wayfinder version and syntax, for many of the examples may still show MODX Evolution and earlier Wayfinder syntax.

Getting Ready To Build Your Own Snippet

After spending so much time "experiencing" what poor documentation can do and delving into the various aspects of the Wayfinder Snippet, we have finally come to a place where we may be ready to experiment with PHP Snippets of our own. For the remainder of this chapter we will be looking at the steps to implement very simple Snippets into a MODX Revolution web project.

To begin, we should first take a moment to mention we are not going to "learn" PHP coding in this short amount of space. To get the most out of this section, the reader should have at least some experience working with PHP, preferably version 5. In any case, this section should remain clear enough for those who simply want to understand the basic steps required to allow someone to build PHP applications / Snippets / Plugins / Widgets for their project or to create their own.

Additionally, if you are a programmer desiring to work on top of a platform, MODX Revolution is a wonderful and amazing framework to build very complex and innovative applications. It can also server as a great "teacher" to learn to code with PHP - especially those new to OOP.

〒 GETTING MORE INFORMATION ABOUT PHP

There are literally hundreds of web sites dedicated to PHP. We would recommend starting at php.net, php.net/manual, php.net/links, planet-php.net and phpclasses.org. Additionally, bn.com and amazon.com have very inexpensive PHP resources for sale. We recently picked up $100 worth of PHP books for $13 shipped.

Coding Advice

Everyone seems to have their own coding style. Much of the advice and insight here is my own and has been established during 30 years of coding, in as many as eleven languages. Some of the older ones, I have long forgotten, such as COBOL and FORTRAN. The opinions in the industry concerning coding practices are wide and varied. Trying to adhere to all of them may prove to be an exercise in futility. I will share a few concepts of my own and also mention expectations of the MODX Project.

As a rule of thumb, I have found the number of bugs and associated issues to be typically proportionate to the amount of code used, essentially its complexity, and the quality of the associated documentation. By simplifying various aspects of the project we may find increased productivity and happier clients. Start with a flowchart or other graphical representation of what the project is to accomplish and the general logic which will be used.

I have been called in as a consultant on projects, where only the lead developer understood what was going on and was not very adept at communicating the needs and goals of his project. I would interview the developer (and usually the client), I "doodled" a flow chart, which was formalized later using software. This quickly resulted in getting more people informed and on board, as programmers and non programmers alike can understand simple flow charts and communicate with one another as to the project's needs and the deliverable content.

Another advantage to flowcharts is a graphical representation is quicker to grasp than thousands or millions of lines of code. Very few of us work on a single project at a time. A quick glance at a flowchart can serve as a very effective self-reminder. For complex team coding, I have seen huge flowcharts displayed on a 12 x 4 foot white board. Somewhere close by would be a permanent marker attached used to cross out sections of the flowchart as they were completed or to indicate issues. The single best advantage to flow charts is, its inherent ability to quickly will reveal logic flaws, which is much cheaper and faster to fix at the beginning of the project than months down the line.

My last few pieces of advice are simple ones:

◆ Make scheduled and unscheduled backups. Assume nothing. We have seen entire projects get destroyed due to a bad drive, or simple user error. One solution to is establish a localized repository or some other distributed storage mechanism.

◆ Separate your development environment from a live environment.

◆ Work on duplicates of an Element, rather than the one site visitors are looking at. This allows more thorough testing and damage control.

◆ Use names which help describe purpose and function. This may even be used in the native language or in the dominant language of coders and the internet, namely US English.

◆ Comment everything. Do not assume the developer is the only one who will ever see and use the code. Even if you are the only user, it may help later to read the comments to remember what was being thought of when the code was written.

◆ MODX Revolution is a framework. It has been designed to be used as a foundation to build upon. When possible, during the conception stage of building Snippets, begin to think of them as the "framework" on which to build other applications.

◆ Only code when it is necessary. The easiest way to do this is to build Snippets which can be used on multiple sites, or simply use Snippets which are in the MODX Revolution Repository. Either of these options will help increase profits and reduce development time.

◆ Learn the xPDO / MODX APIs. This will reap immediate benefits.

◆ Follow the MODX Revolution Coding Expectations, as close as possible. It may, very well help produce better, simpler code.

◆ Wrap all PHP classes and functions with class_exists() and function_exists() respectfully to avoid redeclaration errors and allow multiple in-page usages.

MODX Revolution Coding Expectations

Multiple languages can be used with each of the MODX products, each of which has its own code structure. To help developers new to MODX, the project developers established an entire section of the official documentation to assist people during their programming endeavors. This can be visited by pointing a web browser to: `http://rtfm.MODX.com/display/revolution20/ Developing+in+MODX`.

Contained within this area, is a resource which should provide a baseline set of concepts, to use when working with MODX Revolution `http://rtfm.MODX.com/display/revolution20/ Code+Standards`. This area covers HTML5, JSON, JavaScript, SQL, PHP and others. We shall take a quick look at only a few of them as they directly relate to PHP. Please refer to the site for more information and additional expectations as they are added.

Beginning brackets	Should not begin on a new line
Compression	Should not be used on PHP code
Constructors	Should not contain logic
extract()	Should not be used
File and directory names	Should only be lower case
Global variables	Should not be used
HTML	Should not be in script output
Indentation	Should use 4 Spaces instead of tab
Line Breaks	Should be UNIX format
null, true, false	Should be lowercase
Trailing Spaces	Should be removed from code

Following these simple expectations may help reduce the amount of errors presented to code, when switching back and forth to (X)HTML mode from the PHP Code. It can also reduce the amount of server resources being used and potential security risks. While we will be looking at some examples in the next section, it is also possible to look at the code used in various Snippets and in the MODX Revolution Core files itself for actually working examples.

*MODX Revolution Rule #6: **Only code when and what you have to.***

Using A Basic Structure

For our first Snippet we are going to retrieve and test the current visitors IP address and return it to the screen. There are much simpler ways of doing this, but I wanted to develop a method which would work for both IPv4 and IPv6 addresses using PHP5's FILTER. The original can be found by visiting: http://www.shawnwilkerson.com/MODX-revolution/php-code/php-utilities/getipaddress.html

Listing 06.09: getIPAddress.php

```php
<?php
/**
 * file getipaddress.php
 * created on Mar 12, 2011
 * project shawn_wilkerson
 * @package MODXRevolutionBook
 * @subpackage Chapter06
 * @version 2.0
 * @category network, server variables
 * @author W. Shawn Wilkerson
 * @link http://www.shawnwilkerson.com
 * @copyright 2011, W. Shawn Wilkerson.  All rights reserved.
 * @license
 *
 * This program is free software; you can redistribute it and/ or
 * modify it under the terms of the GNU General Public License as
 * published by the Free Software Foundation; either version 2 of the
 * License, or (at your option) any later version.
 *
 * This program is distributed in the hope that it will be useful,
 * but WITHOUT ANY WARRANTY; without even the implied warranty of
 * MERCHANTABILITY or FITNESS FOR A PARTICULAR PURPOSE. See the GNU
 * General Public License for more details.
 *
 * You should have received a copy of the GNU General Public
 * License along with this program; if not, write to the Free Software
 * Foundation, Inc., 59 Temple Place, Suite 330, Boston, MA 02111-1307
 * USA
 *
 * **************************************************
 * purpose: Discovers, tests, and returns valid IP address
 *
 * requirements: a server running php > version 5.2
```

```
*
* parameters:
*
*   $mode (string)
*           4        for ipv4
*           6        for ipv6
*           both     to test both ipv4 and ipv6 addresses
*           default return all valid and invalid ip addresses
*
*   $showMethod (boolean) 1|0
*           1   display method used to determine the ip address
*           0   hides the discovery method (default)
*
*/

if (!function_exists('test_ip4_address')) {

    /**
     * An array of server-side environment variables
     * @param array $addys      *
     * @return array The first valid ipv4 method and address.
     */
    function test_ip4_address($addys) {
        foreach ($addys as $key => $val) {
            if (filter_var(trim($val), FILTER_VALIDATE_IP, FILTER_
FLAG_NO_RES_RANGE, FILTER_FLAG_NO_PRIV_RANGE, FILTER_FLAG_IPV4)) {
                $out = array(
                    $key => $val
                );
                break;
            }
        }
        return ($out) ? $out : false;
    }
}

if (!function_exists('test_ip6_address')) {

    /**
     * An array of server-side environment variables
     * @param array $addys
     * @return array The first valid method and ipv6 address.
     */
    function test_ip6_address($addys) {
```

```php
        foreach ($addys as $key => $val) {
            if (filter_var(trim($val), FILTER_VALIDATE_IP, FILTER_
FLAG_NO_PRIV_RANGE, FILTER_FLAG_IPV6)) {
                $out = array(
                    $key => $val
                );
                break;
            }
        }
        return ($out) ? $out : false;
    }
}

/**
 * Detected IP Address
 * @var array
 */
$ip = '';

/**
 * Tested IPv4 IP Address
 * @var array

 */
$ipv4 = '';

/**
 * Tested IPv6 IP Address
 * @var array
 */
$ipv6 = '';

/**
 * Run-time Snippet Operation forced to lower case
 * @var string
 */
$mode = isset($mode) ? strtolower($mode) : '';

/**
 * Display the method utilized to get valid IP Address
 * @var boolean $showMethod
 */
$showMethod = isset($showMethod) ? $showMethod : false;
```

```php
/**
 * Server sniffed browser IP addresses utilizing various methods
 * @var array
 */
$srvvals = array(
    'http_client_ip' => $_SERVER['HTTP_CLIENT_IP'],
    'http_x_forwarded_for' => $_SERVER['HTTP_X_FORWARDED_FOR'],
    'http_x_forwarded' => $_SERVER['HTTP_X_FORWARDED'],
    'http_x_cluster_client_ip' => $_SERVER['HTTP_X_CLUSTER_CLIENT_
IP'],
    'http_forwarded_for' => $_SERVER['HTTP_FORWARDED_FOR'],
    'http_forwarded' => $_SERVER['HTTP_FORWARDED'],
    'remote_addr' => $_SERVER['REMOTE_ADDR']
);

switch ($mode) {
    case '4' :
        $ip = test_ip4_address($srvvals);
        break;
    case '6' :
        $ip = test_ip6_address($srvvals);
        break;
    case 'both' :
        $ipv4 = test_ip4_address($srvvals);
        $ipv6 = test_ip6_address($srvvals);
        foreach ($ipv4 as $addy => $val) {
            $ip[$addy] = $val;
        }
        foreach ($ipv6 as $addy => $val) {
            $ip[$addy] = $val;
        }
        break;
    default :
        $ip = $srvvals;
}
foreach ($ip as $method => $address) {
    if (!empty ($address)) {
        $o .= ($showMethod) ? $method . '=>' : '';
        $o .= $address . "\n";
    }
}
return ($o) ? nl2br($o) : false;
```

- -

This Snippet is typical of most of my MODX Revolution contributions and is divided into seven main sections. Approximately half of this code is dedicated to documentation and has been formatted for phpDocumentor (http://www.phpdoc.org), which is not required but provides the basis for clear documentation. Additionally, each section is arranged in either logical or alphabetical order depending on the purpose of the specific area. This is my personal method to provide documentation and structure within the Snippet, especially while under development.

These suggested parts are not mandatory, by any means - but work very well for me.

Part 1: File and Package Information

The first few lines of the Snippet provide the file name and other related information. We very methodically name the file the same as the Snippet will be named within the project. If the file name is snippetName.php, we would name the Snippet snippetName. This allows us to keep close tabs on which Snippets belong to which files. Though this is my company policy, any policy which works for the specific environment can be implemented.

Excerpt 06.10: getIPAddress.php

```
- - - - - - - - - - - - - - - - - - - - - - - - - - - - - - - - - - - - - - - - - - - - -
    * file getipaddress.php
    * created on Mar 12, 2011
    * project shawn_wilkerson
    * @package MODXRevolutionBook
    * @subpackage Chapter06

- - - - - - - - - - - - - - - - - - - - - - - - - - - - - - - - - - - - - - - - - - - - - -
```

Part 2: Legal Declarations

Much of today's society appears to be drawn to allure of courtrooms. To protect my company and our programmers, I typically adhere to the GPL which voids the users right to claim damages or other compensation due to an implied warranty. I personally dislike having to add this much code to each of my Snippets, but I would dislike being in a courtroom even more. Most decent people will not push an issue to court, but there are others who tend to make a living out of it. On the other side, if code is created to intentionally create harm users, I seriously doubt the GPL will cover it or the programmer(s) involved.

Excerpt 06.11: getIPAddress.php

```
 * This program is distributed in the hope that it will be useful,
but WITHOUT ANY WARRANTY; without even the implied warranty of
MERCHANTABILITY or FITNESS FOR A PARTICULAR PURPOSE...
```

Part 3: Snippet Description and Parameter Documentation

In many instances this is all the documentation offered in Snippets. At the minimum, a brief description and a list of acceptable parameters should be provided to inform potential users on the intended implementation options. In Snippets such as Wayfinder with dozens of options, this would probably be best linked to external documentation and can be achieved with a separate file (package/docs) and even part of the Official MODX Revolution Add-ons documentation. My personal preference is to provide the parameters in alphabetical order to aide in readability.

Excerpt 06.12: getIPAddress.php

```
 *   $showMethod (boolean) 1|0
 *        1  display method used to determine the ip address
 *        0  hides the discovery method (default)
```

Part 4: Functions

We typically have two reasons to utilize functions: provide reusable code within a file and clarify specific logic. Even though it is not the intention of this book to teach PHP programming, I can offer some advice on general practices which may save a few errors and moments of frustration.

Please keep in mind, we are not always aware of how people will use our Snippets. Some of them may very well want to place a specific Snippet (such as Wayfinder) in multiple locations within the same page. To remove errors associated with functions being declared multiple times (redeclaration) we would suggest wrapping every function with function_exists to keep the function from breaking a page due to a PHP error if it already exists in memory.

Functions should exist to perform a singular task and should be expected to return only one value. Additionally, there should only be a single return statement in each function. If more are necessary, the code may need to be rewritten. The rule I utilize is simple: one way in and one way out. I also believe every function should return something -- even if it is simply: false.

Excerpt 06.13: getIPAddress.php

- -

```php
if (!function_exists('test_ip4_address')) {

    /**
     * An array of server-side environment variables
     * @param array $addys      *
     * @return array The first valid ipv4 method and address.
     */
    function test_ip4_address($addys) {
        return ($out) ? $out : false;
    }
}
```

- -

Part 5: Variable Declaration

Each variable should be defined before actual usage. It is also acceptable to initialize and define the variable simultaneously. After working with many of the MODX Snippets over the years which implement camelCase variable names and spending quite a bit of time ciphering through the valid parameters, I began forcing all inbound parameters to lower case. This allows the Snippet to function as expected, regardless on the actual case used in the formatting of a specific parameter name. It can also be suggested to declare all variables alphabetically. On some of our larger Snippets, we may even group the variable definitions by general functionality and then alphabetize within that group.

Excerpt 06.14: getIPAddress.php

- -

```php
/**
 * Run-time Snippet Operation forced to lower case
 * @var string
 */
$mode = isset($mode) ? strtolower($mode) : '';
```

- -

Part 6: The Workhorse

Most every Snippet and PHP script has some portion dedicated to the actual purpose of the file. I tend to place this near the bottom of the code, just before the return statement and have found the clearest communication of logic is usually best served up in the form of the PHP switch statement though any logical command can be used.

I use the switch statement for a number of reasons. It can quickly communicate purpose and can easily reflect the documentation (and vice versa). The switch statement also infers a need to have some default response whenever the Snippet is executed. Additionally, it simplifies the method utilized to handle any output which might be on its way back to the browser or server. In our example we had a single variable, $ip, which served as our main vehicle for our data array to begin its process back to the browser.

Excerpt 06.15: getIPAddress.php

```
switch ($mode) {
    case '4' :
    case '6' :
    case 'both' :
    default :
    }
```

Part 7: Return Value

Finally reaching the bottom of the Snippet, a single return statement is found. I believe the best solution for completing a Snippet is a single return value. As was stated in the function section above, I believe every Snippet should return some value. At the very least we should return a false value. This helps us remove assumption as the Snippet will return a value if one has been created or it will simply return false in any other event.

Additionally, there appears to be two camps of thought concerning the return statement. One of these camps believes the return statement should simply return a variable and should not call another function. The other camp seems to think the practice demonstrated below is acceptable -- as long as it is kept very simple. When in doubt, stick to simply returning the variable.

Excerpt 06.16: getIPAddress.php

```
return ($o) ? nl2br($o) : false;
```

Using the Simplest Solution

In honor of William of Ockham, we shall apply the "knife" to our Snippet to provide an even simpler method of obtaining a user's IP Address. The specific needs of the individual project should dictate on how complex the solution is. If the implementation is not mission critical, the IP address may not require extensive testing and validation. The following code is somewhat thorough in its ability to discover a users IP address. Essentially, it tests different mechanisms in order to establish the first occurrence and simply returns the value found at the first opportunity. The final test is the most prevalent solution utilized in many situations to collect the visitors IP address, but may not work where proxy servers or in other networking environments are used:

Listing 06.17: visitorIPAddress.php

```php
<?php

/**
 * Server Sniffed IP Address
 * @var string
 */
$ip = '';

if (!empty($_SERVER['HTTP_X_FORWARDED_FOR'])) {
    $ip = $_SERVER['HTTP_X_FORWARDED_FOR'];
}
elseif (!empty($_SERVER['HTTP_X_FORWARDED'])) {
    $ip = $_SERVER['HTTP_X_FORWARDED'];
}
elseif (!empty($_SERVER['HTTP_X_CLUSTER_CLIENT_IP'])) {
    $ip = $_SERVER['HTTP_X_CLUSTER_CLIENT_IP'];
}
elseif (!empty($_SERVER['HTTP_FORWARDED_FOR'])) {
    $ip = $_SERVER['HTTP_FORWARDED_FOR'];
}
elseif (!empty($_SERVER['HTTP_FORWARDED'])) {
    $ip = $_SERVER['HTTP_FORWARDED'];
}
else {
    $ip = $_SERVER['REMOTE_ADDR'];
}
return $ip;
```

Ockham's Razor has been restated to say, "Of two equivalent theories or explanations, all other things being equal, the simpler one is to be preferred." The elaborate method utilized in `getIPAddress.php` to do something as simple as acquire a visitors IP address can definitely be accomplished in simpler methods. The purpose was to establish a foundation to build upon, by building functions which can handle all of our requirements to validate a user's IP address.

The implementations of the functions found within `getIPAddress.php` have been utilized to build an IP tracking mechanism to keep multiple users from using the same account, as well as to verify identities of users establishing an account at a web site. But not every site needs the foundation for multiple applications to be used for a simple application. In truth, many web sites could use a more direct solution such as the one provided in `visitorIPAddress.php`. Other projects may be able to simplify further and use the following to get the user's IP address:

Listing 06.18: returnIPAddress.php

```
- - - - - - - - - - - - - - - - - - - - - - - - - - - - - - - - - - - - - - - - - - - - - -
        return $_SERVER['REMOTE_ADDR'];

- - - - - - - - - - - - - - - - - - - - - - - - - - - - - - - - - - - - - - - - - - - - - -
```

The simplicity being sought after, may not necessarily be found in the code. It may be located in the specific needs of the project, which may require the most straight forward method to accomplish the site goals. If we are simply wanting to cosmetically display the user's IP address, then any solution may very well suffice. If we are wanting to establish a solid basis of logging an IP address to the point it would hold up in court, then I would probably want to go with a heavier and more demanding implementation.

Additionally, we may need to look at all of the associated site functions working with a specific item of data and ascertain the feasibility to have a single application or create a foundation to deal with that data. In the case of tracking a user's IP addressed, we could have a single application:

♦ Obtain the reported IP address
♦ Verify it's legitimacy
♦ Associate the current user to the address
♦ Log the address to a database, if it is new
♦ Increment a counter if the address is pre existing
♦ Handle any security issues according to our business rules

Suffice it to say, simple coding techniques may not help the "cause" and in fact, may very well hinder the process. Alternately, over thinking a task and creating a highly complex solution could also become an unnecessary weight to the project. The simplest solution is the one that directly satisfies the demands of the project. If a single Snippet can be created to serve at multiple levels, then it could be used as the main implementation to accomplish a task and also be the most familiar. This provides a foundation into any direction necessary.

Each development company will need to establish a baseline of what is deemed as acceptable practice, or simply create a set of acceptable Snippets to be used.

Adding A Snippet To The Project

Once the best solution for our site has been decided, the programming and testing can begin. The process is very similar to those utilized to create Templates, Plugins, and Chunks, though a few extra details should be noted for clarity.

The number of Snippets which can be added to a MODX Revolution site is only limited by the constraints placed on the site itself, either through a web site host, control panel software, or other server established settings. Many web hosting accounts allow for massive amounts of space to be dedicated to a given domain, giving us ample storage for potentially tens-of-thousands Elements to be added to a given installation.

The act of creating a new Snippet does nothing more than place it into the modx_site_snippets table in the database. At this point, if the PHP code has some fatal flaws, syntactical errors, or other issues, it makes little difference. As far as MODX Revolution is concerned, **this "code" is merely text placed into the database** - that is, until we actually try to execute it.

Steps to Creating a New Snippet

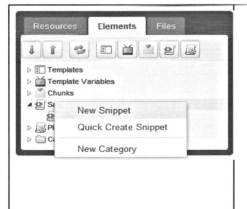

1. Log into the Manager
2. Click on Elements
3. Right-click on Snippets
4. Select New Snippet
5. Provide a meaningful name
6. Provide an informative description
7. Copy the code from a text editor
8. Paste the code into the New Snippet
9. Save the Snippet

Pasting Our Snippet Code

For this example, we opted to use the visitorIPAdress example, mostly because it fit on the screen for the screen capture. Please note, the chosen name and description and how they clearly communicate purpose. The code was pasted, exactly as shown in the code listing for visitorIPAddress.php, though the opening <?php is missing in the display, but was included in the code. I also do not close my PHP snippet with a closing ?>.

This process can be repeated to add additional "home-grown" Snippets to MODX Revolution, until they have been Packaged for distribution. In many instances, it is quite acceptable to make duplicates of existing Snippets for the purpose of editing or creating new versions of the application.

As a safety precaution I would suggest testing all Snippets in a testing environment rather than use a production server. I would not want to inadvertently broadcast a var_dump or print_r of sensitive server or user information to the public. This can be accomplished using a protected section of the site or a dedicated testing environment. Protect yourself, the users, and the data.

Verify Snippet Output

We have hopefully come to the point where we can make informed decisions on how we are going to utilize the output of our Snippet. As a project manager, it may benefit the project to establish a set of questions to be asked when new Snippets are being implemented - and hopefully while they are being developed. Here are a few suggestions to get the juices flowing:

1. What kind of output does the Snippet provide?
2. Does the Snippet require parameters to be sent?
3. Should we use a Property Set with the Snippet or has one already been established by someone else in the team?
4. Who wrote the Snippet, and how has their previous code worked out?
5. Who tested the Snippet?
6. Does the Snippet do things it shouldn't (like access the database or steal credit card information)?
7. Do we need to apply ACLs or user groups to the pages this Snippet executes on?
8. Do any of the functions, methods, properties return content which should not be available for public access? If so, why is this and is this behavior necessary?

Hopefully, the answers to these questions are clearly communicated and investigated before any actual implementation. When in doubt, call the Snippet on a test page, away from the general public to see the actual output before working with it in a live situation. It can not be stressed enough - please get multiple sets of eyes looking at Snippets, as often as possible. Over time a thoroughly tested set of Snippets can be selected and used without this much scrutiny.

Earlier in this chapter, I extensively discussed the way Wayfinder has been implemented on my site. In short, the [[$globalNav]] Chunk creates a non cached call to Wayfinder, creating a global navigation system which is to function across all Templates in the site. Each of the category pages also introduce a vertical Wayfinder menu into the [[*content]] area.

There are two additional Snippets being used in these pages. [[!randomImages]] provides a random header image (or any other image) to be placed at the specified location in the page. As this Snippet not only randomizes the image it shows, but also the positional location of the image, I have chosen to call this uncached, so that it can actually function in a "randomized" manner.

[[crumbz]] simply displays a crumb trail containing each of the ancestors (parents) of the current document. As this will almost never change, I have chosen to call it cached. In the rare event this would actually change, the cache would more than likely be updated in the parent Resource, upon it being saved. Our assumption being, this would subsequently cause a refresh on the current Resource as well, when it is requested by a site visitor.

Many Snippets can be called within a site Template. As you may recall, I typically choose to separate structure from the Resource content. Additionally, I choose to further separate both of those from the actual style which is applied to the page.

Below, I am providing the Template utilized in the pre HTML5 version of the MODX Revolution Section of my web site as an example of how a typical web page Resource may actually call multiple Snippets and Chunks. Next, we will take these concepts to the next level: placeholders.

Listing 06.19: template_MODXSection.html

```
<?xml version="1.0" encoding="UTF-8" ?>
<!DOCTYPE html PUBLIC "-//W3C//DTD XHTML 1.0 Strict//EN" "http://www.w3.org/
TR/xhtml1/DTD/xhtml1-strict.dtd">
<html xmlns="http://www.w3.org/1999/xhtml">
  <head>[[$siteHeader]]<link type="text/css" rel="stylesheet" href="min/g=shc"
/>[[$jQuery:strip]]</head>
  <body class="christian">
      <div id="header" [[!randomImages?folder=`wsw/img/christian/random`&mode=`backgr
ound`&bgPosition=`random`]]>
      [[$globalNav]]<img src="wsw/img/christian/logo.png" alt="logo" />
        <div id="breadcrumbs">
[[breadcrumbs?titleField=`menutitle`&currentAsLink=`0`&showCrumbsAtHome=`1`]]
        </div>
      </div>
      <div id="container">
        <div id="mainContent">
          <h1>[[*pagetitle]]</h1>
          [[*content]]
        </div>
        <br class="clearfloat" />
        <div id="footer">
          [[$siteFooter]]
        </div>
      </div>
    [[$jQueryBeautyofCode]]
    </body>
</html>
```

Working with Placeholders

MODX Revolution coding expectations frown on any (X)HTML code being returned from within the Snippet or any output being presented utilizing echo, print or print_r statements. This does not mean that you absolutely can not do this, or the MODX Project will revoke your license or some other absurd action. It also does not mean debugging and other testing issues can not be completed during development and implementation. It simply means, there may be a better way to get your content from the Snippet into the Resource, than using these methods.

Simple Example

To place the current users IP Address somewhere in the page utilizing a MODX Revolution Placeholder, simply create a new Snippet with the following code:

Listing 06.20: placeHolderIPAddress.php

```
/* ->toPlaceholder('Placeholder_Name_In_Page', $value) */

$modx->toPlaceholder('user.ipadrress', $_SERVER['REMOTE_ADDR']);
```

In this example we simply provide MODX with the name of a Placeholder and an attached value. The MODX Revolution Document Parser will simply replace every occurrence of our Placeholder with the associated value. Somewhere in a Resource, Chunk, Template, or a combination of theses place the following code:

Listing 06.21: placeHolderIPAddress.php

```
[[!placeHolderIPAddress]][[!+user.ipadrress]]
```

The actual placement is irrelevant, so long as the **Snippet appears and is processed before the Placeholder**, as the Parser should have attempted to process the Elements in the order they appear in the page - and would have probably replaced it with nothing. At first glance the syntax of these two Elements is so close, it may be easy to over look or confuse them. A simple way to distinguish Placeholders, is to remember the plus sign (+) indicates the content will be *added* another way.

Why Placeholders?

Someone may be asking, "What's the point? Why can't we just put the Snippet where we want our output to be presented?" The short and inconclusive answer: use whatever works. In many situations simply calling the Snippet where you want the content returned, is more than adequate, in others this could prove to be completely unsatisfactory.

As you may recall, during our chapter on Template Variables, I was able to provide page content directly from each author's Resource page: date of birth, genre, etc. To simplify the content area of the page, I included the associated Template Variable Tags in the main Template file or associated Chunk, which was displayed in a side column on the page. This allowed each of the pages to have a consistent presentation, while also limiting the amount of code our Manager users had to navigate around to do their jobs. Essentially, they only needed to deal with the biographical information in the Resource as the Template Variables working with Placeholders did everything else for them.

I also demonstrated the use of Placeholders in the chapter on Chunks, by greatly simplifying the effort to embed a YouTube video within a page. The use of Placeholders afforded the ability to create a consistent presentation throughout a given site, and required only the video id to work.

What happens when we absolutely are required to have a Snippet run, even if a Manager user may not want it to. Let's assume for a moment we have created a Call Center application built on top of MODX Revolution, and one of the phone representatives has a less than favorable moment of interaction with a potential client.

If they were afforded access to the Snippet call, they could simply remove it. If the Snippet was placed outside of the reach of the call center, this could be remedied. Complete call tracking and associated information could silently be logged into a database. The only thing the user would see is their user identification number on the page, oblivious to the fact the script that put their ID in the page had actually logged the incoming call and the current timestamp.

If they were able to remove the Placeholder showing their ID, the Snippet will still have executed and logged all of the related information, rendering their efforts useless. In some situations we have placed a "honeypot" Placeholder in a page to see if and when it was being removed. The Manager users would typically be completely unaware we could check for the existence of the Placeholder when our Snippet ran.

Placeholders are used for many reasons, a few of which are presented here:

♦ Page structure and presentation consistency

♦ Working with Template Variables, Chunks, Snippets, etc.

♦ Simplify Manager users work flow

♦ Control which aspects of sensitive information is being accessed

♦ When we need our Snippet to return more than one piece of information

Working With Multiple Placeholders and a Single Snippet

MODX Revolution provides two primary methods of returning Placeholders: individually, and as an array. As far as the Resource is concerned - there is no difference, as each individual Placeholder will need to be manually placed within each page, Template, or Chunk where we need them to appear. The simplest method is to return each individual value using the same name and format presented when I only wanted to return a single value, as in the YouTube example:

Listing 06.22: toPlaceholderAuthor.php

```php
$author = array(
    'name' => 'John Milton',
    'dob' => 'Dec 09, 1608',
    'deceased' => 'Nov 08, 1674',
    'bio' => 'Bunch of text here',
    'wiki` => 'John_Milton'
);
    $modx->toPlaceholder('author.name', $author['name']);
    $modx->toPlaceholder('author.dob', $author['dob']);
    $modx->toPlaceholder('author.deceased', $author['deceased']);
    $modx->toPlaceholder('author.bio', $author['bio']);
    $modx->toPlaceholder('author.wiki', $author['wiki']);
```

Listing 06.23: toPlaceholdersAuthor.php

```php
$author_properties = array(
    'name' => 'John Milton',
    'dob' => 'Dec 09, 1608',
    'deceased' => 'Nov 08, 1674',
    'bio' => 'Bunch of text here',
    'wiki` => 'John_Milton'
);

    $modx->toPlaceholders($author_properties, 'author');
```

For the sake of simplicity, I chose to make an array out of the data to illustrate the similarities of both API methods, which can be used to achieve the same result, the main difference being syntax and the requirement of and object or an array to be provided for the toPlaceholders() function. The only people who are probably going to notice are those working with the code.

Please take a moment and consider the syntax of `toPlaceholders()`: the (object | array) value is passed as the first parameter, and a Placeholder prefix is passed as a second. This function is syntactically reversed from `toPlaceholder()`, which requires the actual Placeholder name to be followed by an associated value.

In the case of `toPlaceholder()`, each Placeholder and the associated value will need to be individually coded, whereas `toPlaceholders()` will send everything in the array | object to the page whether there is a Placeholder for it or not - so double check the information being sent.

Placeholders do not need to be present for the PHP script to execute successfully. The Parser performs a simple "search and replace" function on each Placeholder it finds in the Resource. It simply skips through any data it receives it has no where to place. On the other side, if a Manager user can obtain a list of all of the keys in the array | object, they may be able to place sensitive information in a page.

ᛏ *OPTIONAL PARAMETERS FOR PLACEHOLDERS*

An optional third parameter can be sent, to both Placeholder functions: `toPlaceholders()` and `toPlaceholder()` to delineate the separator to be used in the Resources between the prefix and the array key. The default value is a period, which we have never changed ourselves. It is a matter of simplicity: we maintain the object.value nomenclature used in JavaScript and other languages. This gives us one less thing to communicate to our Manager users.

Optionally, you can retrieve a list of values which were replaced. `http://api.modx.com` can be visited for more information.

In most cases, PHP developers utilize objects and arrays with working with data, especially when it comes from a database, JSON, or some other source. The simplicity provided by MODX Revolution to transfer data to a Resource using Placeholders is amazing. If the developer chooses to use `toPlaceholders()` to provide the content for the page, the array keys can be sent directly to the Resource where the Snippet is called and can be captured using the `[[+prefix.key]]` syntax, or `[[+prefixseperatorkey]]` for those who opt to change the separator, from the default period.

Which ever method is used to create the Placeholders, the page will be processed identically the same. In our templateAuthors.xhtml example, The MODX Revolution Document Parser will process the Template and then proceed through the document parsing each of the tags it locates -- in the order it finds them. This is why the Snippet must appear before Placeholders. The following Template provides a working demonstration, when combined with either method: `toPlaceholderAuthor.php` or `toPlaceholdersAuthor.php`.

Listing 06.24:templateAuthors.xhtml

- -

```
[[!toPlaceholdersAuthor]]
<?xml version="1.0" encoding="UTF-8" ?>
<!DOCTYPE html PUBLIC "-//W3C//DTD XHTML 1.0 Strict//EN" "http://
www.w3.org/TR/xhtml1/DTD/xhtml1-strict.dtd">
<html xmlns="http://www.w3.org/1999/xhtml"
    <head>[[$siteHeader]]</head>
    <body class="authors">
        <div id="page">
            <div id="content">
                <h1 id="authorheader">[[!+author.name]]</h1>
                <p id="authorbio">[[!+author.bio]]</p>
            </div>
            <div id="sidebar">
                <div id="stats">
                    <h4>Statistics</h4>
                    DOB: [[!+author.dob]]<br/>
                    Died: [[!+author.deceased]]<br/>
                </div>
                <div class="links">
                    <a href="http://en.wikipedia.org/wiki/
[[!+author.wiki]]" title="Visit [[!+author.name]]">Wiki</a>
                </div>
            </div>
            <br class="clearfloat"/>
        </div>
        <div id="footer">
            [[$siteFooter]]
        </div>
    </body>
</html>
```

- -

⊤ CAUTION

*Developers and project managers need to double check the information they are sending
to the page, and may very well need to sanitize sensitive information before the array is
sent to toPlaceholders(). Never assume, Manager users will not figure out content we do
allow them to. Some people excel at finding loopholes or shortcuts others have taken.*

Using Chunks To Template Snippet Output

Eventually, a project goal may be presented which demands a single Snippet to return an undisclosed number of values. After seeing how easy it is to create a MODX Revolution Snippet and utilize `$modx->toPlaceholders()` or `$modx->toPlaceholder()`, we can feel confident, simply because we may already have a working solution figured out.

Being very happy with ourselves and this simple task, we might meander to the coffee / soda machine and grab our next dosage. Heading back to the desk, we get to work by creating a new PHP file. Half way through the code, the phone rings. The sales representative forgot to mention: the client wants the output fed to a (X)HTML template their staff can implement and would it be possible to have multiple templates? Could the client also define the default values?

Problem: Giving a client with no PHP programming experience access to the data coming from our PHP Snippet without also giving them the ability to break things -- or even worse: direct access to our databases. One of the founding points of PHP, is to control the flow of data and who has access to it. The next few pages will describe how to go about solving this dilemma.

Create a Snippet to Collect The Data

While we were still at the drink machine getting our next refill, we had a decent idea of how to move forward. In fact, until the phone rang we were half way finished with the code. it would probably be a safe bet to finish what we had started and deal with the output last. After all, we are only collecting data, right?

To provide a simple example of using (X)HTML Chunks as templates for MODX Revolution PHP Snippets, we are going to keep this very simple and create a new method of embedding YouTube video in a page. This time we will be providing the ability for clients and any Manager user to edit, create, theme, or otherwise implement the content anyway they choose.

This first item we must understand is the most obvious: the origin of the data. If it is coming from a database or another source, we could simply retrieve a set of values and apply them to the "template". A much larger issue can quickly come into focus when we consider the means to communicate parameters, which can be established as values in the Snippet, runtime parameters, Property Sets, or even by other MODX Revolution Elements.

As developers, we need to discover the balance between functionality and security. To illustrate this point, let us consider inviting someone to handle the section of the back yard we have neglected for the past decade. They arrive early in the morning and begin to hack their way through our "forest" and eventually have a pile by the street three times the size of our fully customized Hummer. When it comes time to offer them a drink, do we offer them a glass of water or the keys to our house? When all is said and done, they only need the money we agreed on and the optional glass of water. Everything else in the house is off limits.

Assuming we need to build an interactive Snippet, requiring users to provide data for the Template's Placeholders, let's assume we will have to deal with run-time user parameters as well as allowing Property Sets. Fortunately, MODX Revolution handles the majority of the work.

Listing 06.25: showYouTube.php

- -

```php
<?php
/**
 *  File      showYouTube.php (MODX snippet)
 *  Created on   Feb 02, 2011
 *  Project    shawn_wilkerson
 *  @package    revoBook-chapter06
 *  @version    1.3
 *  @category   working_demonstration
 *  @author     W. Shawn Wilkerson
 *  @link       http://www.shawnwilkerson.com
 *  @copyright  (c) 2011, W. Shawn Wilkerson.  All rights reserved.
 *  **************************************************
 *  Purpose: Implements a user declared MODX Revolution Chunk as a
 *  template, merging runtime parameters, returning merged content
 *
 *  Requirements: ?template=`chunkname`&videoID=`1234567`
 *
 *  Dependencies: MODX Revolution 2.x +
 *  **************************************************/

/**
 * Create an array of properties users are allowed to interact with
 * THESE MUST BE IN THE SAME ORDER AS THE $placeHolders ARRAY
 */
$_config = array_merge(array(
    'allowFullScreen' => '',
    'allowHiDef' => '',
    'allowScriptAccess' => '',
    'color1' => '',
    'color2' => '',
    'height' => '',
    'videoID' => '',
    'width' => '',
), $scriptProperties);

/**
 * define allowed template placeholders
```

```
    */
$placeHolders = array(
    '[[+allowFullScreen]]',
    '[[+allowHiDef]]',
    '[[+allowScriptAccess]]',
    '[[+color1]]',
    '[[+color2]]',
    '[[+height]]',
    '[[+videoID]]',
    '[[+width]]'
);

/**
 * Grab a MODX chunk from the database
 */
$useChunk = $modx->getChunk($scriptProperties['template']);

/**
 * Perform string replace on the template based on placeholders
 */
return str_replace($placeHolders, $_config, $useChunk);
```

If the data was coming from a database, the first array could simply be converted to process the information retrieved from the corresponding table. The resulting array would then be handed off to the str_replace() function potentially accomplishing similar functionality:

Excerpt 06.26: showYouTube.php modified to use direct input from array

----

```
$_config = array(
    'allowFullScreen' => $row['allowfullscreen'],
    'allowHiDef' => $row['allowhidef'],
    'allowScriptAccess' => $row['allowscriptaccess'],
    'color1' => $row['foreground'],
    'color2' => $row['background'],
    'height' => $row['height'],
    'videoID' => $row['videonum'],
    'width' => $row['width'],
);
```

$scriptProperties	MODX Revolution Internal Array which transports all run-time parameters to Snippets. This variable is limited in scope to the current Snippet and operates in the following order: 1. Adds attached Property Set (if available) 2. Merges values from Snippet Call, overriding pre-existing Property Set values having parameters with the same name
$_config	Array which collects the incoming parameters and merges them with default settings. This is a great technique to simply provide in-script default settings, while allowing Property Set and run-time parameters to over-ride them.
$placeHolders	An array to limit what the developer is allowing to be sent to the page. If the Placeholder does not appear in this list, it will simply not be replaced in the page.
$modx->getChunk()	This is all that is needed to retrieve a Chunk by its name. A default Template name could also be added to the Property Set.
str_replace()	Performs a simple string replace on the template, searching for any Placeholder found in the `$placeHolders` array. This function works its way through the arrays one item at a time. If the order does not match, you will get incorrect output.
allowFullScreen allowHiDef allowScriptAccess color1 color2 height videoID width	We took these values from the embed code provided by YouTube, each of which represents parameters used by the service. Currently YouTube and other video sites are in the process of converting theie embed code to iframes. Hopefully, they will still allow styling of their content.

**Note: $modx->getChunk should be tested to see if it actually returns something.
Never assume, as in this example the user did it right.**

Add An Optional Property Set

With YouTube using so many parameters, one would tend to think we might as well use their embed code, as it is bound to be shorter in the page than stringing together a long list of variables and their values in a Snippet call. Even their new code can leave room for people to mess something up, even though it currently utilizes only four parameters.

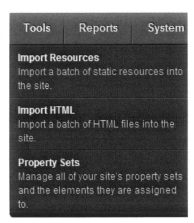

At some point in the planning stage of the web project, "rules" might have been established as to the size and color theme of any embedded videos. With the older YouTube code, we are afforded the opportunity to theme the display to some extent. Note: the current embed code currently limits this customizing behavior.

To address all of these and other situations, we are going to attach a Property Set to our Snippet, so as to provide a solid basis to build on, while reducing the number of parameters designers will be required to define when they implement our Snippet.

To begin, log into the Manager and left-click Property Sets under the Tools menu. [Note: we clicked on a Youtube Property Set, created in another chapter to display the values and then right-clicked on the set name to show the context menu.]

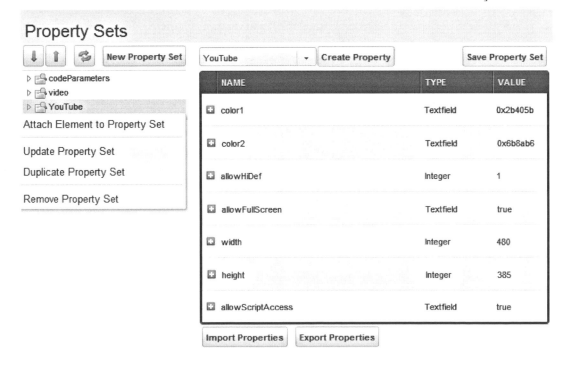

In our chapter discussing the MODX Revolution Manager, we created a Property Set to provide the basis of a consistent presentation of all of the embedded Videos throughout the site. If necessary, take a few minutes and create a new Property Set by following these steps:

1. Provide a name which indicates function
2. Provide a description which will clearly communicate intended purpose
3. Click on Create Property and work through the parameters as shown
4. Save the Property Set when all the items have been added

For those who have the Property Set created in the other chapters, we opted to add a new value: allowScriptAccess. Please feel free to add this value if it does not already exist. Also, notice the export and import buttons, which allows easy transfer of Property Sets between sites and also a simple local backup. It is not uncommon for developers to keep quite a few of these "presets" handy for various providers and utilities, as part of their tool set.

₸ PROPERTIES TAB: SETTING DEFAULT SETTINGS

An alternative to using a site-wide Property Set , is to utilize the Properties tab located with each Snippet. Once the Default Properties Locked button is clicked, the grid will become unlocked allowing dedicated defaults to be established following the same procedure referenced to create a site-wide Property Set.

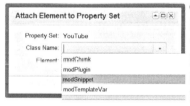

Once the Property Set has been created and saved, right-click on its name in the left column to Attach Element to Property Set. A window will appear, which will provide access to every Element in the web project. For our purposes, we are going to attach this Property Set to a Snippet, though we could attach it to any of the MODX Revolution Elements - even multiple types of Elements simultaneously. To attach our Property Set, simply:

1. Optional: choose the type of Element, by changing Class Name to Snippet (AKA modSnippet). This allows the Element box to be filtered by type, greatly reducing the length of the list. Any class may be chosen, as any Element can be assigned.
2. Required: Select the name of the Element, which will be using the Property Set
3. Repeat for each Element which will be using the Property Set

Building Snippet Frameworks

By now, someone has probably wondered why we don't simply define our default values in the Snippet and be done with the process. Though we can change the $_config array to instantiate designated values, we may find it more productive to allow other users to specify their own implementations of our Snippets, as MODX Revolution is a Content Management Framework after all.

Excerpt 06.27: showYouTube.php with instantiated array values

- -

```
$_config = array(
    'color1' => '0x2b405b',
    'color2' => '0x6b8ab6',
    'height' => '385',
    'width' => '480',
);
```

- -

By hard coding the parameters, we may have inadvertently placed a developer in the role of a front end designer, as they will have to continually create new "display" configurations for the same data as the need arises. We may have also caused other issues.

For a moment, assume a client has a reputation for conducting huge market pushes for new items. Part of their process, is to create new "infomercial" videos for YouTube, which requires a simultaneous request to be sent to project leaders for the video to be included on the front page: at 835 pixels by 505 pixels.

More than likely this type of request would be received by project designers, who would then need to send a secondary request to developers to provide a new Snippet. By locking the Snippet down, we would need a developer to duplicate the preexisting Snippet into one with these new settings. What happens if the client would like to theme each product line with multiple dedicated colors. Quickly this can become a horrid series of request tickets and excessive Snippets stored in the database doing essentially the same task.

The best solution for this example may very well be a combination of everything mentioned in this section. By changing the $_config array to also merge the values of incoming parameters: array_merge($array, $scriptProperties), we can establish default settings in the Snippet, allow Project Administrators the ability to establish site specific overrides, and also allow run-time declarations to be implemented. This may require more effort on the front side of the development, but the benefits of designing a single Snippet to satisfy the vast majority of implementation needs will quickly reduce requests and simplify project work flows. More importantly: it increases production by allowing people to directly perform their job duties.

Create A Chunk To Use As A Template

Regardless of the implementation, Snippets typically have some sort of output. With the advent of new technologies, such as HTML5, utilizing Chunk templates to format the output Snippets returns, is a very simple process and requires minimal updates in the future to match technologies.

During our discussion of using Placeholders with Chunks, in an earlier chapter, we provided a modified version of the YouTube embed code, changing various parameters to Placeholders to provide a consistent site-wide presentation of video. There was a problem with that code. My company currently creates our sites in xhtml strict 1.0, and the provider's code failed to validate. Here is an updated XHTML strict 1.0 MODX Revolution Chunk, developed as the basis of our own embed code template for YouTube videos:

Listing 06.28: template_youtube.xhtml Chunk

```
<object type="application/x-shockwave-flash"
        width="[[+width]]px"
        height="[[+height]]px"
        data="http://www.youtube.com/v/[[+videoID]]&amp;fs=[[+allowF
ullScreen]]&amp;rel=0&amp;color1=[[+color1]]&amp;color2=[[+color2]]&
amp;hd=[[+allowHiDef]]">
    <param name="allowFullScreen" value="[[+allowFullScreen]]" />
    <param name="allowScriptAccess" value="[[+allowScriptAccess]]"
/>
    <param name="color1" value="[[+color1]]" />
    <param name="color2" value="[[+color2]]" />
    <param name="hd" value="[[+allowHiDef]]" />
    <param name="movie" value="http://www.youtube.com/v/
[[+videoID]]" />
</object>
```

Subsequently, YouTube has begun implementing a new format for their embed code. Even though I personally, do not typically enjoy using iframes, I have created a simplified conversion of their current offering. I suspect this will change over time as functionality and parameters are added. Eventually, we should see simple HTML5 <video> tags used to completely theme and customize any web based video, requiring only the source to be updated.

Please visit youtube.com/html5 for more information and updates. Those interested in working with the new code from YouTube which supports HTML5, as well as various older technologies, the above code can be replaced with the following:

Listing 06.29: template_youtube.html5 compliant Chunk

```
<iframe title="YouTube video player" width="[[+width]]"
height="[[+height]]" src="http://www.youtube.com/embed/[[+videoID]]"
frameborder="0" allowfullscreen></iframe>
```

Benefits Of Chunk Templates Used For Snippet Output

Not every Snippet will require or even need a Chunk to present its output. In fact, many of them simply will not. During development and implementation, each Snippet should be evaluated as to associated security concerns, code reusability, and implementation considerations. Here are a few reasons why a developer / project leader may want to allow Chunks to be used as templates:

♦ Keeps non PHP programmers away from the Snippet code

♦ Allows simple updates to content through out the site

♦ Can be cached via MODX Revolution

♦ Allows consistent presentation and implementation

♦ Separates presentation from data

♦ Allows developers to concentrate on PHP Application

♦ Facilitates designers and the construction of the User Interface

♦ Can Enhance communication during development and testing

♦ Allows new platforms to be implemented utilizing output from the same Snippet

♦ Output can be provided allowing experts to handle the data using their specific tools

♦ Multiple presentations can be implemented for a Single Snippet

♦ May provide the basis for real-use example documentation

♦ Attachment of ACLs to the Elements can provide additional layer of protection

♦ Focuses attention of developers to provide the required content

♦ Can provide designers a simple tool to communicate project needs to developers

♦ May reduce support requests, as Templates and Snippets can be used across sites

♦ Can be classified by technology usage html5 , jQuery, JSON, etc

♦ Complex Snippets can be broken down into simpler working Components

♦ Can be based on user group basis providing targeted content

♦ Extremely easy to implement utilizing MODX Revolution's API

♦ Output should more readily consistent and function as expected

Implementing A Templated Snippet

At this point we have established all of the components of our Snippet, which has been developed to implement MODX Revolution Chunks as Template: the Snippet, the parameters via a Property Set, and the template Chunk. All that is left, is to provide a working example to send to the project front end user interface designers.

Snippet Call	Explanation

Note: this is our preexisting Chunk call:
 	
`[[$template_youtube5`
`  @YouTube`
`  ?videoID=`xtjgY-z9QZ8`]]`
	Possible Chunk Call:
	If the Property Set is also attached to the template Chunk, we could allow the Snippet to be bypassed altogether. If this ability is unacceptable and the Snippet is declared by the project, as the only acceptable method to embed video, the Chunk would simply not be attached to the Property Set, leaving output to the Snippet.

`[[showYouTube`
`  @YouTube`
`  ?template=`template_youtube5``
`  &videoID=`xtjgY-z9QZ8`]]`
	Snippet Call Using Property Set: this example calls the Snippet and designates which Property Set is being used. The required Chunk name and videoID also appear.

`[[showYouTube@YouTube` `  ?template=`template_youtube`` `  &color1=`0x234900`` `  &color2=`0x4e9e00`` `  &height=`505`` `  &width=`604`` `  &videoID=`xtjgY-z9QZ8`]]`	**Snippet Call Using Property Set and Over-ridden Parameters**: In this example we are applying a green-tinted theme to the embedded video. The rest of the parameters are used as provided in the Property Set.
`[[showYouTube` `  ?color1=`0x2b405b`` `  &color2=`0x6b8ab6`` `  &showHiDef=`1`` `  &showFullScreen=`true`` `  &height=`385`` `  &width=`480`` `  &allowScriptAccess=`always`` `  &template=`template_youtube5`` `  &videoID=`xtjgY-z9QZ8`]]`	**Fully Qualified Snippet Call**: provides the same functionally as utilizing the Property Set. Designers can be given example Chunks demonstrating each of these implementations, clearly communicating functionality and the associated parameter configuration.

Snippet output

Each of the Snippet Calls returns something very similar to the following expected output:

Listing 06.30: showYouTube Snippet with template_youtube Chunk output

```
<object type="application/x-shockwave-flash"
    width="604 px"
    height="505 px"
    data="http://www.youtube.com/v/xtjgY-z9QZ8&amp;fs=true&amp;rel=0
&amp;color1=0x234900&amp;color2=0x4e9e00&amp;hd=1">
  <param name="allowFullScreen" value="true" />
  <param name="allowScriptAccess" value="true" />
  <param name="color1" value="0x234900" />
  <param name="color2" value="0x4e9e00" />
  <param name="hd" value="1" >
  <param name="movie" value="http://www.youtube.com/v/xtjgY-z9QZ8"/>
</object>
```

Presentation	Summary
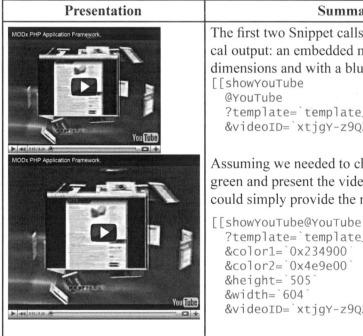	The first two Snippet calls, will produce identical output: an embedded movie at specified dimensions and with a blue theme: `[[showYouTube` `  @YouTube` `  ?template=`template_youtube5`` `  &videoID=`xtjgY-z9QZ8`]]`  Assuming we needed to change the theme to green and present the video at a larger size, we could simply provide the necessary changes:  `[[showYouTube@YouTube` `  ?template=`template_youtube`` `  &color1=`0x234900`` `  &color2=`0x4e9e00`` `  &height=`505`` `  &width=`604`` `  &videoID=`xtjgY-z9QZ8`]]`

Making the Workflow and Snippet Simpler

Once a Snippet is functioning properly, it may be a good time to quickly take a second look, to see if there is anything we can do to make it or eventual implementations more efficient. The single best way typically used to simplify workflow is streamlining.

Currently, there are two glaring ways to streamline our YouTube Snippet. Every Snippet call requires two variables: a Chunk template name and a videoID number. As most web projects will utilize a consistent presentation, providing a default Chunk name in the Property Set can reduce the call down to [[showYouTube@YouTube&videoID=`xtjgY-z9QZ8`]]. The Property Set could also be imported to the Properties Tab of the Snippet itself, further reducing the call: [[showYouTube?videoID=`xtjgY-z9QZ8`]]

MODX Revolution also allows an array to be added to the $modx->getChunk(), which will perform the str_replace() necessary, thereby greatly reducing the Snippet's code. Note: this may remove security restraints and forces us to rely heavily on external documentation.

Listing 06.31: showYouTubeSimple.php

```php
<?php
/**
 * File       showYouTubeSimple.php (MODX snippet)
 * Created on  Feb 02, 2011
 * Project     shawn_wilkerson
 * @package    revoBook chapter06
 * @version    1.3
 * @category   working_demonstration
 * @author     W. Shawn Wilkerson
 * @link       http://www.shawnwilkerson.com
 * @copyright  (c) 2011, W. Shawn Wilkerson. All rights reserved.
 ************************************************
 * Purpose: Uses a user declared MODX Revolution Chunk as a template
 * and merges parameters  returns the merged content
 *
 * Requirements: ?template=`chunkname`&videoID=`1234567`
 *
 ***********************************************/
/**
 * Grab a MODX chunk from the database and apply replacements
 */
return  $modx->getChunk($scriptProperties['template'],
$scriptProperties);
```

In this specific situation, we were able to reduce the code down to a single line. Someone may be wondering why we didn't do that in the first place. The answer is relatively simple: we needed to provide a working demonstration of the various steps and real-world possibilities which may need to be considered from one Snippet to the next. While not at all conclusive, these examples should facilitate a basis to begin implementing Snippets using Chunk as templates.

I have also introduced a few simple methods to help protect the data, while providing a flexible solution which should require very little maintenance on the part of the developer. Simultaneously, we have created a very simple means to facilitate designers in adding site content with very little effort, while maintaining a consistent feel. In essence, we have illustrated many of the steps and processes required to take a concept to an actual application.

Is there multiple ways of embedding a YouTube video in MODX Revolution? Sure there is. We have mentioned this concept in the Chunk chapter, and resurrected it again in this chapter as the concept and goals are relatively simple to grasp. This allows us to focus completely on implementation, without being distracted on why something is the way it is.

It is also completely feasible to use Template Variables to accomplish much of this, though this may require more effort than is necessary to perform such a simple task. For those who want to make this appear even simpler, it might prove beneficial to create a Chunk to house the Snippet Call to reduce the amount of information users need to remember, to something even simpler: `[[$youTube?videoID=`xtjgY-z9QZ8`]]`. Alternately, simply moving the Parameters to the Snippet will also achieve this and allow `[[showYouTube?videoID=`xtjgY-z9QZ8`]]` to be used.

This also limits usage to only the defined parameters, by requiring Manager users to provide only the videoID. Eventually, this may be a personal choice or a "rule" that is based on the decisions of the project leaders and the client. At least we can offer them a range of options with very little effort and time spent on figuring it out or in development. We can now take our beautiful YouTube toolset and shamelessly add it from one site to the next, because it does one thing very well, while not limiting anyone in the project unless directed to do so.

At the beginning of this section we proposed a theoretical problem: Giving a client with no PHP programming experience access to the data coming from our PHP Snippet without also giving them the ability to break things -- or even worse: direct access to our databases. We also needed to define the method we were going to allow Manager users to interact with our Snippet. Since those issues were defined, I have demonstrated how MODX Revolution can be used to provide a very efficient workflow while maintaining data integrity and creating clear job expectations.

This tiny example also introduced many of the solutions implemented in Snippets to obtain run time values. We also got a chance to look at how MODX Revolution combines and subsequently processes various parameters via: 1) Property Set, 2) run-time (in the Snippet Call), and 3) hard coded in the Snippet. Hopefully, developing Snippets as "frameworks" instead of single use implementations will become a valuable tool in your arsenal.

Working With PHP Classes

Coding with a "framework" mentality and seeking the "Holy Grail" of code reusability can both be synonymous with working with PHP Class files. Like many developers, I spent years avoiding them. Once I got the hang of them, I have never looked back. Due to its very eclectic nature, MODX Revolution can be a fascinating playground for teams of developers to test and extend functionality while not having to deal with the "other" administrative functions.

₸ GUIDELINES ON DECIDING TO USE A *PHP* CLASS WITH A SNIPPET

If any of the following can be answered with a 'Yes' then a class would be suggested:

Does this thing have multiple attributes?
Do multiple Snippets need access to a single source of data?
Is data in a custom database table, or tables, being accessed?
Is Security and User Groups a consideration?
Is this code going to be the basis of other projects or Snippets?
Are multiple people going to working with this code?
Will this code eventually be Packaged and distributed?
Is this project going to slowly expand into a larger application?

When reading examples in this section, you may notice a few calls to the MODX API. I choose to get MODX involved with my custom Snippets for a few reasons:

♦ Accessing the MODX Revolution API early, provides immediate benefits

♦ By using the values previously defined in the project, doing so again is unnecessary

♦ Revo will handle quite a bit of the "maintenance" - translating to less code

♦ A Snippet on the file system requiring MODX to work, will not do so otherwise

♦ MODX Revolution is a solid framework, why not build on it?

♦ The immediate inheritance of the xPDO class to work with database tables

As this is not a programming tutorial, we are simply going to illustrate a few foundational concepts to easily implement a class with MODX Revolution. Below we have provided a very straightforward representation of PHP code which accomplishes the primary functions expected from most Snippets. As with all Snippets, this code would be pasted into a Snippet Element within the Manager of a given site, while classes would usually be placed on the file system.

Listing 06.32: example.snippet.php

- -

```php
<?php
/**
 * Descriptive Header goes here
 */

/**
 * Establish the correct path, and then load our class
 */
$example_base = $modx->getOption('example.core_path',null,
                $modx->getOption('core_path').'components/example/');
include_once $example_base.'example.class.php';

/**
 *  Allow MODX Revolution to load the class
 */
if (!$modx->loadClass('Example',$example_base,true,true)) {
    return 'error: Example class not found';
}

/**
 * Create a new object of the Example class
 */
$ex = new Example($MODX);
return $ex->getSomething();
```

- -

This Snippet has the following significant aspects:

1. A header which should contain information regarding the author, purpose, requirements, etc. of this Snippet

2. $example_base which simply defines the path of the Snippet and / or Package on the file System. Using the Core_path setting as the base should eliminate porting issues.

3. $modx->loadClass() which uses the MODX API to load our class. This provides a few benefits, the least of which is ensuring the class does not pre-exist in our page, which would cause an error.

4. $ex becomes an object of our PHP class - keeping variable name close to class name

5. the $MODX object is passed to the class

6. Return a value

7. Other than linking and calling the class, all the real work is done in the class

Listing 06.33: example.class.php

- -

```php
<?php
/**
 * Descriptive Header goes here
 */
if (!class_exists('Example')) {
    class Example {
        function __construct(modX &$modx, array $config = array()) {
            /**
             * import $MODX
             */
            $this->modx = & $modx;

        }

        function __destruct() {
        }

        /**
         * Example method
         * @param none
         * @return  String
         */
        public function getSomething() {
        }
    }
}
```

-      - - - - - - - - -

This Class has the following points of focus:

1. Wrapped in a `class_exists()` function, even though `$modx->loadClass()` does this in the Snippet, to avoid redeclaration errors if loaded for other purposes

2. No global variables (those that occur outside the `__construct` and class methods)

3. The MODX object is passed as a reference and made available to the class

4. There is a `__destruct` function, PHP does this automatically, though we feel we should clean up after ourselves

5. There is plenty of room for adequate documentation, I suggest using phpdoc notation

6. Variable `&references` occur in only the constructor, not the individual methods

7. Should be tested in an `E_STRICT` development environment

These two skeletal examples, demonstrate some of the various components which can be used when developing PHP applications in conjunction with the MODX Revolution environment. While none of this is "required", it should serve as a foundation to build most any application while being somewhat familiar to any seasoned PHP professional.

Developers should find the MODX Revolution API very beneficial to any project, as I have personally seen my code base reduced to an average of 25% of the size required to accomplish similar tasks in other environments and have even benefitted from an occasional 90% reduction. This is directly due to the many methods the API provides facilitating arrays, objects, JSON, Revo Elements, users, and database activities.

The MODX Revolution framework allows people with various levels of ability, to implement solutions at their skill level. Combining the MODX Revolution API with PHP classes can easily help developers streamline their efforts in application development, while also allowing them to increase productivity.

At the end of the day, every project and development situation is different. MODX Revolution provides a flexible enough foundation, each application can mandate how these concepts are implemented. Some organizations may very well shy away from the MODX Revolution API, but I would not understand why that would be necessary. It has been my experience that MODX Revolution supplies tools which I should already have myself. I have found I no longer need to build them, I simply use what MODX Revolution provides: a solid framework to build on.

$modx->runSnippet()

In certain situations, it may prove beneficial to programmatically run a Snippet from within another Snippet. Fortunately, for us MODX Revolution provides this functionality via the $modx->runSnippet() function, as exampled below:

Excerpt 06.34: The template for the calling the another Snippet

- -

```
$snippetOutput = $modx->runSnippet('SnippetName',array(
    'parameter1' => 'value1'
));
```

- -

There are a couple of things to understand when attempting this process. The output of $modx->runSnippet() is always going to be a string. If you are needing an array, object, or some other data type which is not easily type-casted from a string, using a Placeholders may very well serve your purposes better. For simple string output $modx->runSnippet() can come in quite handy.

Exotic Snippet Calls

The following examples are potential Snippet calls which may one day be proven worthy of a production web project. Be advised, some of these may be a little extreme, but are intended to get the reader thinking outside the proverbial box.

Snippet Call	Explanation
[[snippet?dob=`[[*dob]]`]]	[[*dob]] is a Template Variable used to feed the Snippet Parameter
[[snippet?googlesearch=`[[*longtitle]]`]]	Uses the [[*longtitle]] of the current resource as a basis for the query
[[[[*alias]]]]	Uses the current Resource alias to call a Snippet of the same name
[[snippet?ip=`[[!getIPAddress]]`]]	Uses the output of [[getIPAddress]] as the input for this Snippet
[[snippet?userid=`[[+MODX.user.id]]` &resourceAlias=`[[*alias]]` &ip=`[[!getIPAddress]]`]]	Each logged in user, will always have their ID available while on the site. We should note there are much nicer MODX Revolution API methods to obtain all of this information. This is a great demonstration of achieving the same thing, in multiple ways
[[snippet?template=`[[$[[*alias]]]]`]]	Will attach the content of a Chunk having the same name as the current Resource Alias to the Snippet's template parameter.
[[[[snippet]]]]	Can possibly take the output of one MODX Revolution Snippet and use it as the name of the "outside" Snippet to run.
[[[[snippet?alias=`[[[[*alias]]]]`]]]]	This is pretty extreme: uses the Resource Alias as the name of the Snippet to execute which will be used as the value for the alias fed into a Snippet, which will return a value used as the actual name of the "outside" Snippet to execute.

Of course, there are many ways to accomplish the same things - many of them potentially easier. We have actually implemented *some* of these with very impressive results. There are two things to learn here: 1) MODX Revolution allows some very powerful implementations, and 2) just because you can do something, doesn't mean you should. Find the best method for the task.

Plugins

MODX Revolution has dozens of events which execute as different activity occurs through out the site. Plugins, while PHP, differ from Snippets in that they operate on an event basis, by attaching to MODX Revolution System events - some of which occur before an action, while others occur during or after the action.

Plugins can be executed to affect or respond to some action within the Manager or on the visitor face of a site. The thing to keep in mind here, is that these events are MODX Revolution events, not Java, JavaScript or some other event coded for the User Interface by the web project developers. These events are those which have been provided by the MODX Revolution developers, for the eventuality a project will need to use them. Any Plugin installed within the web project is stored in the `modx_site_plugins` table of the MODX Revolution database.

Plugin Example: AntiSpam

To illustrate Plugins we are going to take a look at the steps to provide a very effective level of spam-bot protection – across an entire site. The following public domain Plugin, was originally authored for MODX versions before Evolution, but I have continued to use it on every site built in MODX Revolution. As a result of using this Plugin, I have not experienced any ramifications of spam-bots, as I have never seen any of our projects successfully harvested for e-mail addresses. Your experience may vary, but I am very happy with the results.

This process can be repeated for each Plugin utilized throughout the site. I should also mention that multiple Plugins can be attached to the same event, but additional care may be necessary to ensure integrity and proper flow. Please consider establishing the priority on the Systems Event tab when using multiple Plugins on a single event.

To implement site-wide e-mail obfuscation, log into the Manager, select Elements from the Resource Trees and simply right click on Plugins. For our purposes here we will simply select New Plugin and begin our process. Alternately, check the MODX Revolution repository for ObfuscateEmail-Revo.

As many people may not be aware of obfuscation, it might be easier to simply name the Plugin something more readily understood. In our example I chose antiSpam for our name and provided a description which offered more information. The Plugin comments provide more information, but are typically not going to be viewed by many in our Manager.

〒 <?PHP IS NEVER CLOSED, BUT ALWAYS OPENED

*For security considerations, as well as other issues, it is common practice to allow
MODX Revolution / PHP to close our PHP code for us.*

The original code can be found in its entirety by visiting the extras section of the MODX CMS or
`https://github.com/wshawn/ObfuscateEmail`. I have removed a few of the original comments
and updated the Snippet to be compliant with Revolution 2.1:

Listing 06.35: [abbreviated] ObfuscateEmail plugin originally by Aloysius Lim

```php
<?php
/**
 * ObfuscateEmail plugin for MODX.
 * By Aloysius Lim.
 *
 * Version: 0.9.1 (Apr 15, 2007)
 *
 * This plugin searches for all email addresses and "mailto:"
 * strings in the html output, both inside and outside href
 * attributes. In other words, it also encodes link text.
 *
 * It can find all common email addresses as specified by RFC2822,
 * including all unusual but allowed characters. Any email addresses
 * that satisfy the the construct below will be detected:
 *
 * The plugin than randomly leaves 10% of the characters alone,
 * encodes 45% of them in decimal, and 45% of them in hexadecimal.
 **/
function email_regex() {
    $atom = "[-!#$%&'*+/=?^_`{|}~0-9A-Za-z]+";
    $email_half = $atom . '(?:\\.' . $atom . ')*';
    $email = $email_half . '@' . $email_half;
    $email_regex = '<(' . $email . ')>';
    return $email_regex;
}

function replaceEntities($matches) {
    $address = html_entity_decode($matches[1]);
    $replaced = '';
    for ($i = 0 ; $i < strlen($address) ; $i++) {
```

```
            $char = $address[$i];
            $r = rand(0, 100);
            /* roughly 10% raw, 45% hex, 45% dec */
            if ($r > 90)
            {
                $replaced .= $char;
            }
            else if ($r < 45)
            {
                $replaced .= '&#x'.dechex(ord($char)).';';
            }
            else
            {
                $replaced .= '&#'.ord($char).';';
            }
        }
        return $replaced;
}
$output = &$modx->resource->_output;
$output = preg_replace_callback(email_regex(), "replaceEntities",
$output);
$output = preg_replace_callback('/(mailto:)/', "replaceEntities",
$output);
```

Up to this point this is a simple Snippet of PHP code which alters e-mail addresses found within the content of a web page. The magic happens when we attach the code to the OnWebPagePrerender event, which allows this Plugin to function throughout the entire visitor side of the site, regardless of where the e-mail address originated. The address simply needs to appear somewhere within the page content just before the page is rendered for the visitors web browser.

As we look down the list of events some have groups, while others do not. In my experience, most of our Plugins do not require the changing of the established groups. I simply assume any ungrouped events, were left that way for reasons I may not need to be aware of.

Manager users have the option to disable a Plugin, if the need arises. An example of this could be a "spider" which validates e-mail addresses within a site against a database to ensure accuracy. The spider needs to be able to see the "real" e-mail address as the one in the page is vastly different. Of course we could simply perform a database slight of hand to accomplish this comparison as well. If for nothing else, the Plugin can be disabled if the site begins to function unexpectedly after a Plugin has been activated. That being said, Plugins should thoroughly be tested before being placed within a site, as their entire execution can be completely transparent and hidden from the site visitors -- including any drastic errors.

Anti-Spam Output

`shawn@shawnwilkerson.com?subject=Shawn Wilkerson Website` becomes:

```
&#x6d;&#97;&#105;l&#x74;&#x6f;&#x3a;&#x73;&#x68;a&#x77;n&#64;s&#x68;
&#x61;&#x77;&#110;&#119;&#105;&#108;&#107;&#101;&#114;&#x73;&#x6f;&#
x6c;&#16;c&#111;&#x6d;&#63;&#x73;&#117;&#98;&#106;e&#99;&#x74;&#x3d;
&#83;&#x68;&#x61;&#x77;&#6e; Wilkerson  website
```

Additionally, we are afforded the opportunity to attach a Property Set to the Plugin, so site-specific settings can be applied to the Plugin. Situations arrive where an individual may be required to track new members to a web site as they occur in order to pay out commissions. The ability to attach the appropriate e-mail settings, on a per-site basis could prove invaluable. A plethora of possibilities for application specific needs can exist. The best option is to begin small and test each phase of the project, while keeping it simple as possible.

Assigning Priority to Plugins

MODX Revolution allows multiple Plugins to be attached to the same event. In some instances it could prove beneficial to combine various Plugins into a single element. In others, it would be easier to simply adjust the priority settings, indicating the order they are to be executed with the lower number being executed first – similarly to the method we use to count: 0, 1, 2, 3....

Plugins operate throughout the entire MODX Revolution installation: front end, Manager events, and most everything in between. We do not need to consider how to attach a function to the site to get MODX Revolution to implement it. We simply attach our Plugin to the event which best associates with our need. In many instances, the group column will help us understand which event is attached to which group of events.

When to use Plugins instead of Snippets

There are many examples of using Plugins discussed around the web and in the documentation. These implementations vary from extending the MODX User class, to filtering "bad" words on pages, to domain redirects. The possibilities for using Plugins are quite extensive. The main issue needing to be understood is when it is necessary to use a Plugin instead of using a Snippet.

When something needs to remain consistent across an entire site, Plugins may very well be the simplest and best solution available. Their best benefit: they do not require user implementation or training. They can be assigned by administrators and ran transparently in the "background" without any user intervention or notification of their presence.

Summary

I could have named this chapter, *Everything You Ever Wanted to Know About Snippets* or another similar name, but that would be misleading. The very nature of Snippets is to be dynamic, and as such, they are impossible to approach in their entirety. In this chapter I chose to limit the discussion to those topics which would best serve as a foundation to build upon. We have discussed the following topics:

+ Installation via Package Management and manual entry
+ Deciphering the functionality with little documentation
+ Utilization of Chunks as "templates: for output
+ Creating "frameworks" of our own to solve demanding applications
+ Differences and similarities of Snippets and Plugins

For much of this chapter, I chose to focus on Wayfinder, because it embodies much of what makes the MODX Revolution Content Management Framework so effectively: collaboration, openness, flexibility, support, and relevance. This Snippet has been around for much of the life of the MODX Project and I am still discovering new ways to implement it. In the AJAX and JavaScript chapter we will revisit Wayfinder and show how we create a Kwicks menu created with jQuery.

I have also discussed some of the dangers and benefits of using PHP Snippets on a web project. Be very careful who has access to Snippets, especially their creation, addition, and implementation to a project - the more eyes involved the better. Snippets allow a degree of customization and innovation rarely seen in any Content Management Product.

MODX Revolution was built from the ground up to be extended. Your challenge? To take it as far as you can, and be willing to eventually take it even further. As you do so, share your experiences with the community.

Snippets are indeed like pizza, each of us have the ability to decide what a good one is.

7

:filters - The Art of Manipulating Element Output

Its Valentine's Day and I would really like to do something special for my wife.

With little effort, I pull up the contact list on my phone, move to the very selective Restaurant group, and call "our restaurant": Sapporo Japanese Steak House. I know they will not be opened, but are there, nonetheless, preparing food for tonight's guests, as is their custom. I simply have to let the phone ring long enough, as holidays and events make this place near impossible to get into.

"This is Shawn. I am bringing my wife tonight," I say to the Manager once she answers.

Recognizing my voice, she asks: "When can we expect you?"

I ask: "What slots are open?"

"Just let me know when you want to arrive, I will accommodate you."

"You still open at 5?"

"Yes, 5 o'clock."

"Make it 5 o'clock then."

"I will handle everything Mister Shawn."

"You always do."

I smile as the call ends, because in twelve years, this restaurant has never given us bad food, poor service or any thoughts or trying another. They simply provide an evening filled with excellence in food preparation and a friendly open environment. I only need to tell them what I want in my meal and they create their masterpiece and place it on the plate, very similar to Revo's Filters.

Filters defined

Simply stated: MODX Revolution Filters place a "translation" layer between the processed output of Elements and the Resource they are being parsed from. In other words, Filters allow the output of an Element to be manipulated and translated from one format to another.

In our Valentine's date scenario, there are plenty of examples of real life filters:

♦ Valentine's Day designates the day as special

♦ The Restaurant group in my cell phone represents the best restaurants we frequent

♦ The Manager recognizing my voice may mean I get "preferred treatment"

♦ The appointment means we get seats even if the lobby is full

♦ Selecting the salad dressing, dipping sauce, and meat will define what I am served

♦ The "effort" was filtered leaving only our time together

♦ Wisely calling my wife's favorite restaurant directly translates into a perfect evening

The last of these real life examples represents the very heart of MODX Revolution Filters. We simply want a single thing to go in an intended direction. Elements in MODX Revolution typically return a single response. In some situations, Placeholders are used as a basis to allow a single Element to provide multiple pieces of information, each of which can also be filtered. The end result is greater flexibility for each member of the project team.

The Benefits of Filters

In MODX Revolution, Front-end designers can maximize their efforts and quickly make changes and enjoy faster response times on a number of project demands, because much of the presentation "power" has been left in their hands. A few of the many benefits of MODX Revolution Filters are presented here:

♦ Front-end designers retain the freedom to control presentation

♦ Reduces interaction concerning format issues

♦ Reduces number of Elements required to perform similar related tasks

♦ Provides an additional workflow layer to separate presentation from raw data

♦ Developers can focus on the trasmittal of data, leaving presentation to designers

♦ May reduce the amount of code, simply because presentation is of little consequence

♦ Allows default output data types expectations to be established site wide for Elements

♦ Enables people to do their job, while allowing them to handle the "grey" areas between roles and job descriptions

Implementation Examples

MODX Revolution 2.2.2-pl has over 50 Filters and at least double that number of aliases, which can also be used to implement a filter output function. For these examples, I will be hovering as close to Filter name / alias which closely resembles pre existing PHP commands, though any of the aliases would accomplish the exact same thing for any given Filter.

		Description and Examples

Conditional Overrides and Targeting	*else*	**Performs a function if the test condition is false**
		
		 Simple String Replace:
		 `[[*author_sex:eq=`M`:then=`Male`:else=`Female`]]`
		
		 Targeted content by gender:
		 `[[*author_sex:eq=`M`:then=`[[$Male]]`:else=`[[$Female]]`]]`

	hide	**Removes the Element content if the test condition is true**
		
		 If user is Male hide content:
		 `[[+modx.user.id:userinfo=`gender`:eq=`1`:hide]]`
		
		 Only show the content on Resources which are not containers:
		 `[[*isfolder:eq=`1`:hide:else=`[[Crumbz?startID=`3`]]`]]`

	show	**Displays content only if test condition is true** If user is Female show content: `[[+modx.user.id:userinfo=`gender`:eq=`2`:show]]`

	then	**Performs a function only if the test condition is true**
		
		 We can present this content for males only
		 `[[*author_sex:eq=`M`:then=`[[$Male]]`]]`
		 Using the current MODX User as the source:
		 `[[+modx.user.id:userinfo=`gender`:eq=`1`:then=`[[$Male]]`]]`
		 `[[+modx.user.id:userinfo=`gender`:eq=`2`:then=`[[$Female]]`]]`
		 To alter page content based on its properties:
		 `[[*isfolder:eq=`1`:then=`folder`:else=`page`]]`

	Description and Examples
eq, *is,* *equals,* *equalto,* *isequal,* *isequalto*	**Performs a PHP == comparison, not === version** Provides User 1 with a Chunk, no one else can access: `[[+modx.user.id:eq=`1`:then=`[[$specialMenu]]`]]`
gt, *isgt,* *greaterthan,* *isgreaterthan*	**Does Element have a greater value than the test?** Displays global navigation on all pages except our Home `[[*id:gt=`1`:then=`[[$globalNav]]`]]`
gte, *isgte,* *eg,* *ge,* *equalorgreaterthan,* *greaterthanorequalto*	**Is Element of a greater or equal value than the test?** Displays a warning message if quantity is >= than inventory `[[+ord.qty:gte=`[[+ord.inv]]`:then=`[[$Warning]]`]]`
input, *if*	**Provides an additional test other than Element Output** Display content only on Resource containers / folders. `[[getstring:if=`[[*isfolder]]`:eq=`1`:then=`Yes`]]`
lt, *islt,* *lessthan,* *lowerthan,* *islessthan,* *islowerthan*	**Does Element have a lesser value than the test?** Displays a warning if bid amount is < item minimum `[[+item.bid:lt=`[[+item.min]]`:then=`[[$Warning]]`]]`
lte, *islte,* *le,* *el,* *lessthanorequalto,* *equaltoorlessthan*	**Is Element of a lesser or equal value than the test?** Displays a Chunk if the visitor's login count is <= 10 `[[+modx.user.id:userinfo=`logincount`:lte=`10`:then=``[[$siteTour]]`]]`
ne, *neq,* *isnot,* *isnt,* *notequals,* *notequalto*	**Performs a PHP != comparison, not !== version** Does not display Chunk on containers/folders of other pages `[[*isfolder:ne=`1`:then=`[[Crumbz?startId=`3`]]`]]`

Compare Operators

See: http://www.php.net/manual/en/language.operators.comparison.php

Description and Examples Parsed

cssToHead	**Forces Cascading Style Sheet Content just above </head>** ♦ If the source is wrapped in `<style></style>` tags, the actual source code will be injected to the page head. ♦ All other content will be sent as a link to an external file. `[[+package_css:cssToHead]]` becomes <style>$src</style> or <link rel="stylesheet" href="" . $src . '" type="text/css" />
htmlToBottom	**Injects a block of (X)HTML just above </body>** This is an excellent way to target content and to comply with Yahoo's JavaScript Standard of placing the code after the page content. `[[$jqueryScript:htmlToBottom]]` Will place the scripts in the order they are parsed to the page bottom.

htmlToHead	**Injects a block of (X)HTML to just above </head>**
	This a possible method to add page specific content to the page head.
	`<meta name="keywords"`
	`        content="[[*tags:strtolower:replace=` ` ==,` `]]"/>`
	
	This Chunk could create meta keywords: [[$meta:htmlToHead]]

jsToBottom	**Forces JavaScript Content just above </body>** ♦ If the source is wrapped in `<script></script>` tags, the actual source code will be injected to the page bottom. ♦ All other content will be sent as a link to an external file. `[[+package_js:jsToBottom]]` becomes <script>$src</script> or <script type="text/javascript" src="" . $src . '"></script> `[[+package_js:jsToBottom=`1`]]` treats the source as raw text
jsToHead	**Forces JavaScript Content just above </head>** See: `jsToBottom`
toPlaceholder	**Replaces a [[+Placeholder]] with the content of the Element** Can be used in a variety of way to target page content. `[[$chunk:toPlaceholder=`sidemenu`]]` replaces `[[+sidemenu]]` with the output of `[[$chunk]]`. In JavaScript implementations, I add [[+jquery]] to the end of each chunk, to place subsequent scripts in the same <script> block. Note: The parser places them in reverse order.

Content Injection

Note: Injected Content will appear in the order the Parser encounters the filter: nested first.

<table>
<tr><th></th><th colspan="2">Description and Examples</th></tr>
<tr><td rowspan="8">Date Formatting</td><td>ago</td><td>

Natural language and utilizes lexicon entries

Additional Notes:

♦ Must be convertible to PHP's strtotime() format

♦ Defaults to current lexicon language as defined in: \core\lexicon\{LANGUAGE}\filters.inc.php

To format the resource publication date:
`[[*publishedon:ago]]` becomes 1 week, 4 days ago

</td></tr>
<tr><td>date</td><td>

Formats output utilizing parameters of PHP's strftime function

To format the default Resource publication date:
`[[*publishedon:strtotime:date=`%a, %d %b %Y %T`]]`

Returns the date as: Mon, 14 Feb 2011 05:45:00

</td></tr>
<tr><td>fuzzydate</td><td>

Alters dates occurring within last 48 hours (in 12 hour format)

`[[*publishedon:fuzzydate]]` will appear as: today at 10:34 AM
After the second day: 2011-02-25 10:34:00

</td></tr>
<tr><td>strtotime</td><td>

Returns a UNIX timestamp using PHP's strtotime()

`[[*publishedon:strtotime]]` becomes 1298651640

</td></tr>
</table>

<table>
<tr><th></th><th colspan="2">Description and Examples</th></tr>
<tr><td rowspan="4">Element Filters</td><td>select</td><td>

Returns Element output translated via array map

To "translate" MODX Revolution Gender integer values to single characters:

`[[+modx.user.id:userinfo=`gender`:select=`0=Unk&1=Male&2=Fem`]]`

</td></tr>
<tr><td>tag</td><td>

Allows raw Element tag to be represented in page

A sample Element call, using :tag:
`[[Wayfinder:tag?startId=`0`&level=`1`]]`

Returns an ASCII representation of an actual Element calls for page content:

`&#91;&#91;Wayfinder?startId=&#96;0&#96;&#93;&#93;`

</td></tr>
</table>

		Description and Examples
Logic	*and*	**Utilizes PHP's && logic operator (both tests have to be true)** If user id =1 AND the user is male: `[[+modx.user.id:eq=`1`:and:userinfo=`gender`:eq=`1`:then=`T`]]`
	or	**Utilizes PHP's ‖ logic operator (either test has to be true)** Provide special content to either of two users `[[+modx.user.id:eq=`1`:or:eq=`4`:then=`[[$specialMenu]]`]]`
		See: `http://www.php.net/manual/en/language.operators.logical.php`

		Description and Examples
Math Operations	*add,* *increment,* *incr*	**Increments Element by number provided (defaults to Element + 1)** `[[+price:add=`[[+baseMarkup]]`]]`
	divide, *div*	**Divides Element by filter value** `[[+correctAnswers:div=`[[+numberQuestions]]`]]`
	math	**Allows the use of advanced calculations (use sparingly!)** Strips all characters and white space before eval When possible use the other math functions or a Snippet to return the desired output.
	modulus, *mod*	**Remainder of Element output / Filter value (defaults to % 2)** `[[Snippet:mod:then=`odd`:else=`even`]]`
	multiply, *mpy*	**Multiplies the Element by Filter Value** `[[+price:mpy=`[[+salestax]]`]]`
	subtract, *decrement,* *decr*	**Decrements Element by number provided (defaults to - 1)** `[[+inventory:decr=`[[+orderQuantity]]`]]`
		See: `http://php.net/manual/en/language.operators.arithmetic.php`

	Description and Examples
cat	**Appends the filter string to the end of the element** Simple String Replace: `[[+item.weight:cat=` pounds`]]` Outputs: `9 pounds`

cdata	**Wraps content with <![CDATA [ ]]>**
	`<script type="text/javascript">`
	`[[$javaScriptChunk:cdata]]`
	`</script>`
	
	Produces:
	`<script type="text/javascript">`
	`<![CDATA[`
	`document.write('Hello World');`
	`]]>`
	`</script>`

default,
ifempty,
isempty,
empty
	Provides a default response if the Element output is empty
	Returns the content of a Chunk if the pot of gold is not found by the Snippet:
	`[[snippet:empty=`[[$notfound]]`?find=`pot of gold`]]`
	
	`http://us3.php.net/manual/en/function.empty.php`

esc, *escape*	**Prevents actual (X)HTML tags from being passed into page** Replaces &,",',< and > with HTML entities in `[[$content:esc]]` Takes: `<a href="#">Content</a>` And returns: `&lt;a href=&quot;#&quot;&gt;Content&lt;/a&gt;` See the `htmlent` Filter to use `htmlentities()` and translate all characters all characters with HTML character entities. `http://www.php.net/manual/en/function.htmlspecialchars.php`
ellipsis	**Truncates end of a string attaching an ellipsis if content was lost** To truncate the Gettysburg Address: `[[gettysburg:ellipsis=`50`]]` Returns: `Four score and seven years ago our fathers brought…`

String Manipulation

	Description and Examples
htmlent, *htmlentities*	**Translates *all* characters having HTML entity equivalents** http://www.php.net/manual/en/function.htmlentities.php Notes: ♦ Based on MODX_charset system setting, defaults to UTF8 ♦ Implements ENT_QUOTES affecting both single and double ♦ See esc Filter for htmlspecialchars() implementation ♦ Converts more characters than the five handled by esc Filter
ifnotempty, *isnotempty,* *notempty,* *!empty*	**Returns only the value assigned to !empty** [[*author_deceased:!empty=`Still alive`]]
length, *len,* *strlen*	**Displays the numerical length of the Element Output** Using the text of the Gettysburg Address as a source: [[gettysburg:strlen]] returns 1477 [[gettysburg:cat=` Abraham Lincoln`:len]] returns 1493 To toggle display based on string length: [[+url:len:gt=`8`:then=`yes`:else=`no`]] http://www.php.net/manual/en/function.strlen.php
lcase, *lowercase,* *strtolower*	**Changes case of Element Output to lower case** A simple technique to implement keywords for resource <meta> tags. [[!Crumbz:strtolower]] http://www.php.net/manual/en/function.strtolower.php
limit	**Displays designated number of characters of Element Output** Starts counting at the left most character (or first in string) and defaults to 100 [[gettysburg:limit=`70`]] Returns: Four score and seven years ago our fathers brought forth on this conti http://php.net/manual/en/function.substr.php

String Manipulation

	Description and Examples
md5	**Returns the md5 hash of the Element Output** `[[gettysburg:md5]]` returns e0486fb0267c8c44471a1a46ab8d1769 `http://www.php.net/manual/en/function.md5.php`
nl2br	**Replaces /n with XHTML \<br /\> in Element Output** Assume a Snippet returns a full mailing address for the current user: Fullname\n123 MainStreet\nCity, ST ZIP `[[getAddress:nl2br]]` would return the XHTML line break: Fullname\<br /\>123 MainStreet\<br /\>City, ST ZIP `http://www.php.net/manual/en/function.nl2br.php`
notags, *striptags,* *stripTags,* *strip_tags*	**Attempts to remove PHP and (X)HTML tags from Output** A Chunk containing: `<!-- This is an example --><title>MODX</title>` Becomes: MODX Currently, this does not allow tags to be designated to pass thru unchanged as indicated at `http://www.php.net/manual/en/function.strip-tags.php`
replace	**Exchanges all occurrences of one string with another** Using a navigation bar to create meta tags, we need to add commas: `[[!Crumbz:replace=` ==,`]]` replaces each {space} with {comma space} `http://www.php.net/manual/en/function.str-replace.php`
reverse, *strrev*	**Reverses the Element output** `[[$chunk:reverse]]` MODX Revolution would become noituloveR XDOM `http://www.php.net/manual/en/function.strrev.php`
strip	**Replaces all white space, tabs & line breaks with a single space** To display our header on a single line: `<head>[[$siteHeader:strip]] [[$jQueryTools:strip]]</head>`

String Manipulation

	Description and Examples

stripString	**Removes the designated string from the Element Output**
	Removing "the" from the Gettysburg Address:
	`[[gettysburg:stripString=`the`]]`
	
	Not only removes the word "the" but also all occurrences:
	
	Four score and seven years ago our fars... (instead of fathers)
	`http://www.php.net/manual/en/function.str-replace.php`

ucase, *uppercase,* *strtoupper*	**Changes the Element Output to Upper Case (all caps)** `[[gettysburg:ucase]]` ... FOUR SCORE AND SEVEN YEARS AGO... `http://www.php.net/manual/en/function.strtoupper.php`
ucfirst	**Forces the first character to upper case, if it is a character** `[[+modx.user.username:ucfirst]]` returns: Wshawn instead of wshawn `http://www.php.net/manual/en/function.ucfirst.php`
ucwords	**Forces the first alphabetical character of each word to upper case** `[[gettysburg:ucwords]]` returns: Four Score And Seven Years Ago... `http://www.php.net/manual/en/function.ucwords.php`

urldecode	**Decodes a urlencoded string to its native format**
	`[[gettysburg:urldecode]]`
	...t+hallow+%E2%80%93... becomes: ... hallow –
	`http://us3.php.net/manual/en/function.urldecode.php`

urlencode	**Translate a string to be used as the query component of a URL** `[[gettysburg:urlencode]]` returns ...+hallow+%E2%80%93... encoding `http://us3.php.net/manual/en/function.urlencode.php`

wordwrap	**Politely wraps Element output at a designated length, defaults: 70**
	To display the Gettysburg Address in a 50 character wide "column":
	`[[gettysburg:wordwrap=`50`]]`
	
	`http://www.php.net/manual/en/function.wordwrap.php`

wordwrapcut	**Cuts Element output mid-word if it is very long, defaults: 70**
	To display the Gettysburg Address in a 70 character wide presentation
	`[[gettysburg:wordwrapcut]]`
	`http://www.php.net/manual/en/function.wordwrap.php`

String Manipulation

	Description and Examples
isloggedin	**Returns true if the current user is logged in** The following displays a Chunk respective to current login status: `[[!$islogged:isloggedin:eq=`1`:then=`[[$islogged]]`:else=`[[$notlogged]]`]]`
ismember, *memberof,* *mo*	**Displays Element to members of a designated group** `[[+modx.user.id:mo=`Second Shift`:then=`yes`:else=`nope`]]`
isnotloggedin	**Returns true if the current user is not logged in** See isloggedin for similar example
userinfo	**Returns information, contained in the MODX database.** `[[+modx.user.id:userinfo=`gender`:eq=`1`:then=`[[$Male]]`]]` Many additional fields are available. Check the users and user_attributes tables: <table><tr><td>cachepwd</td><td>logincount</td></tr><tr><td>comment</td><td>thislogin</td></tr><tr><td>country</td><td>mobilephone</td></tr><tr><td>dob</td><td>password</td></tr><tr><td>email</td><td>phone</td></tr><tr><td>fax</td><td>photo</td></tr><tr><td>fullname</td><td>role</td></tr><tr><td>gender</td><td>state</td></tr><tr><td>internalkey</td><td>username</td></tr><tr><td>lastlogin</td><td>zip</td></tr></table> Additional notes: As of this writing: userinfo defaults to username The following are always available for the current user: ♦ `[[+modx.user.id]]` instead of `:userinfo:internalkey` ♦ `[[+modx.user.username]]` instead of `:userinfo:username`

User Filters

Custom Filter

Listing 07.01: filterCheckLastLog Custom Filter Snippet

```php
<?php
/**
 * User: W. Shawn Wilkerson
 * Date: 3/1/11
 * Time: 1:20 PM
 */
if (!empty ($input)) {
  $difference = time() - $input;
  return floor ($difference/86400);
}
```

Upon login a user will be evaluated to see if they have logged in this week:
`[[+modx.user.id:userinfo=`lastlogin`:filterCheckLastLog:gte=`8`:then=`[[$warning]]`]]`

The [[$warning]] Chunk could contain a Snippet call to log the offense, e-mail a supervisor, and finally post some sort of message to the user.

Creating custom filters are extremely easy if you understand the basic Filter functionality.

MODX Revolution Rule #7: **Use the simplest Element output for the greatest flexibility.**

An Ever Growing List:

Over the development life cycle of MODX Revolution, the number of available filters provided within the core files has steadily grown. As of this writing, we have included a summary description of every Filter available in MODX Revolution 2.2.2-pl. It may prove beneficial, to monitor the change.txt files with each new version, as well as periodically looking at the class file associated with these filters to see if any new Filters have been added: `/core/model/MODX/filters/modoutputfilter.class.php`.

Successful Implementation Considerations

Throughout the dozens of filter examples we have seen both simple and complex methods utilized to translate Element output, but have purposely waited until now to explain the actual mechanics of Filter operation, so this chapter can act as a reference and a guide at the same time. The following concepts should greatly simplify utilization.

Filters:

- ◆ Operate from left to right
- ◆ Either evaluate or translate the Element output
- ◆ May change the Element value, so subsequent filters are given a new value to test
- ◆ Are exclusively focused on the current Element value, excluding if / input
- ◆ Should be logically thought through for complex implementations
- ◆ May best be tested one stage at a time

Sample Each Stage

To successfully utilize MODX Revolution filters, it would be very advantageous to ascertain the desired or expected result and select the shortest and simplest implementation to achieve those results. I would suggest the following steps:

1. Create a new Resource with limited access
2. Establish the "natural" output of the Element, especially with dates: [[Element]]
3. Select the first Filter needed to be applied and test it: [[Element:filter]]
4. Continually add filters as needed: [[Element:filter:filter]] and so on, for each stage
5. Once the desired result has been achieved, implement within the site

Summary

This chapter attempts to provide a working example of every known MODX Revolution Filter at the time of this writing and has also introduced the chaining concept where one feeds the next. Filters allow designers the freedom to format Element output on-the-fly, removing the responsibility from developers, facilitating clearer role definition and greater flexibility.

In many ways Filters can streamline projects and create simple solutions to handle everyday problems, such as providing a page specific copyright date, content targeting, and attaching content directly to a group of people or a specific user. In essence, MODX Revolution Filters provide an additional layer of freedom many web projects can benefit from.

PART

II

Live Projects

Using the content from Part I, this section demonstrates real world examples found in many live sites around the globe.

These chapters are intended to present many of the various components which can be implemented in any given web project.

Please do not consider any of these pages mandatory or as a final authority. The majority of this content is entirely optional and is presented as such.

Quick Start

SEO and Site Optimization

Power Blogging

jQuery

AJAX

8

Quick Start:
Putting the Pieces Together

"You're hired."

Those two simple words can be very exciting, intimidating, or a combination of both. Now is the time when "theory" no longer matters and all the experience you may have attained to this point will either serve you well or be proven to be lacking at best.

The first seven chapters discussed many of the foundational concepts necessary to understand and implement a web project utilizing MODX Revolution, which is a very sophisticated product. For those who have made it this far, I believe we have well established the foundation upon which to build most any web-based concept - utilizing the MODX Revolution platform.

This chapter serves two purposes, hence the title. For some readers, this chapter will be the culmination of all the content which has gone before. For others, this chapter will provide a fast-paced walkthrough which will quickly get a site into production. In which ever group you find yourself, please understand the purpose of this chapter is not to discuss or introduce concepts.

At this point in our journey, it is assumed you have some experience using a MODX product, or simply may not be interested in reading seven chapters to get started and are willing to refer back to the related chapter content when necessary and pulling out each of the nuggets found there.

To progress through this chapter, a fully functional installation of MODX Revolution will need to be available and the reader has the proper rights and privileges to develop a web project from the beginning without Access Control List limitations. Eventually, readers should become adept enough to complete these steps in less time than it takes to read about it.

I would personally like to welcome each of you to the fun part of MODX Revolution: using it.

Change System Settings (Chapter 2)

1. Log into the Manager
2. Go to the System Settings located in the System menu
3. Filter the results to Site
4. Make sure each of the settings represents the project's needs
5. Change the **Site Name**
6. Decide whether or not the site will be using **XHTML URLs**
7. Take note of other settings which may need to be changed later, such as **Error Page**

Name	Key	Value	Last Modified
Area: Site (17 Settings)			
Menu indexing default	auto_menuindex	Yes	Dec 31, 1969 06:00 PM
Default Content Type	default_content_type	1	Dec 31, 1969 06:00 PM
Default Template	default_template	1	Dec 31, 1969 06:00 PM
Error Page	error_page	1	Dec 31, 1969 06:00 PM
Hide From Menus Default	hidemenu_default	No	Dec 31, 1969 06:00 PM
URL Generation Scheme	link_tag_scheme	-1	Dec 31, 1969 06:00 PM
Published default	publish_default	No	Dec 31, 1969 06:00 PM
Searchable Default	search_default	Yes	Dec 31, 1969 06:00 PM
Site name	site_name	MODX Revolution	Dec 31, 1969 06:00 PM
Site start	site_start	1	Dec 31, 1969 06:00 PM
Site status	site_status	Yes	Dec 31, 1969 06:00 PM
Site unavailable message	site_unavailable_message	The site is currently unavailable	Dec 31, 1969 06:00 PM
Site unavailable page	site_unavailable_page	0	Dec 31, 1969 06:00 PM
Merge Resource Fields in Symlinks	symlink_merge_fields	Yes	Dec 31, 1969 06:00 PM
Unauthorized page	unauthorized_page	1	Dec 31, 1969 06:00 PM
Use WebLink Target	use_weblink_target	No	Dec 31, 1969 06:00 PM
XHTML URLs	xhtml_urls	Yes	Dec 31, 1969 06:00 PM

Add A Site Template (Chapter 3)

1. Decide which Document Type Definition will be used to display site contents
2. Using an external editor create a basic structure Template for the project
3. Validate the Template
4. Go to the **Elements** tree in the **Resource** menu
5. Overwrite BaseTemplate or right-click Templates to create a New Template
6. Paste (X)HTML code with appropriate Revo Placeholders, then click Save
7. Upload associated images, CSS, and js files to the server verifying correct linkage
8. Assign the default "HOME" resource to the new Template, if not already done
9. Validate the "empty" Home page with W3C at this stage and correct any errors found

Listing 08.01: base MODX Revolution Template

```
<?xml version="1.0" encoding="UTF-8" ?>
<!DOCTYPE html PUBLIC "-//W3C//DTD XHTML 1.0 Strict//EN" "http://
www.w3.org/TR/xhtml1/DTD/xhtml1-strict.dtd">
<html xmlns="http://www.w3.org/1999/xhtml">
    <head>
        [[$siteHeader]]
        [[$jQuery?version=`1.7.2`]]
    </head>
    <body class="MODX">
        <div id="header">
            [[$globalNav]]
        </div>
        <div id="container">
            <div id="mainContent">
                <h1>[[*pagetitle]]</h1>
                [[*content]]
            </div>
            <br class="clearfloat" />
            <div id="footer">
                [[$siteFooter]]
            </div>
        </div>
        [[$javascript]]
    </body>
</html>
```

Create Chunks (Chapter 4)

Every web project is going to have its own requirements. As indicated in the Chunk and Template chapters, we choose to use names and solutions which facilitate communication. Though each of these could actually be included in the main file, or removed to the confines of external CSS and JavaScript files we choose to represent them in this manner for this quick start chapter.

Typically, my company will create reusable entities as much as possible. In this manner, web projects can begin role assignment sooner, as each individual will already be familiar with their part of the process. Additionally, we can assign experts to a specific Element, instead of forcing people to interact with content which they may not be overly familiar with or responsible for.

Listing 08.02: siteheader XHTML Chunk

```
<meta name="google-site-verification" content="get a key" />
<meta http-equiv="Content-Type" content="text/html; charset=utf-8"
/>
  <title>[[++site_name]]'s [[*longtitle]]</title>
  <base href="[[++site_url]]" />
  <meta name="author" content="[[*createdby?userinfo]]" />
  <meta name="copyright" content="Copyright ©[[*publishedon:strtotim
        e:date=`%Y`]] [[*createdby?userinfo=`fullname`]]." />
  <meta name="date" content="[[*publishedon:strtotime:date=`%FT%T%
        z`]]" />
  <meta name="description" content="[[*description:strtolower
        :ucfirst]] on [[++site_name]]" />
  <meta name="keywords" content="[[*introtext:replace=` ==,`
        :strtolower]] />
```

Listing 08.03: jQuery XHTML Chunk

```
<script src="//ajax.googleapis.com/ajax/libs/jquery/[[+jquery_
version:default=`1.7.1`]]/jquery.min.js"></script>
```

Listing 08.04: globalNav XHTML

```
<div id="mainnav">[[Wayfinder?startId=`0`&level=`1`
               &sortBy=`menuindex`&rowTpl=`wfNavBar`]]</div>
```

Listing 08.05: siteFooter XHTML

```
<br /><br /><div id="cpyrght">&copy; [[*copyRight]] <a
href="mailto:shawn@shawnwilkerson.com?subject=[[++site_name]]
[[*longtitle]]">Shawn Wilkerson</a>. All Rights Reserved.</div><div
id="siteDesign">design by <a href="http://www.shawnwilkerson.com"
title="Shawn Wilkerson holder of 10 computer/internet/business
degrees">Shawn Wilkerson</a> </div>
```

Listing 08.06: javascript Chunk

```
jQuery(document).ready(function() {
  /* handle dynamic classes */
  $("a[href*=.pdf]").attr('target', '_blank').addClass('pdf');
  $("a[href*=.zip]").attr('target', '_blank').addClass('zip');
  $("a[href*=.psd]").attr('target', '_blank').addClass('psd');
  $("a").filter(function() {
    return this.hostname && this.hostname !== location.hostname;
  }).attr('target', '_blank').addClass('offsitelink');
});
var _gaq=_gaq||[];_gaq.push(['_setAccount','[[++ggl_
analytics]]']);_gaq.push(['_trackPageview']);(function(){var
ga=document.createElement('script');ga.type='text/javascript';ga.
async=true;ga.src=('https:'==document.location.protocol?'https://
ssl':'http://www')+'.google-analytics.com/ga.js';var s=document.
getElementsByTagName('script')[0];s.parentNode.insertBefore(ga,s);})
();
```

Create Template Variables (Chapter 5)

1. Define possible variables for the site
2. Go to the **Elements** tree in the **Resource** menu
3. Right click on Template Variables and select Create A New Template Variable

Here are a few examples to get you started:

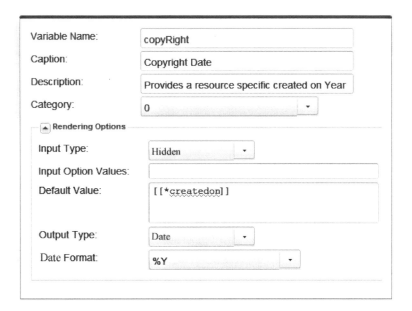

MODX Revolution Rule #8: **Continually build your tool-set and use it generously.**

Variable Name: dateStamp

Caption: Hidden Pub Date

Description: Places a formated Published On date

Category: 0

Rendering Options

Input Type: Hidden

Input Option Values:

Default Value: `[[*publishedon:strtotime:date=`%a, %d %b %Y`]]`

Output Type: HTML Tag

Tag Name: span

Tag ID:

Class: docCounts fltRight

Style:

Attributes:

Variable Name: xpdo

Caption: link to my xPDO section

Description:

Category: 0

Rendering Options

Input Type: Hidden

Input Option Values:

Default Value:
```
<a href="[[~115]]"
 title="[[++site_name]]'s xPDO section">xPDO</a>
```

Output Type: Default

Install Navigation (Chapter 6)

1. Using the **Package Browser**, select the arrow next to MODX Add-Ons
2. Scroll down and open the Navigation group
3. Select Wayfinder and then click the "Download" Button
4. Select "Finished" to leave the download screen
5. Select Wayfinder's "Install" to complete the install process
6. Create a Chunk to be used as a template for the menu:

Listing 08.07: wfNavBar Chunk used as template for Wayfinder Row example

```
<li [[+wf.id]] [[+wf.classes]]><a href="[[+wf.link]]"
title="[[++site_name]] [[+wf.title]]" [[+wf.attributes]]>[[+wf.
linktext]]</a>[[+wf.wrapper]]</li><li class="sep">|</li>
```

Add AntiSpam Plugin

1. Install ObfuscateEmail-Revo via the Package Manager
2. If not using the Package Manager, proceed through these steps
3. Download the file from: https://github.com/wshawn/ObfuscateEmail
4. Open the Element menu
5. Right Click on Plugin
6. Create a new Plugin Named AntiSpam
7. Paste the PHP Code from obfuscateemail
8. Do not use a closing ?> tag
9. Set the OnWebPagePrerender Event for the Plugin
10. Save the **Plugin**

Add Custom PHP Snippets

1. Using an editor, create a block of PHP code to accomplish a single task
2. Test the code as a stand-alone file whenever possible
3. If using the MODX Revolution API please test the code accordingly
4. Open the Element menu in the Resource Tree
5. Right Click on Snippet
6. Create a new Snippet named according to its purpose
7. Paste the PHP Code from the editor
8. Do not use a closing ?> tag
9. Save The **Snippet**

Listing 08.08: visitorIPAddress.php

```php
<?php
$ip = '';

if (!empty($_SERVER['HTTP_X_FORWARDED_FOR'])) {
    $ip = $_SERVER['HTTP_X_FORWARDED_FOR'];
}
elseif (!empty($_SERVER['HTTP_X_FORWARDED'])) {
    $ip = $_SERVER['HTTP_X_FORWARDED'];
}
elseif (!empty($_SERVER['HTTP_X_CLUSTER_CLIENT_IP'])) {
    $ip = $_SERVER['HTTP_X_CLUSTER_CLIENT_IP'];
}
elseif (!empty($_SERVER['HTTP_FORWARDED_FOR'])) {
    $ip = $_SERVER['HTTP_FORWARDED_FOR'];
}
elseif (!empty($_SERVER['HTTP_FORWARDED'])) {
    $ip = $_SERVER['HTTP_FORWARDED'];
}
else {
    $ip = $_SERVER['REMOTE_ADDR'];
}

return $ip;
```

Edit The Home Page

1. Access the Resources Tree
2. Select the Home Resource, which should appear similar to the image
3. Choose the correct **Template** (may already be completed)
4. Change the Title (also used to display the document in the Resource Tree)
5. Provide a Long Title
6. Add a Description
7. Our example siteHeader Chunk utilizes the Summary for meta tag keywords
8. Provide a Menu Title as it might appear in the Navigation Menus
9. Add the Page (X)HTML content in the bottom Resource Content box
10. Decide if the page should be "Published" to a live state for site visitors to see
11. Decide if this page should Hide from Menu Snippets (it is still viewable)
12. Save the Resource
13. Select View

ⴕ *FURL AND AUTO GENERATE RESOURCE ALIAS SETTINGS ARE TURNED OFF*

See the next chapter for information regarding Streamlining Web Projects With SEO, FURLs, and Minify. Currently, each Resource will have to be manually edited to establish the Alias.

Add Additional Resources

1. Access the Resources Tree
2. Right-Click on "web"
3. Hover over Create
4. Select Create a Document Here
5. Possibly create an "About us" page
6. Repeat the procedure on the previous page to create a new page
7. Repeat this process for each additional page to be created, as needed

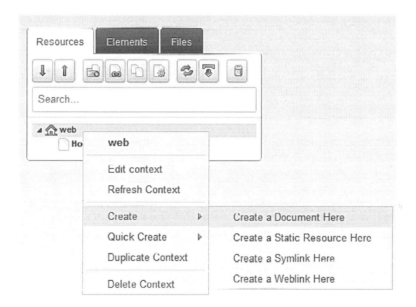

This process can also be used to create a new:

♦ **Weblink** to an existing URL using a redirect, can be off-site or in-site

♦ **Symlink** to an existing URL typically in the same site and does not redirect

♦ **Static Resource**, which is a file based Resource (such as a pdf file)

Create Subdirectories / Containers

1. If necessary, create a new Template for this area of the web project
2. Create a Page specifically for the purpose of containing other pages
3. Under the Page settings tab Select Container, or simply add a page to this new parent
4. If necessary, add page content (use this tab or the Document Tab)
5. Provide some form of navigation to the child pages, under this parent
6. Save the Resource

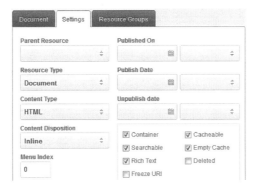

Add Additional Pages To A Container

1. Right-Click on the Document Resource where child Resources will be contained
2. Hover over Create
3. Select "Create Document Here"
4. Choose the correct Template (child Resources should inherit the parent's Template)
5. Create the page as previously described

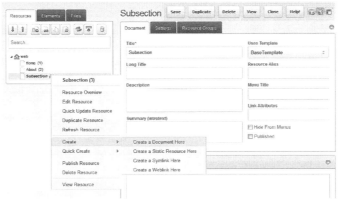

Thinking Forward: Structure and Project Direction

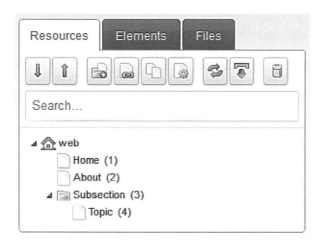

At this stage of the process, it becomes apparent how easy it is to layout an entire site in a matter of minutes.

♦ Navigation is handled by Wayfinder

♦ The page layouts are Templated

♦ Pages now require only the content specific to them

♦ We can graphically demonstrate to the project team and clients the structure we are working with

♦ At this point in the project, personal preference and company policy will probably have a major influence on how the web project will continue

Suggested questions to consider and start asking:

♦ Will multiple users be working on the web project?

♦ Will Access Control Policies need to be enacted?

♦ Will we need to provide dedicated sections of the site to specific groups?

♦ Will we need to allow specific areas of the front page to be edited by specific teams, departments, or external content?

♦ What is the client's message?

♦ What is the central purpose of the project?

♦ Are the topics (nouns) on the site going to have dedicated pages, like an item or a CEO biography? Do we need to implement these links using Template Variables?

♦ Can we design the site and keep the framework open, to facilitate upgrades and allow event themes (like product releases or holidays)?

♦ What is needed to move forward?

♦ Can we get the client to approve this structure?

♦ Are we in danger of missing the client's target expectations?

♦ Who is going to be getting e-mail from the site?

♦ How are they going to be contacted?

Adding A Contact Form

1. Access the Package Manager under the System menu
2. Select Download Extras
3. Select the drop arrow next to Extras to open the category tree
4. Select Forms
5. Download Formit
6. Select Finish

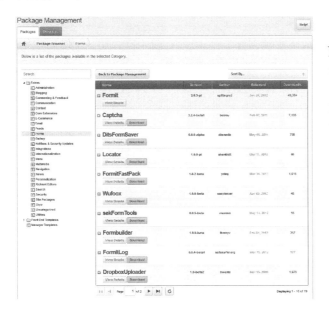

Notice: there are many form related Packages which can be implemented, including a few purposed for easier form creation.

7. Install Formit

8. Once installed, notice how Formit creates a Category of its Snippets. Some Packages will automatically establish Categories to house their various components.

It may prove very beneficial to separate Elements used on the web project into these groups, especially for in-house components being developed for the site.

9. Create a Resource which will serve as a contact page

Listing 08.09: example contact form for use with Formit

```
[[!FormIt?hooks=`recaptcha,spam,email,redirect`&emailTpl=`formitStan
dardEmail`&emailTo=`shawn@shawnwilkerson.com`&emailUseFieldForSubjec
t=`1`&redirectTo=`6`]]
<h2>Contact Form</h2>    <p>[[+fi.error.error_message]]</p>
<form action="[[~[[*id]]]]" method="post" class="form">
    <input type="hidden" name="nospam:blank" value="" />
    <label for="name">
        Name:
        <span class="error">[[+fi.error.name]]</span>
    </label>
    <input type="text" name="name:required" id="name" value="[[+fi.
name]]"/><br />
    <label for="email">
        E-mail:
        <span class="error">[[+fi.error.email]]</span>
    </label>
    <input type="text" name="email:email:required" id="email"
value="[[+fi.email]]" /><br />
    <label for="subject">
        Subject:
        <span class="error">[[+fi.error.subject]]</span>
    </label>
    <input type="text" name="subject:required" id="subject"
value="[[+fi.subject]]" /><br />
    <label for="text">
        Message:
        <span class="error">[[+fi.error.text]]</span>
    </label>
    <textarea name="text:required:stripTags" id="text" cols="55"
rows="7" value="[[+fi.text]]">[[+fi.text]]</textarea>
    <br class="clearall" />
    [[!+formit.recaptcha_html]]    [[+fi.error.recaptcha]]
    <br class="clearall" />
    <div class="form-buttons">
        <input type="submit" value="Send Contact Inquiry" />
    </div>
</form>
```

----

10. Create a Chunk to use for the e-mail template

Listing 08.10: example formitStandardEmail Template Chunk

```
<strong>[[+text]]</strong>
<br />
-- [[+name]] ([[+email]])
```

----

11. Create a Resource to serve as a "Thank You" / landing page and adjust &redirectTo=
    to point to the Document ID

Listing 08.11: example landing page for use with Formit

```
<h2>E-mail send: successful</h2>

<a href ="[[~1]]" title="return to my home page">Return Home</a>
```

----

12. Test the contact form

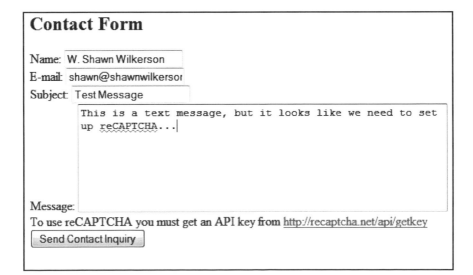

13. Optional: Visit `http://recaptcha.net/api/getkey` to receive a pair of keys and enter them in Setting Settings (pay close attention to the key order) or simply remove `recaptcha` from the `hook` parameter in the FormIt Snippet call

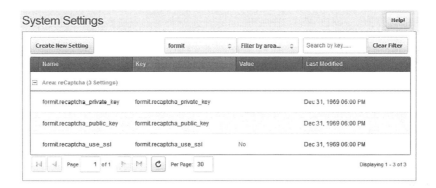

14. Retest the form, once reCAPTCHA is functioning (if the site uses it)

15. Successful: e-mail was sent

16. Troubleshoot e-mail failure to send as some server setups require SMTP user and password authentication for all outbound e-mail, in those cases it may be necessary to change the following settings, at a minimum:

Use SMTP, SMTP User, SMTP Password

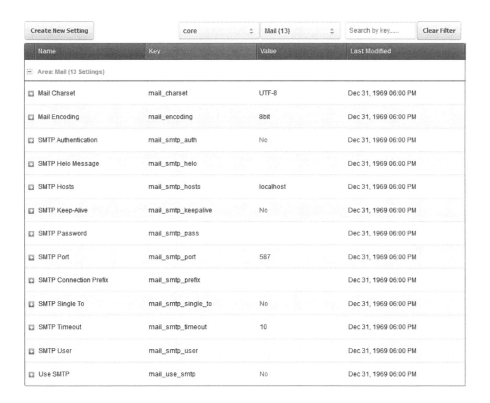

If you are unsure, please contact your system administrator or hosting company for the correct details. In many cases, it is simply an issue of the full e-mail address is the user name and the SMTP port may have been changed in the e-mail exchange software.

Adding Site Search (For Static Content Only)

1. Access the Package Manager under the System menu

2. Select Download Extras

3. Select the drop arrow next to Extras to open the category tree

4. Select Search

5. Download SimpleSearch

6. Select Finish

7. Create a dedicated resource to display the Search results

8. Add [[!SimpleSearchForm]][[!SimpleSearch]] to the dedicated search page

9. Optionally add [[!SimpleSearchForm?landing=`9`]] to the header with id of dedicated search page to display and paginate the results.

10. Test functionality and add CSS

Summary

In a very few pages, we have "raced" through the various aspects of getting a site up and running, culminating the material which took hundreds of pages to cover. We have demonstrated each of the steps typically associated with building a MODX Revolution web project: Templates, Chunks, Template Variables, Snippets, and installing Packages from the Package Manager.

For those who finished this chapter understanding much of the content, you are now ready to move on to a very enjoyable experience with MODX Revolution. The first seven chapters may now serve as your reference for moving further.

Others may have used this chapter as a litmus test to determine their overall understanding of this amazing Framework. How do you feel about taking the driver seat now? There is no better teacher in technology than simply working with it. Start with the areas you understood and are comfortable with and begin experimenting with the other areas.

Nearly every step and process presented herein can be considered completely optional and only a specific method to accomplish any given task, which can also be accomplished in many other ways. I tried to presented methods in use by many individuals utilizing MODX Revolution, though I have myself implemented many others. It is now time for you to being developing your own tools, methods, and processes.

This is your moment: Go forth and build the web your way.

9

Streamlining Web Projects With SEO, FURLs, and Minify

I was summoned to a meeting, in Spring 2000, with Russ Truelove, a race car driver from the days before today's organized racing organizations existed. His years of racing cars are long over, but his life of successfully crossing many "finish" lines was not.

"Shawn, I represent the worlds largest supplier of ring metals and we need your help."

"What exactly do you have in mind", I responded.

"We produce 75% of the worlds notebook ring mechanisms and no one knows who we are. We want to get our name out there, and to establish a brand recognized around the globe."

"Have you considered a web site?", I asked.

"That's exactly what I was thinking about. I want you to do for us, what you did with the racing club. I want you to get us out there. I want people to know who we are and what we do."

We began to work together and continued for eight years. At the height of its popularity, the site dominated the first four pages of Google results and the first pages of most other relevant search engines. We "owned" the top positions. Sadly, the global economic downturn of 2008 forced the company to develop inhouse, resulting in the other SEO - Search Engine Obscurity.

If there is a dark art on the internet, I do not believe it is cracking, or other malicious activity. I believe it comes down to Optimization: Search Engine and the physical site itself. This much debated topic has as many theories as those regarding good pizza: everyone seems to have one.

This chapter will discuss the methodology surrounding the site content as it relates to Search Engine Optimization (SEO) from a perspective used successfully for over a decade.

Understanding The Search Engine

The following concepts attempt to communicate my understanding of search engine methodology. I offer these perspectives with the hope it may provide an informative foundation for those who would like to benefit from search engines indexing their web project:

Search Engines attempt to:

♦ view a web site the way humans would

♦ discern origins of a given topic (such as everything **MODX** originates at MODX.com)

♦ associate site content with a topic to establish relevance

♦ measure content with that of the originators to ascertain relevance

♦ calculate the percentage of the current page relating to a specific topic

♦ assign a relative value which a "typical" informed visitor would to specific content

♦ synthetically "act" and "think" the way humans do when presented with content

♦ get to things quickly, but actually appear to take their sweet time

♦ count the occurrences of specific text in a Resource

MODX Revolution Rule #9: **A web project only has one purpose: the visitor.**

Optimizing a Site For Search Engines

I am going to make a statement, which is probably bound to upset quite a few people. I would ask for those individuals to continue reading, as I will quickly prove the basis of my statement and then we can move forward to understanding some of the "whys" of web projects .

As internet technology professionals, we must admit that we have been lied to. The entire Search Engine Optimization (SEO) process is unrealistic and even impossible. The very name itself implies we have access to the inner workings of respective internet-based search engines and the ability to manipulate those systems to our benefit. For many of us, this is simply not the case.

The truth is, most of us on this planet will never have access to these systems and will never be able to optimize any search engine. Special abilities, simply do not exist to manipulate the search engines to benefit our clients or ourselves the way many so-called "experts" tell us they can.

We must understand why search engines work the way they do, and how we can help them do it. Simply stated, our job is to create web projects valued by people, because search engines try very hard to "view" our sites the way people do.

All we have to do, is build sites people will enjoy and value. Search engines will typically agree.

Configuring: Friendly URLs

We have all heard it: "the internet is forever." In other words, once content is indexed in the search engines, it will stay there. We do not want search engines, "remembering" the last place they saw content on our site, as much as we want them to get accustomed to finding it where they last saw it and continually look for where we discuss it next on the site.

The first thing I typically set up for a web site, are Friendly URLs, so we are not "moving" content from `index.php?id=5` to `about.html`. People like them and search engines tend to like what people do. Fortunately for us, Friendly URLs (FURLs) can be configured and operational in just a few minutes on most [Apache] servers by following a simple four step process.

Modify .htaccess file

MODX supplies an ht.access file which requires minimal editing to match server settings. There are many ways to access this file, but remember on Linux / UNIX/ BSD operating systems a file beginning with a period (or dot) is hidden.

The MODX Browser provides a very quick means to edit this file without needing to open an (S)FTP client, ssh session, or web development software package. Simply click on the ht.access file and follow the directions below. This file will need to renamed to `.htaccess` when editing has been completed and can usually be placed at the location shown or anywhere above the MODX installation on the web server.

干 *BE CAREFUL WHERE THE .HTACESS FILE IS PLACED*

Be aware some control panels like to write their own .htaccess just above the site level so the best place to put it is where the home page of the site points to (view image above).

Alternate locations: /www, /htdocs, /public_html or even in the main Apache configuration file for servers hosting only a single domain. The .htacess has to be at the same level or above the main index.php MODX is presenting documents from.

Listing 09.01: .htaccess file

```
# Friendly URLs Part
RewriteEngine On
RewriteBase /
RewriteCond %{HTTP_HOST} .
# Force all pages to go to www.domain.com for SEO
RewriteCond %{HTTP_HOST} !^www\.DOMAIN\.TLD [NC]
RewriteRule (.*) http://www.DOMAIN.TLD/$1 [R=301,L]
# Friendly URLs
RewriteCond %{REQUEST_FILENAME} !-f
RewriteCond %{REQUEST_FILENAME} !-d
RewriteRule ^(.*)$ index.php?q=$1 [L,QSA]
```

To get FURLs operational, simply:

1. Find DOMAIN and replace it with your actual name (ex. shawnwilkerson)
2. Find TLD and replace it with your extensions (ex. com)
3. There are two of each, ensure all are changed
4. Remove the beginning hash symbol so the lines are no longer commented out, as shown above
5. Do not edit more than you need, as web servers can be very picky with mistakes
6. Save the file
7. Replace the original
8. Rename the file to .htaccess
9. Verify front of site is still loading, as any errors in this file may cause Apache to fail
10. If necessary, check the web server software error log to discover errors

T **RewriteBase considerations**

The RewriteBase should typically end with a /

Subdomains or other settings may require additional editing, depending on domain settings. A subdomain may need to have RewriteBase of MODX/ or simply /.

Configure MODX Revolution To Use Friendly URLs

Next we need to change the MODX Revolution for Friendly URLs. Fortunately they have been grouped together so they can easily be changed, by setting the "Area" filter to Friendly URL and retrieve the FURL settings, typically similar to these as found in Revo version 2.2.2-pl:

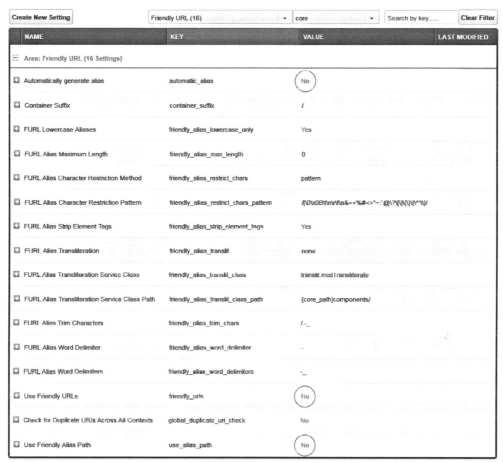

For the vast majority of sites we simply set Automatically generate alias, Use Friendly URLs, and Use Friendly Alias Path to Yes. I have never needed to adjust any of the other settings for a FURL implementations, though you may want to reference them to see if they apply to your situation.

Alternately, if the site should appear as if all the documents are on the site root, then Use Friendly Alias Path would be left as No, which will disregard any paths used by the Resource Tree of the Manager to organize pages. For the majority of my web projects, I typically set this to Yes, to allow targeting for search engines and site visitors to specific topical areas.

Check All Templates and Header Chunks For a <base href> Tag

Make sure the following line appears between the <head></head> section of each of the pages which will appear on the site. Typically, this meta tag will be found in Templates or in assocated Chunks which contain those portions of the <head>. The inclusion of this directive should be considered mandatory, as the entire site is actually being served from a single file, and the "physical" contents do not exist. This directive enables MODX Revolution to efficiently link all of the site content. You may also notice the [[!++site_url]] is set to be uncached by MODX Revolution. This can come in quite handy when multiple contexts are being used or when multiple domain names point to the same site. If this is not the case, feel free to cache the setting.

Excerpt 09.02: (X)HTML base href should be considered required

- -

```
<base href="[[!++site_url]]" />
```

- -

⊤ *[[++site_url]] System Setting*

The [[++site_url]] is supplied directly from the web server software and as such can not be located in the System Settings area of the MODX Revolution Manager.

Clear the MODX Revolution cache

The last step requires the MODX Revolution cache to be cleared as to remove any references to the previous locations to existing Resources. If this step is skipped, Page Not Found Errors (404) and other issues may be experienced by site visitors.

If pages are not working after completing this process, there is a very good chance the offending page may not have an alias. Edit each page as needed and ensure each of them has an alias. Once, we have set Automatically generate alias to yes in the System Settings, these will be generated for subsequent additions to the site - just not those which existed before the value was changed.

The Friendly URLs procedure is now complete. If pages are still not working, try using another web browser or emptying the cache on the computer. These steps have successfully been performed on every Apache web server where we have installed MODX Revolution.

You may also need to check the error_log of the web server and see if it contains hints.As we mentioned before: Apache is not very forgiving for typos or mistakes - even those in filenames.

Minified JavaScript / Cascading Style Sheets

A few years ago, the Yahoo Developer Network released approximately thirty-five "rules" for building web projects. This list has been posted in its entirety at: http://developer.yahoo.com/performance/rules.html. In this section we will install the PHP5 Minify script, and allow it to transparently address many of these for us, namely:

JavaScript Related	CSS Related
♦ Make JavaScript External	♦ Choose <link> Over @import
♦ Minify JavaScript	♦ Make CSS external
♦ Put Scripts after Content	♦ Minify CSS
♦ Remove Duplicate Scripts	♦ Place images in cached CSS
	♦ Put Stylesheets at top of page

Content Related
♦ Add an Expires or a Cache-Control Header
♦ Avoid 404s
♦ Gzip Components (discussed in next Section)
♦ Make Ajax Cacheable
♦ Make Fewer HTTP Requests
♦ Reduce DNS Lookups
♦ Reduce the Number of DOM Elements

Installing Minify

Currently there are two methods to install Minify to the MODX Revolution web project: via the Package Manager and manually. These concepts should be consistent for both methods, though I had difficulty with the Package version. For our purposes, we will be using the manual installation and showing the steps currently in use on many of my web sites to better illustrate functionality.

1. Visit http://code.google.com/p/minify/
2. Download or wget the newest zip file
3. Extract the file
4. Upload only the min directory to the root of the web project

Match Settings to Server Configuration

I have removed all of the comments from the configuration file for presentation purposes. Please view the file included in the Minify download for more information. To get Minify working we simply have to adjust a couple of settings:

Excerpt 09.03: edited config.php for use with Minify

```php
<?php
/**
 * Configuration for "min", the default application built with the
 * Minify library
 *
 * @package Minify
 */
$min_errorLogger = false;
$min_allowDebugFlag = false;
$min_enableBuilder = true;
$min_cachePath = '/home/user/tmp/minify/';
$min_documentRoot = '';
$min_cacheFileLocking = true;
$min_serveOptions['bubbleCssImports'] = false;
$min_serveOptions['maxAge'] = 31104000;
$min_serveOptions['minApp']['groupsOnly'] = false;
$min_symlinks = array();
$min_uploaderHoursBehind = 0;
$min_libPath = dirname(__FILE__) . '/lib';
ini_set('zlib.output_compression', '0');
```

This configuration example is from a Red Hat 5.6 Apache web server. Other users may need to read through the config.php comments and adjust settings according to their hosting environment. Typically, only the first four options are required to be configured during our implementations, though we also adjust $min_serveOptions['maxAge'] to set a far off date of one year (60x60x24x30x12), even a month would work (2592000).

The $min_enableBuilder is usually set to true, to provide a "build" script to be used to assist a developer to link JavaScript or Cascading Style Sheets to the Minify PHP script. For more information on using Builder visit the Minify Project at http://code.google.com/p/minify/. Once Minify is working properly, you can probably set this to false.I found out it

To establish the $min\_cachePath$, you may have to consult with a server administrator, possibly take a look inside MODX Revolution /core/config/config.php and locate the $MODX\_core\_path$ setting the Revo installer auto detected, or look in the site's Control Panel Software to ascertain the physical file path to the top of the site. Usually somewhere near the root of the path, a site will have a dedicated /tmp directory which is "owned" by the site's user and group.

T̄   *PERSONAL PREFERENCE*

On most of our sites we will create a directory for $_SESSIONs, and a directory matching each script name being implemented, if it is expected to store data on the site. In this example, we have created a dedicated minify directory inside the site's tmp folder.

I typically choose to use the individual sites "locked down" tmp directory for all temporary storage for a specific site, as indicated in the $min\_cachePath$ Minify setting in our example. Though it is possible to use the server wide /tmp partition, we would strongly recommend against storing $_SESSION or any site information there. If necessary, ask your server administrator for more information.

After the first time or two using Minify, many users will typically only need to edit the options: $min\_enableBuilder$, $min\_cachePath$, and $min\_serveOptions['maxAge']$. As always, every implementation has its own specific rules.

Once you have made the changes, save the file. If (S)FTP is being used, I would suggest renaming the unedited original from /min/config.php on the server to /min/config.original.php and upload the edited config file to the server. This is typically all that is necessary to configure Minify for use on the majority of my web projects.

T̄   *MINIFY CONSIDERATIONS*

Once fully operational, many users will find themselves VERY pleased with the results of minify, if for no other reason than its speed benefit to most web projects.

We must offer a word of caution:
If any file is edited and sent to the site after it exists in the $min\_cachePath$ directory, it may not be refreshed in the Minify cache until $min\_serveOptions['maxAge']$ has passed. Any associated cache files may need to be manually deleted from Minify's temp folder to reflect subsequent updates. Ensure the source files are functioning correctly before committing them to Minify.

Implement Minify via a MODX Revolution Template

The easiest way to test Minify is to use it. By now, most sites will have already established some sort of site css file. If you already have a template file with a working CSS attached, this should prove to be relatively easy. Simply access any given template via the MODX Revolution Manager, or a duplicate if the project is already live, and look for a line similar to the following in the page header:

Excerpt 09.04: typical external css file linked to a page

- -

```
<link type="text/css" rel="stylesheet" href="site.css" />
```

- -

Typically this requires the addition of only a few characters to the line above to activate Minify and have it produce cached copies of our css files for web browsers. This example assumes the cascading style sheet is located at the top of the site. If this is not the case, simply try adding /min/f= in front of the path currently working and then save the template.

Excerpt 09.05: minified external css file linked to a page

- -

```
<link type="text/css" rel="stylesheet" href="/min/f=site.css" />
```

- -

The <link></link> line may also appear in a site header MODX Revolution Chunk, and in some instances it may even appear in a Resource with a blank template attached. The above changes can be placed wherever the external style sheet is linked and should always appear between the page <head></head> tags.

▼ BROKEN SITE WARNING

As most modern web projects have isolated the style away from the contents, the site may appear broken if Minify is not configured correctly. We would recommend testing this configuration and associated functionality on a hidden section of the site, or on a development server with similar path structure.

Testing the Minify Implementation

Clear the MODX Revolution cache and reload any page using the template with the updated `<link type="text/css" rel="stylesheet" href="/min/f=site.css" />` statement implementing Minify. Upon viewing the page source in Firefox, we are able to click on the new link, Minify should have taken a typical external CSS file:

Excerpt 09.06: typical css file

```
@charset "utf-8";
.shawnwilkerson,.credentials,.christian,.code,.computers,.topNotHome
{
  font: 100% Geneva, Arial, Helvetica, sans-serif;
  background: #fff;
  margin: 0;
  padding: 0;
  text-align: center;
  color: #000;
}
```

And rendered a minified version of it, which would look similar to the following:

Excerpt 09.07: minified css file

```
charset "utf-8";.shawnwilkerson,.credentials,.christian,.code,.
computers,.topNotHome{font:100% Geneva,Arial,Helvetica,sans-serif;ba
ckground:#fff;margin:0;padding:0;text-align:center;color:#000};
}
```

By default Minify, will create two versions of the original file: a minified version with the majority of white space removed and a subsequent gzipped version which can be offered to a web browser. In either case the files created by Minify are much smaller than the originals which directly translates in lower bandwidth utilization and faster site presentations.

Additionally, using an (S)FTP, SCP, or ssh log into the site and switch to the directory we designated for Minify to use as its temporary storage: `$min_cachePath`. We should see files which have been created and cached for Minify to offer to site visitors.

Here we see two main types of files, a singular css file and groups of JavaScript files. Any supported file type can be sent to Minify in groups or individually, though currently it is not feasible to mix JavaScript and Style Sheets in the same group.

Desiding to process a single file or to group them depends on the implementation, which will usually indicate the direction to follow. Additionally, in some situations it is even feasible to minify all CSS used in a given web project into one group, and all the JavaScript into another. In the file listing above, the largest JavaScript group is only 16k when gzipped, which translates to mere seconds on a 56k modem. The files are set to cache for a year. With such a small footprint, I would personally violate the "don't load un needed content rule" if the need arose.

Establishing Groups

Some sites will utilize separate Cascading Style Sheets in a site depending on the media being utilized to view site content. Each of those files would count as an additional http request on the server, and the rule states we are to keep this number to a maximum of 5.

JavaScript is even more notorious for being loaded in pieces from multiple files, such is the case of the Syntax Highlighter Code, which requires a core file to be loaded and then an additional file for each programming language "brush" to be used.

Listing 09.08: from chapter 3 to load our syntax highlighter JavaScript

```
<script type="text/javascript" src="js/shCore.js"></script>
<script type="text/javascript" src="js/shBrushBash.js"></script>
<script type="text/javascript" src="js/shBrushCss.js"></script>
<script type="text/javascript" src="js/shBrushJScript.js"></script>
<script type="text/javascript" src="js/shBrushPhp.js"></script>
<script type="text/javascript" src="js/shBrushPlain.js"></script>
<script type="text/javascript" src="js/shBrushSql.js"></script>
<script type="text/javascript" src="js/shBrushXml.js"></script>
<script type="text/javascript">SyntaxHighlighter.all();</script>
```

Simply looking at this list, it is not too difficult to image how easy it is to violate a number of Yahoo's Recommendations: excessive http requests, the scripts combined weight is approximately 40k, and none of these scripts are minified or gzipped. Fortunately for us we can correct all of this in a matter of a few short of minutes, by following these steps:

1. Open the /min/groupsConfig.php file
2. Add a new array element
3. Use any name you would like, in this case we chose "sh"
4. Add the full relative path from the site root
5. Take special note of the extra "/" in front of the paths, this instructs Minify to start at the document root of the site
6. Add each file as an array value of the name previously selected
7. Save the file
8. Upload to the server

Listing 09.09: /min/grouspConfig.php

```php
<?php
return array(
    'sh' => array('//js/shCore.js',
        '//js/shBrushBash.js',
        '//js/shBrushCss.js',
        '//js/shBrushJScript.js',
        '//js/shBrushPhp.js',
        '//js/shBrushPlain.js',
        '//js/shBrushSql.js',
        '//js/shBrushXml.js'),
);
```

We next need to edit what ever MODX Revolution Chunk, Template, or Resource content responsible for loading our 8 Syntax Highlighting files. For now, comment out those lines using the (X)HTML <!-- comment -> and insert the following lines:

Listing 09.10: Minified JavaScript group call

```html
<script type="text/javascript" src="min/g=sh"></script>
<script type="text/javascript">SyntaxHighlighter.all();</script>
```

Empty the Site Cache and reload any page which utilizes your JavaScript group. Clicking on the link, in Firefox page source should produce a single file consisting of each of the files listed in the 'sh' group Minified: combined into a single smaller file.

If everything is working, we will now have a very tiny 14k file being sent to the browser if gzipped is enabled on the server (and the browser supports it) or a single 31k file. We have resolved each of the issues previously mentioned: excessive http requests, 40k file which can be reduced, etc. We have also decreased the amount of overhead required to load the current page, due to each http request. You may now return and move the commented code replaced above. For those of you who opted not to use a Chunk to load your JavaScript in your Resources, maybe now it is understood why I choose to do so - I have nothing left to edit.

Please keep in mind most modern web sites will probably violate Yahoo's list at one junction or another. If an implementation "requires" our violating the list, we simply need to understand when and why it is necessary and that we actually intend to do it.

You now have all the information required to implement Minify -- experiment and enjoy.

Forcing JavaScript To The Page Bottom

Yahoo recommends all Javascript to be loaded after page content. Additionally, it should be noted: Cascading Style Sheets should also be linked prior to Javascript to reduce page reflows. This can be accomplished via output filters [[+jqueryLibrary:jsToBottom]] and [[+plugincss:cssToHead]]. Snippet's can also be created to inject content in these areas:

Listing 09.11: javascriptToFooter Snippet

```php
<?php
$srcArray = explode(',', $src);
foreach ($srcArray as $javascript)
{
    $modx->regClientScript($javascript);
}
```

Listing 09.12: load required JavaScript libraries (can be placed at Template top)

```
[[javascriptToFooter?src=`//ajax.googleapis.com/ajax/libs/
jquery/1.7.2/jquery.min.js,//cdn.jquerytools.org/1.2.5/all/jquery.
tools.min.js,min/g=js&amp;1`]]
```

Utilizing multiple Snippet calls or any of the MODX Revolution content injection Output Filters, we can implement Yahoo's load Javascript last recommendation. Each subsequent call, places additional lines beneath those already inserted with previous Snippet and content injection calls. At best, this is a balancing act of page reflows verses download latencies, so experiment!

Listing 09.13: Page Output of javascriptToFooter

```
<script type="text/javascript" src="//ajax.googleapis.com/ajax/libs/
jquery/1.7.2/jquery.min.js"></script>
<script type="text/javascript" src="//cdn.jquerytools.org/1.2.5/all/
jquery.tools.min.js"></script>
<script type="text/javascript" src="min/g=js&amp;1"></script>
```

Note: By removing the Protocol, https mixed content errors can be avoided.

Basic .htaccess Optimizations

Discussion of Apache .htaccess files are all over the web. Apache can be extensively configured and as such has led to many debates over the years as to best practices. I will simply be looking at methods which can quickly benefit a majority of web projects at a basic level.

Previously in this chapter I demonstrated how to achieve Friendly URLs by instructing the web server and MODX Revolution to produce Resources which have "real world" words for page names and / or directories. Essentially, we would like to add "expiration dates" to image files and gzip as much of the content sent to the site visitors browser as possible. Simultaneously, we need to keep in mind the dynamic nature of MODX Revolution, even on static content:

We want:

 ◆ to avoid needlessly caching dynamic content
 ◆ to keep from caching content already in MODX Revolution's cache
 ◆ to supplement the Revo cache for content it does not actually process
 ◆ to gzip and compress as much as possible
 ◆ to choose which option is being used with each file type
 ◆ "permanent" files to remain cached on visitors computers for quite a while
 ◆ to be able to establish a default mechanism to speed up a site
 ◆ to maximize the benefits afforded by the server software

Listing 09.14: example .htaccess file for use with MODX Revolution

```
# Establish site root
RewriteEngine On
RewriteBase /

# Establish 30 day life spans on images
ExpiresActive On
ExpiresByType image/gif A2592000
ExpiresByType image/jpeg A2592000
ExpiresByType image/png A2592000
BrowserMatch "MSIE" brokenvary=1
BrowserMatch "Mozilla/4.[0-9]{2}" brokenvary=1
BrowserMatch "Opera" !brokenvary
SetEnvIf brokenvary 1 force-no-vary

# Force all pages to go to www.domain.com and not domain.com
RewriteCond %{HTTP_HOST} .
RewriteCond %{HTTP_HOST} !^www\.domain\.com [NC]
```

```
RewriteRule (.*) http://www.domain.com/$1 [R=301,L]

# Move content from code folder to site root
RewriteRule ^code/xpdo(.*)$ /xpdo/$1 [L,R=301]
RewriteRule ^code/MODX-revolution(.*)$ /MODX-revolution/$1 [L,R=301]
RewriteRule ^code(.*)$ /MODX-revolution/$1 [L,R=301]

# The Friendly URLs part
RewriteCond %{REQUEST_FILENAME} !-f
RewriteCond %{REQUEST_FILENAME} !-d
RewriteRule ^(.*)$ index.php?q=$1 [L,QSA]

# If mod_zip is present the gzip the following content
<IfModule mod_gzip.c>
  mod_gzip_on                   Yes
  mod_gzip_can_negotiate        Yes
  mod_gzip_dechunk              Yes
  mod_gzip_minimum_file_size    600
  mod_gzip_maximum_file_size    0
  mod_gzip_maximum_inmem_size   100000
  mod_gzip_keep_workfiles       No
  mod_gzip_temp_dir             /usr/local/apache/gzip
  mod_gzip_item_include         file \.html$
  mod_gzip_item_include         file \.txt$
  mod_gzip_item_include         file \.css$
  mod_gzip_item_include         file \.js$
  mod_gzip_item_include         file \.jsp$
  mod_gzip_item_include         file \.php$
  mod_gzip_item_include         file \.pl$
  mod_gzip_item_include         mime ^text/.*
  mod_gzip_item_include         mime ^application/x-httpd-php
  mod_gzip_item_include         mime ^httpd/unix directory$
  mod_gzip_item_include         handler ^perl-script$
  mod_gzip_item_include         handler ^server-status$
  mod_gzip_item_include         handler ^server-info$
  mod_gzip_item_exclude         mime ^image/.*
</IfModule>
```

Use these settings at your own risk. They work on our servers, but yours may not allow, or even understand these settings. This is intended to serve as a starting point to build from, but as presented should establish a fairly decent working environment for your web site.

For additional .htaccess ideas visit https://github.com/smooth-graphics/modx-boilerplate

Strategic Utilization of System Settings and Elements

MODX Revolution provides ample opportunities to use and reuse various System Settings and Elements to present a common topic, word, phrase, noun, idea, etc., multiple times in a page with very little effort on our part.

Using the following excerpt from my site as an example, please take note how many times the site name appears in the header. Also, consider the fact the [[++site_url] also contains the same information, namely: shawn wilkerson. Essentially, by reusing the [[++site_name]] and [[++site_url]] in this manor my name appears over half a dozen "legal" times before the page content even appears.

Excerpt 09.15: related page header content

```
<title>[[++site_name]]'s [[*longtitle]]</title>
<base href="[[++site_url]]" />
<link rel="canonical" href="[[~[[*id]]:replace=`//"==/"`]]"/>
<meta name="author" content="W. [[++site_name]]" />
<meta name="description" content="[[*description:empty=`[[*intr
otext]]`:empty=`[[*longtitle]]`:empty=`[[*pagetitle]]`:ellipsi
s=`150`]]"/>
<meta name="keywords" content="[[++site_name:replace=` ==,`:strtolow
er]],[[!Crumbz:replace=` ==,`:strtolower?textOnly=`1`&seperator=`,`&
removeSiteHome=`1`]]" />
```

Make no mistake, the most valuable real estate on a web page is arguably the domain name. If the name is the actual topic, or closely related to the topic of the site, it helps immensely. It serves to make the site easier to find for humans and more intelligible to search engines.

Additionally, Resource settings such as [[*pagetitle]], [[*longtitle]], and [[*menutitle]] can be used to consistently present a string of words on a page in key points, such as in the various headers used in the page: <h1>[[*pagetitel]]</h1>.

The wonderful aspect of configuring Element output once and having it dynamically created by MODX Revolution makes it a very effective platform for SEO implementations. Additionally, Snippets such as Wayfinder can use Templates "salted" with System Variables and Resource Settings to pass along, the main point of a given page or topic, as illustrated below.

Listing 09.16: wfNavBar Chunk used as template for Wayfinder Row example

```
<li [[+wf.id]] [[+wf.classes]]><a href="[[+wf.link]]"
title="[[++site_name]] [[+wf.title]]" [[+wf.attributes]]>[[+wf.
linktext]]</a>[[+wf.wrapper]]</li><li class="sep">|</li>
```

SEO Benefits From the Site Structure

In addition to utilizing MODX Elements and settings, project leaders can very strategically decide on placement of site content. Typically, a considerable amount of thought goes into the structural layout of a web project's directories, files, and page names. While MODX Revolution does not necessarily utilize the "physical" characteristics of traditional web sites, it easily presents content using very a similar composition, based on the various Friendly URL settings previously discussed in this chapter.

When Use Friendly Alias Path is set to yes, MODX Revolution presents each Container document as a "directory" to site visitors. By using simple logic, this structure can be used to supplement page content and attach a "bigger picture" to the actual content.

Essentially, as a person moves further into a directory tree, they are simply viewing a smaller and more precise aspect of a parent folder. By moving up or down the "structure" all the content should be directly related to some degree. Assume we are working an a web application which will present information based on geographical data concerning the United States, a "bread crumb" navigation bar would also serve well to give the page a recognizable connection to associated content.

T *AN EXAMPLE OF LOGICALLY LAYING OUT CONTENT:*

Country, State, County, City, Zip Code would translate to
United States, Florida, Volusia, Daytona Beach, 32117

Also, take note how we used the Crumbz Snippet combined with the :replace and :strtolower Filters in the XHTML header code excerpt on the previous page to create key word meta tags. In this regard the simple act of adding Resources to a site can directly facilitate SEO.

If the site structure isn't completely clear, try visiting various search engines which use categories and subcategories and take a look at how they view topics centered around the message of your web project. One of the largest can be found by visiting at: http://www.dmoz.org/,

Webmaster Resources

If for some reason you do not have a Webmaster Tools account, I would strongly urge you getting one by visiting http://www.google.com/webmasters/tools/ and/or http://www.bing.com/toolbox/webmaster/. You may also want to get a Google Analytics account. These resources provide an objective perspective of web projects and can serve site developers and owners in many ways. For our purposes we are simply looking at the optimization aspects, which become very tangible when provided with the information of what people value about your project.

Weekly reading through the various reports have the benefit of removing any assumptions about the effectiveness of the project, the value of its content, or the items of visitor interest. In short, project leaders can view how people are using Google in association with the site.

Creating a Site Map

One aspect of the Webmaster Tools, is the direct association with a site and a dedicated sitemap.xml file. Once a site has been added to the Webmaster Tools, simply click on its name to go to its Dashboard. Submit a sitemap.xml file to these services, is as simple as accessing the Site Configuration menu and adding it to the Sitemaps.

To create a sitemap on the web project:

1. Install the **GoogleSiteMap** package via the Package Manager.
2. Create a Resource utilizing an **empty template** at the top of the site
3. Title the Page Site Map (or what ever you want)
4. Manually give the page the **alias of sitemap**
5. Select **Publish and Hide from Menus**
6. On the Page Settings Tab **remove check marks** from all boxes except Empty Cache
7. Switch the **content type to XML**
8. For the page contents, use only: [[!GoogleSiteMap]]
9. **Save** the document
10. Select the View button to verify page is working (at domain.com/sitemap.xml)
11. Add the site map URL to the Webmaster Tools services
12. Read through the reports at regular intervals and incorporate what has been revealed

The GoogleSiteMap Snippet will notify the search engines of any content added added, updated, or modified on site upon every visit. For sites under active construction, this can prove highly beneficial because some search engines attribute increased development activity to possible relevance. Both Bing and Google can take advantage of the GoogleSiteMap Package.

robots.txt

Ethical search engines will comply with any stipulations placed in the robots.txt file located at the root of the web project. I typically view this file as a way to instruct search engines to not waste their time viewing content on the site, which is not relevant to its purpose.

There are those who may look at the robots.txt file as a means to control what search engines do on a web site. To quote Tolkien's Galadriel, "But they were all of them deceived." Search engine bots can be created to do anything they need to do and access whatever they can. The only way to "control" what they access is to use technologies specifically designed for that purpose, such as Apache's <Directory> directive.

Listing 09.17: example MODX Revolution robots.txt file

```
# Default modx exclusions
User-agent: *
Disallow: /assets/
Disallow: /core/
Disallow: /manager/
Disallow: /min/
Disallow: /setup/

# For sitemaps.xml autodiscovery.
Sitemap: http://www.domain.com/sitemap.xml
```

humans.txt

There is an initiative which has recently begun to gather more attention, which essentially allows a web project to be defined for humans (http://humanstxt.org/). Part of this initiative is to declare the last time the site was updated. I choose to create a new Resource with an alias of humans, hidden from menus and published. On the page settings tab, I switched the type to text, which will provide the necessary humans.txt file. I then used a template containing only [[+editedon]] and the following getResources Snippet call to create the dynamic date:

Listing 09.18: example MODX Revolution humans.txt implementation

```
[[!getResources?tpl=`humanstxt`&parents=`0`&limit=`1`&depth=`20`
&showHidden=`0`&hideContainers=`1`]]
```

Dynamic Content

Many web projects currently under construction, as well as an unfathomable number of sites left to their own devices, include some aspect of Ajax or other technology which dynamically places content into a page, based on user interaction. The information contained in these implementations is seldom seen by any search engines, as no thought was given to the significance of intentionally feeding search engines results from data bases and other sources.

 A simple technique is to create a link to a Resource providing Ajax responses and then attaching a JavaScript to intercept or otherwise manipulate the presentation to the user, while still allowing search engines to fall through and get to the same information presented to the user.

Listing 09.19 Sample Link for Search engines to be fed information

```
<a href="index.php?id=17&songid=64&djaction=getsong" rel="#overlay"
        style="text-decoration:none">
      <button type="button" value="64">Revelation Song</button>
</a>
```

Listing 09.20 Same jQuery implementation to Ajaxify a fall through link

```
$(function() {
    $("a[rel]").overlay({
        mask: 'darkblue',
        effect: 'apple',
        onBeforeLoad: function() {
            var wrap = this.getOverlay().find(".contentWrap");
            wrap.load(this.getTrigger().attr("href"));
        }
    }).button();
});
```

In some situations, in may be prudent to keep search engines from being able to index information, such as a clients credit card or private information. In many situations it simply makes sense to give the same opportunity to search engines to value the site for a specific reason. Carefully consider if a project is losing possible topic relevance simply because search engines can not get to the content available.

Summary

This chapter covers quite a bit of content and is barely a stones throw through the various topics. They are presented here to expose people to the techniques and resources discussed and to allow them to research and implement each as they will, if they even choose to do so. It was not meant to be all inclusive, nor could it be. Though it should be very beneficial to begin site optimization.

Following the steps in this chapter will help get the design components out of the way of search engines, and expedite their introduction to the content on any given page. Search engines do not like waiting around for the "real" content to get loaded any more than people do. By placing content before JavaScript, search engines are afforded the opportunity to index content and move on through the site, without having to wait for User Interface directives to load.

Enabling Friendly URLs (FURLs) presents a site as being more "intuitive" to humans, who search engines attempt very hard to mimic during their various methods of indexing and rating sites. The better we build our site for our visitors to easily utilize, the more they will visit. Search engines, seem to correlate this activity as meaning the site is relevant. The frequency of visits to a site and links to site content tend to cause search engines "to think" the content is relevant.

Web server configurations can be customized to a surgeons precision. For our purposes we simply provide a mechanism to produce as much cached content as possible, using the MODX Revolution cache as the foundation, while off-loading some of the permanent caching of external files to better mechanisms: Minify for JavaScript and Cascading Style Sheets, and .htacess which can implement a wide array of server configurations for caching and on-the-fly compression of site content, such as images and other downloadable files.

Minify can be used to remove excessive white space from files, as well as comments. This allows the "original" file to remain in a very normal format for future editing, while providing an optimized version to the site visitor. This helps in a myriad of ways: large percentages of page content is not dedicated to loading external files (possibly lowering perceived relevancy), reduces overhead on server to process each of the requests associated with the files, and vastly increases page load time on Resources with large amounts of JavaScript and CSS files. In essence, we are getting the content to the visitor faster, which is why sites are usually developed.

The combination of all of these methods should provide a satisfactory foundation of site optimization. These techniques also benefit search engine considerations because they allow them through our "mazes" faster, as the pages are cleared of excessive code and external files. As such, each resource can be kept very clean and more tightly focused on content instead of presentation or function.

By intentionally building the web project from the perspective of maximizing the benefit of each available tool, we can quickly learn to automate key "milestones" or stages of development, effectively keeping the project moving forward. When all is said and done, having access to a bunch of tools is better than using one to do everything.

10
Power Blogging

When I was a young boy, we would occasionally have the opportunity to ride horses. On one of those occasions a friend of mine did something which resulted in his getting kicked in the chest by the horse. Afterwards, he was limited to riding ponies for quite some time. Being the older "caring" boy that I was, I would always ask him if he wanted to race. For whatever reason he always declined the invitation. I never really understood his reasoning. When you get down to it, aren't they both horses?

As you might have guessed, my friend was riding on a colt or filly, while I was riding on well trained adult horses. I was allowed to ride around within the boundaries given to me: "Don't get lost in the woods and be back here on time." My friend was confined to the limits of riding a colt led on a leash as someone walked along side or attached to a rod which spun on a center point. No matter how it happened, he ended up simply walking in circles, until he grew up.

Years later, my wife and I went horse riding. Some how or another we had both learned to ride horses, while growing up and living in Florida - of all places. Of course she wanted to race. We did and I lost as I had opted to give her the fully trained horse, while taking the younger "green rope" horse for myself. We both had adult horses, but mine had not achieved the confidence to work with a rider yet. When I asked for a rematch, with our trading horses, she wisely and summarily denied my request. At least she smiled with a beautiful gleam in her eye as she galloped back leaving me to continue working with my horse.

Unlike some blogging software which is simply created with the intent of using leashes to lead the user around, MODX Revolution provides a full framework necessary to turn a blog into an application, a social community, or even an on-line symposium of experts sharing similar content. MODX Revolution can serve as a individual's users blog or provide a blog component to a much larger application.

Sample Project Requirements

1. Global navagation containing "blogged" and regular content
2. Allow comments from authenticated users
3. Directory structure for blog content will be contained in categories
4. Actual Blog Content will be contained within one directory of category
5. Site is to be optimized
6. Friendly URLs are to be implemented
7. Archives of blog content, Tag navigation, as well individual author pages
8. Empty Comment and Tag fields should not be displayed
9. Blog Content is not to go below the third tier: Home | Category | Content

Blogging Foundations

To establish a blogging platform utilizing the MODX Revolution framework, the combined effort of *at least five* separate Packages is needed: **Archivisit**, **getPage**, **getResources**, **Quip** and **tagLister**. These can be easily and quickly obtained utilizing the Package Manager. In this chapter we will create a blog without Articles and then build another one with the Package.

I chose to present this content in this manner to help readers better understand and implement the technologies related to blogging, I believe we should first take a hands-on approach with the various pieces of software which are typically utilized for the purpose. Currently, there are over two dozen Packages in the Blog Category - many of which being optional, though very effective.

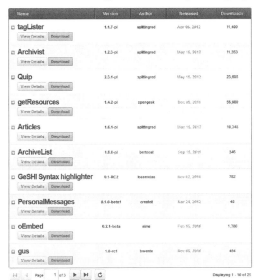

Over the next few pages we will learn how to create a blog from scratch, by selecting Packages to perform specific tasks, such as representing categories, tagging, and creating templates for our pages and the various presentation components.

Afterwards, we will install the Articles Package, and be in a better position to customize its components to meet the needs of any blogging project.

Note: I would suggest working through this chapter using two different sites, even though Articles can import and otherwise interact with the traditional style blog. Many of the techniques contained herein can be used in other implementations.

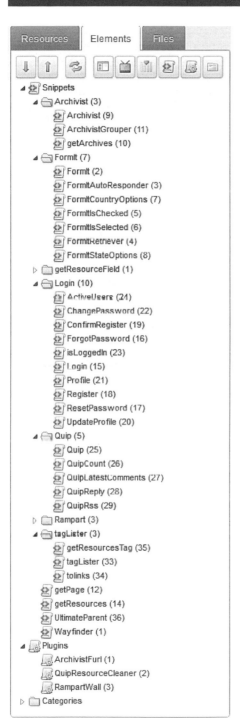

For this walk-through, it should be assumed the project may eventually utilize the features offered by a blog, as well as the benefits of a fully functional web application. This *is* MODX Revolution, we can have the best of both.

In preparation for this, two additional Packages will be installed: **Wayfinder** for site-wide navigation and **FormIt** to handle any form-based interaction with site visitors. The list of Packages is becoming quite large and appears on the next page. For now, take a minute to notice how many Elements are implemented before we even get started blogging.

As you can see, there are dozens of Snippets installed at this stage, as well as a few Plugins and the additional formitStandardEmail Chunk which was created in the Quick Start chapter for use with the e-mail hook of the FormIt Snippet.

Now, take a few minutes to visualize a visitor working their way through the site and the means they will interact with it. Begin making decisions on possible content, and how to get people visiting the site. Will we be targeting content towards given audiences? Is so, who? Specifically, which content?

One of the best things to consider at the beginning stages of a web project is the viability of having site members and possibly user groups. Many sites, provide only limited functionality in hopes to draw people into varying levels of membership.

Accordingly, "member-only" features may be desired on a web project, which will require the ability for users to actually log into the presentation side of the site. One such "member only feature" could be the simple ability to post comments to the blog articles. There are many ways within MODX Revolution to use the current user's "logged-in" status as a basis to actually display the content on the site allowing them to post comments on the site. Alternately, "non-members" could be presented with a "join today" link. For this we also need to install the **Login** and **Rampart** Packages.

Summary of Installed Packages For "Power" Blogging

So far, we have alluded to quite a few packages to use on our "blogified" web project. The packages previously mentioned are all that is required for a "normal" blog site. The parameters for this sample blog site infers that we will need to support multiple authors as well as an normal web content.

Though I do not presume to present the "only" way to build a blog in MODX Revolution, I do intend on showing each of the components used in a current project I have recently completed. Essentially, I will be demonstrating the means to build a blogging foundation to be integrated into a corporate or community site.

To better understand the significance of each package used in this example, I have provided a summary list with a brief description of what each Package does. Please be advised Crumbs and getUserID are not currently released in Package Form.

Creating a Blog Implementation

♦ **Archivist** an archive navigation Extra for MODX Revolution. It allows for wordpress-style navigation of Resources, as well as month/year/day archive listing and automatic FURL generation

♦ **getPage** is used for presenting, navigating, and optionally caching, multi-page views from any Element that accepts a limit and offset properties for limiting a data set

♦ **getResources** a Resource listing and summarization snippet

♦ **Quip** a simple commenting Snippet for MODX Revolution. It allows you to quickly and easily put up comments on your web site, including threaded support, moderation, url to link conversion, automatic thread closing, and more. It also allows for full comment management via the back end system in the Revolution manager.

♦ **tagLister** is a simple tag listing Snippet, that can be used with a 'tags' TV to generate tag-based navigation. This requires the creation of a **Autotag** or **Tag** Template Variable, as prescribed in chapter 5. For this implementation, the TV is named `tags`, input type: Autotag, and Output type being left at default.

General Web Project

♦ **Crumbz** an extremely versatile and light breadcrumb Snippet, available from `http://github.com/wshawn/crumbz/`, though any similar Snippet would do

♦ **FormIt** a dynamic form processing Snippet for MODX Revolution. It handles a form after submission, performing validation and follow-up actions like sending an e-mail or any developer enabled function, such as logging to a database table.

- **getUserID** a very simple Snippet which retrieves a user's ID number, based solely on their user name and is created in this chapter, but not found in the Package Manager
- **getResourceField** is a simple Snippet which can be used to display a single field of any Resource for MODX Revolution, including its Template Variables.
- **injectJSLinksToBottom** introduced in Chapter 10
- **randomImages** Custom Snippet designed to present random images in page element backgrounds, banners, etc. Available from `https://github.com/wshawn/randomImages`
- **UltimateParent** Returns the ID of the ultimate parent of the current Resource
- **Wayfinder** is a Snippet by kylej that scans a specified portion of the MODX document tree, finds all documents that satisfy a certain criteria (determined by the Parameters), and outputs a formatted list of those documents.

User Authentication

- **Login** a security Extra for MODX Revolution, which allows for front-end login capabilities, as well as profile updating, registration, and forgotten password functionality.
- **Rampart** a robust anti-spam tool and can be used to help prevent spam registrations and postings on your MODX Revolution site.

As you may have noticed, there are over a dozen Packages in use on our "Power Blog" comprising dozens of Snippets and Plugins. Using the Package Manger to install the majority of them, can be completed in just a few minutes. Crumbz can be installed manually from my Github repository, and getUserID can be simply entered via the keyboard.

T CHAPTER CONSIDERATIONS

The content presented throughout the rest of this chapter may contain implementations, which may be considered by some to be advanced. Though some explanation may be expected, an assumption has been made by the author that the reader is familiar with the basic concepts utilized herein. When necessary, feel free to refer to the appropriate content in Part 1: Foundations of MODX Revolution and in the Streamlining Web Projects - chapter 9.

This is the method used to implement an actual live web site: http://www.1truth.net.

Manually Building a Blog

For this example, I created five folders: Archives (published and hidden from menus), Authors, Contact, Articles, and Research. The last two are intended to house our first two blog containers.

I also created a page to handle thread replies and a thank you page for individuals utilizing the main contact form. For the final foundational page, I simply used the Home page as provided by the MODX Revolution installer.

From this meager start, I believe it possible to build massive community blogging sites and even corporate web projects with associated blog content.

Site Templates

In this project we will be utilizing only two Templates: one for all non blog content and the other which will present the blog articles. Please note: some users may prefer the use of additional Templates for the category level and individual author pages. I have chosen to use only two Templates, albeit harder, to provide increased exposure to the various methodologies behind many web projects, as well as greater insight into working with MODX Revolution.

Listing 10.02: base_blogContent.xhtml Template

- -

```
[[injectJSLinksToBottom?src=`[[$jQuery]],[[$jQueryTools]],
                         min/g=js&amp;1`]]
<?xml version="1.0" encoding="UTF-8" ?>
<!DOCTYPE html PUBLIC "-//W3C//DTD XHTML 1.0 Strict//EN" "http://
www.w3.org/TR/xhtml1/DTD/xhtml1-strict.dtd">
<html xmlns="http://www.w3.org/1999/xhtml">
<head>
    [[$siteHeader:strip]]
    <link type="text/css" rel="stylesheet" href="/min/f=site.css"/>
</head>
<body>
```

```
<div id="header" [[!randomImages?bgPosition=`random`
                   &folder=`assets/img/christian/random`
                   &mode=`background`]]>
    [[$globalNav:strip]]
    <h1>[[++site_name]][[*id:neq=`[[++site_start]]`:then=`:
        [[!getResourceField?id=`[[!UltimateParent?topLevel=`2`]]`
                             &field=`pagetitle`]]`]]</h1>
</div>
<div id="container">
    <div id="mainContent">
        <h2>[[*pagetitle]]</h2>
        <p class="info">Posted [[*publishedon:strtotime
                                          :date=`%b %d, %Y`
                                          :fuzzy]]
        by <a href="[[~4]][[*publishedby:userinfo=`username`]]"
            title="&copy; [[*publishedon:strtotime:date=`%Y`]]
            [[*publishedby:userinfo=`fullname`]].">
            [[*publishedby:userinfo=`fullname`]]</a><br/>
            [[!QuipCount:gt=`0`:then=`
                <a href="[[~+id]]#comments" class="comments">
                Comments</a> ([[!QuipCount?thread=`blog-post-
                [[+id]]`]])`
              ?thread=`blog-post-[[+id]]`]]
            [[*tags:notempty=`Tags: [[!tolinks?items=`[[*tags]]`
                                            &key=`tag`
                                            &target=`1`]]`]]
        </p>
        [[*introtext:strip]] [[*content:strip]]
        <hr/>
        <div id="comments">
            [[!QuipCount:gt=`0`:then=`
                        [[!Quip?thread=`blog-post-[[*id]]`
                                &replyResourceId=`3`
                                &closeAfter=`30`]]`
              :else=`<p>Be the first to comment on this page!`]]
            <br/><br/>
            [[!QuipReply?thread=`blog-post-[[*id]]`
                        &notifyEmails=`my@email.com`
                        &moderate=`1`&requireAuth=`1`
                        &moderatorGroup=`Moderators`
                        &closeAfter=`30`]]
        </div>
    </div>
    <div id="archives">
```

```
                <p> </p>
            </div>
            <div id="rightMenu">
                <h3>Menu</h3>
                <ul>[[!Crumbz?format=`list`
                        &removeLastID=`1`
                        &lastChildAsLink=`1`
                        &reverse=`1`]]
                </ul>
                <h3>[[!getResourceField?id=`[[!UltimateParent?topLevel=`
    2`]]`&field=`pagetitle`]]<br/>Tags</h3>
                <ul>
                    [[!tagLister?tv=`tags`
                        &parents=`[[!UltimateParent?topLevel=`2`]]`
                        &target=`[[!UltimateParent?topLevel=`2`]]`
                        &tpl=`tagListerListItems`
                        &activeCls=`current`
                        &cls=``
                        &altCls=``
                        &weightCls=``]]
                </ul>
            </div>

            <br class="clearfloat"/>
            <div id="footer">[[$siteFooter]]</div>
        </div>
    </body>
</html>
```

- -

+ Actual Page Title will be display just above blog content

+ Date Posted information has been filtered with the MODX Revolution fuzzy filter

+ Dynamic link created to dedicated author's page / area of site based on user name

+ Comments, links to comments, and tags will not appear if they are empty

+ my.email.com would have to be changed to a real e-mail address

+ **Once the site is live, set the Default Site Template to this in the System Settings**

Listing 10.01: base_template.xhtml

```
[[injectJSLinksToBottom?src=`[[$jQuery]],[[$jQueryTools]],
                        min/g=js&amp;1`]]
<?xml version="1.0" encoding="UTF-8" ?>
<!DOCTYPE html PUBLIC "-//W3C//DTD XHTML 1.0 Strict//EN" "http://
www.w3.org/TR/xhtml1/DTD/xhtml1-strict.dtd">
<html xmlns="http://www.w3.org/1999/xhtml">
<head>
    [[$siteHeader:strip]]
    <link type="text/css" rel="stylesheet" href="/min/f=site.css"/>
</head>
<body>
    <div id="header" [[!randomImages?bgPosition=`random`
                    &folder=`assets/img/christian/random`
                    &mode=`background`]]>
        [[$globalNav:strip]]
        <h1>[[++site_name]][[*id:neq=`[[++site_start]]`:then=`:
            [[!getResourceField?id=`[[!UltimateParent?topLevel=`2`
                            ]]`&field=`pagetitle`]]`]]</h1>
    </div>
    <div id="container">
        <div id="mainContent">
            [[!UltimateParent:eq=`4`:then=`<h2>[[*pagetitle]]</h2>`
                                        ?topLevel=`2`]]
            [[*content]]
        </div>
        <div id="centerMenu" class="posts">
            <div id="newestPosts">
                <h5>Recent Additions</h5>
                [[!getResources?tpl=`blogNewPosts`
                &parents=`[[!$categoryList]]`
                &limit=`10`            &depth=`10`
                &includeContent=`1`    &includeTVs=`1`
                &showHidden=`0`        &hideContainers=`1`
                ]]
            </div>
            <div id="archives" class="posts">
                <h5>Archives</h5>
                <ul>[[!ajaxArchives?target=`2`
                                &tpl=`archives`&limit=`6`
                                &parents=`[[!$categoryList]]`]]
                    <li class="ajaxarch"><a href="#">-More
```

```
                                                        Archives-</a></li>
                </ul>
                [[injectHTMLToBottom?src=`
                <script type="text/javascript">
                    $('li.ajaxarch a').click(function() {
                        $.get('[[~38]]', { months: 60 },
                            function(data) {
                                $('#archives ul').html(data);
                            });
                        return false;
                    });
                </script>
                `]]
            </div>
        </div>
        <div id="rightMenu">
            <h5>Categories</h5>
            [[!Wayfinder:strip?startId=`0`
                            &level=`1`
                            &sortBy=`pagetitle`
                            &rowTpl=`wfRightMenu`
                            &excludeDocs=`1,2,3,4,5,6`]]
            <h5>Site Tags</h5>
            <ul>
                [[!tagLister?tv=`tags`
                            &target=`1`
                            &parents=`[[!$categoryList]]`
                            &tpl=`tagListerListItems`
                            &activeCls=`current`
                            &cls=``
                            &altCls=``
                            &weightCls=``]]
            </ul>
        </div>
        <br class="clearfloat"/>
        <div id="footer">
            [[$siteFooter:strip]]
        </div>
    </div>
</body>
</html>
```

- ◆ jQuery libraries and scripts are injected to the Page Bottom per Chapter 10
- ◆ Page displays the site name and the top level page titles / containers in header
- ◆ Only shows the [[*pagetitle]] of third tier documents in the authors folder
- ◆ Wayfinder is directed to ignore the majority of the root level documents, showing only categories in the right menu

Blog Related Chunks

Listing 10.03: blogCategoryPage Chunk uses the baseTemplate site Template

----

```
[[!getResourcesTag?tpl=`blogPosting`
  &parents=`[[*id]]`        &limit=`5`
  &depth=`5`               &includeContent=`1`
  &includeTVs=`1`          &showHidden=`0`
  &hideContainers=`1`      &elementClass=`modSnippet`
  &element=`getResources`
  &pageVarKey=`page`
]]
[[!+page.nav:notempty=`
<div class="paging">
<ul class="pageList">
  [[!+page.nav]]
</ul>
</div>`]]
```

Essentially, the blogCategoryPage Chunk provides the additional contents to the base site Template to allow a Resource to become a blog category page. It would be completely reasonable to simply create a dedicated site Template for these pages, but I wanted to keep the site as slim as possible. Once a category page has been created, simply insert the Chunk call and save the page: [[$blogCategoryPage]].

- ◆ &parents is set to the current page
- ◆ &limit specifies when the paging functionality activates
- ◆ &depth dictates how far down the site structure content should be retrieved from
- ◆ &hidecontainers allows content to be displayed without regard to the Containers utilized in the Manager to create our Categories
- ◆ if navigation is not needed the actual code will not be written to the page

Listing 10.04: blogPosting Chunk (template for blog posts on non blog pages)

- -

```
<div class="post">
    <h3 class="title"><a href="[[~[[+id]]]]">[[+pagetitle]]</a></h3>
    <p class="info">Posted [[+publishedon:strtotime:date=`%b %d,
%Y`:fuzzy]] by <a
            href="[[~4]][[+publishedby:userinfo=`username`]].html"
            title="&copy; [[+publishedon:strtotime:date=`%Y`]]
                    [[+publishedby:userinfo=`fullname`]]">
                [[+publishedby:userinfo=`fullname`]]</a><br/>
        [[!QuipCount:gt=`0`:then=` <a href="[[~[[+id]]]]#comments"
class="comments">Comments</a>
        ([[!QuipCount?thread=`blog-post-[[+id]]`]])`?thread=`blog-
post-[[+id]]`]]
        [[!QuipCount:gt=`0`:then=`[[+tv.tags]]`:notempty=`
|`?thread=`blog-post-[[+id]]`]]
        [[+tv.tags:notempty=`<span class="tags">Tags:[[!tolinks?item
s=`[[+tv.tags]]`&key=`tag`&target=`1`]]</span>`]]
    </p>
    <div class="entry">
        <p>[[+introtext]]</p>
    </div>
    <p><a href="[[~[[+id]]]]" class="readmore">Read more</a></p>
</div>
```

- -

- ◆ Dynamic link created to dedicated author's page / area of site based on user name
- ◆ Comments, links to comments, and tags will not appear if they are empty
- ◆ my.email.com would have to be changed to a real e-mail address
- ◆ This template displays a summary of blog content outside of typical blog pages

Listing 10.05: categoryList Chunk (comma separated list category Resource IDs)

- -

```
7,8
```

- -

This route was chosen, so as to target all Elements requiring category information to a single data source. Subsequent expansion to the site can occur by editing this single Element providing getResources and other Elements with the new category list without edits to their individual calls.

Wayfinder Related Chunks

Listing 10.06: globalNav Chunk (provides links to only top of the site)

```
<div id="mainnav">[[Wayfinder?startId=`0`&level=`1`&sortBy=`menuindex
`&rowTpl=`wfNavBar`&excludeDocs=`[[$categoryList]]`]]</div>
```

Listing 10.07: wfListChildOrSibs Chunk (used on main /Authors page)

```
<li [[+wf.id]] [[+wf.classes]]> <a href="[[+wf.link]]" title="[[+wf.
title]] by [[++site_name]]" [[+wf.attributes]]>[[+wf.title]]</a>:
[[+wf.linktext]] [[+wf.wrapper]]</li>
```

Listing 10.08: wfNavBar Chunk (used for global navigation)

```
<li [[+wf.id]] [[+wf.classes]]> <a href="[[+wf.link]]"
title="[[++site_name]] [[+wf.title]]" [[+wf.attributes]]>[[+wf.
linktext]]</a>[[+wf.wrapper]]</li><li class="sep">|</li>
```

Listing 10.09: wfRightMenu Chunk (used for a right menu category link)

```
<li class="catLink"><a href="[[+wf.link]]" title="[[++site_name]]
[[+wf.title]]" [[+wf.attributes]]>[[+wf.linktext]]</a></li>
```

Taglister Related Chunks

Listing 10.10: tagListerListItems Chunk (item links to tag content in right menu)

```
<li><a href="[[~[[+target]]? &[[+tagVar]]=`[[+tag]]`]]">[[+tag]]</a>
([[+count]])</li>
```

Site - Wide Chunks

Listing 10.11: siteFooter Chunk

```
<br/><br/>
<div id="cpyrght">&copy;[[*publishedon:strtotime:date=`%Y`]] 1truth.
net and respective authors. All Rights Reserved.
</div>
<div id="siteDesign">Site design and development:
    <a href="[[+site_url]]"
        title="Site design and development by W. Shawn Wilkerson">W.
Shawn Wilkerson</a>
</div>
```

Listing 10.12: siteHeader Chunk

```
<title>[[++site_name]] [[*longtitle:empty=`[[*pagetitle]]`]]</title>
<base href="[[++site_url]]"/>
<link rel="canonical" href="[[~[[*id]]:replace=`//"=="/"`]]"/>
<meta name="author" content="W. Shawn Wilkerson"/>
<meta name="copyright"
      content="&copy; [[*createdon:strtotime:date=`%Y`]] [[!*created
by:userinfo=`fullname`]]], All Rights Reserved"/>
<meta name="date" content="[[*editedon:strtotime:date=`%FT%T%z`]]"/>
<meta name="description" content="[[*description:strtolower:ucfirst]]
by [[++site_name]]"/>
    <meta name="keywords"  content="[[*tags:notempty=`[[*ta
gs]]`:empty=`[[!Crumbz:striptags?textOnly=`1`]]`:replace=`
==,`:strtolower]]"/> [[! use article tags or breadcrumb as source]]
```

Individual Author's Resource Page

Listing 10.13: Resource contents for individual author

```
[[!getPage?
        &elementClass=`modSnippet`
        &element=`getResources`
        &parents=`[[$categoryList]]`
        &depth=`2`
        &limit=`10`
        &pageVarKey=`page`
        &includeTVs=`1`
        &includeContent=`1`
        &tpl=`blogPosting`
        &where=`{"publishedby:=":[[!getUserID?user=`[[*alias]]`]]}`
        ]]
[[!+page.nav:notempty=`
<div class="paging">
    <ul class="pageList">
        [[!+page.nav]]
    </ul>
</div>`]]
```

Custom Snippets

For this project I chose to utilize two of my Snippets, crumbz and randomImages, which can be installed by visiting my site (http://www.shawnwilkerson.com) or my Github repository (https://github.com/wshawn/). The other Snippet written for this application is absurdly simple, due to MODX Revolution's API., which allows us to link directly to a dedicated author's page based on the id of the user who published the Resource (blog article) in the first place.

Listing 10.14: getUserID

```php
<?php
// Retrieves User id associated with their username

$user = $MODX->getObject('modUser',array('username' => $user ));
return $user->get('id');
```

Screen Shots Taken from 1truth.net

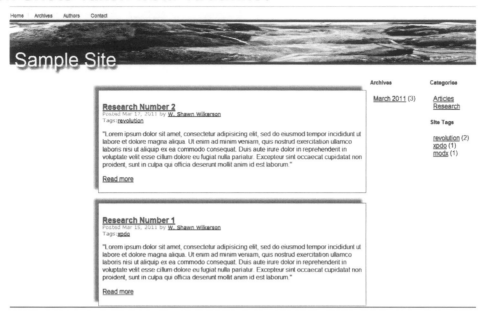

Home Page

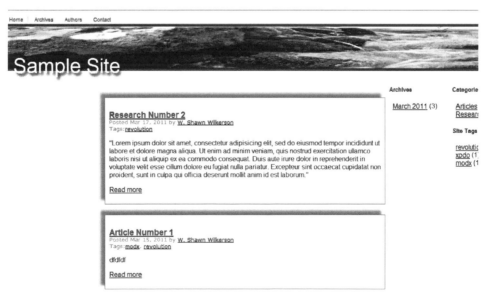

Tag browsing across categories

Archive

Author's Page one year later

Final Notes on Creating a Blog From Scratch

The blog demonstrated over the last pages, was specifically built during March 2011 to be included in this book. Since that time, hundreds of Articles have been posted in public and private areas. Eventually the Resource tree became populated to the point I began seeking alternative MODX Revolution methods to provide the functionality necessary.

With over three dozen Snippets, multiple Plugins, and fifteen installation Packages, building a blog from scratch appeared much more difficult than it needed to. Over the years, many people have posted "how-tos" on the web in the hopes of sharing the process, as they figured it out, but many of these posts simply led to more questions.

Essentially, we could create a blog with MODX Revolution, but not in a straight forward manor. This implementation required a working knowledge of many Packages, as well as an excessive amount of work - though once understood and functional, could be transferred from one site to the next with little effort.

To succinctly illustrate the point, one of the project parameters included the necessity of author specific content. I wanted a secure and simple method to provide their information without exposing unnecessary or sensitive information. The trick was, to provide a method to feed the MODX Revolution API which would return the results necessary to satisfy both conditions.

As indicated in Listing 10.13, the content used for each author's page, I opted to use the current page alias as the basis from which to feed the getUserID Snippet. As you may know, MODX Revolution can be configured to automatically generate the alias and does so based on the *pagetitle field. In this instance, I used the actual MODX Revolution full name for the *pagetitle and *longtitle, while manually entering the specific author's username for the page *alias, thereby matching the output provided from the getUserID Snippet.

In application, this was a very straightforward and secure solution. Implementation is quite another matter. How many of you actually understood the previous paragraph? Would this help: `&where=`{"publishedby:=":[[!getUserID?user=`[[*alias]]`]]}`?

Many of the components utilized in this implementation, are stand alone applications. Which is great for us, as they are highly flexible due to template mechanisms and runtime parameters. Fortunately for use, they are easily accessible via Package Management. The examples in this chapter can still prove very effective and invaluable, as they can be used to create implementations in their own right, but should all of this be required for a simple blog?

It became very apparent a solution was needed for the vast number of "non-programmers" which could be be released to the masses. It should also do most of the work for the Manager User, and require very little programming experience, while staying true to MODX Revolution and facilitate the freedom to take the project in any direction.

On November 29, 2011 Shaun McCormick answered the call and released Articles.

Implementing the Articles Add-on

Articles provides an innovative blog implementation which greatly simplifies the creation and maintenance of blogs - regardless of the user's ability. If a Manger User is able to install Articles via the Package Manager, they can literally have a blog up and running in, as little as, ten minutes - even on a completely empty web site.

This section assumes the web project is essentially devoid of content and has the Articles Package installed. As we have previously discussed the individual components utilized in blogging with MODX Revolution, I will only present information which is unique to the implementation being presented, thereby streamlining the next few pages to only relevant code and related images.

To begin, let us tale a few minutes to understand what Articles actually is. For some of you, Articles is simply a very effective tool to establish a blog anywhere within a web project. For others it could serve as a tutorial on how to extend the core functionality of MODX Revolution. The following items should be of interest to readers for various reasons.

The Articles Package:

- ◆ installs each of the Components and sub packages it requires to operate
- ◆ extends the modResource Object creating an Article Object
- ◆ utilizes a customized user interface for blog content
- ◆ provides per Container and per Category settings
- ◆ allows Access Control Lists to be assigned to each blog category and article post
- ◆ streamlines the Resource Tree with Category containers, instead of individual posts
- ◆ facilitates the administration of visitor comments
- ◆ can directly import preexisting content into blog categories
- ◆ functions very similar to normal MODX Revolution Resources

Developers may very well find Articles to be a great training aide for those who are interested in extending MODX Revolution and learning how to offer some of its "behind-the-scenes" functionality to your Packages, namely: core extension, sub package installation, and /or offering a custom user interface.

For those of you desiring to set up a personal blog for yourself, or to provide the same functionality for a client, just follow the steps I am about to present. Please note: much of the content in the remainder of the chapter, can be considered optional and simply "for informational purposes only."

Note: The following pages will show the implementation used on `shawnwilkerson.com` during June of 2012, as it directly relates to the Articles Package and blogging.

Templates

Articles installs everything it needs, to get a blog up and working quickly. For those who would prefer using their own Templates, it is recommended to create new Templates in the Element Tree as upgrades to Articles could subsequently overwrite any changes. To keep our blog safe from this sort of event happening, we will be creating three HTML5 / CSS3 Templates: the first of which is for all non-blog content on the site, the second is for use with Blog Categories, and the last is for the Article pages themselves.

Listing 10.15: template_articles_baseTemplate.html for non blog content

----

```
<!DOCTYPE html>
<html>
<head>
    <base href="[[++site_url]]"/>
    <meta charset="utf-8"/>
    <title>[[*pagetitle]]</title>
    <link type="text/css" rel="stylesheet" href="min/g=shc"/>
    <!--[if gte IE 9]>
    <style type="text/css">
        body {
            filter: none
        }
    </style>
    <meta name="description" content="[[*description]]"/>
    <meta name="keywords" content="[[*longtitle:replace=`,==`
                                        :replace=` ==,`]]"/>
    <meta name="author" content="W. Shawn Wilkerson, Sanity LLC"/>
    <meta name="revised" content="W. Shawn Wilkerson,
[[*editedon:default=`[[*publishedon`]]:default=`[[*createdon]]`]]"/>
    <!--[if IE]>
        <script src="//html5shiv.googlecode.com/svn/trunk/html5.js">
        </script>
    <![endif]-->
    [[++jquery_load:eq=`0`:then=``:else=`
    <script src="//ajax.googleapis.com/ajax/libs/jquery/[[++jquery_
version:default=`1.7.2`]]/jquery.min.js"></script>
    `]]
    [[++jquerytools_load:eq=`0`:then=``:else=`
    <script src="//cdn.jquerytools.org/[[++jquerytools_
version:default=`1.2.6`]]/all/jquery.tools.min.js"></script>
```

```
    `]]
    <script>var _gaq=[ ['_setAccount','UA-YOURKEY-1'],['_
trackPageview']];(function(d,t){var g=d.createElement(t),s=d.
getElementsByTagName(t)[0];g.src='//www.google-analytics.com/
ga.js';s.parentNode.insertBefore(g,s)}(document,'script'))</script>
</head>
<body>
<header style="background: #fff url(assets/images/randomHeaders/
halifaxRiverBoats.jpg) no-repeat bottom center;">
    <nav>
        [[!Wayfinder:strip?startId=`[[+site_start]]`
                        &level=`1`
                        &sortBy=`menutitle`
                        &rowTpl=`wfNavBar`]]
    </nav>
    <div id="header_middle">
        <br><br><br><br><br><br><br>

        <h1></h1>

        <div class="container">
        </div>
        <div id="secondary">
            <div id="slogan">
                <div id="primary">[[+jquery.header]]
                </div>
            </div>
        </div>
    </div>
</header>
<div class="main_content">
    <div id="container_wide">
        [[*id:neq=`[[++site_start]]`:then=`
        <article class="medium-corners">`]]
            [[*content]]
            [[*id:neq=`[[++site_start]]`:then=`
        </article>
        `]]
    </div>
    [[*id:neq=`[[++site_start]]`:then=`
    <aside class="forth medium-corners">[[Wayfinder?startId=`[[Ultima
teParent?level=`2`]]`&sortBy=`pagetitle`]]</aside>
    `]]
</div>
```

```
<br class="clear">
<footer>
    <div class="container light">
        <div class="box forth">
        </div>
        <div class="box forth"></div>
        <div class="box half">
        </div>
        <br class="clear"/>
        <div id="ownership">
            <section class="box">&copy;[[*publishedon
                        :empty=`[[*createdon]]`:strtotime:date=`%Y`]]
                [[++site_name]]. All
                Rights Reserved. | Site design and development: <a
href="//www.sanityllc.com" title="Site design and development by
Sanity LLC">Sanity LLC</a>
            </section>
            <section class="boxright">
                Powered By: <a href="//www.modx.com" target="_
blank">MODX Revolution
                [[++settings_version]]</a>, <a href="//www.xpdo.org"
target="_blank">xPDO</a>, <a
                    href="//www.jquery.org"
                    target="_blank">jQuery</a>,
                <a href="//alexgorbatchev.com/SyntaxHighlighter/"
target="_blank">SyntaxHighlighter</a>
            </section>
        </div>
    </div>
</footer>
<script type="text/javascript" src="min/g=sh"></script>
</body>
</html>
```

- -

♦ Establishes a page header
♦ Defines a content area
♦ Provides a site-wide page footer for non-blog content
♦ Optionally loads jQuery and jQuery Tools
♦ Preloads Syntax Highlighter so blog pages with code will load quicker

Listing 10.16: template_articles_categoryPage.html

- -

```
<!DOCTYPE html>
<html>
<head>
    <base href="[[++site_url]]"/>
    <meta charset="utf-8"/>
    <title>[[*pagetitle]] articles by [[++site_name]]</title>
    <link type="text/css" rel="stylesheet" href="/min/g=shc"/>
    <style type="text/css">
        body#[[*alias]], body#[[*alias]] .divider {
                                    filter: none
                                }
    </style>
    <![endif]-->
    <!--[if IE]>
        <script src="//html5shiv.googlecode.com/svn/trunk/html5.js">
        </script>
    <![endif]-->
    <meta name="description" content="[[*description]]"/>
    <meta name="keywords" content="[[*pagetitle:cat=` [[+tags]]`:str
iptags::strtolower:strip:replace=` ==,`]]"/>
    <meta name="author" content="W. Shawn Wilkerson, Sanity LLC"/>
    <meta name="revised"
        content="W. Shawn Wilkerson, [[*editedon:default=`[
                    [*publishedon`]]:default=`[[*createdon]] ]]"/>
    [[++jquery_load:eq=`0`:then=``:else=`
    <script type="text/javascript"
            src="//ajax.googleapis.com/ajax/libs/jquery/[[++jquery_
version:default=`1.7.1 ]]/jquery.min.js"></script>
    `]]
  <script type="text/javascript" src="assets/js/jquery.tagcloud.js">
    </script>
    <script type="text/javascript">
        $.fn.tagcloud.defaults = {
            size:{start:10, end:18, unit:'pt'},
            color:{
                start: '#[[*alias:select=`modx-revolution=00FF00
                                    &xpdo=1F93FF`:empty=`999999`]]',
                end: '#[[*alias:select=`modx-revolution=006e2e
                                    &xpdo=15317E`:empty=`000000`]]'
            }
        };
```

```
        $(function () {
            $('#tagcloud a').tagcloud();
        });
    </script>
    <script>var _gaq=[ ['_setAccount','UA-YOURKEY-1'],['_
trackPageview']];(function(d,t){var g=d.createElement(t),s=d.
getElementsByTagName(t)[0];g.src='//www.google-analytics.com/
ga.js';s.parentNode.insertBefore(g,s)}(document,'script'))</script>
</head>
<body id="[[*alias]]">
<header>
    <nav>
        [[!Wayfinder:strip?startId=`[[+site_start]]`
                        &level=`1`
                        &sortBy=`menutitle`
                        &rowTpl=`wfNavBar`]]
    </nav>
    <div id="header_middle">
        <img class="fltleft" src="assets/images/[[*alias]].jpg"
alt="[[*pagetitle]]"/>
        <section class="wide">
            <h1>[[*pagetitle]] [[*id:eq=`3`:then=`<sup>TM</sup>`]]
            </h1>
            [[*id:eq=`4`:then=`<br class="clear">`]]
            <div class="twothird">
                <p id="description">[[*description]]</p>
            </div>
        </section>
    </div>
</header>
<div class="main_content">
    <div id="container_wide">
        <section class="wide">
            <br>
            [[*content]]
        </section>
        <section class="forth">

            <p><a href="http://feeds.feedburner.com/
[[*pagetitle:replace=` ==-`:replace=`comPuters==computerz`]]?format=
xml" class="button gradient small-corners">RSS Feed</a></p>
            [[+comments_enabled:is=`1`:then=`
            <h3>Latest Comments</h3>
            <ul>
```

```
                    [[+latest_comments]]
                </ul>
                `]]
            </section>
        </div>
    </div>
</div>
<br class="clear">
<footer class="[[*alias]]">
    <div class="container">
        <div class="box fltleft">
            <h3 class="css-vertical-text">Tag Cloud</h3></div>
        <div class="box third">
            <div id="tagcloud">
                [[+tags]]
            </div>
        </div>
        [[+projectlinks:notempty=`
        <div class="box fltleft">
            <h3 class="css-vertical-text">Links</h3>
        </div>
        `]]
        [[+projectlinks:default=`
        <div class="fifth"><p></p></div>
        `]]
        <div class="box fltleft">
            <h3 class="css-vertical-text">Archives</h3></div>
        <div class="box third">
            <section id="archives">
                <ul>
                    [[+archives]]
                </ul>
            </section>
        </div>
        <br class="clear">
        <div id="ownership">
            <section class="box">&copy;[[*publishedon
                    :empty=`[[*createdon]]`:strtotime:date=`%Y`]]
                [[++site_name]]. All
                Rights Reserved. | Site design and development: <a
href="//www.sanityllc.com" title="Site design and development by
Sanity LLC">Sanity  LLC</a>
            </section>
            <section class="boxright">
                Powered By: <a href="//www.modx.com" target="_
```

```
blank">MODX Revolution
                [[++settings_version]]</a>, <a href="//www.xpdo.org"
target="_blank">xPDO</a>, <a
                href="//www.jquery.org"
                target="_blank">jQuery</a>,
            <a href="//alexgorbatchev.com/SyntaxHighlighter/"
target="_blank">SyntaxHighlighter</a>
            </section>
        </div>
    </div>
    <br class="clear"/>
</footer>
</body>
</html>
```

- -

- ◆ Implemented a body class based on the Category alias
- ◆ Added a jQuery Tag cloud utilizing the Autotag values for the current Resource
- ◆ Created a Category base coloring scheme for the tagcloud using a :select filter
- ◆ Utilize the pagetitle to attach a Feedburner RSS feed to the category page

Listing 10.17: template_articles_blogPage.html

- -

```
<!DOCTYPE html>
<html>
<head>
    <base href="[[++site_url]]"/>
    <meta charset="utf-8"/>
    <title>[[!getResourceField?id=`[[*parent]]`&field=`pagetitle`]]:
[[*pagetitle:strtolower]] by
        [[*publishedby:userinfo=`fullname`:strtolower]]</title>
    <link type="text/css" rel="stylesheet" href="/min/
g=shc&f=assets/components/quip/css/web.css"/>
    <!--[if gte IE 9]>
    <style type="text/css">
        body#[[!getResourceField?id=`[[*parent]]`&field=`alias`]],
body#[[!getResourceField?id=`[[*parent]]`&field=`alias`]] .divider {
        filter: none
        }
```

```
    </style>
    <![endif]-->
    <!--[if IE]>
    <script src="//html5shiv.googlecode.com/svn/trunk/html5.js"></
script>
    <![endif]-->

    <meta name="description" content="[[*description]]"/>
    <meta name="keywords"
        content="[[!getResourceField:cat=` [[*articlestags]] `:str
iptags:strtolower:strip:replace=` ==,`?id=`[[*parent]]`&field=`pageti
tle`]]"/>
    <meta name="author" content="W. Shawn Wilkerson, Sanity LLC"/>
    <meta name="revised"
        content="[[*createdby:userinfo=`fullname`]], [[*editedon:d
efault=`[[*publishedon`]]:default=`[[*createdon]]`]]"/>
    [[++jquery_load:eq=`0`:then=``:else=`
    <script type="text/javascript"
        src="//ajax.googleapis.com/ajax/libs/jquery/[[++jquery_
version:default=`1.7.1`]]/jquery.min.js"></script>
    `]]
    <script type="text/javascript" src="min/g=sh"></script>
    <script type="text/javascript" src="assets/js/jquery.tagcloud.
js"></script>
    <script type="text/javascript">
        $.fn.tagcloud.defaults = {
            size:{start:10, end:18, unit:'pt'},
            color:{
          start: '#[[!getResourceField:select=`modx-revolution=00FF00
              &xpdo=1F93FF`:empty=`999`?id-`[[*parent]]`
                                      &field=`alias`]]',
            end: '#[[!getResourceField:select=`modx-revolution-006e2e
              &xpdo=15317E`:empty=`000`?id=`[[*parent]]`
                                      &field=`alias`]]'
            }
        };
        $(function () {
            $('#tagcloud a').tagcloud();
        });
    </script>
        <script>var _gaq=[ ['_setAccount','UA-YOURKEY-1'],['_
trackPageview']];(function(d,t){var g=d.createElement(t),s=d.
getElementsByTagName(t)[0];g.src='//www.google-analytics.com/
ga.js';s.parentNode.insertBefore(g,s)}(document,'script'))</script>
```

```
<script type="text/javascript">SyntaxHighlighter.all();</script>
</head>
<body id="[[!getResourceField?id=`[[*parent]]`
                            &field=`alias`]]">
<header>
    <nav>
        [[!Wayfinder:strip?startId=`[[+site_start]]`
                        &level=`1`
                        &sortBy=`menutitle`
                        &rowTpl=`wfNavBar`]]
    </nav>
    <div id="header_middle">
        <a href="[[~[[*parent]]]]"
            title="[[!getResourceField?id=`[[*parent]]`
                                        &field=`pagetitle`]]">
        <img class="fltleft"
src="assets/images/[[!getResourceField?id=`[[*parent]]`
                                &field=`alias`]].jpg"
alt="[[!getResourceField?id=`[[*parent]]`&field=`pagetitle`]]"/></a>
        <div class="wide">
        <h1><a href="[[~[[*parent]]]]" title="[[!getResourceField?id=`
                                        [[*parent]]`
                    &field=`pagetitle`]]">[[!getResourceField?id=`
                    [[*parent]]`&field=`pagetitle`]]
                [[*parent:eq=`3`:then=`<sup>TM</sup>`]]</a></h1>
            <br class="clear">
  <div class="twothird"><p id="description">[[*introtext]]</p></div>
    </div>
    </div>
</header>
<div class="main_content">
    <div id="container_wide">
        <div class="full"><p>Posted in: [[!Crumbz?lastChildAsLink=`1
`]]</p></div>
        <article class="medium-corners">
            <div class="twothird">
                <h2>[[*pagetitle]][[*parent]]</h2>
                <p class="info">by
            <a href="[[~2]][[*createdby:userinfo=`username`]].html"
            title="&copy; [[*publishedon:strtotime:date=`%Y`]]
            [[*createdby:userinfo=`fullname`]]">
        [[*createdby:userinfo=`fullname`]]</a> | Views: [[!+hitss]]
                <br/>
                [[*articlestags:notempty=`
```

```
                      <span class="tags fltleft">Tags: [[+article_
tags]]`]]</span></p>
              </div>
              <div class="seventh">
                  <div class="entryDate">
<span class="postMonth">[[*publishedon:strtotime:date=`%b`]]</span>
<span class="postDay">[[*publishedon:strtotime:date=`%d`]]</span>
<span class="postYear">[[*publishedon:strtotime:date=`%Y`]]</span>
                  </div>
              </div>
              <br class="clear">
              <hr>
              <section>
                  [[*content]]
              </section>
          </article>
          <aside class="medium-corners">
              <h3>In this article:</h3>
              <div id="toc" style="padding-left:25px">
              </div>
              [[+myModxRepo]]
              [[+github]]
              <br><div style="padding-left:35px">
              [[+comments_enabled:is=`1`:then=`<a
href="[[~[[*id]]]]#comments" class="button gradient small-corners
fltleft">Jump to Comments ([[+comments_count]])</a>`]]</div><br>
              <h3>Tags for [[!getResourceField?id=`[[*parent]]`
                                &field=`pagetitle`]]:</h3>
              <div id="tagcloud">
                  [[+tags]]
              </div>
          </aside>
          <br class="clear">
      </div>
      <div id="container">
          <div class="post-comments" id="comments">
              [[+comments]]
              <br/>
              <h3>Add a Comment</h3>
              [[+comments_form]]
          </div>
      </div>
  </div>
  <br class="clear">
```

```
<footer class="[[!getResourceField?id=`[[*parent]]`
                                   &field=`alias`]]">
    <div class="container">
        <div class="box third"></div>
        <div class="third"></div>
        <div class="box third"></div>
        <div id="ownership">
            <div class="box">
&copy;[[*publishedon:empty=`[[*createdon]]`:strtotime:date=`%Y`]]
[[++site_name]]. All Rights Reserved. | Site design and development:
<a href="//www.sanityllc.com"
   title="Site design and development by Sanity LLC">Sanity LLC</a>
            </div>
<div class="boxright">Powered By: <a href="//www.modx.com" target="_
blank">MODX Revolution [[++settings_version]]</a>, <a href="//www.
xpdo.org" target="_blank">xPDO</a>,
<a href="//www.jquery.org" target="_blank">jQuery</a>,<a
href="//alexgorbatchev.com/SyntaxHighlighter/" target="_
blank">SyntaxHighlighter</a>
            </div>
        </div>
    </div>
    <br class="clear"/>
</footer>
<script type="text/javascript">
    $(document).ready(function () {
        $("article h1, article h2, article h3, article h4, article
h5, article h6").each(function (i) {
            if (i > 0) {
                var current = $(this);
                current.attr("id", "toc" + i);
                $("#toc").append("<a id='link" + i + "'
href='[[~[[*id]]]]#toc" + i + "' title='" + "Jump to " + current.
html() + "'>" + current.html() + "</a><br>");
            };
        });
    });
</script>
</body>
</html>
```

- -

- Header image for blog page uses the alias of the Category Container for the name
- Incorporates the Hitts Package for counting Page views
- Implements placeholders for my Github and MODX Repo contributions
- Retrieves the current version of MODX Revolution used on the site
- Removes protocol from anchors to avoid https mixed content errors
- Creates an in-page Table of Contents, base on actual article headers

Template Variables

Once we have the page Templates in the Element Tree, we can then move on to adding the Template Variables necessary for our pages to function. The best place to look, is the two Templates supplied in the Articles Package: sample.ArticlesContainerTemplate and sample. ArticleTemplate.

Currently, the only Template Variable required for Articles is articlestags, which enables Taglister and other functions to perform their tasks. Currently, this TV has a Hidden Input Type and is handled directly in the Resource. Personally, I would eventually like to see an Autotag implementation to ensure identical tags are being used on applicable Resources.

Access articlestags in the Template Variable section of the Element tree and navigate to the Template Access tab. Provide access to this TV by enabling the Templates created in the previous section, as well as any others which may be receiving a list of tags used throughout the site, or simply one or more of its categories. Save the articlestags Template Variable.

Another component which may be of interest is to provide passive feedback on the popularity of a given article in the Blog. Practically speaking, the majority of people taking the time to read a Blog article will seldom respond or otherwise comment on the article itself - making it difficult to demonstrate to other visitors the relevance of the specific content. A simple way to provide some basis of feedback, is by providing a "hit counter" for the specific page. As hit counters are typically a very bad idea, we change the name to Views and it seems to have a different meaning to people. Instead of , "No one has looked at this page", we may get "I'm first to read this article."

Take a minute and install the hitspage package via Package Management. I would also suggest adding the actual blogPage Template to the HitsPage Template Variable, using the steps described for the articlestags TV. For our purposes, Category Pages, and the rest of the site are completely optional, as RSS and other means of visitor landing typically associated with Blog content will simply skip over the category and parent pages to arrive on the article itself.

Note: there is absolutely nothing wrong with adding a counter to all your pages, I simply would not broadcast those numbers to non-authorized site visitors - competitors visit sites too.

Creating a Chunk for Category and Other Pages

Listing 10.18: chunk_articles_ArticleRowTpl.html

```html
<article class="medium-corners blog_wide">
    <div class="seventh">
        <div class="entryDate">
            <span class="postMonth">[[+publishedon:strtotime
                                        :date=`%b`]]</span>
            <span class="postDay">[[+publishedon:strtotime
                                        :date=`%d`]]</span>
            <span class="postYear">[[+publishedon:strtotime
                                        :date=`%Y`]]</span>
        </div>
    </div>
    <div class="twothird">
        <h2 class="blogtitle">
        <a href="[[~[[+id]]]]">[[+pagetitle]]</a></h2>
        <p class="info">by
            <a href="[[~ID]]/[[+createdby:userinfo=`username`]].html"
                title="&copy; [[+publishedon:strtotime:date=`%Y`]]][[+c
reatedby:userinfo=`fullname`]]">[[+createdby:userinfo=`fullname`]]</
a><br>

            [[+comments_enabled:is=`1`:then=`<a
href="[[~[[+id]]]]#comments" class="comments">[[%articles.comments]]
                ([[!QuipCount? &thread=`article-b[[+articles_
container]]-[[+id]]`]])</a>`]]
            [[+tv.articlestags:notempty=` | <span class="tags">
            [[%articles.tags]]: [[!toLinks?
                    &items=`[[+tv.articlestags]]`
                    &target=`[[*id]]` &useTagsFurl=`1`]]</span>`]]
        </p>
    </div>
    <br class="clear">
    <div class="intro">[[+introtext]]</div>
    <p><a href="[[~[[+id]]]]" class="button gradient small-corners
                                fltright">Read more</a></p>
</article>
```

Note: This Chunk will be used in the Articles Container on the Templates Tab.

Creating Category Pages

By now, most of the preliminary activities have been completed to implement Blog content into our site: the Installation of Articles, creation of Templates, and the attachment of the articlestags Template Variable. If this process is being worked out on an otherwise empty site, the Manager viewport, from the Package Management Page, should look like the following:

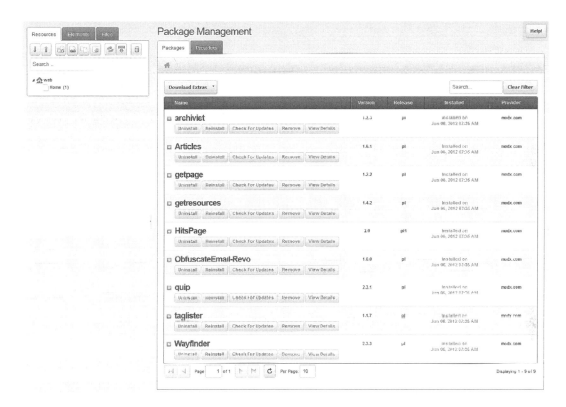

Many of you might be tempted to create all of the category containers before moving through this section. I would suggest, a momentary pause, and the creation of a skeleton to be used as a "template" for each of the Blog's categories, especially in those areas were the Category settings will be replicated from one Articles Container to another. In the end, this will save valuable time and ensure consistency in content presentation, as well as, third-party services, such as Feedburner, Twitter, and Facebook. Additionally, it may serve as a gentle reminder to attach the Blog to an author's or site's Twitter feed and other similar activity.

Note: Now is the time to enabled Friendly URLs (FURLs) and the automatic generation of the Resource alias in the System Settings. See chapter 9 for details.

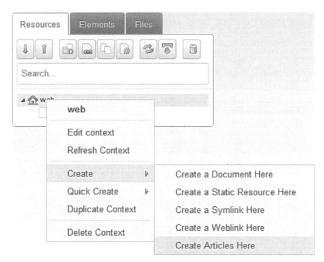

The initial steps used in the creation of a new Articles Container is identically the same as those used to create a Resource, Weblink, or Symlink. Simply select the section of the Resource tree where Articles is to appear and choose "Create Articles Here" in the Create sub menu.

For now, choose a name which is very generic, as this "Container" may never see the front end of the site. The choice of names is yours, but finish setting up one category before moving forward to the next. There are plenty of reasons to get one category working first, as we shall soon see.

MODX Revolution Rule #10: **Future-proof web projects as much as possible.**

The initial presentation is slightly different from the one shown here, as the Comments tab does not appear, but will once the Article Container has been saved. Up to this point, there is relatively little difference in the creation of an Articles Container and a regular Resource. An Articles container can appear anywhere within a site, though I would recommend placing it as close to the site root as possible to present a logical flow for visitors browsing by tags or Article date.

In a few minutes, some of you may even be thinking, "Using Articles may be a better way to lay out a project than using regular Resources." This could actually be done, though it may limit some of the perceived "freedom" presented in typical Resources. Keep in mind, Articles extend the modResource object, so it contains all of the functionality of a typical Resource.

If you take a moment and consider my shawnwilkerson.com site, it should not take very long to understand, I indeed treated each blog article as if it was a Resource. How else could I have pulled off Syntax Highlighting, the injection of source code, and the insertion of an in-page, on-the-fly, table of contents?

Further discussion of this topic should be a topic considered on a per-project basis, and should take into account the skill-sets available to the project. At the very minimum, this requires a general understanding of MODX Revolution. I will leave this topic for your own development team to discuss and consider, though I personally do not limit myself just to Articles.

Assign Templates to the Article Container

Simply use the drop-down lists to select the Templates we specifically added to the site for this implementation. I should also mention the ability to create as many Templates as you would like, even ones dedicated to a certain topic or audience. I simply chose to use the same structure across all of the Blog Categories, while utilizing Resource Settings and CSS to modify the content.

Take note of the Article Row Chunk name: ArticleRowTpl, which replaces the default Articles SampleArticelRowTpl. As of this writing, this field has to be manually entered. Additionally, the site cache may need to be cleared after any changes are made to these settings for updates to appear in the site if a page has already been visited on the front end of the site. At this point we should be completely separated away from the default Templates and using our own theme.

Advanced Settings

General

Pagination

Archives

Tagging

RSS

Latest Posts

Notifications

Comments

— Display

— Security

— Latest

— Other

As of this writing, there are twelve setting groups available for customizing the various aspects of the Blog Container, containing approximately eighty settings covering everything from in-line templates to the inclusion of third-party services. This is why I suggest for a skeleton to be created on multi-category sites.

For many web projects, the default settings will achieve a fully functional application, but do not let this keep you from exploring these groups as there are settings which could easily switch Articles from a blog implementation to something quite different.

Feel free to explore and experiment, as each setting has an in-line description of its purpose and occasionally provides hints of actual usage. Additional information can be found by looking through the other settings to discover Placeholder names, as well as, any setting required to establish a wide array of applications.

Do not mistake these Advanced Settings for making it easier to blog, or even as a means to reach out to the site visitor. These settings are from the perspective and position of a site owner and administrator to facilitate the administration of each Articles container.

When I get around to switching 1truth.net to Articles in the coming months, I have additional considerations, simply due to hidden blog categories, which are not available to the public. Fortunately, Articles will allow me to designate the Moderator Group and actual Moderators on the security tab, allowing me to keep each author in control of their content and subsequent comments.

For shawnwilkerson.com, only a few adjustments are required to connect the project to Feedburner, Facebook, and Twitter. As time goes on, I expect to see additional implementations discussed in the community. Before we move on to third-party services, let us take a few moments and look at a few highlights found within the Advance Settings.

Advanced Settings Highlights

General Tab

- To create a knowledge base, simply change Sort Field to pagetitle
- The Articles URL Format establishes the path to each Article. Blogs typically utilize the default setting, while it is plausible to utilize: %Y%m%d%alias/, %alias/, or some other design of your own
- To add additional TVs to each Page place them in Include TVs List. Consider using HIDDEN input types.
- Other Listing Parameters provides the ability to send additional Parameters to getPage and getResources Snippet calls: &showHidden=`1`&showDeleted=`1`

Pagination Tab

- Establishes the minimum number of Articles on the page
- Defines how many pages to show in the pagination list

Archives

- Articles can be grouped by year, for sites with multiple years of content
- Contains optional settings to template and limit the number of listings

Tagging

- Provides the css class names to style against in the site Cascading Style Sheet

Comments

- Allows for comments to be threaded, which requires an additional Resource
- Optionally force each comment to be previewed
- Limits the number of days for comments
- Allows comments to be paginated

Security

- Establishes Category Administrators, Moderators, and who is allowed to comment

Other

- Provides Gravatar integration for blog comments (as of this writing)

Third-Party Services

For our purposes, there are two easy ways to interact with third-party services: a dedicated API and through Really Simple Syndication (RSS) feeds. We will be looking at how to implement both of these technologies in conjunction with the Articles Package. In this section I will demonstrate three different technologies, including a "forth-party" service which autonomously updates users around the globe as to recent additions to your site.

Feedburner for RSS Feeds

The RSS tab of the Advanced Settings informs us of a fully functioning RSS freed existing at {article_container_name}/feed.rss, in my case: http://www.shawnwilkerson.com/modx/ feed.rss, established in preparation of the recently announced 2013 release of MODX 3.0. We could utilize this feed, but I would also like the benefit of tracking subscribers, the number of hits on the feed, and increased "reader" support. Instead of creating all of these myself, I will simply utilize Google's Feedburner Service: http://feedburner.google.com.

If you already have a Google account, simply use it to log in and "claim your feeds." If not, take a few minutes and create one and add Google Analytics while you are at it. Once, logged in to your Google account, you will be presented with a screen asking for the URL to your feed. Using the format shown above, visit your feed in another tab and copy the URL to the Operating System clipboard and then paste it in the box as shown:

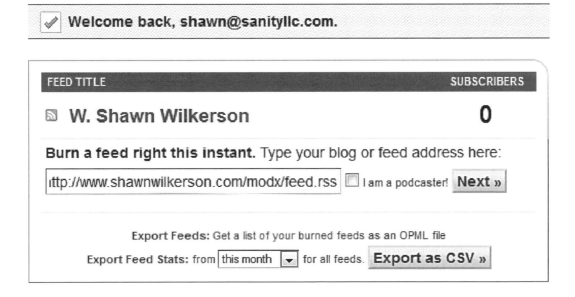

Give your feed its title and feedburner.com address:

Feed Title: MODX

Enter a title to help identify your new feed in your account.

http://feeds.feedburner.com/

Feed Address: MODX3

The address above is where people can find your new feed.

Next »   Cancel and do not activate

Create an addresses to your feed, keeping it specific and easy to remember

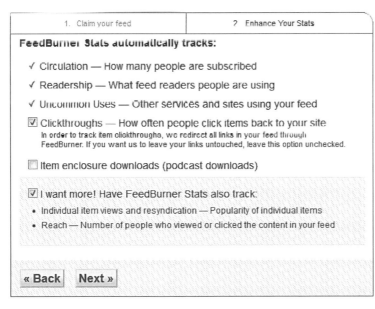

| 1. Claim your feed | 2 Enhance Your Stats |

FeedBurner Stats automatically tracks:

√ Circulation — How many people are subscribed

√ Readership — What feed readers people are using

√ Uncommon Uses — Other services and sites using your feed

☑ Clickthroughs — How often people click items back to your site
In order to track item clickthroughs, we redirect all links in your feed through FeedBurner. If you want us to leave your links untouched, leave this option unchecked.

☐ Item enclosure downloads (podcast downloads)

☑ I want more! Have FeedBurner Stats also track:

• Individual item views and resyndication — Popularity of individual items

• Reach — Number of people who viewed or clicked the content in your feed

« Back   Next »

After clicking next on this Stats screen you should have a fully functional Feedburner RSS Feed.

If you chose a feed name matching the pagetitle of the Article container, then the Templates provided in the Articles section of this chapter will automatically point to the correct Feedburner RSS feed.

If not, you may very well have to intercept the pagetitle and change it, as I had to do with my Computers section.

Alternately you can simply change the Resource pagetitle to match the feed name: `http://www.shawnwilkerson.com/modx3/feed.rss`.

Twitter

𝕋 *TIP: DUPLICATE YOUR SKELETON BEFORE INTEGRATING TWITTER*

Note: If you are using a skeleton to create future categories, you may now want to create a category as a duplicate before integrating Twitter. Currently, there is no simple way to undo this process. It is possible to create a new category with the correct settings and move all of the Resource to the new Parent in the database. Once an Articles category has been attached to Twitter all subsequent Categories may also retain the same connection.

Moving on to the Notifications tab of the Advanced Settings, we find a simple quick process to connect our blog category to Twitter. Essentially, we can click a text link and, sign in to Twitter, authorize the MODX Articles Application, and toggle the "Send to Twitter" setting to yes.

At the beginning of this chapter, we established our Sample Project Requirements. As you may recall, the ability to facilitate multiple authors was in the list. The Articles add-on facilitates this need, as **each category can be individually authorized with Twitter - unless it has been previously authorized**. Fortunately, this entire process takes only a few seconds, but it also offers site administrators a choices on how best to integrate to Twitter.

Let us assume for a moment, our project has multiple authors. Each category could be attached to a specific author's Twitter feed, or a generic feed for the entire category or even site. If we were to switch our focus to a company, with multiple products or interests, each category could represent a group of products or section of the company. Another scenario, which could be played out here, is a single Twitter feed spread across all of the Article Containers within a given site. This would create a public time line of content, and provide a central location to retrieve information of a given site. Additionally, it allows us to create an Articles implementation without any Twitter interaction. Regardless of the scenario, Articles will allow you to create any sort of Twitter feed.

Some of you might be asking, "What if I have multiple authors in a single Category?" This is a very good question. Simply follow this process and attach the Article Container to a generic

Twitter feed for the site or topic. On the individual author's page, create a `feed.rss` link to an underlying page, which implements the concepts presented in Listing 10.13.

Mark Hamstra details many of the specific steps required to create a RSS feed in the official MODX Documentation, which can be viewed by visiting `http://rtfm.modx.com/display/` `ADDON/getResources.Building+a+RSS+feed`. Follow his recommendations to begin with as it should get you going - the article even demonstrates how to cross Category boundaries.

You may need to add a few pieces of specific information to Mark's code: a means to establish which author we are looking for - demonstrated in Listing 10.13, a "container" to wrap each article, and a template to present each listing to the RSS feed. I would suggest using the Articles RSS chunks as a starting point, which can be found in `core/components/articles/elements/` `chunks/`.

Tweet Template

This setting is very easy to over look. Further down on the Notification tab, space is provided which allows site administrators to adjust the presentation of each Tweet as they will. The template provided in Listing 10.19 will typically get the Tweets flowing like music from the depths of a tropical rain forest. Other implementations, may actually hard code certain aspects, such as the hashtags, with something like: #modx. Typically, hastags are comprised of the first three tags attached to the individual article.

> ### Listing 10.19: In-line template for use with Tweets

```
[[+title]] [[+url]] [[+hashtags]]
```

Up and Running

At this point, a site should have a fully functional Tweet notification system. I would recommend setting up another browser or tab and check the content being Tweeted. This way you can delete any Tweets if they are not what you expected or if you forget to add the appropriate Tags to the page for hashtag creation. Note: currently the best way to publish an article is to by doing so on the article page itself. I've had mixed results using other methods.

This whole process can take a few short minutes to work out across an entire site. With Twitter's 140 character limit, you can expect around seventy to eighty characters to remain after three hashtags and a url, As you might have guessed, 80 characters is not very much to completely inform Twitter followers concerning each of your articles. Please choose your titles accordingly, unless you happen to have a client with millions of followers who will click on any link posted.

Building a Twitter Application

There are situations where a client may insist on using their own Twitter application to attach Article Containers, and not necessarily utilize the default MODX configuration. It also doesn't hurt the image of a web company to have applications of their own for Twitter and other social networks and online services. I have created such an application for my company which allows all of my sites to integrate MODX Revolution Articles to a single authentication source of my own choosing. The following information is a "bare essentials" presentation on this task.

- ♦ Go to https://dev.twitter.com/apps/new and if necessary, login
- ♦ Create a name
- ♦ Add a link to your domain
- ♦ Give it a nice logo
- ♦ For this implementation we only need read and write access
- ♦ The callback URL should point to your domain - the path shown here is to the Articles installation on my company web site, it would be best to use your own site
- ♦ Add your organization information

OAuth settings

Your application's OAuth settings. Keep the "Consumer secret" a secret. This key should never be human-readable in your application.

Access level	Read and write About the application permission model
Consumer key	
Consumer secret	
Request token URL	https://api.twitter.com/oauth/request_token
Authorize URL	https://api.twitter.com/oauth/authorize
Access token URL	https://api.twitter.com/oauth/access_token
Callback URL	http://www.sanityllc.com/assets/components/articles/twitter.auth.php

♦ Retrieve the Consumer Key

♦ Retrieve the Consumer Secret

♦ Return to the Articles Category Notification Tab

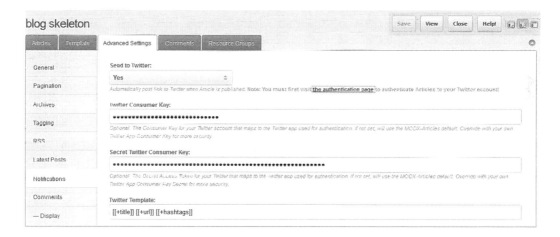

♦ Paste in each of the keys in the respective location

♦ Save the Page

♦ Click the "the authentication page" text link

You can use your Twitter account to sign in to other sites and services.
By signing in here, you can use TweetSanity without sharing your Twitter password.

Authorize TweetSanity to use your account?

This application will be able to:

- Read Tweets from your timeline.
- See who you follow, and follow new people.
- Update your profile.
- Post Tweets for you.

TweetSanity
By Sanity LLC
www.sanityllc.com

Sanity LLC application to tweet from our projects to Twitter

← Cancel, and return to app

| Username or email |

| Password |

☐ Remember me · Forgot password?

Sign In   **Cancel**

This application **will not be able to**:

- Access your direct messages.
- See your Twitter password.

Success!

By following this basic steps a simple Twitter application can be created for the sole purpose of excluding any possibility of unexpected Twitter activity from a third-party. It will also look nice to have a small token of your company in front of the user whenever they access the Account settings in their Twitter account or even as part of each Tweet sent from the site.

Listing 10.20: In-line template_for use with Tweets point to our app

```
[[+title]] [[+url]] [[+hashtags]] via SanityTweet
```

Facebook Integration

With Facebook constantly making changes to their API, I chose to use a third-party application, name RSS Graffiti. Essentially, I have it poll the web site one an hour, to ascertain if there has been any new articles created in a given category. Currently, it retrieves information from only the MODX Revolution content on the site. Eventually, I may get around to creating a site-wide Really Simple Syndication (RSS) feed.

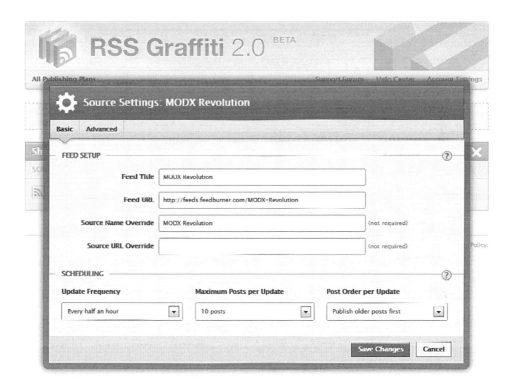

- ◆ Attach the Graffiti application to the account to receive updates
- ◆ Enter the information to the "official" RSS feed - I utilize feedburner
- ◆ Save the changes. Now links to the articles will also appear on Facebook

Summary

There are plenty of articles on the web specifically discussing the use of MODX Revolution for a blog web site. I chose to present this topic in a community / corporate scenario as the benefits of navigation typically associated to blogging can prove a huge benefit to any web site.

The easier a visitor can move around a site exploring information of interest, the more they tend to value the site. For companies this can mean repeat business, or a better Return on Investment (ROI) for the resources invested in the web project. It could also mean increased visitor retention.

Concepts were also presented in this chapter regarding some implementations which can be used in a wide array of projects. The method used to link an author's individual page to every mention of their name of their site, can be used to represent items, events, or anything else worth mentioning. Essentially, it is a great way to drive traffic to items of interest.

Throughout Manually Building A Project, techniques were utilized to only present links and content to users which actually had value. Empty tags and comment areas were replaced with content asking the visitor to log in or simply no placed in the page at all. If I had demonstrated an actual implementation of the Login Package, this content could easily contained a link for the user to log in or join the web site at their point of interest.

In the Articles implementation, I discussed simple changes to the sort order which should enable a project to extend Articles beyond a simple blog into knowledge bases and other information archiving technologies - with a simple change to the Arcticle Container settings. We then moved on to third party implementations.

Admittedly, I could have taken a much easier route to demonstrate MODX Revolution blogs, but in doing so I would have violated the intended purpose of this book: providing clear examples to enable readers to build the web their way. I endeavored to present plenty of concepts which could be implemented in other applications, as well as establish MODX Revolution as an amazing platform.

Anyone can blog. MODX Revolution users have the ability to Power Blog.

11

Dynamic JavaScript, CSS, and jQuery Essentials

Thinking back over the decades of my life, I can recall many events, but find it interesting how some of them seem to stand out in my mind as significant events, while others were simply activities I endured. There appears to be a universal truth: some experiences remain with us.

Like most people I went to elementary school and can even name all of the schools I attended during those years, but remember very little about them other than their location. Only a few moments during those six years stand out: first kiss, first "girlfriend", third grade learning about the Japanese culture, and singing in Chorus under Mrs. Twerp. Most of the rest of those years are mere shadows of memories which require effort to see again in my mind.

During some part of my childhood we moved to California and for a certain amount of time we lived at Point Mugu Naval Air Station. Constantly, military jets were taking off, filling the air with the noise of those powerful engines and shaking the ground and buildings with their raw power. Periodically, air shows at the base dominated everything around us for days. The annual air shows held in my home town do not begin to compare with those of the the Naval Air Station.

As a child, I also went to Walt Disney World many times. It was enjoyable and I had fun with those who took me: my mother and occasionally my uncle. When I first went there with the woman who was to be my wife, it became an entirely "new" park and remains special to us even decades later. When I began taking my children there, it transformed again. I have literally been there hundreds of times.

I share these stories, with the hope we can begin enjoying the moments in our lives and our work. Doing so, will enable us to grasp that little extra flavor to put into our web projects to make them more meaningful and even memorable to the visitors - giving them something they want to visit.

Loading JavaScript into the Resource

There are plenty of JavaScript libraries available on the web. For what ever reason I settled on jQuery years ago and have never really had a need to utilize any of the other offerings. This is my personal preference, though I believe many of the implementations presented in this chapter should be easily translated to other JavaScript libraries.

Forcing JavaScript and HTML to the Bottom of a Resource

To address Yahoo's recommendation of placing all JavaScript after the page content is loaded, and also to resolve the dilemma of controlling the order the Scripts are parsed, I have created two very simple Snippets to facilitate an elegant solution to both issues.

The MODX Revolution API includes a method to inject JavaScript into the bottom of the page, just above the closing </body> tag. It also includes a method to place any HTML code at the same location. The beauty of this simple implementation, is how it accomplishes this task by utilizing the order the names are provided to insert the desired content into the page bottom. I will be using the following two Snippets extensively through the remaining of this chapter:

Listing 11.01: injectJSLinksToBottom Snippet

```php
<?php
/* Places <link> statements above </body> from comma delimited list
*/
$srcArray = explode(',', $src);
foreach ($srcArray as $javascript)
{
    $modx->regClientScript($javascript);
}
```

Listing 11.02: injectHTMLToBottom Snippet

```php
<?php
/* Can be used to inject any HTML just above the closing </body> */
 $modx->regClientHTMLBlock($src);
```

Forcing CSS, HTML and JavaScript to the Page <head>

MODX Revolution also supports the ability to force various types of content to the page header, as defined by the (X)HTML closing </head> tag. There are quite a few possible reasons for doing this, especially when using a JavaScript implementation contains dedicated CSS style sheet definitions, which do not need to be loaded on every page.

Listing 11.03: injectCSSLinkstoHead Snippet

```php
<?php
/* Places <link> statements above </head> from comma delimited list
*/
$srcArray = explode(',', $src);
foreach ($srcArray as $externalStyleSheet)
{
    $modx->regClientCSS($externalStyleSheet);
]
```

Listing 11.04: injectHTMLToHead Snippet

```php
<?php
/* Can be used to inject any HTML just above the closing </head> */
 $modx->regClientStartupHTMLBlock($src);
```

Listing 11.05: injectJSLinksToHead Snippet

```php
<?php
/* Places <link> statements just before </head> from comma delimited
list -- JavaScript should be loaded at page bottom when possible */
$srcArray = explode(',', $src);
foreach ($srcArray as $javascript)
{
    $modx->regClientStartupScript($javascript);
}
```

Note: See the Content Injection Output Filters for additional implementations.

Using Chunks to Create Version Specific Dynamic Links

JavaScript libraries are in constant development, which may suggest Chunks to be used matching a specific version for a given application. To accomplish this, two dedicated MODX Revolution Chunks can be created with associated properties on the Properties allowing us to specify the version we are wanting to use: jquery_version and jt_version. Note: I opted to hard code the default values in the Chunks so they could be viewed by the implementation team, but they could also have simply been placed in the respective Chunk Property itself or overridden in the call.

Listing 11.06: jQuery Chunk

```
//ajax.googleapis.com/ajax/libs/jquery/[[+jquery_
version:empty=`1.7.2`]]/jquery.min.js
```

Listing 11.07: jQueryTools Chunk

```
//cdn.jquerytools.org/[[+jt_version:empty=`1.2.7`]]/all/jquery.
tools.min.js
```

Laying the JavaScript Foundation

Using the injectJSLinksToBottom Snippet and the two jQuery Library Chunks, we can add the following code to the very top of any Template utilized on the site. This provides jQuery, jQuery Tools and a group of files to be implemented on each page using that specific Template.

Listing 11.08: loads all required JavaScript (placed at Template top)

```
[[injectJSLinksToBottom?src=`[[$jQuery]],[[$jQueryTools]],min/
g=js&amp;1`]]
```

Once we have saved the Template, possibly clearing the Site cache, and refreshed the visitors page on the front of the web project, we should see something similar to the output shown in Listing 11.09. At this stage, it may prove beneficial to view the page source and scroll down to the links created by injectJSLinksToBottom and verify they are indeed correctly linked and loaded for further use. Alternately, we could have used [[$jQuery?jquery_version=`1.4.2`]].

Listing 11.09: Page Output of injectJSLinksToBottom

- -

```
<script type="text/javascript" src="//ajax.googleapis.com/ajax/libs/
jquery/1.7.2/jquery.min.js"></script>
<script type="text/javascript" src="//cdn.jquerytools.org/1.2.7/all/
jquery.tools.min.js"></script>
<script type="text/javascript" src="min/g=js&amp;1"></script>
```

- -

If everything is linked correctly, feel free to remove any preexisting JavaScript code from the Template's header, which is now being handled by injectJSLinksToBottom Snippet. This may also be a good time to test the various JavaScript files being loaded and make sure no errors are being reported. Note: on many of my recent Templates, I load the libraries in the page header, while loading page specific content in the page itself - typically at the bottom to avoid page reflows.

Testing the Foundation

As we move through the examples in this chapter, the author is assuming the necessary libraries have been loaded and are not preventing subsequent code from being parsed and implemented correctly. If any of the files are not being loaded or if errors are occurring during parsing, subsequent JavaScript may behave in an unexpected manner or simply fail to function at all.

There are many tools available for testing and debugging JavaScript. Many people use a Firefox addon named Firebug to accomplish this task, which can be obtained via `https://addons.mozilla.org/en-US/firefox/addon/firebug/`. This addon should only be enabled while debugging, you definitely do not want to visit the MODX Revolution Manager or other resource intensive site with this addon enabled, as it can easily slow down the web browser.

On occasion, I will utilize Internet Explorer's Developer Tools User Interface as I have found it less forgiving than other applications, which *may* translate into cleaner code. Internet Explorer's Developers Tools User Interface is accessed by pressing F12 while viewing the page.

Regardless of the toolset utilized to debug JavaScript, it can prove very helpful to make sure each section of code is thoroughly tested on an individual basis as well as part of the whole page interface being presented to the user, in the off-chance variable collision or other errors occur.

⊤ *Expectations for Chapter examples*

Associated libraries must be linked and functional for the chapter examples to work.

Implementing Site Wide JavaScript

I intentionally, keep the JavaScript required on every page of the site to the very minimum, so as to only load necessary functions. As with all *easy* implementations, there is always a temptation to load more than what is necessary to have it available. It is typically suggest to keep this type of code limited to only the essentials.

Listing 11.10: googleAnalytics.js using asynchronous page tracking

```
var _gaq = _gaq || [];
_gaq.push(['_setAccount', 'MY ID NUMBER']);
_gaq.push(['_trackPageview']);
(function() {
    var ga = document.createElement('script');
    ga.type = 'text/javascript';
    ga.async = true;
    ga.src = ('https:' == document.location.protocol ? 'https://ssl'
: 'http://www') + '.google-analytics.com/ga.js';
    var s = document.getElementsByTagName('script')[0];
    s.parentNode.insertBefore(ga, s);
})();
```

Listing 11.11: site.js to handle various link scenarios (requires jQuery)

```
$(document).ready(function() {
    $("[href$='.pdf']").each(function() {
        $(this).attr('target', '_blank').addClass('pdf');    });
    $("[href$='.zip']").each(function() {
        $(this).attr('target', '_blank').addClass('zip');    });
    $("[href$='.psd']").each(function() {
        $(this).attr('target', '_blank').addClass('psd');    });
    $("[href$='.phps']").each(function() {
        $(this).attr('target', '_blank').addClass('phps');    });
    $("a").filter(function() {
        return this.hostname && this.hostname !== location.hostname;
        }).attr('target', '_blank').addClass('offsite');
});
```

Using Minify's To Combine External JavaScript Files

Minify is an awesome asset to any site, especially when using external JavaScript And Cascading Style Sheet files. Below is an example of how to implement a Minify group, just by adding and configuring our group as indicated:

Listing 11.12: groupsConfig.php (located in Minify's min directory)

```php
<?php
return array(
    'js' => array('//assets/js/googleAnalytics.js','//assets/js/
jquery.site.js'),
);
```

As discussed in our *Streamlining Web Projects* Chapter, Minify can process our JavaScript code allowing us to directly benefit in quite a few ways:

- ♦ Combined files reduces http requests and associated overhead
- ♦ gzip compression can reduce a file to 18k from an originating size of 207k
- ♦ Web browsers are instructed to hold a file on the users system longer
- ♦ Minify groups allow the hiding of file paths and file names
- ♦ Minify allows original non compressed and unaltered files to be stored on the server
- ♦ Visitors only receive the compressed and minified versions of files
- ♦ The creation of application specific groups

Please refer to the *Streamlining Web Projects* Chapter for more information on implementation and links to the Minify Project.

᛭ *TAKE NOTE OF THE DOUBLE SLASHES IN THE PATH*

Minify may require the use of double slash ('//') for relative inking from the site root.

jQuery Foundational Concepts

To best understand jQuery, it would be beneficial to establish a baseline perspective, though we will only be looking at jQuery in regards to MODX Revolution. The following code block represents the standard method to implement jQuery once the library has been loaded:

Default document.ready Container

Listing 11.13: jQuery asking "if the document is ready for it to function"

```
$(document).ready(function() {
    /*
        All jQuery code is typically implemented
        within this container.
    */
});
```

Ŧ SOME IMPLEMENTATIONS MAY REQUIRE LONG HAND JQUERY CALLS

If other libraries are in use or planned to be used it may be necessary to utilize jQuery longhand: `jQuery(document).ready(function() { }`*. For more information, visit* `http://docs.jquery.com/Using_jQuery_with_Other_Libraries.`

jQuery is

♦ simply JavaScript
♦ cross browser compliant and tested
♦ utilizes CSS type selectors: # for id="" and . for class=""
♦ a library of functions which can target any aspect of the DOM or its elements
♦ usually represented by the use of a dollar sign: $ at the beginning of code
♦ intended to allow one function to feed the next - similar to MODX Revolution Filters
♦ typically understood from left to right - especially during chaining of functions
♦ called after the page content is loaded it is intended to manipulate
♦ usually found in the DOM source, and not in the page source once it executes
♦ best implemented after the document is ready to function (finished loading)

MODX Revolution jQuery Implementations

This section contains actual working examples of jQuery being utilized in different capacities on live MODX Revolution web projects. For those who have not had the pleasure of working with this wonderful library, a simple word of caution should be given: jQuery is called the "write less do more, JavaScript library" for a reason - it takes very little effort or code to get it working.

Manipulating Hyperlinks

Excerpt 11.14: from site.js

- -

```
$(document).ready(function() {
    $("[href$='.pdf']").each(function() {
        $(this).attr('target', '_blank').addClass('pdf');      });
    $("a").filter(function() {
        return this.hostname && this.hostname !== location.hostname;
        }).attr('target', '_blank').addClass('offsite');
});
```

- -

This code was "borrowed" from the previous section on site-wide JavaScript and demonstrates how various site content and off-site links can be handled. As you may recall, a few years ago opening Adobe PDF documents in browsers begin causing assorted issues with visitor browsers. When a situation like this occurs, the vendor is typically never blamed by the site visitor - the web site is. This misplaced "charge" typically translates in lower visitor retention and loyalty.

There is debate on whether we should force off-site content to open anywhere other than the current page. I choose to leave the choice to the visitor by providing access to both. Along with the off-site links, I selected various file extensions and force them to utilize a `_blank target`.

The first of the hyperlink manipulations in Listing 11.14, simply tells jQuery to look at all the strings associated with `href` and look for links targeting a `pdf` file. The second function reads all of the links in the page and looks for any off-site links.

Additionally, each of the manipulations has a class assigned which can be enhanced with css styles, such as: icons, color changes, decoration changes, or even other jQuery functions, such as content hiding and display animations.

jQuery Tools, jQuery UI, Flowplayer and many other tools can also be used to manipulate the target, display, and overall user interaction with simple hyper links, thereby creating an innovative user experience. Over the next few pages we shall take a look at a few jQuery MODX Revolution implementations demonstrating the simplicity in which these products can be used together.

Limiting The Number of List Items Displayed

Listing 11.15: page content (X)HTML via Wayfinder output

```
<ul class="shortList">
    <li>Item 01</li>
    <li>Item 02</li>
    <li>Item 03</li>
    <li>Item 04</li>
    <li>Item 05</li>
    <li>Item 06</li>
    <li>Item 07</li>
< some items removed for brevity >
    <li>Item 18</li>
    <li>Item 19</li>
    <li>Item 20</li>
</ul>
[[injectJSLinksToBottom?src=`min/f=assets/js/jquery.
limitNumberOfItems.js`]]
```

Listing 11.16: (jQuery) limitNumberOfItems.js

```
$(document).ready(function() {
    showonly = 6;
    $('ul.shortList>li').each(function(i) {
        if (i > (showonly-1)) {
            this.style.display = 'none';
        }
    });
    $('ul.shortList').append('<li class="css_link">Click for more
items<\/li>');
    $('ul.shortList li.css_link').click(function () {
        $('ul.shortList li').each(function(i) {
                this.style.display = 'list-item';
        });
        $('ul.shortList li.css_link').css('display', 'none');
    });
});
```

Before

- Item 01
- Item 02
- Item 03
- Item 04
- Item 05
- Item 06
- Click for more items

After AJAX Injection

- Item 01
- Item 02
- Item 03
- Item 04
- Item 05
- Item 06
- Item 07
- Item 08
- Item 09
- Item 10
- Item 11
- Item 12
- Item 13
- Item 14
- Item 15
- Item 16
- Item 17
- Item 18
- Item 19
- Item 20

Occasionally, we may find ourselves working with very long lists of of data wrapped in <li></li> XHTML tags. This can present two issues:

1. The page may now require site visitors to scroll for quite some time and be forced to navigate and locate an item. This can be very much like a "needle in the haystack" scenario. Visitors are happiest when we can simply hand them what they are wanting, so the shorter the list we can provide them the better. People tend to dislike scrolling through page content.

2. If we are forced to remove content from a page to reduce or eliminate scrolling, we take the chance of reducing its relevancy, which may be directly attached to the number of occurrences in a given page.

Fortunately, the simple technique shown in in Listings 11.15 and 11.16 can provide the content in the page, while simultaneously hiding it from the visitor until they are actually wanting to view it.

We have allowed them to make the decision to scroll as the page requires it, simply by giving them something to do which causes the page to extend to a longer length. In a sense we have now shared the responsibility with the visitor for the page becoming so long.

So how does this relate to MODX Revolution? For example, let us assume for a moment, Wayfinder has been implemented on a site and has been templated to provide "Wiki" type links with short descriptions, each wrapped in <li></li>.

If that list were sorted by the *publishedon date and set so the twenty newest were presented first, we could provide the ten most recent, while allowing the option to immediately show the rest.

Sortable Tables and Working With Runtime Configurations

Historically used for page structure, HTML tables have been reduced to simple display mechanisms of data, typically pulled from databases, XML, or other data sources. As many of these lists can become quite large and eventually confusing to visitors, a simplified interactive presentation may be required to allow them to format the data to their personal preferences.

Before:

Table Sort

Week	Date	Size	Length	Speaker	Title
01	Jan 02	24MB	53:12	Jim Pelletier	Focus in 2011 4: Next Things
02	Jan 09	29 MB	63:53	Jim Pelletier	Pursuing Greater Glory
03	Jan 16	28 MB	64:17	Jim Pelletier	Pursuing the Call 1: Walking In It
04	Jan 23	29 MB	64:17	Jim Pelletier	Pursuing The Call 2: Answer The Design
05	Jan 30	14 MB	30:28	Jim Pelletier	Pursuing The Call 3: Four Dimensions Of God's Call
06	Feb 06	25 MB	61:02	Jim Pelletier	Pursuing The Call 4: The Eternal Height
07	Feb 13	26 MB	62:41	Jim Pelletier	Pursuing The Call 5: A Steward's Width
08	Feb 20	20 MB	48:56	Jim Pelletier	Pursuing The Call 6: The Elect Depth
09	Feb 27	19 MB	48:36	Jim Pelletier	Pursuing the Call 7: Our Final Response To God's C
10	Mar 06	35 MB	76.27	Richard Remington	The Power of Unity
11	Mar 13	31 MB	67:47	Jim Pelletier	Exceeding Greatness
12	Mar 20	26 MB	63:50	Jim Pelletier	Exceeding Glory

After:

Table Sort

Show 10 ▾ entries

Search: [   ]

Week	Date	Title
12	Mar 20	Exceeding Glory
11	Mar 13	Exceeding Greatness
10	Mar 06	The Power of Unity
09	Feb 27	Pursuing the Call 7: Our Final Response To God's Ca
08	Feb 20	Pursuing The Call 6: The Elect Depth
07	Feb 13	Pursuing The Call 5: A Steward's Width
06	Feb 06	Pursuing The Call 4: The Eternal Height
05	Jan 30	Pursuing The Call 3: Four Dimensions Of God's Call
04	Jan 23	Pursuing The Call 2: Answer The Design
03	Jan 16	Pursuing the Call 1: Walking In It

Showing 1 to 10 of 12 entries

Listing 11.17: Sample Table Data

```
<table id="messages">
<thead>
    <tr>
      <th>Week</th>
      <th>Date</th>
      <th>Size</th>
      <th>Length</th>
      <th >Speaker</th>
      <th>Title</th>
    </tr>
</thead>
<tbody>
 <tr>
    <td class="sweek">01</td>
    <td class="sdate">Jan 02</td>
    <td class="ssize">24MB</td>
    <td class="slength">53:12</td>
    <td class="sspeaker">Jim Pelletier</td>
    <td class="stitle">Focus in 2011 4: Next Things</td>
  </tr>
<tr>
    <td class="sweek">02</td>
    <td class="sdate">Jan 09</td>
    <td class="ssize">29 MB</td>
    <td class="slength">63:53</td>
    <td class="sspeaker">Jim Pelletier</td>
    <td class="stitle">Pursuing Greater Glory</td>
</tr>
 -- Some content Removed --
<tr>
    <td class="sweek">12</td>
    <td class="sdate">Mar 20</td>
    <td class="ssize">26 MB</td>
    <td class="slength">63:50</td>
    <td class="sspeaker">Jim Pelletier</td>
    <td class="stitle">Exceeding Glory</td>
</tr>
</tbody>
</table>
```

Resource: datatables.net

A very streamlined and sortable table can be provided to site visitors, by including the jQuery library, an HTML table, the dataTables plug-in, and associated settings within the page. Though many table sorting mechanisms are available for jQuery I chose DataTables (http://www.datatables.net) due to its ability to work with JSON, AJAX, and immense data sets (20 million records).

I downloaded the current version and uploaded the Minified version to my JavaScript directory. I still call the file with Minify to receive the benefits of caching and gzip deflation as version 1.7.6 is a massive 207 kilobytes. After Minify is done with it, it becomes a tiny 18k. DataTables 1.9.2 is even smaller.

Listing 11.18: Link DataTables jQuery file

```
[[injectJSLinksToBottom?src=`min/f=assets/js/jquery.dataTables.min.
js`]]
```

Configuration:

HTML tables utilizing DataTables will typically not appear as their generic counterparts. Both tables are using the exact same data. This can be contributed to the settings applied to the current page in the Chunk we utilized to initialize DataTables, [[$tablesort?tableid=`messages`]]:

Listing 11.19: $tablesort Chunk (Page Specific Configuration attached to id)

```
<script type="text/javascript" charset="[[++modx_charset]]">
    $(document).ready(function() {
        sortTable = $('#[[+tableid]]').dataTable();
        sortTable.fnSetColumnVis(2, false);
        sortTable.fnSetColumnVis(3, false);
        sortTable.fnSetColumnVis(4, false);
        sortTable.fnSort([ [0,'desc']  ]);
    });
</script>
```

Notes:

- A Chunk was used for the settings to accomplish a few things: code reusability, cleaner implementation, and providing the ability for Revo to feed runtime parameters to JavaScript values.

- The contents could have been fed directly to the `[[injectHTMLToBottom?src=`` `<script type="text/javascript" charset="[[++modx_charset]]">...`]]` with very similar results. This would require '`#[[+tableid]]`' to be replaced with '`messages`'.

- I decided to provide the table name dynamically, to illustrate integrating MODX Revolution Elements into JavaScript. This ability can come in quite handy when AJAX is being implemented on a page.

- Three rows are made invisible to the site visitor (counting starts with 0).

- The final setting, simply establishes a default sort order. Multiple rows could have been selected.

- Take special note of the syntax: `[ [0,'desc'] ]`. If the spacing is removed from between the brackets MODX Revolution would see this as an Element and parse it, probably rendering it as empty.

- A properly formed table must exist for Datatables to function:`<table><thead></thead><tbody>*rows*</tbody></table>`

- The table must have an id or class to attach Datatables to.

MODX Revolution Rule #11: **Web browsers only see the results of MODX Elements.**

One application created for my wife's site, involved the use of MODX Revolution Chunks to house the actual table rows for content based on the needs of respective pages. In her scenario, she was creating a section for Sir Arthur Conan Doyle, who has many literary works to his credit. The information for each work was collected and then grouped. Once that process was completed she placed each group into table tows `<tr><td></td></tr>` data sets and saved it to a dedicated MODX Revolution Chunk.

On a parent page all of the chunks were combined into a single display. A default sort based on the year each work was released, was implemented for all of the pages associated with the author. This allowed a consistent user experience throughout the section, while providing logical separation of the information for sub pages containing only the Chuck specific to the page.

Essentially, the data is only entered in the Chunks and placed into the pages needing them.

Toggle the Display of Page Content by Element Class

Default Display ("All"):

All | Business | Club | Corporate | Event | Gaming | Ministry | Non-profit | Personal

Content Filtered ("Corporate"):

All | Business | Club | **Corporate** | Event | Gaming | Ministry | Non-profit | Persc

Listing 11.20: page content of Click Event filters and portfolio items

---

```
<ul id="filter">
    <li class="current"><a href="#">All</a></li>
    <li><a href="#">Biz</a></li>
    <li><a href="#">Club</a></li>
    <li><a href="#">Event</a></li>
    <li><a href="#">Gaming</a></li>
    <li><a href="#">Personal</a></li>
</ul>
<ul id="portfolio">
    <li class="club"><img src="pic_01_thm.jpg" /></li>
    <li class="personal"><img src="pic_02_thm.jpg" /></li>
    <li class="biz"><img src="pic_03_thm.jpg" /></li>
    <li class="event"><img src="pic_04_thm.jpg" /></li>
    <li class="biz club"><img src="pic_05_thm.jpg" /></li>
    <li class="biz club"><img src="pic_06_thm.jpg" /></li>
    <li class="biz"><img src="pic_07_thm.jpg" /></li>
    <li class="gaming"><img src="pic_08_thm.jpg" /></li>
    <li class="biz"><img src="pic_12_thm.jpg" /></li>
    <li class="gaming"><img src="pic_13_thm.jpg" /></li>
    <li class="club"><img src="pic_15_thm.jpg" /></li>
    <li class="biz"><img src="pic_16_thm.jpg" /></li>
</ul>
```

Listing 11.21: inject external JavaScript to page bottom

```
[[injectJSLinksToBottom?src=`min/f=assets/js/jquery.
manipulateByClass.js`]]
```

- ♦ injectJSLinksToBottom adds the class to the end of the page just above </body>
- ♦ jquery.manipulateByClass.js attaches a click function to <ul id="filter"> items
- ♦ <ul id="portfolio"> are hidden/shown based on a <ul id="filter"> click event
- ♦ Selecting "All" in <ul id="filter"> results in showing all <ul id="portfolio">
- ♦ Some items in the <ul id="portfolio"> will appear in multiple filters: biz or club
- ♦ Can be seen in action at: http://sanityllc.com and http://shawnwilkerson.com

Listing 11.22: jquery.manipulateByClass.js

```
$(document).ready(function() {
  /* Attaches to the ul with the id of filter for click events */
  $('ul#filter a').click(function() {
    $(this).css('outline','none');
    $('ul#filter .current').removeClass('current');
    $(this).parent().addClass('current');

  /* Establishes a filter based on what was clicked above */
    var filterVal = $(this).text().toLowerCase().replace(' ','-');
    if(filterVal == 'all') {
      $('ul#portfolio li.hidden').fadeIn('slow').
removeClass('hidden');
    } else {
      $('ul#portfolio li').each(function() {
        if(!$(this).hasClass(filterVal)) {
          $(this).fadeOut('normal').addClass('hidden');
        } else {
          $(this).fadeIn('slow').removeClass('hidden');
        }
      });
    }
    return false;
  });
});
```

This very simple technique can be applied to any MODX Revolution content. On a blog site, we can save a hit on the server if we attach the "tags" to the <li> on a given page. Clicking the trigger could simply filter that page to only those articles containing a specific tag. At the bottom of the list jQuery can easily append a link asking the visitor to "Click here for more" articles on using a specific tag.

Additionally, we can utilize this technique on <tables> or other page content we would like to allow the current site visitor to filter to their needs. The categories used in this example could as easily have been "photograph", "painting", and "video", thus providing the visitor with the ability to reduce the thumbnails to only the content they are interested in viewing.

Extremely Simple Lightbox

jQueryTools provides many user interface enhancements, one of which is *overlay*. I have created a very simple example here, which can easily extended in many directions, as there are a wide array of options available. Extensive examples and sample css styling can be found by visiting the project web site at : `http://flowplayer.org/tools/overlay/index.html`

Normal Presentation:

Lightbox

Lightbox:

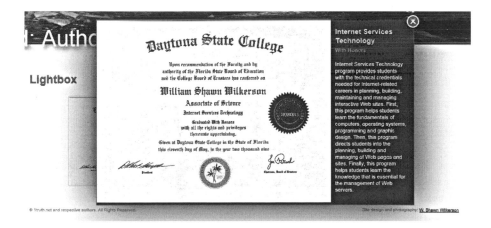

Listing 11.23: $lightbox Chunk Configuration Container

```
[[injectHTMLToBottom?src=`
<script type="text/javascript">$(document).ready(function() {
$("img[rel]").overlay();
});</script>
`]]


<!--From http://static.flowplayer.org/tools/css/overlay-basic.css -->
[[injectCSSLinkstoHead?src=`/min/f=overlay.css`]]



[[injectHTMLToHead?src=`
<style type="text/css">
#triggers {
text-align: center;
}
#triggers img {
cursor: pointer;
margin: 0 5px;
background-color: #fff;
border: 1px solid #ccc;
padding: 2px;
-moz-border-radius: 4px;
-webkit-border-radius: 4px;
}
.details {
position: absolute;
top: 15px;
right: 15px;
font-size: 11px;
color: #fff;
width: 150px;
}
.details h3 {
color: #aba;
font-size: 15px;
margin: 0 0 -10px 0;
}
</style>
`]]
```

The lightbox configuration Chunk contains three main components:

1. An injection to the page bottom which simply calls to the overlay function packaged together with the full version of jQuery Tools.

2. An injection of an external Cascading Style Sheet link at the top of the page

3. A third injection of companion css code which is also placed in the page header file. This example simply injects raw source code in the header and could come in quite handy for users which do not have access to the site Templates or CSS files, while still allowing the placement of CSS and other relevant code into the HTML <head></head> section.

Listing 11.24: LightBox Sample Page Content

```
<div id="triggers">
    <img src="http://farm4.static.flickr.com/3597/3597042731_
a7a61cc4eb_m.jpg" rel="#pic1"/>
    <img src="http://farm4.static.flickr.com/3392/3597038791_5ba2120a
29_m.jpg" rel="#pic2"/>
</div>
<div class="simple_overlay" id="pic1">
    <img src="http://farm4.static.flickr.com/3597/3597042731_
a7a61cc4eb.jpg"/>
    <div class="details">
        <h3>Software Engineering</h3>
        <h4>With Honors</h4>
         <p><strong>Computer Programming and Analysis - Software...
        </p>
    </div>
</div>
<div class="simple_overlay" id="pic2">
    <img src="http://farm4.static.flickr.
com/3392/3597038791_5ba2120a29.jpg"/>
    <div class="details">
        <h3>Internet Services Technology</h3>
        <h4>With Honors</h4>
        <p><strong>Internet Services Technology</strong> program...
        </p>
        </div>
</div>
[[$lightbox]]
```

Wayfinder Combined With jQuery

A couple of years ago, I got to thinking of how jQuery and Wayfinder have one very interesting thing in common: they both utilize list items <li> extensively. So, this logical progression lead me to create a cool menu with Wayfinder and spice it up with jQuery. The following is what I did on CreativeInfusions.com before I reformed my company into Sanity LLC.

Wayfinder Presentation:

jQuery Implementation:

I decided to implement a "Kwicks" style expanding menu, but immediately ran into a snag: I needed to be able to have Wayfinder create unique ids to attach jQuery to. My solution should help you implement any sort of jQuery Wayfinder combination, not to mention HTML 5 designs.

Utilization:

As this is a site wide application, I would suggest adding all of the associated JavaScript files to the js array in the groupsConfig.php located in the Minify directory. I would also integrate the relevant CSS to the site css file, or consider grouping it with the main Cascading Style Sheet also in the Minify groupsConfig.php. **Note: CSS and JavaScript must be in separate groups.**

Resource: jeremymartin.name

It is my understanding, the original concept was implemented on the Mootools home page. Jeremy Martin (http://www.jeremymartin.name/projects.php?project=kwicks) decided to do the same thing with jQuery. In keeping with progress, I subsequently endeavored to port Jeremy's concept to MODX Revolution. Please note, I would recommend downloading the full, un minimized, version from his site, as Minify will handle gzipping and compression for us.

Components:

Listing 11.25: wfKwicksOuter Wayfinder Outer Template:

```
<div class="kwickswrap">
    <ul class="kwicks">[[+wf.wrapper]]</ul>
</div>
```

Listing 11.26: wfKwicksItem Wayfinder Row / Item Template

```
<li id="kwick[[+wf.docid]]"[[+wf.classes]]> <a href="[[+wf.link]]"
title="[[++site_name]] [[+wf.title]]" [[+wf.attributes]]>[[+wf.
title]]</a>: [[+wf.linktext]] [[+wf.wrapper]]</li>
```

Some of you may have already noticed the method I utilized to create the unique names necessary for jQuery to attach to. For those that may have missed it, I simply asked Wayfinder to provide the individual document ID of each Resource the menu was pointing to. This is possible because MODX Revolution ensures each document does, in fact have a unique ID, which provides us the foundation to build from.

The simple inclusion of [[+wf.docid]] allowed this entire mechanism to work. If someone chooses to alter the id number, the kwicks configuration file will need to be updated to reflect the change, or part of the menu will fail to expand.

Listing 11.27: jquery.kwicksconfiguration.js file

```
function main_kwicks() {
    $(".kwicks").kwicks({maxWidth:190,duration:800,easing:"easeOutQu
int"})
}
function starhover() {
    var b = $(".kwicks  li");
    var a = $("#particles_hover");
    b.mouseover(function() {
        switch ($(this).attr("id")) {
            case"kwick1":
                var c = 10;
                break;
            case"kwick2":
                var c = 116;
                break;
            case"kwick3":
                var c = 222;
                break;
            case"kwick4":
                var c = 328;
                break;
            case"kwick10":
                var c = 434;
                break;
            case"kwick11":
                var c = 540;
                break;
            default:
                var c = 0
        }
        a.css({left:c,display:"block"})
    });
    b.mouseout(function() { a.css({display:"none"}) })
}
main_kwicks();
```

----

mainmenu.png CSS Sprite

The `main_kwicks()` attaches the entire implementation to the HTML Element with the class of "kwicks". This could easily have been attached to an id instead. I chose to use `class="kicks"` over using `id="kwicks"` as someone may want to have the same menu on a page twice. This method also defines the maximum width of each link to 190 pixels and the duration of any effect to last .8 (4/5) seconds. Lastly, it establishes the effect as `easing` and the type of that easing to be: `easeOutQuint`.

Please take a moment and look at each of the case statements. As you may have surmised, the "kwick1" - "kwick11" reflect the id names Wayfinder provides for the individual <li> Elements. These designators allow Kwicks to understand the offsets to use to line up correctly with our sprite image. Below I have provided the CSS definitions and with that, you now have a fully working example combining Wayfinder output with jQuery.

Listing 11.28: kwicks.css

```css
.kwickswrap{padding:0;}
.kwicks{list-style:none;position:relative;width:840px;height:50px;z-index:2;margin:0;padding:0;}
.kwicks li{display:block;float:left;overflow:hidden;width:120px;height:50px;z-index:2;cursor:pointer;padding:0;}
.kwicks li a{height:50px;text-indent:-9999px;outline:none;display:block;background-image:url(ci/img/mainmenu.png);background-repeat:no-repeat;z-index:2;cursor:pointer;}
#kwick1 a{background-position:0 0;}
#kwick1 a:hover,#kwick1 #aktiv{background-position:0 -50px!important;}
#kwick2 a{background-position:-190px 0;}
#kwick2 a:hover,#kwick2 #aktiv{background-position:-190px 50px!important;}
#kwick3 a{background-position:-380px 0;}
#kwick3 a:hover,#kwick3 #aktiv{background-position:-380px -50px!important;}
#kwick4 a{background-position:-570px 0;}
#kwick4 a:hover,#kwick4 #aktiv{background-position:-570px -50px!important;}
#kwick10 a{background-position:-760px 0;}
#kwick10 a:hover,#kwick5 #aktiv{background-position:-760px -50px!important;}
#kwick11 a{background-position:-950px 0;}
#kwick11 a:hover,#kwick6 #aktiv{background-position:-950px -50px!important;}
```

flashembed()

Embedding Adobe Flash content in a web page can be extremely simple. Included in the "all tools" version of jQueryTools, or in a very tiny, stand-alone JavaScript file which can be accessed by visiting: http://flowplayer.org/tools/toolbox/flashembed.html. The following is what is necessary to embed the majority of flash content and even handles browser specific requirements:

Listing 11.29: HTML Container hold the video linked to the id="intel"

```
<div id="intel" style="width:752px;height:442px"></div>
```

Listing 11.30: flowplayer Implementation

```
[[injectHTMLToBottom?src=`
<script type="text/javascript">$(document).ready(function() {

flashembed("intel", "http://www.intel.com/itcenter/demo/corefamily_
perf/demo.swf");

});</script>
`]]
```

Listing 11.31: flowplayer Implementation (W3C compliant code)

```
[[injectHTMLToBottom?src=`
<script type="text/javascript">$(document).ready(function() {

flashembed("intel", {src: "http://www.intel.com/itcenter/demo/
corefamily_perf/demo.swf", w3c: true});

});</script>
`]]
```

Final Thoughts on Content Injection

MODX Revolution has undergone hundreds of changes, since I began writing this book. Once of the most recent, and suggested by me, is the ability to directly inject any Element to just above the page </head>, above the </body> tag, and directly to a Placeholder via Output Filters, instead of our needing to write many of the PHP scripts found at the beginning of this chapter.

Listing 11.32: Samples of using Output Filters for content injection

```
[[$jquery:jsToBottom]]
[[$scriptBlockFromlisting11.30:htmlToBottom]]
[[$matchingCSS:cssToHead]]
```

As an added treat I also came up with this little idea to place all my jQuery JavaScript in the same document ready function. The only caveat is you need to be mindful of the order, as the parser will place them in the order they are requested. If nested items appear in the Elements, they could very well appear before you may want them and before the ones listed in the Element itself. At the end of every jQuery MODX Revolution Chunk add the same placeholder and then use the following example for injection.

Listing 11.32: Grouping Injected Items To a "Single" Placeholder

```
[[$jquery.flowplayer:toPlaceholder=`jquery.chunk`]]
[[$jquery.embed:toPlaceholder=`jquery.chunk`]]
```

Listing 11.33: Example jQuery Chunk to allow Injection Grouping

```
sortTable = $('#[[+tableid]]').dataTable();
[[+jquery.chunk]]
```

Listing 11.34 Template Aspect of Injection Grouping

```
$(document).ready(function() { [[+jquery.chunk]]  });
```

Summary

One of the benefits of using jQuery and the MODX Revolution API is simply the ability to allow each to do what that are extraordinarily good at, without hindering either product. As stated in other chapters: MODX Revolution has a distinctive ability to stay out of the way of our implementations while providing developers the framework to do very impressive things.

With content injection recently added to the MODX Revolution Output Filters, many of the examples presented in this chapter, can be streamlined even further. What some of you may have surmised, is there is nothing limiting you from creating an assets/jQuery folder and simply installing one implementation after another into sub folders. This can allow a high degree of flexibility and exploration, as each tool can have multitudes of settings, css, and images directly within a parent folder dedicated to a single purpose, such as assets/jQuery/flowplayer. MODX Revolution Chunks can become simple injection lists for a specific purpose.

Many of the examples discussed in this chapter have additional functionality than was represented here. Feel free to visit the various links provided in this chapter to discover methods which are much more complex than these.

The wonderful aspect of this chapter, is all of the content is freely available on the web from the project resources. The author of jQueryTools blatantly states," there is no copyright -- do what individual you want." Hopefully, this chapter has shown you how simple it is to implement jQuery (and other libraries) with MODX Revolution.

For those of you, who specialize on other libraries, the MODX Revolution aspect of the techniques presented herein, should work for almost anything you can think up or interact with. Feel free to contribute examples and Packages to the community as you are able.

12
AJAX Content Injection

Many of us have seen the television commercials over recent years, which depict a person or a couple wanting to purchase a car. They begin by standing in an empty white room. Suddenly, the room is filled with a large assortment of cars of varying make, model, and color. As the buyer(s) supply information, the available choices are filtered to reflect their updated preferences. Eventually, the perfect vehicle sits shiny before the very excited and "fulfilled" buyer(s).

Typically, the rest of us have a different experience while shopping. Take the simple process of ordering food in a drive-thru at any given restaurant. As soon as the employee understands they have you trapped in line and stuck between cars, they immediately begin "suggesting" the featured item, which is rarely what the customer even wants.

In the middle of these two situations is a much more fluid and simple experience we can easily reference: dine in restaurants. Typically, a host(ess) will escort the party to a table and provide a customary introduction speech and informs the party of the name of the server. The situation immediately becomes one of exchange.

Granted there is suggested selling inside of a restaurant, but seldom does it have the "oppressive" feel of the same technique implemented in a drive-thru experience. Instead, it becomes part of the exchange and is intended to support the environment and the customer. The server offers a menu, which the customer typically orders from. During the meal drinks are refilled and other needs are met. At the end of dinner, desert and/or coffee may be offered.

When the topic of AJAX comes into a conversation or into someone's thoughts, typically one of two extremes are presented: give the visitor everything and let them choose how to find what they need or force the visitor to make a choice and then respond with the requested information. I believe the best use of AJAX is somewhere in the middle and should always be viewed from the perspective of the site visitor as it relates to the site purpose, also known as its environment.

AJAX (Asynchronous JavaScript And XML)

In essence, AJAX is simply a method a visitor can communicate to the web server by way of page elements to a server, A response can then be injected into the current page at a specified location. All of this takes place *in the midst of a user visiting a single web page.*

Essentially, the communication from both directions happens in relation to the current page and does not typically require the browser to change URI locations, though there are implementations which provide "quick jump" menus which utilize an AJAX transaction to bypasses a lot of clicking and places visitors directly on the desired page. This differs from a typical hyperlink, in that once it is clicked *a sequence of events* begin which typically completes by the web browser being sent to a new Uniform Resource Identifier which displays an entire new web page in the browser. Frequently, AJAX simply works within the boundaries of a single web page.

One of the determining factors for using AJAX is whether it is better to move the visitor to a page dedicated to specific content or to keep them on a single resource while updating an area of that page to display contents as a result of their actions. A solid set of rules regarding the implementation of AJAX has never been established, but there are quite a few opinions.

With the "power" associated with the use of any technology, there is always ways to abuse or manipulate it in ways never intended. For example, I have had clients choose to send all of their media to an e-mail account instead of using the client area, DVD, or other storage medium. Its a wonderful thing to not get any e-mail for two days because the box is tagged full, because the Sendmail daemon knows there is a 700 MB file sitting in the spooler. Fortunately, I had another technology configured to clean the spooler every night at midnight - and now every 3 hours.

In regards to AJAX abuses, some people have attempted to serve the contents of entire other sites, or at least the data retrieved from their databases. Fortunately, most servers are now configured to forbid AJAX transactions from occurring outside the same domain which originates the request, but that does not keep cURL or other back end technologies from bridging the gap. MODX Revolution allows most any application to be developed, even abusive ones, which is not the intention of the Project Leaders or the author of this book.

Historically, abuses were not the only AJAX related problem, as developers have had to deal with associated web browser and protocol issues. Some browsers adhere to one format while others tend to favor an alternative method. Before I started using jQuery I would have to implement JavaScript which would proceed through a series of Try/Catch Blocks to handle my applications.

In this chapter I will present jQuery as the foundation for AJAX requests, as it handles all of the protocol variables, as well as actual implementation. The MODX Revolution setup and Snippets present herein should serve as a foundation for the majority of AJAX implementations. MODX Revolution provides an amazing framework which can quickly and easily become "AJAX enabled" within a few minutes, but first we need to decide if we actually need AJAX.

To AJAX Or Not To AJAX

Understanding when and why to implement AJAX into a solution has been argued by many. On one end of the spectrum are those individuals who simply want to be associated with the newest fad or buzzword. "Purists" can be found on the other end, which find very little value with any implementation of AJAX.

After a decade of working with many aspects of Internet Technology, I have come to a few conclusions on the matter of AJAX, and humbly offer my *opinion*s. My mind set believes technology is intended to serve people, not become a cruel taskmaster. So how can we be served?

Argument For Implementing AJAX

As a rule, I use the following grading scale for considering the implementation of AJAX in a web project. By selecting all of the numbers which apply to the current application and subsequently totaling the sum. Any score over 18 should be considered the basis of an AJAX implementation.

AJAX should only be used if:

1. Sales / Information needs targeting
2. Server load utilization is excessive without it
3. Restricted Access to data is desired, even kept from search engines
4. The possible data set is quite large and needs to be filtered via user interaction
5. The visitor perceives they are receiving direct benefit from it
6. The User Interface requires it for simplicity
7. It benefits the visitor and the project

Argument Resistant to AJAX

There are those who believe that all links on a site should point to actual content and even go as far as suggesting an AJAX implementation and an additional fall-through static solution. By choosing **a single solution** and maximizing its effectiveness, the best implementation will typically result hopefully handling all the project goals efficiently.

For example: many online retailers, first attempted to implement AJAX user interfaces, only to discover the simplicity of using blog-type tags for filtering. In other words, site visitors are more than capable of targeting content themselves, if given the opportunity. Designers simply need to provide the user an interface to facilitate their needs and provide a flow of information which is as intuitive as possible. Simplicity is usually what visitors value the most. In the end, it is usually better to add AJAX functionality to a project once the static content has been established. In short, if a task can be completed without AJAX, it probably isn't needed.

Component Essentials

There are many possible methods to utilize AJAX on a MODX Revolution web project. The best of which will utilize the MODX API, separate tasks to those skilled to perform them, and clearly communicate implementation needs. Each of the examples in this chapter require Manager access and very little programming experience, though they are intended to offer a solid AJAX foundation.

MODX Revolution provides a very simple method for AJAX implementations: simply use the Manager to create each of the various Elements and direct the AJAX calls to a Resource containing the necessary Components. Larger projects may also use file system based resources.

An AJAX Template

The first item we need is a Template which can be used to service all of our AJAX functions. As with most AJAX implementations, information will need to be received and sent back to the calling page, while excluding any additional content from contaminating the data. In essence, an "empty" Template is easiest and has been provided with MODX Revolution.

AJAX Resources

The next item necessary is a Resource dedicated to fulfilling a specific AJAX implementation. This Resource can literally be placed anywhere in the site tree, as only its ID number will be needed for our examples, as MODX Revolution can easily complete the path and filename.

If multiple AJAX implementations are being used, I would suggest creating an AJAX Container in the Manger: published, hidden from menus, and assign it the Empty Template discussed previously. Each AJAX implementation can now be added under this Parent Resource, with the same settings and the added Benefit of inheriting some of the settings from the parent.

Assorted AJAX Implementations

The best AJAX solutions typically resemble static content, while providing a very clean and intuitive extension to that content. Throughout the rest of the chapter, we will look at a variety of AJAX implementations, which serve both the user and the project purpose. Please keep in mind, there are probably many other methods which can be used to provide similar or identical functionality.

The examples contained herein are intended to illustrate the simplicity of using AJAX with MODX Revolution, as well as various implementation methods. You are invited to skim or scour the examples shown, according to your skill level and need.

Manipulating Snippet Presentation: Extending The Archivist Tree

After finishing the site built by hand described in the *Power Blogging* chapter, I discovered the Archives were only showing the default number of entries, and I have content 14 years old. I needed to provide a simple way to extend the default number of archives to a much larger number, while presenting only the last six months, unless a user wanted to see more.

In the *Dynamic JavaScript, CSS, and jQuery Essentials* chapter, I demonstrated how to limit the number of list items displayed on a page, with a little slight of hand. Regardless of the current presentation, all of the list items were always there. With the Archives, I needed to actually access new content and replace the small list with a much larger list, but only if the user chooses.

As you may recall, the output of Archivist was housed in a dedicated column, as indicated by the code below. I will be demonstrating how to convert this into an AJAX presentation, using a very straightforward technique.

Convert Static Content to Dynamic

Listing 12.01: excerpt from Power Blogging base_template.xhtml

```
<div id="archives">
    <h5>Archives</h5>
    <ul>[[!Archivist?parents=`[[!$categoryList]]`&target=`2`]]</ul>
</div>
```

Listing 12.02: Chunk ajaxArchives derived from Listing 12.01

```
[[!Archivist?parents=`[[!$categoryList]]`&target=`2`]]
```

Listing 12.03: revised excerpt from Listing 10.02 base_template.xhtml

```
<div id="archives">
    <h5>Archives</h5>
    <ul>[[!$ajaxArchives]]</ul>
</div>
```

To begin, I want to ensure the presentation remains consistent between the two Archivist data sets we will be working with. The easiest way to accomplish this is to utilize the same Element to create both sets of data, in this case a MODX Revolution Chunk will be used to house the Snippet Call. We then replace the original Snippet Call in the base_template with a call to our newly created Chunk.

Once the Chunk has been created and saved and the base_template edited, clear the MODX Revolution cache and retest the page to verify the page still presents the Archivist output as it did before we performed these changes.

Create The Resource to Return the AJAX Result

Next we create a Resource which will return the response back to the AJAX Request. Make sure the appropriate settings are on each new AJAX resource: published, hidden from menus, and assign it the Empty Template. Failure to apply these settings could result in strange behavior, such as Manager users logged in can see the content, but site visitors can not.

Listing 12.04: ajaxResource (with ID of 38 linked to AJAX)

```
[[!$ajaxArchives]]
```

Create A Helper Snippet

The purpose of AJAX is dynamic content, which is where PHP becomes involved. To process the transactions, AJAX utilizes $_POST and $_GET. It has been my experience, $_GET is the transport object of choice for many of our simple implementations and the one we will using here. For this example to work, we need to "catch" a request value to hand to the Archivist Snippet to change the number of Archivist months displayed in the page.

Listing 12.05: getMonths.php

```php
<?php
$months = (!empty($_GET['months'])) ? $_GET['months'] : 0;
return intval($months);
```

Attach A Listener To A Page Element or Event

We are just about finished. The entire <div id="archives"> section of code has been rewritten and updated to implement AJAX. and uses the [[injectHTMLToBottom]] Snippet introduced in the *Dynamic JavaScript, CSS, and jQuery Essentials* chapter:

Listing 12.06: revised archives <div> from base_template.xhtml

- -

```
<div id="archives">
    <h5>Archives</h5>
    <ul>[[!$ajaxArchives]]
        <li class="ajaxarch"><a href="#">-More Archives-</a></li>
    </ul>
    [[injectHTMLToBottom?src=`
    <script type="text/javascript">
        $(document).ready(function() {
            $('li.ajaxarch a').click(function() {
                $.get('[[~38]]', { months: 60 }, function(data) {
                    $('#archives ul').html(data);
                });
                return false;
            });
        });
    </script>
    `]]
</div>
```

- -

1. The Archivist Snippet call has been replaced with the ajaxArchives Chunk

2. A <li class="ajaxarch"> was added to attach a click event

3. We inject the required JavaScript code to the end of the page

4. Before the injection occurs [[~38]] is completed by MODX Revolution to point to a Resource within the current site, and a link is creating replacing the [[~38]] tag

5. The number of months is set to 60 (5 years) and then sent to our ajaxArchives Chunk via the Resource with the id number of 38

6. The result can then be fed back to archives div and placed inside of the <ul> tags

7. The default click action is set to false as to not allow the page to change, or reload

Modify Chunk To Accept AJAX Request

At this stage, we get to decide the default and AJAX values, by manipulating the &limit Archivist Snippet parameter, which allows us to adjust Archivist's default number of items. To convert this Snippet call to AJAX we simply feed the limit parameter the results of our help Snippet. If that is empty, we set a default of six items. As a reminder, [[!$categoryList]] is a Chunk which holds a comma delimited list of our blog category Resource IDs, which is subsequently read by various Element calls all over the site to establish and interact with the category parents.

Listing 12.07: Chunk ajaxArchives

- -

```
[[!Archivist?parents=`[[!$categoryList]]`&target=`2`&limit=`[[!getMonths:empty=`6`]]`]]
```

- -

Archives

March 2011 (1)
February 2011 (3)
November 2010 (1)
August 2010 (1)
May 2010 (1)
November 2009 (1)
-More Archives-

Archives

March 2011 (1)
February 2011 (3)
November 2010 (1)
August 2010 (1)
May 2010 (1)
November 2009 (1)
October 2009 (1)
August 2009 (1)
February 2009 (1)
August 2008 (2)
July 2001 (1)
April 2001 (1)
March 2001 (2)
March 2000 (1)
May 1997 (1)

Resulting Implementation

As shown here, we have accomplished all of our goals:

♦ Consistent Presentation
♦ The rest of the page remains intact
♦ Clean interface
♦ Provides the current content
♦ Immediate access to more content
♦ Doesn't change the feel of the page
♦ Enhances the purpose of the page
♦ Intuitive

Essentially, many MODX Revolution AJAX implementations are created in a very similar manor as the one shown here. Surprisingly, the entire process is comprised of only five components:

1. A Snippet to Process the request
2. A Resource for the AJAX Snippet
3. A Snippet to "catch" values
4. A Chunk for Presentation
5. A trigger to activate the request

Using $modx->runSnippet()

An alternative method to extending the Archivist presentation can be implemented using MODX Revolution's runSnippet() function. Essentially, we create a wrapper Snippet to handle the majority of the components required in the previous implementation:

Listing 12.08: ajaxArchives Snippet (wrapper for Archivist)

```php
<?php
/* override snippet limit with AJAX $ GET value if available */
$scriptProperties['limit'] = (!empty($_GET['months'])) ?
    $_GET['months'] : $scriptProperties['limit'];

/* if limit is empty remove it to use Snippet Defaults */
if (empty($scriptProperties['limit'])) {
    unset($scriptProperties['limit']);
}

/* Run the Snippet and Return its content to the Page */
return $modx->runSnippet('Archivist', $scriptProperties);
```

Listing 12.09: ajaxResource content for implementing AJAX wrapper Snippet

```
[[ajaxArchives?parents=`[[!$categoryList]]`&target=`2`&limit=`6`]]
```

Simply replace the contents of the ajaxResource Document and the [[!$ajaxArchives]] Chunk Call in the base_template with the above code. This will provide the exact same functionality we had using the Five Components in the last section.

ajaxArchives Snippet

1. Provides a consistent interface with established settings
2. Defaults to $scriptProperties['limit'] if $_GET['months'] is not received
3. Removes $scriptProperties['limit'] if empty, allowing Archivist defaults
4. Simply acts as a pass through utilizing Archivist Parameters
5. Utilizes the same click event, as it is supplying the same data to the same location
6. Allows us to eliminate the Chunk [[$ajaxArchives]] (of the same name)

User Details

Our last example will simply interact with the MODX Revolution User Object for the current logged in user. This example demonstrates enhanced functionality on the page and in the AJAX Implementation. To keep things simple, only those aspects of the implementation which directly relate to AJAX will be discussed. The MODX API will be introduced later in this book.

Page Contents

Listing 12.10: userDetails.xhtml

```
<ul id="filter">
    <li><a href="#">User</a></li>
    <li><a href="#">Profile</a></li>
    <li><a href="#">Groups</li>
    <li><a href="#">User Docs</a></li>
</ul>

<div id="ajaxContent"></div>

<script type="text/javascript">
$(document).ready(function() {
    $('ul#filter a').click(function() {
        var userChoice = $(this).text().toLowerCase().replace(' ',
'');
        $.get('[[~228]]', { mode: userChoice }, function(data) {
            $('#ajaxContent').html(data);
        });
        return false;
    });
});
</script>
```

This page requires jQuery and provides the following:

1. filter: which will serve as our click event triggers to filter the content by
2. ajaxcontent: which will display the AJAX data
3. javascript : uses the text in the filter to traverse a PHP switch statement
4. User Docs is translated to userdocs in the userChoice declaration
5. { mode: userChoice } is a JSON styled parameter array sent to the AJAX processor

AJAX Back End

Listing 12.11: userDetails.php Snippet

- -

```php
<?php
if (!function_exists(formatUserData)) {
    function formatUserData($arry = '') {
        foreach ($arry as $key => $val) {
            $val = (!empty($val)) ? $val : 'not provided';
            $str .= $key . ': ' . $val . '<br />';
        }
        return $str;
    }
}
$userObj = $modx->user;
switch ($_GET['mode']) {
    case 'groups':
        $o = formatUserData($userObj->getUserGroupNames());
        break;
    case 'profile':
        $profile = $userObj->getOne('Profile');
        $o = formatUserData($profile->toArray());
        break;
    case 'user':
        $o = formatUserData($userObj);
        break;
    case 'userdocs':
        $docsArray = $userObj->xpdo->context->aliasMap;
        sort($docsArray);
        foreach ($docsArray as $doc => $id) {
            $o = $modx->makeUrl($id) . '<br />';
        }
        break;
}
return $o;
```

- -

To implement this example, create a Resource containing Listing 12.10 for site visitors. Next create a Snippet with the code in Listing 12.11 userDetails.php Snippet to process the AJAX request. Finally, create a Resource to hold the Snippet call: [[!userdetails]] which will be linked to, such as the [[~228]] found in Listing 12.10. Once functioning correctly, the current user data will appear in the <div id="ajaxContent"></div> - depending on log in status.

Summary

We have only scratched the surface of everything that can be done with AJAX in a MODX Revolution web project, but we have actually covered the foundation required to implement almost any AJAX concept imaginable. Chapter 18, actually provides a multi-faceted third-party applications which utilizes AJAX extensively - with some MODX Revolution flavoring.

We have seen how an event of some sort is required to trigger the AJAX Request. Keep in mind there are dozens of events which can be used. I chose to represent very simple ones to demonstrate the flow of the entire transaction, which typically require two Resources and a Snippet - at the very minimum.

Our first example used more components than the others and demonstrates how AJAX can be implemented from even a simple Manager Users perspective, without the need of any real programming. The second example combined many of the components of the first example into a cleaner Snippet wrapper, which transparently acts as a middle man to the main Snippet.

Our last example demonstrated how to interact with a customized PHP back end which was directly attached to the actual text on the page. Acting as a bridge to limitless implementations, this example demonstrates how a simple Snippet can provide a doorway to much greater data sources - including data bases.

Two aspects remain consistent across all AJAX implementations, triggers and targets. A skilled developer can inject code into as many targets as necessary on a single AJAX transaction. I invite you to explore, extend, and implement as much creativity as possible.

Finally, please consider giving back to the MODX Revolution community as you implement new and exciting tools.

MODX Revolution Rule #12: **Presentation should be clean, simple, and intuitive.**

III

Administration

This section discusses the basic principles of developing a web project with teams of people, document permissions and different "front ends" .

Project leaders and site administrators should find these pages informative and the examples easily understood as straightforward methods are demonstrated.

This section is geared to provide a working foundation to learn from and build on.

Grouping

Access Control Lists

Contexts

13

An Overview of Grouping: Category, User and Resource

Each of us is born in a given city, province, state, territory, country, and even planet. So were a lot of other people, but how many were born to our specific parents? As people age, they typically go through a series of schools, colleges, and / or universities, as do many others. But how many people were born of those parents, went to those schools, took the exact same classes, graduated, were employed at a given company, became married, and eventually had their specific children? How many of those individuals write MODX Revolution books?

In the United States, an individual is born as a group of one, with their Social Security Number serving as a reference point to where many aspects of their lives overlap into a huge collection of assorted data. An individual can also belong to many groups. This ideal is so "normal" for many of us, it is never given a second thought. We simply move through life flowing though these groups as opportunity and events take place, such as a simple trip to a public rest room.

Huge sections of our lives have been outlined as a result of grouping, with many of these groups having existed so long, no one really knows where they originated. Seldom are we aware of just how much each of the various groups in our lives have defined us from birth. We simply take this aspect of life for granted.

In the case of web projects, the vast majority are comprised of a minimum of two groups: those that built the site and those that visit it. Additionally, project leaders may be asked to group users and documents in such a manner as to be transparent to the individual user.

To accomplish this, MODX Revolution provides Manager users the ability to assemble people, documents, and Elements into groups or Categories. This chapter introduces many of the concepts necessary to successfully implement this functionality into a web project.

Element Categories

One of the simplest grouping mechanisms found in MODX Revolution, is the ability provided to Manager users and Package Developers to categorize Elements, thereby identifying some delineation of relationship. Any reason or division can be specified, and typically center around the Package name, specific functionality, User Group ownership, or a combination of these.

Essentially, the function of Categories within the MODX Revolution Manager is simply to allow grouping of Elements within the Manager remotely similar to the way "Tagging" works on the front of the site, albeit only using a single "tag". These categories could also be considered as a "label" or "brand" designating "ownership" similar to major corporations which offer items located in different areas of stores.

This can help designers and developers recall the purpose of a specific function without additional communication, by simply noticing the name of the Category it belongs to. This is very similar to a Social Security Number and how it crosses boundaries. Manager Users can easily identify related Elements no matter which section of the Element tree they are found.

To create a new **Category**, simply right click on Category in the Element Tree and select New Category. At this stage simply choose a name which clearly communicates general functionality. Eventually, it may become necessary to use sub-Categories to further denote function, such as: AJAX, DOM, menuEnhancement, and tableManipulation. Each of these could easily reference a jQuery "main" Category as their parent.

Create as many Categories as needed, keeping in mind each of them will only appear in an area of the Element tree where the Category has been assigned to any of its respective Components. Additionally, Categories operate without consideration of which type of Element it is attached to, namely: **Snippet**, **Plugin**, **Chunk**, **Template Variable**, and/or **Template**.

For example, a Chunk may contain a jQuery section of code which implements an AJAX call to a MODX Revolution Snippet, both the Snippet and the Chunk can belong to the same Category, as well as any other Elements which are also used to support this implementation, such as any Chunks being used to template the Snippet output. Once the Category has been created and the Chunk and Snippet are assigned to it, the Category will appear under the Chunk and Snippet areas as a sub set of those Element types, but it will not appear before this assignment has taken place or in any Element Sections it is not used.

This simple little tool can prove to be of great value to facilitate clear communication of site functions, in its ability to streamline the Element Tree in the Manager. By providing Manager users subcategories represented by folders, the display is left cleaner - especially for complex sites with a large number of Elements and/or "offices" working.

Personally, I tend to utilize a couple of default Element groups on many of my web projects. The first of these being a jQuery Category which nicely groups all of the Chunks, CSS, AJAX, and associated PHP Snippets into a single Category so all of the content contained therein is directly related to jQuery.

Another Category I like to use, contains the many menu implementations utilized with the Wayfinder Snippet, which does not currently use any Categories of its own. I have dozens of Chunk templates for use with Wayfinder which produce a wide array of output from drop down menus, static global navigation menu, and even jQuery enhanced menus. In the assumption Wayfinder could eventually begin using a Category of the same name, I chose to use the more generic "menu_Implementations".

A central development server may have a few dozen of these Wayfinder templates. The ability to close all of those Chunks into a single line is priceless, especially when we take into consideration the amount of screen real estate a large web development company with a central test server / repository with dozens of menus and even more jQuery chunks.

The use of Categories is by no means mandatory. For smaller projects and when Manager security is low in priority, a simple Element naming convention may be used to satisfy the "group", such as: wfBreadcrumbs, wfGlobalNavBar, wfDropDown, etc.

The ability to create groups crossing Element "lines" can prove immensely valuable. Project leaders interested in forward proofing a site, may very well find the implementation of Categories a powerful ally. For a moment, assume the project is run by a Marketing team, but a section of the site belongs totally to Human Resources. All of the HR Elements could be assigned to a dedicated Category with attached Access Control List permission, allowing only the respective group access to the areas of the project they are responsible for. Marketing could utilize their own areas, but not even see or update the HR Department areas. Each could simply be allowed to update their Elements without a series of requests or the necessity of having any concern of prying eyes.

Consider using Categories to group Elements to clearly communicate functionality, streamline the Element Tree, and / or as the beginning of planning the future implementation of Contexts and/or ACLs. Categories can serve the web project well in any of these capacities.

Resource Group Considerations

Security

Manage Users
Add, update, and assign permissions to users.

Access Controls
Manage user groups, roles, and access policies.

Resource Groups
Manage the groups resources belong to.

Form Customization
Customize manager forms by security permissions.

Flush Permissions
Flush all permissions and reload the cache.

Flush All Sessions
Flush all sessions and logout all users.

A Resource is *"a type of container that is interpreted by the Parser to fetch content: mostly accessed as a Document or Page"*.

A **Resource Group** is a collection of Resources, which can be found anywhere within the web project. Resources can be grouped together for any purpose: as part of a very structured plan, or as sporadic additions to the main content.

Any Resource being added to the Resource Group will need to be individually added. For larger sites, it is completely feasible to create a Snippet to add an entire directory to a Resource Group.

The act of creating a Resource Group using the "Create Resource Button" only provides a container to reference the documents by and does not automatically provide any protection. Resources may still be available to Anonymous users, until they are fully attached to a User Group.

Access protection may be available once a Resource Group has been attached to a User Group and Access Control Lists established. Don't assume all Snippets will honor the Access Control List attached to them, as many currently do not. Test the implementation thoroughly.

Typically, Resource Groups will be implemented in one of the following ways:

1. Under a single parent
2. As individual documents appearing throughout the site, with availability centered on the specific user's access to them
3. Based on specific needs of the users or client, such as a "support" page linked to a previously purchased item
4. As a combination of the above, where Chunks can be placed in web pages based on User Group Membership, with dedicated menus linking to additional content
5. Split off into entirely new MODX Revolution Contexts, based on language, domain name, product class, or other specified purpose - technically not a Resource Group

Adding a Resource to a Resource Group

The first method provided in the Manager to add Resources to Resource groups is located on the Access Permissions tab of each Resource. Simply access the tab and provide access to any Resource Groups the document is to be included in.

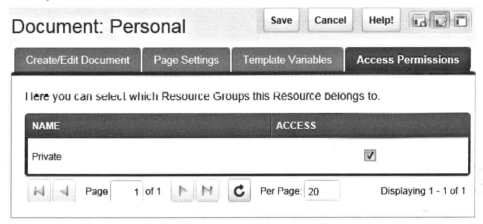

The second can be located on the Resource Groups page, and simply requires a drag-and-drop of the respective page to the appropriate group.

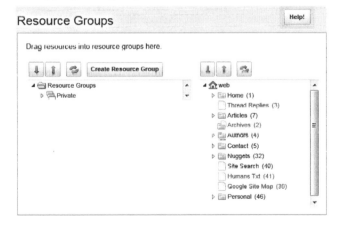

☞ **WARNING: THESE DOCUMENTS MAY STILL BE "PUBLIC"**

All Resources should be considered "Public" until the Resource Group has been attached to a User Group, Access Control Lists established, and the Sessions Flushed. Before placing sensitive information in the document, thoroughly test the implementation.

User Groups

While many web projects may not have any requirements associated with site visitors being required to log in, others may offer dedicated content and/or capabilities to those individuals who have been previously placed in a group which grants additional access and/or enhanced functionality. At first, this may appear more complicated than it actually is.

Examples of this ability can be seen throughout many e-commerce sites, where authenticated individuals are allowed to create wish lists, comment on recent purchases, interact in forums, as well as a myriad of other possibilities. At some stage of a project, leaders must assess the project's purpose and if an implementation is needed to provide additional access and content for authenticated users in specified manners.

The MODX project serves as a good example of a typical business, as it allows its users anonymous access, logged-in enhanced functionality, wider site access with the signing of a Contributor License Agreement, and/or dedicated forum access for participants in the Solution Partner Program. The main project leaders have access far above any of the project users.

In a sense, all of the MODX project's users could be considered a group of MODX Users, but as the entire project assumes the users have some commonality with MODX, the larger group is broken into smaller - more defined groups. In this case, "MODX" could be simply assumed and each user subsequently categorized based on their participation level within the project.

Essentially, each User Group represents varying levels of trust, which is typically the need being addressed when any thought is given to the implementation of groups within a web project. **The amount of access given to a group of users, or any individual should directly represent the level of trust being given to them.** For many web projects, the first discussion of user implementation may immediately demand an answer to simple questions:

1. Does the project need User Groups?
2. Why does the project need these groups?

In the introduction to this chapter, a statement was made on how a person can be a "group of one." While this may sound like an oxymoron, it only requires a slight change of perspective to understand the concept and how it directly relates to the development of a web project.

A simple way of discerning potential User Groups, may be to consider what a typical user represents, instead of thinking about the person directly. Now extend the associated characteristics of a single individual represented in a specific manner to a group of others: "They work in the Advanced Research and Development Laboratories."

This is where a discussion can begin on grouping users and their associated content. Once a discernible group has been recognized, it becomes only a matter of laying out a mutually beneficial structure to be used in the web project.

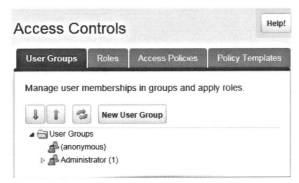

Every MODX Revolution project consists of at least two groups or containers of people:

1. Anonymous (the visitors) which have access to all published and non "protected" content, typically only on the public face of the site

2. Administrators (the builders) which typically have full access privileges to both the MODX Revolution Manager and the front areas

The same database table maintains the records for all users, without regard to their function, greatly simplifying the code requirements when developing "home grown" Snippets and Packages. A User simply refers to any individual accessing a site's content and/or Manager. A User Group is a set of users with some definable characteristic or set of characteristics.

For example, a group may simply be a collection of employees working for a specific client. The client may very well want to provide "in house" content to only their employees, without anyone else in the world having any inkling the information even exists on the web project. For many clients, a "protected read-only area" will serve their needs very well. In these scenarios, simply having the ability to successfully log into the web project would allow the "employees" to gain access to the information.

I can not possibly, overemphasize the necessity of keeping group names and their construction as generic as possible. Over the years, I have found an unnecessary increase in the level of complexity when the User Group is overly specific. Additionally, Site Administrators will need to clearly communicate the group and its purpose with as few words as possible.

Typically, a client will provide the phrase themselves, if we are paying attention. When the conversation turns to the goals and needs of the project, statements made by the client can define entire work flows required for the project: "I need our employees/associates to be able to monitor news and announcements on a weekly basis."

A Site Administrator may summarize this requirement to the Project team simply by saying "We need to give the [User Group] access to the [Resources] containing [Privileged] content." They could provide the actual names previously implemented within the project, or simply establish those simultaneously to stating the client's goal.

⊤ *TIP: KEEP IT SIMPLE FOR EVERYONE INVOLVED*

If you can't describe the User Group with a simple sentence, rethink it until you can.

User Groups: A World Unto Themselves

To readily understand the functionality of User Groups, it is imperative to be exposed to the differences experienced inside a group versus the surrounding environment. Many of these concepts can be understood in a relative short time by referencing a movie and listing specific contrasts.

The factory in *Willy Wonka and the Chocolate Factory* represents many of the concepts of User Groups, as each area represented a world unto itself - with its own subset of reality. In essence, a User Group must be perceived as a microcosm of the hole. Take note of some of the differences between a typical Manager User and a User Group member:

Manager Users	Inside the User Group
Anyone having the Administrator Role has complete access to all aspects of the web project	Only those Users, given the Administrator Role will have it, whether they are a site administrator or not
A user of the site, is a user of the whole site as defined by associated ACLs	A member of one Group, may or may not, have access or membership in another
The default Roles work across an entire context	A User Role will only function in the User Groups in which it occurs
Permissions are "global" until overridden	Permissions do not automatically transfer from one User Group to another. A user may be an Administrator in one group, a member of another, and be excluded from others
The Administrator and Anonymous roles embody each of the permissions required for users within a functioning project	User Groups are empty, and therefore need each aspect of it to be defined, even on the simplest implementations
Only Administrators can do anything	Anyone can be made a Group Admin
Site Administrators can be added at any time to a User Group, though are not required to be a member in any of them	Group Admins will not inherit the privileges of a Site Administrator, unless they are a member of the Site Administrator group

At one point of the movie, Wonka quotes Arthur William Edgar O'Shaughnessy: *"We are the music makers, And we are the dreamers of dreams"*. This single quote describes the role most Project Leaders play in a web project: visualizing applications and solutions to client needs.

The issue faced by many, is how to utilize the "rules" of individual subcomponents to accomplish the client's goals. This is very significant in the area of Users, because we are now specifically thinking of users as the client sees them. There were many areas of the factory, four of the ticket winners never saw and no indication was given Oompa-Loompas had free access to everything.

Using the Access Wizard for User and Resource Group Creation

MODX Revolution 2.2.2-pl introduced the Access Wizard which can be accessed via the Resource Group and User Group pages. Essentially, this streamlined innovation provides a simple method to simultaneously create a User Group, Document Group, and assign the basic permissions for the relationship.

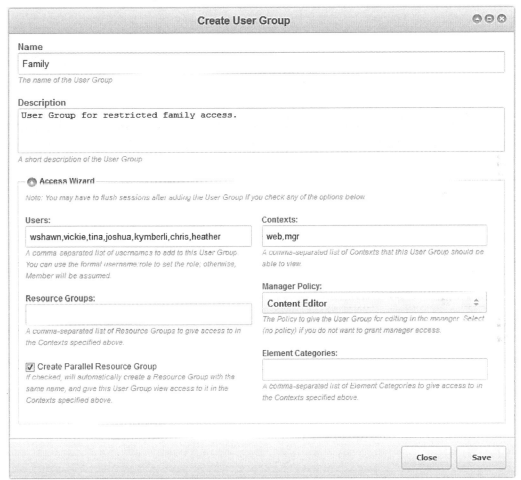

- ◆ The Resource and User Groups will both be named "Authors"
- ◆ wshawn has been added to the Group
- ◆ The Authors group will only exist in the web context - mgr will have to be added for any users in the Group to have Manager Access
- ◆ Manager access requires a User Role of at least a Content Editor

Please verify all settings, minimum roles and Access Policy once groups are created.

Adding Users To A User Group

Pay close attention to the very important missing component in the User tab of any newly created User Group: a user name. **When a User Group is created it may contain no users - not even the Site Administrator,** which means it is a whole new world with nobody in charge.

I would strongly suggest, adding a Site Administrator as soon as possible when any User Group is created. Failing to do so, can have the ill effect of locking the content neatly away from their control. It should be noted, all Site Administrators will not necessarily need to be attached to every group. One is typically more than sufficient. If necessary, Site Administrators have the ability to add or remove themselves from a group whenever they need to.

Additionally, to best understand the significance of this step, we must remember **to adjust our perspective to only this particular group** by thinking: "In this User Group, wshawn will act as a Super User."

A web project in the early stages of development, will typically have only a few user accounts. Once a site has over a few dozen users, this particular interface could lead to mistakes being made or in excessive time being required to add users.

Site Administrators may find it easier to directly access a user's account, located in the Manage Users area located in the Security Menu when they need to add them to a group.

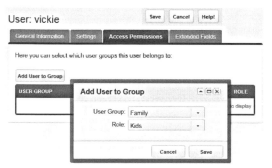

By updating a user, they can easily be added to a User Group and assigned a Role, by utilizing the Access Permissions tab. During the initial stages of establishing a User Group it may be best to assign everyone minimum roles.

User Roles

By the time most web projects get to the stage of defining actual User Roles, the project leaders have usually decided which User and Resource Groups to attach. The focus will subsequently turn to issues of trust: who and how much. MODX Revolution provides 10,000 possible positions of Authority to be utilized for this purpose, which is far more than most of us will ever need.

To understand the interrelationship of these various Authority Levels, simply visualize a typical dart board with a dart placed exactly in its center representing a distance of zero ("0") from the center and the Administrator Role of the web project. Attaching a string to the dart, left dangling straight down, the following User Role concepts apply:

◆ All permissions apply in a liner fashion - they are all on the same string

◆ The closer to the dart (or zero) a role is, the more it is trusted

◆ An Authority Level will proportionately take on characteristics of the default Roles based on its distance from them - relative closeness can imply greater influence

◆ As there is only one length of string, the Administrator Role will inherit all permissions on the string, as they are "tied" to it

◆ Any position on the string will inherit all the permissions on the string as it dangles after it - a position of 100 will inherit 101 - 9999, but not 0 - 99

◆ As a string can reflect the shortest distance between two points, so Roles should represent the most basic structure possible

◆ Role definitions should indicate function and be kept as generic as possible

Project goals may expect User Roles be implemented with those having the greatest amount of access first, as those are the positions which will typically be adding site content and working with user accounts. When possible, I work from the least access upwards and tend to create Role structures which indicate trust levels by the number of digits used in the Authority level. A typical project may require only a handful of Authority positions.

The following represents possible base structures to begin with:

◆ 0 Administrator (CTO?)	◆ 0 Super Administrator
◆ 5 Executives	◆ 5 Me Only
◆ 50 Managers	◆ 50 Spouse
◆ 500 Team Leaders	◆ 500 Kids
◆ 5000 Team Members	◆ 5000 Site Member
◆ 9999 Anonymous	◆ 9999 Anonymous

Policy Templates

To define the actual "trusts," MODX Revolution contains eight base Policy Templates, which can be used to establish very specific Access Control Lists for any "security" implementation. Each of these Templates contain the available permissions for a specific class, while additional Policy Templates may be provided by Packages, as found with the installation of Quip.

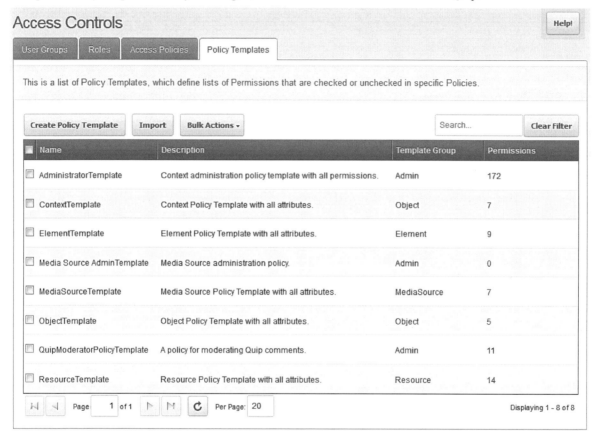

Policies are established using one of these Templates as a base, and the subsequent selection of the various permissions which a User Role is entrusted. Site Administrators can quickly attach a Template to a Policy, by simply recognizing which facet of MODX Revolution is being addressed.

---

7 *NEVER DIRECTLY EDIT A POLICY TEMPLATE - CREATE DUPLICATES*

To ensure the proper functionality of the web project, please edit only Duplicate Policies.

Summary of Policy Templates:

AdministratorTemplate contains the permissions related to accessing and utilizing specific areas and functions of the Manager. This policy is typically duplicated and edited to provide lesser functionality and access in the Manager, as demonstrated in the Content Editor Policy.

ContextTemplate contains the foundational permissions available within any given Context and interaction with the objects it contains. In effect, a Policy can be created giving a user Read-Only access to the Manager: load, list, view, and view_unpublished.

ElementTemplate contains the possible actions which can be performed on an Element.

MediaSourceTemplate contains the possible actions which can be performed on an Media Source objects.

ObjectTemplate contains the possible actions which can be performed on an Object. The Anonymous Role is defined using the "Load" Only Object Template

QuipModeratorPolicyTemplate contains the possible actions which can be performed on Comments and Threads posted on a site via the Quip and/or Articles Package. Note: This Template is not part of the default MODX Revolution installation.

ResourceTemplate contains the possible actions which can be performed on a Resource.

MODX Revolution Rule #13: **Only duplicates of the MODX Policies should be edited.**

Policies

Access Control Lists require a Policy to define the actual aspects of the trust being given to a User Role. MODX Revolution provides multiple Policy Templates for Site Administrators to utilize during the definition of any action or access associated with any "trusted user" implementation, whether a Manager User or simply a site visitor.

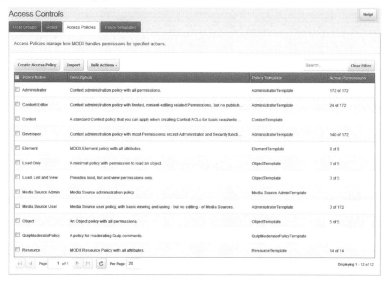

MODX Revolution 2.2.3-pl provides two Policies for users (Administrator and Content), one for Elements, three for objects, and one for Resources. Quip adds a Policy of its own, so Site Administrators can add comment moderation with very little effort.

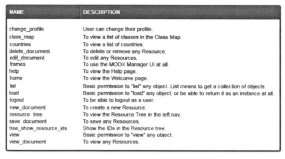

The Active Permissions column indicates the number of permissions the Policy is using out of the total number provided in the **Policy Template** it is based on.

For example, the Site Administrator has 172 possible permissions, while the Content Editor Policy, is simply the Administrator Policy with 148 permissions no longer enabled.

Site Administrators should pay close attention to why the Policy is needed in the first place. If a User Role requires access to the Manager, they will probably need some derivative of the Administrative Policy. If they are going to be working with Resources and/or Elements, the associated Policies will have to be added in the User Group in order to provide the necessary access and permissions to the group. Essentially, a Policy is typically linked to a specific user function and is utilized in preestablished ways.

How the Pieces Work Together

So far, this chapter has provided a large amount of information, with very little practical application. Essentially, each of the topics in this chapter are combined to create very specific permissions and abilities for specific roles within User Groups. This sounds much more complicated than it is, as it all comes together when a User Group is being defined:

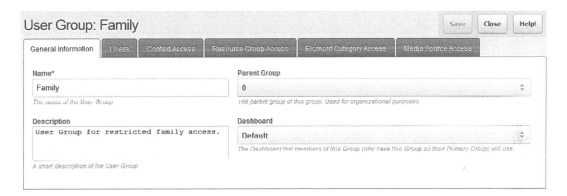

Combining the pieces:

The General Tab is a summary of the User Group name and description and the associated dashboard for the Group.

The User Tab is populated with each member of a User Group and their respective role.

The Context Access Tab is used to define the minimum role a user must have in order to perform an operation. This is where the Roles assigned to users actually begin to take on substance. In the "web" and "mgr" Contexts any policy based on the "object' template can be used, though a Policy based on the AdministratorTemplate should be used for the "mgr" context.

The Resource Group Access Tab establishes the minimum Role in the User Group a user must have to access its Resources in any given Context. This tab utilizes any Policy based on the Resource or Object Policy Templates.

The Element Category Access Tab allows a Category of Elements to become accessible to members of the User Group, if their Role has sufficient permissions. This tab utilizes any Policy based on the Element or Object Policy Templates.

The Media Source Access Tab establishes those Media Sources directly accessible to any given User Group, as well as the minimum Role associated with the access.

Summary

This chapter discussed concepts typically reserved for huge sections of college semesters and hopefully provides the necessary foundation to effectively implement Users and Groups on a MODX Revolution web project. The purpose of this chapter was to present a broad overview of the use of Categories, User Groups, and Document Groups.

I will be presenting an actual real-world implementation in the next chapter. Essentially, I wanted to introduce the areas involved in Access Control Lists without distracting the actual application, with a myriad of definitions, warnings, and explanations.

Key points:

- To be on the safe side, Site Administrators should consider all Users and Resources to be "Anonymous" if they have not had Policies attached.
- Thorough testing should be conducted before any content is made available on the "public side" of the web project.
- Sensitive information should not be placed in untested areas
- Elements, Users, and Resource can be grouped for any reason
- A Resource is typically viewed as a web page
- A Resource Group can consist of Resources located anywhere on the project
- Users are people visiting a web site, either in the Manager or the public side
- User Roles define the function a member of a User Group has within a specific area of the project
- Policy Templates encapsulate the permissions which are allowed to be performed
- A Policy is based on one of the four default Policy Templates and is used to establish specific permissions within User Groups and its User Roles
- Users and Roles are combined in the User Group Definition and attached to Contexts

14
Access Control List Implementation

My family enjoys going to the Smoky Mountains. Typically these getaways begin around 2:30 A.M. with my driving through the early morning. If all goes well, a late breakfast at the foot of the mountains awaits us - usually around the time the passengers wake up. The first order of business on these trips is simply to turn off radios, phones, and televisions. We love the rustic, slow-paced, peaceful lifestyle many of the "locals" enjoy, which reflect some of our core values.

For those who have never experienced the Smoky Mountains, head over to my Flickr account where over 10,000 pictures have been uploaded. It doesn't take much to understand why my wife and I want to live in a "modern" log cabin with all the accoutrements of both worlds, essentially creating a world of our own imagination.

In the last chapter, *An Overview of Grouping: Category, User and Resource,* I discussed many of the concepts associated with the creation of "trusted" areas within a web project. In this chapter, I will focus primarily on implementation and creating user accounts, leaving explanation to the previous chapter.

Unlike many other "CMS" software, MODX Revolution provides a fully functional and solid foundation to establish and implement all aspects of site security as part of its very core. The boundaries of which, are limited only by the stipulations placed on the project and the skill set of those involved in the implementation.

Essentially, Site Administrators simply need to consider which tasks require privileged access, define where this access should be granted, and what people are allowed to do once they successfully log in. Initially, a clean MODX Revolution installation consists of a single Administrative User, with all others being assigned the Anonymous Role.

Implementing The Login Package

The primary component required for any Access Control List implementation is typically considered to be the site's users. MODX Revolution has a user account workhorse known as the **Login Package**, which places many of the basic demands of account creation and maintenance directly on the user, rather than administrators. I would definitely recommend installing the Login Package on any site implementing any form of front-end user permissions.

Steps	Code
1.) Create a Published Document to allow users to login to the site and to act as a container for all user account services. *Choose* Published *and* Hide From Menus *to keep links to these pages from appearing in global menus.*	None: Return to this document in Step 5.
2.) Create an Account Activation Resource, taking note of the Resource ID Number. *The optional* redirectTo *parameter can be used to send the user directly to a page.*	`[[!ConfirmRegister]]`
3.) Create a Resource to notify people their information was received, taking note of the Resource ID Number. *A Chunk can also be implemented, using a format, similar to the* lgnActivateEmailTpl *template utilized for the account activation e-mail.*	`[[!Register?successMsg=`Thanks for registering! Check your e-mail for further directions.`]]`
4.) Create a Resource allowing people to Register, taking note of the Resource ID. *Replace 1st ## with the Resource ID number from Step 2. Replace 2nd ## with the Resource ID number from Step 3.*	`[[!Register?activationEmail Tpl=`myActivationEmailTpl` &activationEmailSubject=`Please activate your [[++site_name]] account in the next 3 hours!` &activationResourceId=`##` &submittedResourceId=`##` &submitVar=`registerbtn`]]`
5.) Edit Resource created in Step 1 *Replace ## with the Resource ID number from Step 4.*	`[[!Login]]` `<a href=`[[~##]]` title=`Create a [[++site_name]] account`>Register to create a new account</a>`

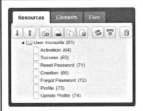

At this point you should have a fully functional Registration / Login System. The following steps provide the finishing touches, resulting in a set of 8 files allowing visitors to work with their own accounts, as much as is typically needed.

Steps	Code
6.) Create a Resource to point e-mails sent to users to reset their password, taking note of the Resource ID Number. *Replace ## with the Resource ID number of Steps 1 and 5 (Login Page).*	```[[!ResetPassword?``` ```&loginResourceId=`##`]]```
7.) Create a Resource for people who have forgotten their password. *Replace ## with Resource ID from Step 6.*	```[[!ForgotPassword?``` ```&resetResourceId=`##`]]```
8.) Create a Resource allowing people to view their profile. *View the file mentioned in Step 9 and the* `modx_user_attributes` *table to view the majority of possible placeholders, as there are over two dozen available.*	```[[!Profile?prefix=`user.`]]``` ```<h2>[[+user.username]] ([[+user.fullname]])</h2>``` ```[[+user.email:notempty=`E-mail: [[+user.email]] `]]``` ```[[+user.phone:notempty=`Phone: [[+user.phone]] `]]```
9.) Create a Resource allowing users to update their profile without Manager access.	```[[!UpdateProfile]]``` *Note: Use the template located at* `core/components/login/chunks/lgnupdateprofile.chunk.tpl` *as a base to create your template from.*

10.) Optional: Create a Wayfinder menu to point to various Login Snippets from the main Login Page, created in Step 1.
 	
Exchange the ## with the Resource IDs from Steps: 2, 3, and 6
	```[[Wayfinder?startId=`[[*id]]`&```
	 ```ignoreHidden=`1`&excludeDocs```
	 ```=`##,##,##`]]```

11.) Create a means to allow people to login and logout of the project.
 	
Replace ## with the Resource ID number from Step 1.
	```[[!+modx.user.id:isloggedin:eq=`1````
	 ```:then=`<a href="[[~##]]?service=```
	 ```logout">Logout</a>```
	 ```:else=`<a href="[[~##]]">Login</```
	 ```a>`]]```

User Account Considerations

When faced with the reality of implementing User accounts in a web project, a very sobering finality begins to set into the minds of many Site Administrators. In effect, user implementation is simply gauged as pass or fail, because users are usually attached to the very purpose of the web project and the profitability and competitive advantage of a company.

In many situations, Customer Relations and Human Resources rely heavily on web technologies to enhance and develop relationships. It only takes a single "glitch" in the system to potentially damage a valued relation or expose critical data, as major corporations such as Sony and Amazon found during the early months of 2011 when services where hacked or seemingly disconnected.

This is the realm of law suits, potential job loss, and the highest responsibility typically attached to a web project. For these reasons, company policies should be clear in the handling of new users, before they are actually implemented in the web project and should directly reflect the values of the company, as well as the proper amount of protection required for company assets.

Site Administrators have three primary options of creating User accounts:

1. Utilize Manage Users located in the Security menu to manually enter each user account, which is fine for projects with just a few users or if a web project has a dedicated "User Administrator" responsible for creating new accounts.

2. Installation of the Login Package, allowing users to register for the site and immediate group membership: `[[Register?usergroups=`Family`]]`. For some clients, this is unfathomable, simply because of possible abuse. There are a variety of ways to handle this situation, the simplest would be to have the user register for a low level account and have an Administrator subsequently add them to a User Group and assign them a User Role. It is also feasible to have someone already in the group access a "protected" version of the page which would allow them to create the account for the new user.

3. Create a Snippet which catches form data and injects a user object into the database utilizing the MODX Revolution API, which might be considered overkill as the other two options are much simpler.

On many of my projects I start with the first option, implement the second as the site goes "live", and actually add a touch of the third when necessary. More advanced techniques can also be used: extending the User Object, using a domain controller, or others discussed at rtfm.modx.com.

This chapter will demonstrate the simplicity in which Access Control Lists can be created, as such it may prove tempting to assume an implementation is solid and trustworthy. I can not possibly over stress the significance of thoroughly testing any application regarding users, intellectual property, and sensitive information. This testing should include every Snippet, Package, and Chunk being used in the associated documents, as well as MODX Revolution itself if needed.

Implementing a "Trusted User" Read-Only Area

In the *Power Blogging* chapter, I mentioned how the techniques utilized in blogging could benefit sites of any size for any client. While preparing for this chapter I was wondering why I had never implemented blogging functionality for my private content, by simply attaching names and general groups making it much simpler to catalog and reference.

The purpose of this group will be to allow private content to be stored on the site, with only my immediate family having access. With this definition in mind, I can begin moving forward by creating the necessary components which will be utilized in this simple Access Control List "Member Area".

The majority of ACLs are comprised of these components:

1. Resource Group
2. Resources
3. User Group
4. User Role
5. Users
6. Contexts
7. Media Sources

Create A Resource Group

The Resource side of an ACL is much more straightforward to establish than the User side. Not only are they simple, they are much faster to establish. I could have just as easily started on the User aspect of Groups, but we will be spending more of our time there.

Drag resources into resource groups here.

Step 1: Access the Manager, and click on **Resource Groups** in the Security menu.

Step 2: Click the Create Resource Group button and create a "Private" Group. As mentioned in the last chapter, I would strongly suggest keeping the names as generic as possible.

Create a Resource and add it to the Resource Group

Step 3: Create a New Resource named Personal and add it to the Private Resource Group on the Access Permissions tab.

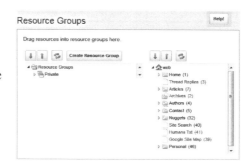

Alternately, drag-and-drop the Personal page to the Private group using the Resource Groups menu found in the Security menu.

Create a User Group

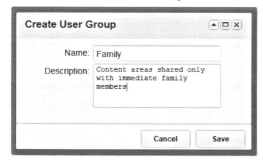

Step 4: Under the same Security Menu used to create a User group, click on Access Controls to get started with a custom group of people.

My goal can be easily translated to a sentence: "I want to give my Family access to the Personal area of the web project containing Private content".

🖛 **WARNING: PRIVACY HAS NOT BEEN ESTABLISHED AT THIS TIME**

At this stage, any document created and assigned to the Private group is still public and viewable to the world at large. Additionally, Users will still be "Anonymous" until Roles have been assigned. I am simply building a foundation to use.

Create the Minimum User Role

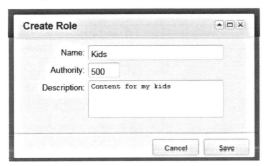

Step 5: Select the Roles tab under Access Controls and create a User Role which will establish the minimum user which will be trusted within the new User Group.

The Minimum Role in my family would be the one held by the kids.

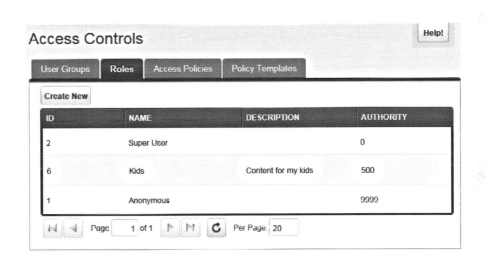

The Super User Role will have "unlimited" power within the User Group

The Kids Role will be the minimum level of trust allowed access to the User Group

The Anonymous Role will not be allowed any access to the User Group whatsoever

Add a Site Administrator to the User Group

Step 6: Once the User Group is created and the screen updates with the newly formed group, simply right-click on the group name to add a Site Administrator to the Group.

Alternately, Site Administrators may find it easier to update their account via the Manage Users area of the Security Menu where they can easily be attached to a User Group and assigned a Role, by utilizing the Access Permissions tab.

Any user can be added or removed from a group.

☞ *Tip: ADDING A SITE ADMINISTRATOR TO A GROUP AFTER LOSING ACCESS*

Site Administrators, can simply use either of the techniques to add themselves to a User Group, at any time: edit their own User Account, or simply edit the User Group and add themselves as a user. At the minimum they may try to "Flush Permission" but may need to log out of the Manager and back in for the changes to take effect.

"In the Family User Group, wshawn will act as a Super User."

If the Resource Group unexpectedly "disappears" from the view of a Site Administrator, start by verifying the correct Role was assigned and the user actually has membership assigned to the group.

MODX Revolution Rule #14: **Site Administrators have to be manually added to groups.**

Add Additional Users

Step 7: Add a user to the Minimum Role. "In The Family User Group, my wife will act as a Kid."

I initially plan to use her account to test the minimum User Role within the group. As new Authority Levels are added, I could slowly increase her Authority to test new permissions, while adding users to take the actual roles which were established for them. In any case, I am intentionally using a trusted user to test accounts.

Assign Minimum Roles to Contexts

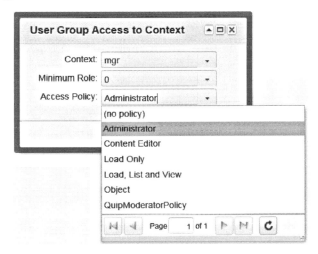

Step 8: Establish the minimum User Role required for Manager Access. Select the Policy which provides sufficient permissions for this User Role.

This process will have to be repeated for each Context being accessed by any given User Role.

If the Manager is the only Context being given as access, then we can stop here.

Step 9: If desired, establish the minimum User role to be given access to the content on the "web" face of the project.

For our purposes we simply want to provide minimal access to users, thereby providing a read-only area.

Note: Quip and other Snippets can be used for the purpose of user feedback, without requiring Manager Access.

Add Resource Access

Step 10: Add the newly created Resource Group to the "mgr" Context and define the Super User Role as the minimum Role able to access these Resources - to begin with.

Note: if a user is a Super User in another Group, they will not have access to these Resources unless they also have sufficient permissions to this User Group via a User Role.

Step 11: Attach the Resource Group to the minimum User Role to be used in the "web" Context.

Note: anyone with an Authority level lower than a User Role of 500 (501 - 9999) will not have access to this content, which can be an effective method to limit unwanted search engine indexing and content pilfering from various Internet bots.

By this time, all of the basic settings, assignments, and definitions should be completed to have a dedicated Read-Only content area. I would suggest any User Group involving the "web" or any front facing Context to begin in this manner: utilize very generic content to ensure security and establish the Minimum User Roles which is to have access. **Double check everything with multiple browsers and sessions.**

These steps can be repeated as many times as necessary to create the foundation of any MODX Revolution User Group. After creating a few of these User Groups, most users can do it from memory with very little outside influence, but there remains a vital step which should never be taken for granted or ignored.

Verify Settings

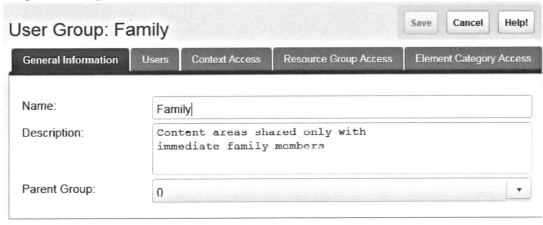

Is the correct User Group Being worked on?

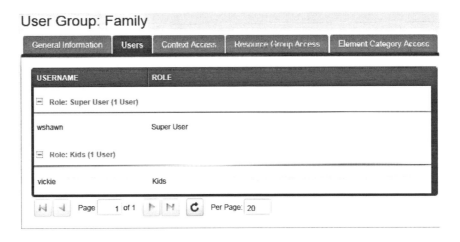

Are the Correct u7sers in the User Group?

Do they have the correct Role assigned?

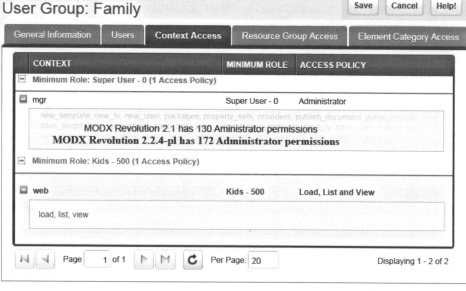

Has the User Group been attached to the necessary Contexts?

Are the minimum Roles appropriate to accomplish project requirements?

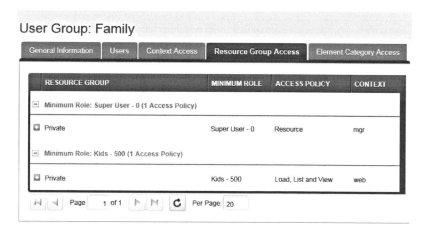

Has the correct Resource Group been assigned to the User Group?

Do the minimum roles reflect the lowest group to have access to the content?

Does the access policy reflect the upper and lower permissions defined in the projects goals?

Is the User Group and its Resources going to be available in the correct Context?

Are there any Element Categories attached to this User Group?

Are they supposed to be? Are any missing?

Are any Media Sources going to be used by this group?

Has the access to a Media Source been restricted to the required location?

Have we limited the access to specific file types? Do we need to?

Have we designated the correct minimum role for Media Source Access?

When Everything is Satisfactory, Click The Save Button.

Hopefully at this point, a fully functional limited-access area has been established. This is the best time to thoroughly test the Minimum Role and ensure access on the "web" and "mgr" Contexts - preferably before any sensitive data or information is displayed on the page. Typically, I will create a page in the designated Resource Group with the text, "This is protected content."

Additionally, I would suggest the use of an alternative web browser to check permissions, than the one utilized to create the Access Control List in the first place. This will help protect against an assumption being made as to the overall successful creation of the ACL due to a Super User administrator's permission accidentally being tested against, rather than the actual Minimum User Role created for the User Group.

Site Administrators may even choose to create user accounts named "Minimum Role", "Tier2", or whatever name they deem necessary to thoroughly establish and test their Access Control List Permissions. Only when Anonymous and underprivileged users are unable to access the protected content should we begin thinking to the next stages. As a final precaution, it is recommended to log all users off of the site.

Force All Users to Log Back Into Site

Click on Flush All Permissions to force all authenticated users, including yourself, to be logged out of the Manager and off of each Context of the site.

Whenever a User Group is established or major changes are implemented, it is typically best to force everyone to log back into the web project to allow all of the affected accounts to receive the new permissions.

If a single user is moved from one role to another, they can be asked to log out and back in. In some instances, it may simply be easier to Flush All Permissions to ensure proper access of each user account- including site administrators.

⊤ *IF A MANAGER USER IS TESTING ACLS AS THEMSELVES*

Using one browser to log into the Manager as a "Site Administrator" and a second web browser to log into the front of the site as the "lowest" User group role may be required, as PHP Sessions carry permissions across web browser tabs.

Testing the Read-Only Implementation

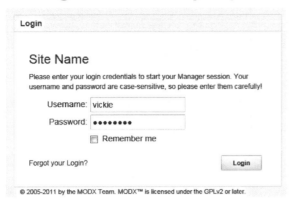

To begin, attempt to log into the Manager via the lowest level User Role in the newly create User Group.

MODX Revolution should allow the user to log in, but Respond with:

Permission denied!
You do not have the proper access policy permissions to view this page. If you feel this is in error, please contact your systems administrator.

If Vickie had previously, been added to another group and given a User Role which provided Manager access, she should have successfully logged in, though nothing would have changed for her, as this current group did not provide her any additional access within the Manager.

To ensure she does have the appropriate access, return to the front of the web site, without logging out, Vickie should now have access to the "Personal Resource" created in Step 3 of the Implementing a "Trusted User" Read-Only Area section of this chapter. Wayfinder should present a link to the Resource, hidden from lesser User Roles, if it was configured to do so.

Once access has been verified, we will want to ensure no one below her Authority Level shares the same access. Using the browsers back button, return to the "Permission denied" page and proceed to logout by clicking on the "Log Out" button.

After being returned to the Manager login screen, simply visit the front of the site and verify the absence of any Protected content. If the Protected content is still visible, make sure the current user is indeed logged out and try again. You may also want to try another web browser, a new browser tab may not work.

Using an account with a User Role in the new User group with Manager access, log into the Manager and verify it has access to the Personal Resource. Next ensure, the account has the ability to edit the Resource and add child Resources under the Personal container. **Note: each may have to be added to the "Private" Resource Group.**

For those who are experiencing difficulties, I would suggest checking the Wayfinder Snippet call to make sure it is, indeed an uncached call. I would also try clearing the site cache and Flushing Permissions again. If these still do not correct the issue, recheck each of the associated settings, especially where minimum User Roles are concerned. Lastly, ensure the Resource was Published and not hidden from Menus. If everything is working as expected, you should have a fully functional Read-Only trusted user area. Congratulations.

Extending the User Group

Many projects will have multiple users responsible for work with site content. The issue many clients may have with this very beneficial situation, is the idea of people being given a User Role with the name of "Super User". Clients may not feel very comfortable with anyone on the site with a Role which remotely infers they have supreme authority, even if it is limited to a specific User Group.

Clients may go to great lengths to ensure the ability for multiple bloggers to work from a single site, but restrict those users to only their areas. In keeping with that design concept, I am going to add some additional roles to provide additional functionality for specific users.

Add New User Roles to the Project

Super User: User Group Admin

Private: For the creation of content without releasing it before it is ready

Spouse: Content for my wife and I

Kids: Preexisting Minimum Trusted Role

Site Members: "Anonymous" users who will be allowed to "comment" and utilize future additional functions

Anonymous: Search Engines and typical unprivileged users

ᵮ Tɪᴘ: Uᴘᴅᴀᴛᴇ ᴀ Usᴇʀ Gʀᴏᴜᴘꜱ ʙʏ ꜱɪᴍᴘʟʏ ᴍᴏᴠɪɴɢ ᴛʜʀᴏᴜɢʜ ᴛʜᴇ ᴛᴀʙꜱ ɪɴ ᴏʀᴅᴇʀ

I have found the simplest means of updating a User Group, is to move from the first tab, through each tab, concluding with the fifth. By working through these tabs in order, required settings will be established before they are requested on later tabs. For English speaking languages, this process proceeds left to right.

Place Users Within The Newly Created Roles

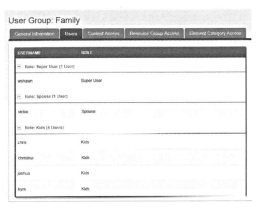

Once the new User Roles have been added to the MODX Revolution web project, it becomes a simple matter of updating the User Group and assigning those roles to users.

As the "Kids" User Group was previously "tested" to work for "Read-Only" access, I went ahead and added our kids to the group.

Additionally, I moved "vickie" to the higher, and increased trusted Authority Level of Spouse.

Adjust the minimum User Role for Manager Access

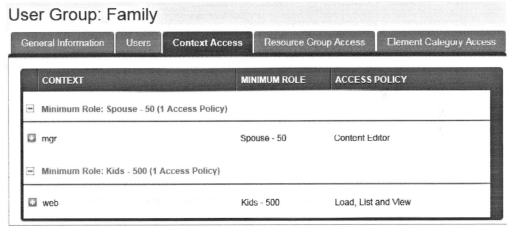

In order to allow "vickie" to log into the Manager and be able to work with Resources, we must make a few changes to the Context Access. To begin with, the minimum role being allowed access to the Manager, will need to be reduced from "Super User" to "Spouse".

The "Spouse" User Role requires specific content editing capabilities, which are provided by attaching the Content Editor Access Policy. An additional benefit of using this Access Policy, is clients can relax when Site Administrators are giving out Access Policies with 24 permissions, instead of the approximately 172 available to site Super Users.

Adjust the minimum User Role to access Resources

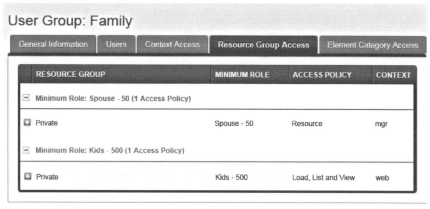

In the Context Access tab, the Spouse role was given the ability to interact with Resources in the Manager, but we need to allow the role access to the Resource Groups assigned to this specific User Group. To provide the "Spouse" with access to the Family Resources, the minimum role needs to be reduced to the appropriate Authority Level.

Access on the front end, does not require any changes, as the requirements on the front end have not changed from being "Read-Only" to the "Kids" at trust level 500. In those situations where feedback or other types of input is required - Quip, Formit or other MODX Revolution Snippets can provide an additional layer of interaction from the lowest Role in the Resource Group to those with users with greater trust levels.

Add Associated Element Categories

This tab may actually be optional for many User Groups. In the event, a Resource Group assigned to a User Group has dedicated Elements involved, a Category can be utilized to provide specific access to Elements to the User Group. In this group, there is a possibility of additional areas or blog categories being added to a site. Providing access to the Chunks which implement the various Wayfinder and site navigation can quickly increase the production of those areas.

Attach a Dashboard to the User Group

The ability to customize user login landing pages was introduced in MODX Revolution 2.2 allowing Widgets to be created to present predetermined information to a specific group or groups of users on the web project. Essentially, Dashboards provide the means to immerse Manager users into their tasks by presenting information which is catered to their specific task and area of operation. They can also be used for a variety of other purposes, such as a constant reminder of current projects or organizational goals.

For all of their potential, I believe Dashboards to be in their infancy and hope to eventually see the ability to group them within a "container" and assign Minimum Role values so as to further target User Roles within each specific User Group. It will prove interesting to see the directions taken by the MODX developers with this innovative user interface in the future.

Currently, it is best to keep these implementations simple and very straightforward as Widget output will need to be formatted as it will appear on the screen. As of MODX Revolution 2.2.4-pl, I attempted to use user-defined Placeholders, Element Filters and other MODX Revolution features and found them to not work as I would like. This is as I expected it to turn out, as Manager pages are not currently processed like the Resources which appear on the front of the site. In fact, I do not believe their may ever be treated like actual web pages.

Additionally, it appears any Widget not returning content will simply be discarded from the presentation - including the Widget header. I would strongly suggest the thorough testing of each Widget in its native format, perhaps on a normal page *before* utilizing it in a Dashboard. It may also be advisable to create a Test Dashboard for the purpose of implementing Layout and verifying Widget content.

Creating a new Dashboard

♦ Log into the Manager

♦ Hover over the Dashboard menu

♦ Select Dashboards from the dropdown

♦ Click on the Create Dashboard Button

♦ Provide a name and definitive description

♦ If applicable add available Widgets

♦ Click Save

In the current implementation, MODX Revolution Dashboards are very straightforward to create and attach to User Groups. Widgets on the other hand, may initially tend to be problematic if developers lose sight of the purpose of the Dashboard: to serve as a foundation to create customized Manger user interfaces and to provide information.

Creating Dashboard Widgets

Site administrators seldom wear the "developer" hat, so I will be presenting simple Widgets which should be easily implemented - hopefully with little regard to their programming prowess. Developers, on the other hand, should be able to completely change the Dashboard in a myriad of ways. Currently there are four types of Widgets which can be used to *provide formatted output* to populate a Manager user Dashboard:

File

Listing 14:01 File Widget - can be of any type delivered by the web server

```
<h2>Top Secret - Eyes Only</h2>
<p>Please take the following steps to protect out client: </p>
<ul>
    <li>Do not access this project outside of our facilities.</li>
    <li>Utilize only approved channels of communication.</li>
    <li>Follow Physical Security SOP
        <ul>
            <li>Limit Access to physical room housing computer</li>
            <li>Do not store access passwords on computer</li>
            <li>Clear browser cache on computer shutdown</li>
            <li>Have an auto desktop lock feature set to one minute</li>
            <li>Keep abreast of security memorandums</li>
            <li>Verify and identify the daily password</li>
        </ul>
    </li>
</ul>
```

HTML

Widget: widgetHTML

General Information | Dashboards | Save | Close | Help!

Name
widgetHTML

Description
Provides a sample HTML Widget

Widget Type
HTML

Size
Half

Namespace
core

Lexicon
core:dashboards

Widget Content
```
<h2>Scheduled Events</h2>
<p>2012 Oct 01 Field testing of experimental hardware<br>
2012 Oct 02 Debriefing of field testing with emphasis on <span style="color:green">pass</span> / <span style="color:red">fail</span> scenarios<br>
2012 Oct 03 Designate teams to resolve <span style="color:red">fails</span><br>
2012 Oct 08 Retest all <span style="color:green">pass</span> criteria for validation<br>
2012 Oct 09 Begin field testing of all <span style="color:red">fails</span> for recertification.</p>
```

Listing 14.02 HTML Widget - Can contain most any (X)HTML syntax

---

```
<h2>Scheduled Events</h2>
<p>2012 Oct 01 Field testing of experimental hardware<br>
2012 Oct 02 Debriefing of field testing with emphasis on <span
style="color:green">pass</span> / <span style="color:red">fail</span> scenarios<br>
2012 Oct 03 Designate teams to resolve <span style="color:red">fails</span><br>
2012 Oct 08 Retest all <span style="color:green">pass</span> criteria for validation<br>
2012 Oct 09 Begin field testing of all <span style="color:red">fails</span> for
recertification.</p>
```

File Widgets are not necessarily going to be HTML, if they were exclusively intended to be HTML files it would be redundant to also have a Widget dedicated to the type. In this implementation, I thought it beneficial to place the HTML on the file system which could be placed outside of the "reach" of Manager users and also shared as a Chunk on the front facing web project.

I opted to place "dynamic" content in the Manager, as it would require occasional updates, probably by a project leader or site administrator. These could have been task switched, with the File Widget being a PHP File returning the hard-coded schedule of events seen in Listing 14.02 and the Standard Operating Procedure being a simple HTML Widget as seen in Listing 14.01.

Inline PHP

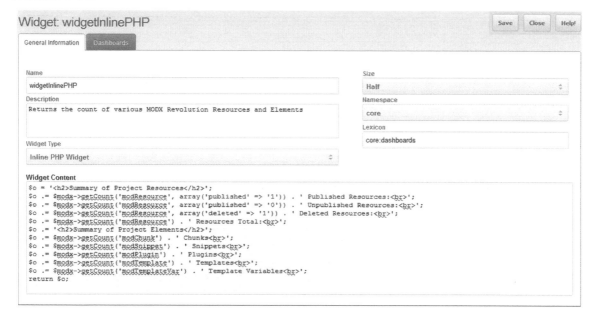

Snippets

Inline PHP and Snippet Widgets utilize PHP code to provide the ability of presenting real dynamic content to Manager users, though their output must be pre-formatted for display. The official documentation also examples on how to utilize a File Widget to extend the dashboard class and thereby create elaborate Dashboards utilizing xPDO and MODX objects.

Change the User Group's Dashboard

Once a Dashboard is ready for use, simply return to any User Groups which will be using it, and change their Dashboard to the modified implementation. This process can be repeated as often as necessary, depending on the needs of the project. In this situation I opted to change th Administrators group with site content, rather than the default MODX RSS feeds and other preinstalled Dashboard Widgets - though they could also be utilized at any time.

Example Modified Dashboard

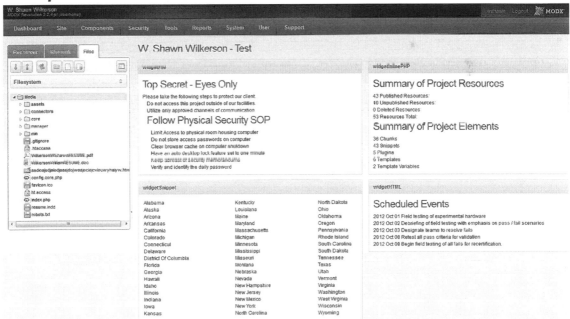

Targeted Application

MODX Revolution has one of the most effective CMS User APIs I have ever seen. If an implementation requires functionality not directly supplied by the predefined Access Policies, simply edit one and create one that does. Additionally, the User Accounts themselves can easily be enhanced by using the additional Extended fields available in each user account, or by programmatically extending the user class via PHP.

The simple act of allowing site visitors to log into some aspect of the site, may seem trivial or even mechanical to some Site Administrators, but a drop of perspiration and a dash of imagination can create very interesting applications:

- ◆ Shaun McCormick introduced a method to combine MODX Revolution with a Domain Controller

- ◆ Jason Coward and others have demonstrated and/or released Packages to allow visitors to log into a MODX Revolution web site using Facebook, Twitter and other Social Networking accounts

- ◆ I have created the framework of a social networking system which is directly attached to geographical data

Assume a web project has multiple login mechanisms. Now if someone were to conceptualize the possibility of targeting the site content to the type of login used, the beginning of a very innovative web presence could be implemented. Facebook users could be greeted with content implementing the Facebook API, and styled after the method utilized by the service to provide their content. This could provide a "clean" transition from the social networking giant to the client site which gently transitons the visitor and allows the content to presented to be directly targeted and formatted based on the service they arrive from.

The same site could have a "business" Context accessed via a Domain Controller providing them content consisting of news, announcements, and functionality directly related to the daily operations of the client. Additionally, department only sites could be implemented.

Potentially greater benefit could be achieved, by placing pieces of these Contexts on the "main" site so as to present visitors with the various components of Social Networking sites used by hundreds of millions or even billions of users around the globe. This becomes even more relevant when we consider many of these APIs are bidirectional: the web project could also be placing content as Tweets, Wall Posts, or some other user notification mechanism and thereby create the foundation of a very effective and targeted marketing campaign - at relatively little cost beyond initial development.

It is also completely feasible to create varying levels of access via Media Sources where User Group Administrators have full access to a specified directory tree, whereas others may only see specific types of files in a folder. Each of these User Groups could also have Snippets, or other Widgets placed into a dedicated Dashboard - such as hit counters, or other relevant information.

Summary

Implementing User Accounts and associated Access Control Lists utilizing MODX Revolution, can be pretty straight forward, not to mention lucrative. Outside of some very small web projects, the vast majority of my clients prefer to have some form of control on who can see sections of content on their sites.

Other clients would like to be able to give selected employees the ability to perform updates on the site without, providing them access to PHP Snippets, scripts, or sensitive customer information. By following the procedures presented in this chapter, clients can be empowered to handle the daily updates to their sites, without feeling as if they are forced to rely on an outside "expert" to get simple changes made.

I have also found clients to be much more involved in the production of the site, if they know they will actually be using it. This translates to higher customer satisfaction, but more importantly a greater respect, appreciation, and understanding of Site Administrators and developers.

The key to establishing a successful Access Control List, is to be able to clearly translate the needs of the client into Roles and subsequently communicate those to the Users who are tasked with performing the required tasks. Much of this communication, should be self-evident when the User accesses the Manager and only "sees" what "they" are given to do.

I chose to use the simplest structure known to man and recognizable to the majority of us to illustrate the thought process behind Access Control Lists, namely a family. I could have used more business-like terminology, but my experience has shown that the simple term of "manager" can prove ambiguous - even within the confines of a single company.

As demonstrated in *An Overview of Grouping: Category, User and Resource*, the following could have just as easily been the case:

♦ 0 Administrator (CTO?)	♦ 0 Super Administrator
♦ 5 Executives	♦ 5 Me Only
♦ 50 Managers	♦ 50 Spouse
♦ 500 Team Leaders	♦ 500 Kids
♦ 5000 Team Members	♦ 5000 Site Member
♦ 9999 Anonymous	♦ 9999 Anonymous

The names are irrelevant, and are there for Site Administrators to define which group is being referred to. MODX Revolution focuses on the Authority Levels - not the names. For those wanting a more "business related" implementation, simply update the User Group and User Roles and change the names and descriptions..

15
Contexts: Implementing Sites with Multiple Faces

When last in the Smoky mountains taking thousands of pictures, as I am apt to do, I noticed how the locals seemed to take their beautiful environment and lifestyle for granted. Then I reflected on how we do the same in Daytona Beach, Florida, where we typically avoid racing events, bike weeks, spring break, and even seem to forget about our 23 miles of beaches.

Occasionally, my wife and I will go down to the beach during the early evenings and walk through the white sands. It usually doesn't take long before someone mentions the pleasant texture or the warm temperature of the ground beneath our feet. Eventually, we have to travel home to the house which we have slowly been remodeling for years to have the relaxed atmosphere of a mountain cabin. As we step inside, the hard wood floors reflect the place our hearts really yearn for: the mountains of Tennessee and the simple life associated with them.

From the outside, a context can be a new and awe inspiring thing, but on the inside it can simply become "business as usual". Many of us never really take time to understand the context of something until it becomes contaminated or we leave the environment we are in.

One of the most disruptive sensations, which can crash through any of us, is to expect one experience while another intrudes into the sanctity of the moment. Sand is the last thing we want to feel beneath our feet on our beautiful wooden floors. At the beach, walking on broken glass or discarded trash disrupts the mood, as do the increasing number of cell towers in the Smokys.

MODX Revolution provides a very power ally to facilitate all aspects of any context required for web projects. Completely isolating them from one another, while allowing crossover only where it is desired. For site administrators, Contexts really can be everything - and more.

Laying a Foundation

The first consideration for many site administrators concerning Contexts, is to discern their viability on their project. For many web projects, the two provided by MODX Revolution are all that is needed: web and mgr. For others who are considering using Contexts for the first time, a new set of concepts may need to be considered.

When asked to help someone understand why Contexts are actually used in a web project, the simplest answer I can offer is to focus on potential site visitors and Manager users and think through where they are going on the site and why they are doing it. For simple web projects, this is easy: Manager users create content and visitors simply view it. Increasingly complex sites may require more definition and even very broad sections to be established.

For example, let us consider the Smoky Mountains of Tennessee. In all the years I have been going there, I have never seen a surfboard loaded on top or a car. I also do not recall seeing snow shoes and parkas on the beaches of Daytona Beach, FL. People traveling to these environments have completely different needs, resources, and expectations. Essentially, site administrators may find themselves creating "virtual" environments for people to experience content which directly addresses these same issues.

MODX Revolution Contexts are very similar to the mind sets associated with going on vacation or showing up for work: there is a location being visited for a specific purpose. Outside of this focus, it is typically understood there are peripheral and secondary considerations: gas stations, stores, restaurants, etc.

Contexts can be completely isolated from the rest of the project, similar to isolated islands in the middle of ocean, with limited or no outside influences. They can also implement methods to utilize the same Elements across each of the Contexts within the web project.

Once a purpose has been defined for Contexts within the web project, the next topic to decide is who will be given access and if they will be needing "trusted" levels of access. For this reason, it is assumed the topic of MODX Revolution Access Control Lists is understood by the reader, as discussed in the last chapter.

During this chapter I will be presenting:

- ♦ practical applications concerning Contexts based on real world needs
- ♦ implementations which adhere to MODX Revolution "rules"
- ♦ solutions not requiring any of the core files to be edited
- ♦ adherence to MODX coding expectations
- ♦ simple straightforward examples

Possible Malfunctions

There are many issues which can arise in Contexts. For example, many of the people having trouble with multi-domain name Contexts in MODX Revolution simply do not understand there are perquisite steps to be followed. Without these steps being completed, it would be impossible to succeed at having Revo "catch" the domain name - as it will never get to the server.

While some of these steps may require server configuration, System Administrators may also implement direct functionality with the domain registrar or in various software processes running on a typical web server. In either case similar issues could arise:

- Typographical errors are a major culprit. IP Addresses, domain names, and the name servers all have to be exactly correct on the web server and the domain name registrar
- By automatically adding a domain name "renewal service" as part of your package, it will avoid very bad impressions if the name "expires' at the beginning of a project
- The client's ISP updates their name servers, only daily or weekly causing additional time to be added, making clients very unhappy - especially when their clients can see the project, while your client, the project owner, can't
- Be aware if e-mail or telephonic authorization is required for any updates to the domain name, causing potential confusion or unproductive development time
- Untested server configurations can cause issues, when the server or software is restarted
- The last web master may still have access to the domain in the registrar - which may prove to be problematic if they decide to use this access to reverse any changes made
- The domain was not added to the web server or parked on a preexisting domain

Simple Precautions

The vast majority of these mistakes can be avoided altogether, with a few simple steps enacted as the first steps of the project work flow. The following relates a summary of these and is offered for your consideration:

- Be patient - the process relies on systems not in your control
- Handle all domain name transactions with as few people as possible
- Establish all of the correct account settings in a single setting / sitting
- Preexisting domains should be visited to verify the spelling and ownership
- Cut and paste the domain name from the registrar or the operational site
- Cut and paste the name servers, even for simple ones like ours: ns1.sanityllc.com
- Make sure the main domain is correctly functional at the appropriate location

Understanding Context and User Group Differences

When a site administrator first considers implementing Contexts or User Groups, many of them seem to have an issue discerning the underlying reason each is typically used. Subsequently, many requests for help end up having to describe the purpose before any real aide can be offered. The following real world examples should help clarify their specific roles in a project.

Goal	Simplest Solution
Create a protected area	User Group
Create multiple faces of a single site, with users having transparent access to all content	User Groups and / or subdomains via Contexts
Create multiple faces of a site, so the public views one aspect of the site, while authenticated users essentially have the site replaced with an entire new site	User groups landing in a container to house the member area is suggested. Context also a viable solution.
"Host" multiple client projects	Individual Contexts
Create a two "face" project. The public face will have unprotected content and authenticated user enhanced functionality.	A User Group attached to the "web" Context or simply checking if they are logged in.
The private face demands all users to belong to a Primary User Group, while each of those groups will have varying levels of capability and even Sub-User Groups based on department or other company policy	Individual Contexts with dedicated User Groups

Contexts tend to cater to the needs of the project and its respective client and may be considered an entry port to access sensitive information or dedicated applications utilized in the daily operations of a specific company. Typically, users are not the primary purpose of a Context.

User Groups tend to center around a specific set of people, which have been placed into a collection around a given purpose. The primary purpose of a User Group, is to define a structure of people within the site and is essentially user centric as it deals with their collective function.

Implementing a Context where a User Group will suffice, may greatly increase the complexity involved in the project. Likewise, a User Group will not easily facilitate a completely different face being provided to the employees of a given company, when the client needs to have a full functional "portal" for their employees. Discerning whether the main purpose is satisfying a client need or placing users is key to success.

Often Contexts are established around a need, and User Groups are implemented within them.

Creating a New Context

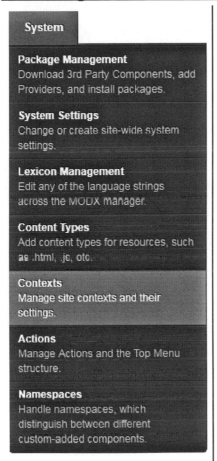

1. On a clean Revo install, it is possible to duplicate the "web" Context and skip to Step 5

2. Alternately utilize the System menu to access the Contexts configuration area

3. Create a new Context, using a definitive name

4. Right-click on the new Context and create a new "Home" Resource. If necessary, refresh the screen to view the new Context. Alternately, a Resource from the "web" Context "Home" can be duplicated and dragged into place.

5. Right-click the new Context in the Resource Tree and select Edit.

6. Override a few of the default System Settings, by creating localized Context Settings using the same keys:

Make sure the new settings are actually stored in the database, by selecting the Save button. These are all the settings required to move forward. Additional settings can be added if necessary, and might even be suggested for Context-wide "variables" which can be utilized throughout a client's page's, such as their contact information.

Another thought to consider, if a project is going to "host" multiple web sites, a skeleton Context can be used as a "template" subsequently duplicated for each domain which will be served by the installation of MODX Revolution. Similar to Elements, Contexts can be duplicated, which copies the settings, which will need to be updated, as well as the Resources into the new version.

With a little forethought and planning, additional small sites can be implemented quickly and efficiently, as we shall see in the next section.

Implementing a Context "Skeleton"

Before delving very far into creating a bunch of Contexts, it might be wise to create the basis for any additional web sites or other implementations *before* they are actually created. The following steps should quickly provide a nice site skeleton:

1. Duplicate any functioning Context, to use as a "Context Template" - preferably a clean "web" Context, as the Resources can also be duplicated in their published state
2. Right-click and edit the "skeleton" Context
3. Remove all values from user-created Context Keys, excluding the default Context
4. Create additional keys as needed, some multi domain name values are shown below
5. Save The Context
6. Create any additional Resources to be subsequently used on new web projects
7. Edit associated MODX Revolution Elements to use the Context Keys, as necessary

Example Site Skeleton Components

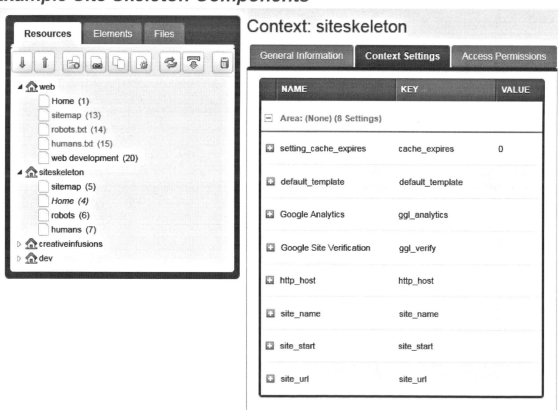

Listing 15.01: Sample Site Template Using Context Variables:

```
<?xml version="1.0" encoding="UTF-8" ?>
<!DOCTYPE html PUBLIC "-//W3C//DTD XHTML 1.0 Strict//EN" "http://
www.w3.org/TR/xhtml1/DTD/xhtml1-strict.dtd">
<html xmlns="http://www.w3.org/1999/xhtml">
[[injectJSLinksToBottom?src=`[[$jQuery]],[[$jQueryTools]]`]]
<head>
    [[$siteHeader:strip]] <link type="text/css" rel="stylesheet"
href="assets/[[getContextName]]/site.css"/>
</head>
<body>
<div id="header">
    <div class="fltRight">[[$globalNav:strip]]</div>
</div>
<div id="container">
    <div id="mainContent">
        [[*content]]
    </div>
    <div id="rightMenu">
        [[$rightmenu:strip]]
    </div>
    <br class="clearfloat"/>
    <div id="footer">
        [[$siteFooter:strip]]
    </div>
</div>
</body>
</html>
```

Using `[[getContextName]]` allows Context specific CSS insertions, etc.

Listing 15.02: getContextName Snippet

```
<?php
return $modx->context->key;
```

A simple Snippet to obtain the current Context Name, which can be used in paths and file names. The output could also be sent to Placeholders via the *toPlaceholder* filter or changing the code.

Listing 15.03 Establish Global Top Navigation for each Context

----

```
<div id="mainnav">
    [[Wayfinder?startId=`[[+site_start]]`
                &level=`1`
                &sortBy=`menuindex`
                &rowTpl=`wfNavBar`]]
</div>
```

Each Context uses the `[[+site_start]]` setting to target the Wayfinder Snippet.

Listing 15.04 Establish a generic cross-Context Site Footers

```
<div id="cpyrght">
    &copy;[[*publishedon:empty=`[[*createdon]]`:strtotime:date=`%Y`]]
[[++copyright_name]]. All Rights Reserved.
</div>
<div id="siteDesign">
    Site design and development by [[++designedBy]]
</div>
```

Uses the `publishedon` or the `createdon` date to establish copyright date, and utilizes a `[[++designedBy]]` System Setting to link to my company from any Contexts on which it appears. Alternately, footers can be named `contextNameFooter` and retrieved using the `[[getContextName]]` Snippet: `[[$[[!getContextName]]Footer]]`.

Global Site Header

Each of the lines in the site header containing the meta tags, page title, etc., could have associated Context Settings which would then simply complete the value. For small web sites, each Resource's [[*introtext]] field could be used for the keywords and its [[*description]] field for the meta description, as well as Auto Tag Template Variables.

The navigation, footers, and headers could just as easily be placed in the Template itself. I simply choose to have as few Elements as possible, while providing a large amount of options to the clients. The main point here, is to simply show the various components utilized across all of the domain Contexts in a single MODX Revolution installation.

Utilizing the Site Skeleton Context

A good portion of future Contexts can easily be completed, by simply right-clicking on the siteskeleton Context and selecting Duplicate. An exact copy of all the skeleton's Resources and Context Settings can be placed neatly in the newly created Context. MODX Revolution may also provide each of the Resources in an Unpublished state. By design I have chosen to call many of the Elements cached due to the static nature of the majority of our smaller sites.

Additionally, a "To-do" list can be placed on the "Home" page of the Skeleton Context to remind Manager Users of the actual process required for each new project, as new web sites are brought online. For my company, it would simply consist of:

♦ Determine the Template to be used on the site

♦ Duplicate the Skeleton Context

♦ Obtain appropriate web provider accounts: Google Analytics, etc. (may require domain name to already be functional on the server for e-mail access)

♦ Configure the new web site, by updating the Context and supplying the correct values in the Context Settings tab

♦ Edit the domainGateway Plugin, discussed next, to reflect the new domain name

♦ Point/park the Domain Name in the server configuration

♦ Move the Domain Name at the registrars.

Typically, each of these steps can be completed in under ten minutes, including the Resources being Published and the Search Engine Optimization files configured and functional. Any significant "downtime" is usually associated with the time the domain name takes to propagate. To ensure a smooth introduction of the new web site, I will usually have a single person perform all of these tasks or directly supervise their completion. Using this process and the associated Components, site development can be greatly reduced to hours instead of days.

Due to the new web site being hosted on a fully functional primary domain name, much of the site can be built before the domain name even fully propagates. It is even possible to discuss page structure with clients, allowing them to select the basic layout of their web site utilizing previously tested MODX Revolution Element implementations. Once a Template has been selected it can be set as the default_template for the Context, saving even more development time.

In situations where a number of small clients are housed within a single MODX Revolution installation, the cache_expires setting can be extended upwards to a week (604800), a month (2592000), or even longer. The default setting of 0, allows the cache to utilize built-in settings of 1 hour (3600). Any of these will greatly reduce the load on the server.

Take a few moments to look through the default System Settings and implement them as needed.

Prerequisites For Domain Name Specific Contexts

Typical "web companies" tend to have quite a few clients which have simple 8 page, or less, web sites. The construction of those sites for a number of these clients, subsequently requires repetitive uploading of the same "home grown" Snippets and Chunks, as well as the basic set of Packages installed by the MODX Revolution Package Management. The insistent nature of this "work model" can simply be reflected as higher development cost and reduced efficiency.

In some situations, clients may actually have multiple domain names attached to a given project, and would like to be able to target site visitors to a specific "face" of their given company. This technique could facilitate media blitz campaigns or the use of product centric domains to directly focus attention of site visitors. Eventually, many of these types of web projects, inadvertently result in redundant data and the associated man hours to create it.

Contexts allow each of these situations to be addressed with a single installation of MODX Revolution, as various Elements can be shared across the entire installation reducing the need for redundant work flow. It also allows, data to be shared across web sites. The key here is simply getting all of the domain names to point to the same installation of MODX Revolution.

The majority of articles I have read concerning this implementation, typically do not mention the prerequisites necessary to successfully operate multiple domains from a single installation of MODX Revolution. The basic steps are introduced here, but the actual methodology will probably vary depending on the registrar and hosting environment.

Domain Name Considerations

Before any domain-specific Context can be implemented, the actual domain must be "pointed" to the MODX Revolution installation. Typically, this is a very straight-forward process, requiring an authenticated user to log into a domain name Registrar's site and make changes. The process usually flows as follows:

1. Either purchase the domain, or coordinate with the client to make changes
2. Point the primary domain to the project's name servers
3. Wait for the domain name to propagate (can take from a few minutes to 48 hours)
4. Test the primary domain name and install MODX Revolution, if necessary
5. Point any additional domains to the same Name Servers
6. Wait for propagation

Set Nameservers

Nameserver 1: *	Nameserver 2: *	Nameserver 3:	Nameserver 4:
NS1.SANITYLLC.COM	NS2.SANITYLLC.COM		

OK   Cancel

Hosting Considerations

We typically create the client's account on our servers during the propagation phase. Companies fortunate enough to have System Administrators on staff, can simply provide the list of domains and the requirement to point them all to the same hosted space on the server.

On Linux based servers, this could take a few seconds, as many administrators have Bash shell scripts, which automates this process for them. Typically, a minimum of three configurations will need to be edited: hosting, binding the name to the server, and local dns attaching the domain name back to the parent dns servers. Firewall and other security based configurations may also be necessary. As individual hosting environments tend to be very specific, I will leave the actual details to the specific administrator.

As many web hosting providers offer their clients control panels, they will typically have a similar interface for their own domains. In the case of MODX Revolution, this places web hosting providers in an interesting position. My company has 7 domains with quite a few sub domains.

This offers me multiple choices:

1. Install MODX Revolution on each domain
2. Place all of my company domains on one installation of MODX Revolution, allowing me to share data and reduce development time
3. Separate my domains and use them to "host" the small web projects, where clients do not want a control panel or access to anything on their site, other than e-mail
4. Dedicate one, or more of my domains to "host" these tiny sites on separate servers, while leaving the rest on a single MODX installation
5. Purchase a "do nothing" domain and install Revo there, adding each client as necessary
6. Host sites according to contract terms and longevity; in other words - it would be possible to have a 10-year hosting contract and use that domain as primary

Many of these choices will be answered by the server configuration, before MODX Revolution is ever installed. Others will be answered by policy, as some hosting providers simply do not allow these activities. There is also the potential for bandwidth abuse, which can cause multiple sites to be shut down, thereby upsetting many clients, but this can easily avoided by those responsible to build the site in the first place.

On shared hosting, which utilizes cPanel or some other control panel, it is typically an issue of simply adding a parked domain to the site. This can be done at any time, but should typically be done before the initial propagation occurs, so as to not cache an "unavailable" response in any, or all, of the 13 global name servers.

Configuring Domain Names on Shared Hosts

To begin, I create a cPanel account utilizing my company's primary domain name: www. sanityllc.com. I next utilize the "Parked Domains" utility to point the alternate domain name to the same web site and document root.

I have recently started a Limited Liability Company, and have decided to keep my old domain name active for the next two years. By adding www.creativeinfusions.net as a "Parked Domain", both sites will land on the same document root, and thereby will be able to utilize the same MODX Revolution installation.

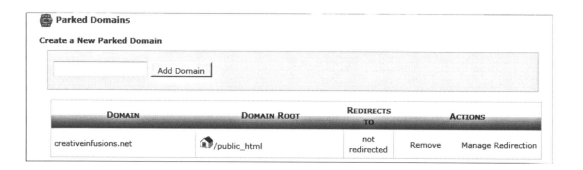

Additional names can be added at any time, and should typically be tested to correctly land on the front of the "web" Context, until site administrators find themselves comfortable with this process. Caution should be considered at this point, as many clients will have already been "spreading" the world concerning their new web project, it could lead to some awkward situations if the domain is perceived to have been pointed to another site - even temporarily.

In my particular situation, I usually see domain names propagate in fifteen minutes and almost always under one hour. This is far from normal. Our server is located in Texas and sits on the same backbone as our local internet provider, so we only have to wait for our ISP's internal name servers to update, before we can directly access the site to begin development.

The client is told to start looking 48 hours from the time the project begins, as that is typically the maximum amount of time the process should take. Internally, we handle the changes to the name servers and know we have to be ready to catch requests for it, almost immediately.

In essence, we typically do not point the name servers to our dns system until we are ready to catch the requests. In our workflow, we simply consider this the first step of the development process, once the client has approved the project, the appropriate contracts have been signed, and initial payment received.

Hosting Many Web Sites

Once the primary domain is pointed to the server correctly, MODX Revolution should be installed and "normal" begin-stage operations performed. Each developer will typically have their own methods for getting a server "ready" to begin. Note: cPanel utilizes cpanel3-skel, which is located in the primary account - just above the site root, allowing MODX Revolution to be pre loaded on new accounts, reducing ftp time for each new site added to the server space.

For my company this process begins with

- ◆ Insertion of basic in-house Elements, manually, via Packman or Database query
- ◆ Installation of the following MODX Revolution Packages: Wayfinder, Login, Getresources, Google Site Map, ObfuscateEmail-Revo
- ◆ Creation or Insertion of a Template

At this point, any domain names aliased, parked, or pointed to this document root, should all show the same page and have access to each of the site components. The first steps should be those which will be utilized through all of the contexts, such as the use of Friendly URLs , discussed in the Streamlining Web Projects aka: SEO, FURLs, and Minify chapter.

.htaccess Multi-domain Modifications

The .htaccess example file provided with MODX Revolution, is typically utilized for a single domain. The following changes force all incoming URL requests to their fully represented www. domain.tld form, regardless of which domain name is being received. These changes will need to be made to the .htaccess file to ensure correct operation across each of the domain names. Also, note the necessary Friendly URL declarations remain identical to those of a single domain.

Listing 15.05: muti-domain .htaccess file

```
# Force all requests to go to www.domain.com and not domain.com
#RewriteCond %{HTTP_HOST} .
RewriteCond %{HTTP_HOST} !^www\.
RewriteRule ^(.*)$ http://www.%{HTTP_HOST}/$1 [R=301,L]

# The Friendly URLs part
RewriteCond %{REQUEST_FILENAME} !-f
RewriteCond %{REQUEST_FILENAME} !-d
RewriteRule ^(.*)$ index.php?q=$1 [L,QSA]
```

robots.txt and humans.txt Considerations

Typically the robots and humans files are left as actual files on the site, and can remain as such for the primary domain utilizing the "web" context. They can also be made into MODX Revolution Resources, with a type of "text" and saved in the Manager as part of each domain, and can be "published" and "hidden from menus" to perform identically to their file based counter parts.

Listing 15.06: robots.txt content for a MODX Revolution Resource / Chunk

```
# Default modx exclusions
User-agent: *
Disallow: /assets/
Disallow: /core/
Disallow: /manager/
Disallow: /min/
Disallow: /setup/

# For sitemaps.xml autodiscovery.
Sitemap: [[++site_url]]sitemap.xml
```

Listing 15.07: humans.txt content for a MODX Revolution Resource / Chunk

```
/* TEAM */
    Chef: W. Shawn Wilkerson
    Contact: shawn REMOVE-AT-THIS sanityllc.com
    Twitter: @shawnwilkerson
    From: Daytona Beach, FL (United States)
    Photographer: W. Shawn Wilkerson
    PHP Programming: W. Shawn Wilkerson
    Standard Man: W. Shawn Wilkerson
    UI developer: W. Shawn Wilkerson
    Web designer: W. Shawn Wilkerson

/* SITE */
    Last update: [[!getResources?tpl=`humanstxt`&parents=`[[++site_st
art]]`&limit=`1`&depth=`20`&showHidden=`0`&hideContainers=`1`]]
    Language:English
```

Create or Duplicate a New Context

Once we have a new Context, and are ready to move forward, make note of the name for the final steps - I typically match the Context name to the incoming HTTP_HOST, Additionally, ensure the minimum Context settings: `http_host`, `site_start`, and `site_url` are correct for the Context.

Activating The New Context

Create a new Plugin and attach it to the OnHandleRequest system event. Once the Plugin is saved, Clear the Site Cache and Flush all Sessions to make sure the new Context is available to all users, as the Minimum Role is set to 9999 / Anonymous.

> *Listing 15.08: domainGateway Plugin*

```php
<?php
switch ($modx->getOption('http_host')) {
    /*
     * Uncomment any of the following lines
     * if the server configuration requires it
     */

    // case 'creativeinfusions.net:443':
    // case 'creativeinfusions.net:80':
    // case 'creativeinfusions.net':
    case 'www.creativeinfusions.net':
        $modx->switchContext('creativeinfusions');
        break;
    default:
        // MODX will load the "web" context automatically
        break;
}
```

🖅 **WARNING: RESOURCE TREES MAY DISAPPEAR ON NEXT LOGIN**

If the next Loging into Manager has missing Element trees, try deleting the Browser cache. In certain situations, a manual deletion of the /core/cache/context_settings directory may be required, to restore complete Manager functionality. In rare instances deleting the entire /core/cache folder has proven successful to restoring functionality.

Subdomain Contexts

Configuring subdomains to work with a single installation of MODX Revolution follows the same basic sequence provided for fully qualified domains, with only a few additional steps: forcing the subdomain to land at the site root, and bypassing the .htaccess rewrite rules.

Forcing the Subdomain to the Site Root

Server administrators should easily be able to "alias" or point the subdomain, in much the same manner used to host fully qualified domains. In many cases, using the primary domain as a template, administrators can simply cut and paste the www.domain.com section under the preexisting data and change the www.domain.com to subdomain.doman.com., as well as create a www.subdomain.domain.com record. Please make a backup copy of the configuration, before editing or modifying existing server configurations.

For users of control panel software, issues may arise due to the automation of some stages of the process, as the software has been set to "guess" the location for the subdomain. Typically this will be selected for /public_html/subdomain or /subdomain. Care must be taken to point the subdomain to /public_html, or whatever the current DOCUMENT_ROOT, as utilized during the installation of MODX Revolution, the control panel itself, or phpinfo() - located by clicking the View link in the Manager, by accessing the Reports Menu | System Info screen.

SUBDOMAINS	ROOT DOMAIN	DOCUMENT ROOT	REDIRECTION
dev	.sanityllc.com	/public_html	not redirected

In some instances, the web server will need to be restarted to reflect the new changes. Most control panels will handle this by performing a "localized" restart. Once a "success" message is given, attempt to visit the main domain to verify it is still functioning correctly. Next, attempt successful connection to the newly added subdomain url and ensure it is correctly pointing to the main MODX Revolution installation index.php.

⚠ *WARNING: REMOVE ANY PHYSICAL DIRECTORIES MATCHING THE SUBDOMAIN*

Just about every major control panel I tested, automatically created a directory to catch the request for the new subdomain. Typically, these will have to be deleted in order for MODX Revolution to catch the request, as physical directories may take precedence over simple .htacess rewrites.

.htaccess subdomain Modifications

Previously, I created a rewrite rule forcing all requests to www.domain.tld, regardless of the domain requested, which includes subdomains. This would have the effect of creating www. subdomain.domain.tld rewritten requests, which is a ugly. The following represents appropriate changes to inform the web server software of what is needed.

Listing 15.09: subdomain and domain modified .htaccess file

```
# Rewrite subdomain requests to remove www
RewriteCond %{HTTP_HOST} .
RewriteCond %{HTTP_HOST} ^www\.legal\.creativeinfusions\.net
RewriteRule ^(.*)$ http://legal.creativeinfusions.net/$1 [R=301,L]

RewriteCond %{HTTP_HOST} .
RewriteCond %{HTTP_HOST} ^www\.dev\.
RewriteRule ^(.*)$ http://dev.sanityllc.com/$1 [R=301,L]

RewriteCond %{HTTP_HOST} .
RewriteCond %{HTTP_HOST} ^www\.legal\.sanityllc\.com
RewriteRule ^(.*)$ http://legal.sanityllc.com/$1 [R=301,L]

# Force all pages to go to www.domain.com and not domain.com -
ignore subdomains
RewriteCond %{HTTP_HOST} .
RewriteCond %{HTTP_HOST} !^(legal\.creativeinfusions\.net)?$
RewriteCond %{HTTP_HOST} !^(dev\.sanityllc\.com)?$
RewriteCond %{HTTP_HOST} !^(legal\.sanityllc\.com)?$
RewriteCond %{HTTP_HOST} !^www\.
RewriteRule ^(.*)$ http://www.%{HTTP_HOST}/$1 [R=301,L]
```

Checks for content in the request: %{HTTP_HOST} . in each block

First we clean www from each respective subdomain

Any request to the dev subdomain that hits the project will be redirected to dev.sanityllc.com

Any subdomain can exist on any domain - just designate them

In the last section all subdomains are listed, so they will be ignored by the rewrite rule

Note: The domains associated with your project will need to be used in place of mine

Create or Duplicate a Context for the Subdomain To Use

Depending on the needs of the Context, either follow the process outlined in the Skeleton implementation in this chapter, or create a new Context. Pay attention to the name used, as it will be used in the next section.

Implement or Edit the domainGateway Plugin

If necessary, create a new Plugin and attach it to the OnHandleRequest system event or simply edit the preexisting Plugin. Enter a "test" case to the PHP switch block attaching the incoming host request to the associated receiving context.

Listing 15.10: domainGateway Plugin with subdomains

```php
<?php
switch ($modx->getOption('http_host')) {
    case 'dev.sanityllc.com':
        $modx->switchContext('dev');
        break;
    /*
     * Additional example
     */
    case 'legal.creativeinfusions.net':
    case 'legal.sanityllc.com':
        $modx->switchContext('legal');
        break;
    default:
        /* by default, the web Context will return Sanityllc.com */
        break;
}
```

dev.sanityllc.com represents a typical subdomain implementation

Both legal.domain.tld requests are sent to the same Context

Once the Plugin has been saved, the subdomain Context should become completely functional. Don't forget to empty the browser and site caches, if needed.

Congratulations! Your Contexts should be fully functional.

domainGateway with Domains and Subdomains

After extensively testing my final .htaccess file, I am able to make sure MODX Revolution is getting only requests formatted in expected ways, I was able to streamline the Plugin to house the main domains of my company.

Listing 15.11 Streamlined Gateway plugin

```php
<?php
switch ($modx->getOption('http_host')) {
    /* Fully qualified domains */
    case 'www.creativeinfusions.net':
        $modx->switchContext('creativeinfusions');
        break;
    case 'www.sanityllc.info':
        $modx->switchContext('info');
        break;
    case 'www.sanityllc.org':
        $modx->switchContext('org');
        break;

    /* Subdomains */
    case 'dev.sanityllc.com':
        $modx->switchContext('dev');
        break;
    case 'legal.creativeinfusions.net':
    case 'legal.sanityllc.com':
        $modx->switchContext('legal');
        break;
    default:
        /* the web Context will return Sanityllc.com */
        break;
}
```

Listing 15.12: Optional .htaccess Category / directory to subdomain redirect

RedirectMatch 301 ^/dev/(.)$ http://dev.sanityllc.com/$1*

A redirect to keep people from going to www.sanityllc.com/dev.

Protecting the Manager Context

Working with domain and subdomain centric Contexts is typically straightforward. In some implementations, additional attributes can be established via the domainGateway Plugin, which could adversely affect the ability of Manager Users. An easy example of this, is when Contexts are used in applications which center around changes in user language. These changes, will typically be unwanted in the Manager, at least as far as the typical Super Administrator is concerned. Steps should be taken to protect the Manager Context from language changes or access from "secondary" domains and subdomains being served via the MODX Revolution installation.

Listing 15.13 Language based contexts and Protecting the manager

```
if($modx->context->key != "mgr"){
    switch ($modx->getOption('http_host')) {
        case 'en.example.com':
            $modx->switchContext('en');
            $modx->setOption('cultureKey', 'en');
            break;
        case 'fr.example.com':
            $modx->switchContext('fr');
            $modx->setOption('cultureKey', 'fr');
            break;
        case 'es.example.com':
            $modx->switchContext('es');
            $modx->setOption('cultureKey', 'es');
            break;
        case 'jp.example.com':
            $modx->switchContext('jp');
            $modx->setOption('cultureKey', 'jp');
            break;
        case 'ru.example.com':
            $modx->switchContext('ru');
            $modx->setOption('cultureKey', 'ru');
            break;
        default:
            break;
    }
}
```

Examples of using Snippets and Chunks with Contexts

The following code examples represent foundational components to implement broader applications and their testing:

Listing 15.14: contextNames Chunk (may require anonymous user access)

```
alpha,bravo,charlie,delta,echo,web
```

Listing 15.15: Login Snippet call using a Chunk to provide Context names

```
[[!Login?contexts=`[[$contextNames]]`&loginResourceId=`30`]]
```

Listing 15.16: Example Wayfinder Call Across Contexts

```
[[!Wayfinder?startTd=`[[+site_start]]`&level=`1`&sortBy=`menuindex`
&contexts=`[[$contextNames]]`&startIdContext=`2`]]
```

Listing 15.17: getContextName Snippet - returns the current Context Name

```
<?php
return $modx->context->key;
```

Listing 15.18: getSessionContexts - returns all of the Contexts for this user

```
<?php
print_r($modx->user->getSessionContexts());
```

Summary

MODX Revolution provides a solid foundation to simplify even the reusability of code. By utilizing Contexts, Manager users can quickly add new web sites, sub sites, and even alternate sites based on any number of configurations to an installation and have immediate access to a large portion of the "in-house" tool set.

For many people, the implementation of Contexts can cause confusion if the primary purpose is forgotten or not understood. Contexts tend to cater to the needs of the project and its respective client and may be considered an entry port to access sensitive information or dedicated applications utilized in the daily operations of a specific company. Even in multiple language applications, the focus is providing content in a variety of languages - not on the users being required to speak those languages. Typically, users are not the primary purpose of a Context - the content is.

Far too often, Manger users find themselves frustrated over permissions and access when working with Contexts. Although each of these can play a major role in Contexts, an over emphasis on them may indicate the need for more attention to User Groups. Essentially, the most common mistake I have seen, is people attempting to implement a Context where a User Group will serve them much easier. Others attempting to use User Groups where Contexts will work better, will also end up working through their frustration.

Contexts should be thought of as individual buildings, which can simply be clones of other buildings or extensively defined entities of its own. If the current work flow continually pulls the Manger user back to Users, there is a very good possibility User Groups are the answer.

If the primary purpose of the project is the presentation of Content, then begin looking into Contexts, where User Groups may or may not be necessary, but where containers of site content are desired.

MODX Revolution Rule #15: **Contexts focus on content - users are secondary.**

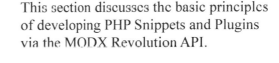

Development

This section discusses the basic principles of developing PHP Snippets and Plugins via the MODX Revolution API.

This section serves as a primer intended to provide a functional foundation for most any Project: from the simplest to those which are more complex.

This section is intended to provide a developers a foundation to learn from and build upon.

Quick Start

SEO and Site Optimization

jQuery and AJAX

The author's final words

16
MODX Revolution API Concepts

I have a natural propensity to explore, which is probably the reason I like taking pictures of secluded locations. The effort required to search out and get to a picturesque location, gives the image much more meaning - especially when it required a few descents down various sections of a mountain and a trek through underbrush rarely seen or visited by anyone.

Two of my favorite locations to take photographs are located in Chattanooga, Tennessee: Rock City and Ruby Falls. Both of which have plenty of "exploring" to be done, even though the paths and routes are "pre-defined". Further east in North Carolina, Raven Rock State Park also provides a nice environment to walk through with many opportunities to catch the "perfect shot".

My all time favorite getaway photography shoot is located in the Smoky Mountains. With dozens of water falls and trails spanning hundreds of miles, weeks could be spent relaxing, hiking, and exploring. Soon, I would like to be able to take my kids and hike through some of those mountain trails, as I have been told it is too dangerous to keep doing it alone.

When all else fails, I happen to live in Florida, where we have an abundance of terrain and water locations to serve as a day-trip or long weekend allowing the benefit of being as rustic or comfortable as the mood requires. The terrain here is so varied, the U.S. Army Rangers have the last phase of their school in Florida, allowing the students to see and experience Florida in all of its natural glory - hopefully not at the expense of being dropped from the course.

Development using the MODX Revolution API is very similar to the way I perceive photography: the final result is not nearly as important as the experience itself. The issue becomes which way do I want to accomplish the task, rather than how do "the developers" allow me to do it.

Of all of the platforms and Content Management Systems I have used, only MODX Revolution allows me: to develop the way I am accustomed, explore new techniques, and package Components for easy distribution. Welcome to raw power and total freedom.

Concerning Object Oriented Programming

MODX Revolution is a great place to warm up to OOP for those who have never learned the associated programming techniques and nomenclature. The entire platform is constructed of objects and can be used as an example of how to "correctly" develop complex web applications. Additionally, there are plenty of MODX Revolution Packages available which can be used to illustrate single purpose OOP implementations, providing a foundation to learn from.

To help facilitate the concept of Object Oriented Programming, a simple example should help. If you needed to borrow a pen from someone, what would you ask for? This question is, of course, overly simplistic though it does illustrate the point. Most of us would easily understand what a pen is - even without anyone explaining it to us. In essence, a pen is a writing utensil which places ink on paper or other surfaces.

For a programmer, the pen may have a model number, ink color, a mechanism, diameter of tip, price, description, etc. Each of these attributes are associated with almost all pens, though most of us are unconcerned with them when we simply need to get something written down.

By extension, a pen object is simply a pen with attributes which can be defined to specify an individual unit. The same object can be used to define any pen in existence, as it simply represents a "framework" of qualities belonging to any of them. When we use a pen to write down a note or other information, the actual characteristics of the pen are of little consequence. After all, it is just a pen and we simply need it to work.

Other examples which can be defined by objects: the car we drive, the place we work, the job we perform, even the spouse we choose. In essence, anything with characteristics and attributes can be defined as objects.

Many experienced PHP programmers should already be familiar with Object Oriented Programming and comfortable with classes, objects, instantiation, and the like. I would strongly suggest anyone serious about PHP development to make the investment to learn these practices, so they can reduce development time and increase their productivity.

There are many tutorials on the web concerning PHP Object Oriented Programming. A simple Google search should yield a plethora of links which can help those who desire to greatly enhance their coding abilities. The following are currently available resources found via Google. I have not used nor do I directly endorse these sites, though I have seen them recommended.

OOP in Full Effect (First of three parts):
http://www.phpfreaks.com/tutorials/oo-php-part-1-oop-in-full-effect

Object Oriented PHP Tutorial for Beginners (videos and multiple parts) :
http://www.killerphp.com/tutorials/object-oriented-php/

Google search: "php oop tutorials":
http://lmgtfy.com/?q=php+oop+tutorials

The $modx Object

To my knowledge MODX Revolution is the only Content Management Platform designed from the ground up as an actual extension to a database Object Relational Bridge. In essence, this means developers can map database structure to their application, providing a very efficient and streamlined work flow process. More information about this amazing platform can be found by visiting Jason Cowards project site: http://www.xpdo.org/.

The $modx object extends, and thereby inherits, all of the xPDO functions, providing developers immediate access to the many database tables, data, and extensive number of class functions for working with various forms of data. Essentially, this translates to less programming to interact with the MODX database or its associated data, as the actual classes used to build MODX Revolution, are the same as those utilized to access the database and other sources of data.

An overly simplistic summary of the $modx object: it is everything MODX Revolution at a given moment, for a given user, and in a given session. In essence, it is the very environment and means a user has to interact with the web project.

Benefits of utilizing the MODX Object

The vast majority of code written in many programming projects, involves the "normal" functions of accessing databases and working with various forms of data. Much of the time, this code can be redundant from one class to another. This issue becomes more complex as projects require translation from one technology to another, or developing related implementations which will present some sort of output for the visitor's web browser from each of those technologies.

The simple act of connecting to a database, or performing queries can amount to hundreds or even thousands of lines of code across an application and vastly increase the time to get a project completed. By utilizing the MODX Revolution API, immediate access is granted to any table housed within the main MODX installation database, as well as additional functionality for working with arrays, objects, and JSON. Even the introduction of third-party databases and tables into the web projects can be greatly simplified by utilizing xPDO and the MODX API.

Essentially, much of the "foundation" has been established within MODX Revolution, which removes the necessity of repeatedly establishing structures to gain access to various data sources and manipulating it. On-the-fly conversions of JSON, arrays, objects, and data contained in database systems have been readily simplified, allowing developers to concentrate their efforts directly on the task at hand, instead of peripheral supporting code.

For many developers, MODX Revolution becomes an array of tools allowing a very fast turn around on projects. I have personally experienced projects requiring only ten percent of the code utilizing the MODX Revolution API, compared to very similar functionality not using the API.

The Dangerous Side to the MODX Revolution API

Any code implementing the $modx object, will also have direct access to the very core of MODX Revolution, including: database, file system, private user data, and other potentially sensitive information. Project leaders should be very cautious and aware of exactly who has the ability to add PHP Snippets to their MODX Revolution project.

Concern for what site visitors see, or what data is exposed to the public side of a web site is only one part of the problem. Snippets can run transparently in the background accomplishing any of a myriad of methods to transfer data from one server to another.

MODX Revolution has built in methods to send e-mail. It also has a very powerful foundation in xPDO which could easily be utilized to duplicate data to another database. These and other issues are not isolated to MODX Revolution. Most any Content Management System in use can be abused or effectively utilized in these manners. The simplest protection is to limit Manager access to only those individuals which need it, and subsequently restrict their access to only necessary areas.

Verify PHP Functionality and Output

Once something appears on a page and is seen by the public, it can not easily be taken back. For some of us, things tend to work out in such a way, Google or some other search engine will index the site just at the moment which may prove the most problematic. It is much better to be 100% certain of what is going on, than to take someone's word for it or to move forward on assumption.

In some situations one developer may be asked to implement and work on a Snippet another created, as a second set of eyes could prove very beneficial. One of the reasons for this is to ensure a given Snippet / Class does not wander far from its intended purpose.

Due to its inheritance of xPDO, MODX Revolution was built from the ground up to directly interface and map data to applications. It affords raw, unlimited power which can yield amazing results with very little effort. As far as web projects go, this is a huge plus when presenting a concept to a client for their consideration. It is a huge confidence builder to be able to walk into a meeting with the knowledge your chosen platform really can be made to do most anything.

Over the coming pages, I will be demonstrating the simplicity of utilizing the MODX Revolution Application Programming Interface. Please keep in mind, this information is a two-edged sword: *"From everyone who has been given much, much will be required; and to whom they entrusted much, of him they will ask all the more (Luke 12:48 NASB)."*

MODX Revolution Rule #16: **Be very careful of who has access to the project.**

$modx Object Implementation - importing the API

PHP classes which utilize the MODX Revolution API, typically begin in an almost "standard" fashion. A reference to the $modx object is passed into the class, as well as associated runtime parameters. The following demonstrate the simplicity involved to take full advantage of Revo, while more complete examples will be shown in the coming pages.

Listing 16.01: PHP 5 class structure implementing the MODX Revolution API

- -

```php
class Myclass {
    function __construct(modX & $modx, array $config = array()) {
        /*
         * Import $modx reference
         */
        $this->modx = & $modx;

        /*
         * Establish default parameters allowing user parameters
         */
        $this->config = array_merge(array(
                'param1' => 'value1',
                'param2' => 'value2',
                'param3' => 'false',
        ), $config);
    }
}
```

- -

Listing 16.02: Accessing the $modx object in a PHP Snippet

- -

```php
if (!function_exists('func') {
 function func() {
   global $modx;
   }
}
    $_config = array_merge(array(
            'param1' => '',
            'param2' => '',
    ), $scriptProperties);
$modx->someFunction($varFromThisSnippet, $parameters);
```

- -

Secondary MODX Revolution Classes

The secondary classes utilized in MODX Revolution can be grouped into three primary groups, which are loaded in the following order allowing subsequent classes to extend previously loaded classes. Note: inheritance works to the right and upwards.

Security / Access Policy		
modAccess	xPDOSimpleObject	xPDOObject
modAccessibleObject	xPDOObject	
modAccessibleSimpleObject	modAccessibleObject	
Content		
modResource	modAccessibleSimpleObject	
modElement/	modAccessibleSimpleObject	
modScript	modElement	
User / System Access		
modPrincipal	xPDOSimpleObject	xPDOObject
modUser	modPrincipal	

There are many other secondary classes, utilized by MODX Revolution, many of which tend to extend or support one of those listed here. For example, modElement is extended by modChunk, modSnippet, modTemplate, modScript, and ultimately modPlugin.

It should be assumed by developers, any interaction with the MODX Revolution API infers the utilization of objects, as indicated by the chart above. Many of these objects can be traced back to xPDOObject through their inheritance chain.

MODX Revolution extends xPDO, while many of its "subclasses" extend xPDOObject. The primary difference is that xPDO maps a database structure to an application, while xPDOObject reflects a single row of data from a table in that database.This is why there are references to functions within modx.class.php which relates to groups of Resources or other collections. An object is a single instance of something. As many of the secondary classes only represent the current access to the project, they are objectifying the User, Resource, Element, etc., being interacted with. Essentially, these objects are reflecting one of something.

For now, simply keep in mind: an object represents a single row in a database table. An object map focuses on the relationships between tables and the way they are supposed to interact with one another. The remainder of this chapter should greatly clarify these concepts.

Avoid Garbage In / Garbage Out Scenarios

Occasionally, it may be helpful to take a glimpse at the database structure to see what type of data is being interacted with. The majority of MODX Revolution objects are stored in variable length character fields. While this offers plenty of flexibility, it does not directly restrict the structure used for each entry as it is stored to the database table.

For example, the phone number is a user's profile is stored as entered. If that information belonged to organizations creating call sheets or internal contact lists, the resulting presentation might look like an amateur had put it together. To further complicate things, phone numbers in the United States can come in lengths of 7, 10, 11, or even longer derivatives with extensions.

I would typically consider formatting the information before it is stored using the same format throughout the project. The Login Package allows the use of hooks (Snippets) which allow for this sort of standardization.

Example Steps to Standardize Phone Numbers

◆ Create a second form field for extensions

◆ Disallow entry of anything over 11 characters

◆ Strip all non numeric content: return preg_replace('(\D+)', '', $str);

◆ Combine $phone .= ($extension) ? 'x' . $extension : '';

◆ unset ($extension) and store consistent format into User's Profile

Other formatting issues can take place when users are asked to enter their address and other contact information. For example, years ago we had a huge problem getting users of a certain online service to understand their screen name and an e-mail address were two different things.

With regards to addresses, I may utilize two helper Snippets from the FormIt package, [[FormItStateOptions]] and [[FormItCountryOptions]], to supply geographical names. Additionally, an AJAX lookup can be used to populate the city name, county, state, and area code from a Zip code lookup database. This provides a consistent presentation simply because it was "entered" by the same source and in a relatively identical format. It also, greatly reduces the number of typographical errors contained in the data, which greatly increase its integrity.

Care should be taken in applications where subsequent implementations using the data is not necessarily known. In these situations it is typically best to reduce the information to the most basic of formats - facilitating greater flexibility, reduced resource consumption, and increase overall efficiency which is appreciated by clients.

I typically have two types of clients: those who need things done and have no idea what they are doing, and those understanding their requirements and are in need of a solid foundation to build upon. As for my development process: I utilize the same methods and reasoning for both groups, making my job simpler in the long run. I simply keep things simple and consistent.

Retrieving Values From Object Attributes

It is my hope the examples contained in this chapter will facilitate an expedited learning process for those delving into PHP OOP for the first time, as well as provide the information needed for those simply desiring to learn the MODX Revolution API and methodology. Each topic should have enough commentary to explain the basic premise and should help non-OOP developers to bridge the gap and begin making streamlined, tightly integrated MODX Revolution Packages.

These examples should help coordinate efforts and expectations by providing simple explanations and descriptions which can easily translate to other real world situations. For non-developers, the ability to create a somewhat informed conceptualization of an idea, should reduce issues with communication. At the very least, these examples should provide a clear explanation of what can be accomplished in a MODX Revolution project.

To simultaneously accomplish these tasks, I have chosen to center much of the content in this chapter around a single MODX Revolution Object: the user. This topic represents something readily understood by a majority of people, regardless of Object Oriented Programming skills, with should facilitate greater understanding and communication.

The $modx->user object is undoubtably one of the most frequently implemented MODX Revolution objects, but its name should be considered a bit of a misnomer. The user object extends the modPrincipal class which applies to humans, as well as systems which are accessing the project, hence the official explanation: *"A User is simply a representation of a login in MODx Revolution"*.

The $modx->user object largely interacts with the PHP $_SESSION and associated database tables in the areas of the Principal's account, attributes, user group membership, document group membership, password functions, member-to-member messaging, and the sending of "system" messages. Essentially, the $modx->user object is centered around a specific "user", and relates all associated information and affiliation with the MODX Revolution installation. For readability, many of the examples in this section have been processed with PHP's ksort().

Our focus will remain primarily on MODX Revolution API functionality and should facilitate developer interaction with those items. Many of the topics presented will transfer directly to "in-house" objects specific to the project - especially those which implement single object functionality. Some of the functions, require tables in a database to function, which is discussed in the next chapter.

A word of caution: don't over think or complicate the examples or what they represent. Each is fully functional, regardless of how tiny or simple the code may seem. The MODX Revolution API really is this powerful.

I believe the MODX Revolution API is the doorway for many developers to come into their own.

Object Instantiation

Implementing an application which interacts with users on the site is typically placed into one of two categories: the current user object or another user. This is typical of all objects, as MODX Revolution instantiates the current user, Resource, and various other objects automatically for the active session. For now, we should focus on accessing a single object:

Listing 16.03: PHP Snippet to access the current user object

```php
$user = $modx->user;
```

Listing 16.04: PHP Snippet to access users via a runtime parameter - the user id

----

```php
$user = $modx->getObject('modUser', $uid); // id is the default
```

Listing 16.05: PHP Snippet to access any user by other table field(s)

```php
$user = $modx->getObject('modUser', array(
                            'username' => $username,
                            ));
```

Listing 16.06: PHP Snippet to specify a user or default to current user

----

```php
$user = (!empty($userId)) ? $modx->getObject('modUser', $userId)
                          : $modx->user;
```

Listing 16.07: the format to access MODX Objects by attributes

----

```php
$pseudoVar = $modx->getObject('modSubClass', $criteriaArray);
```

----

get(): Directly Accessing Object Attributes

Tight integration with the MODX Revolution API is possible, in part, because many of its methods attempt to respond with data types similar to that of the request or in an expected data type. This "seamless" integration with an object can be easily seen when targeting attributes / table columns / fields using get().

Listing 16.08: PHP Snippet targeting specific columns in the Object's table
----

```
echo $user->get('hash_class') . '<br/>';
echo $user->get('salt');
$fieldNamesArray = array('hash_class','salt');
$userFieldsAry = $user->get($fieldNamesArray);
print_r($userFieldsAry);
```

Listing 16.09: Example string / array results of Listing 16.08

```
hashing.modPBKDF2
3a2ed0f373474b84a038437daa482775Array
(
    [hash_class] => hashing.modPBKDF2
    [salt] => 3a2ed0f373474b84a038437daa482775
)
```

For example, when a string is used to tell get() to return a value, the API returns with a string. Alternately, when an array is supplied as the parameter, a response in the type of an array is returned. Each method in the API has its own means to provide output. Take time to become familiarized with each API function being implemented in the application. The code you save could be your own.

Listing 16.10: PHP Snippet accessing extended fields demonstrating 1:1 relation
----

```
// instantiated user
$profile = $user->getOne('Profile');
// retrieve extended fields from their profile
$fields = $profile->get('extended');
```

This example represents one of those times, it is a good idea to look at the way data is being stored in the database. Unlike a user's settings which are stored in a one-to-many relationship, a user's Extended Fields are stored in a JSON array, but formatted as a string in a single field in the `modx_user_attributes` table.

Listing 16.11: PHP array representation of optional extended fields (ksorted)

```
Array
(
    [College] => Array
        (
            [Degree] => BAS Supervision And Management
            [Name] => Daytona State College
            [SecondaryDegrees] => Array
                (
                    [secDegree1] => AS Computer Programming and
                                       Analysis - Software Engineer
                    [secDegree2] => AS Internet Services Technology
                    [secDegree3] => AS Network Administrator
                )
        )
)
```

In this example, get() "decides" to return the results in a PHP array, which appears to be its way of dealing with JSON from a database table. Make sure to test the output of each of your applications when working with the MODX Revolution API.

Many developers will typically be able to successfully anticipate the type of data which will be returned from a method call, in a relatively short amount of time. Repetitive usage and consistent coding practices will definitely help.

☞ *THE MODX REVOLUTION API WAS CREATED WITH EXTENSION IN MIND*

Keep in mind that a user object represents a Login, and so should extended user classes. This is discussed in the official MODX Documentation, http://rtfm.modx.com/display/ revolution20/Extending+modUser, which I wrote some time ago.

Also see the modActiveDirectory and other Packages with extended user application.

toArray(): Returning PHP Arrays of Object Contents

Regardless of the technique utilized to obtain a user object, information similar to the example below is typical to what is directly accessible with $modx->user. MODX Revolution via xPDO provides multiple formats to retrieve object data: string, array, and JSON.

Listing 16.12: PHP Snippet using toArray();

```php
$u = $user->toArray();
print_r($u);
```

Listing 16.13: PHP array representation of an anonymous user object

```
Array
(
    [id] => 0
    [username] => (anonymous)
    [password] =>
    [cachepwd] =>
    [class_key] => modUser
    [active] => 1
    [remote_key] =>
    [remote_data] =>
    [hash_class] => hashing.modPBKDF2
    [salt] =>
    [primary_group] => 0
    [session_stale] =>
    [sudo] =>
)
```

In terms of PHP, arrays are the historical method utilized to transport a collection of data from one implementation or variable to the next. An over simplified description of an object, could be summarized as an array with built-in programmed functionality. I have heard PHP objects described as a distant cousin to arrays, but I tend to think of them as the fullness of array functionality.

toJSON(): Returning JavaScript Object Notation

Many JavaScript libraries and other technologies natively understand and easily manipulate the user interface using JSON. This functionality becomes especially apparent when lists or collections of information are presented to a visitor, offering them the ability to filter, sort, and otherwise manipulate the presentation.

By using the MODX Revolution API, the process of providing an implementation on the front side of the web project a JSON source becomes almost a non issue. PHP developers can simply grab the appropriate objects and create a JSON response to hand off to their JavaScript counterparts, with little communication being required between the two teams. This can greatly expedite AJAX and other cross-technology applications.

For user interface / experience (ui/ux) developers, simple functions like `jQuery.getJSON()` provide a very straightforward workflow from database to screen presentation with very little effort by any of the developers involved. This allows each team to maximize their effectiveness without communication delays or excessive documentation creation.

For those projects with a single developer, this allows a seamless ability to change from a PHP to a JavaScript role and back again, with very few mental acrobatics. This can help reduce frustration, stress, and exhaustion during those long days spent in development.

Listing 16.14: PHP Snippet using toJSON();

```
return $user->toJSON();
```

Listing 16.15: JSON representation of a typical user (note: table order retained)

```
{"id":0,"username":"(anonymous)","password":"","cachepwd":"","
class_key":"modUser","active":true,"remote_key":null,"remote_
data":null,"hash_class":"hashing.modPBKDF2","salt":"","primary_
group":0,"session_stale":null,"sudo":false}
```

PHP provides extensive array functionality and provided additional JSON support with version 5.2. The MODX Revolution API provides four primary means for working with these data types: `toArray()`, `fromArray()`, `toJSON()`, and `fromJSON()`. Using either `toArray()` or `toJSON()` on a MODX Revolution object will result in having all of the database fields being returned, typically in the order they appear in the database table and retaining the same names as the table headings.

Retrieving Multiple Related Objects

MODX Revolution Objects retain a consistent naming conventions from database to object, while transparently associating the database data type with each attribute. This should result in simpler object utilization, as an object's attributes simultaneously represents the mapped table column of a particular row and the identically named attribute in every respect.

Essentially, this provides an immediate level of application development streamlining, as the data type of each database field is automatically handled via the xPDO Class. This frees developers from having to create translation mechanisms to associate the data as individually belonging to respective data types. Long sections of code, such as the following are no longer necessary:

Listing 16.16: PHP Unnecessary traditional-style code

```
$address = (string) $row['address'];
```

Regardless of the retrieval method used, the values retrieved from the API can be manipulated at run time just like any other variable or traditional database query result, though permanent changes back to a storage medium have to be saved() and be compatible with the datatype defined in the xPDO schema. In the best of situations datatypes should exactly match or be easily and automatically "converted" through type casting, such as an int to a string.

As a rule of thumb, I directly utilize the MODX Revolution API, except in situations multiple lines of code are accessing the object's value. This is personal preference, but I believe it also aides in readability in either application. If I am looking at $profile-get('address'), I do not have to look very far to understand the entire object inheritance.

Instead of needing to "remember" what I was thinking when I wrote the code in the first place, I simply can think, "Oh, xPDO and MODX are handling that," and move on. The more this situation occurs in my projects, the simpler my application become to develop and implement.

╤ *TIP: MANIPULATION OF DATA DOES NOT TRANSLATE TO PERMANENT STORAGE*

An instantiated object will only reflect the object at the moment it was created, plus any programmed changes to its attributes. Any updates to the database are not necessarily reflected in the object after it has been instantiated, unless it is retrieved after the update. Likewise, value manipulation does not necessarily translate into updates to the database.

getOne(): Accessing a 1:1/0 Relationship

This example introduces the getOne() method, which is available to all MODX Revolution objects. Essentially, it operates across a 1:1 or 1:0 relationship as defined in the database schema, and is discussed in greater detail in the chapter on xPDO. A direct relationship, as in this situation where one user has only one profile, can be easily accessed via getOne().

Listing 16.17: PHP Snippet to access the profile of an instantiated user object

```
/*
 * Using an object to retrieve an associated database object
 * with the following syntax:
 * $object = $modClass->getOne('Alias');
 */
$profile = $user->getOne('Profile');
$arry = $profile->toArray();
print_r($arry);
```

The beauty of this method, is that a single function can easily replace multiple lines of traditional code. $user->getOne() utilizes our database connection, creates a join query, executes the query, and returns a Profile object. xPDO directly hands us the result set with little thought of manually coding all of those processes ourselves.

This basis of implementation allows developers to establish a consistent mechanism for working with 1:1/0 relationships, with the added benefit of retrieving an object with all of the associated functionality of an xPDOObject. In essence, the object itself carries a major amount of functionality, saving developers from spending time on those items and reducing the level of learning curve associate with new objects created in a typical PHP Class.

𝕋 TIP: AN EASY MISTAKE

Over the years, I have been asked why something similar to the following doesn't always seem to work:

Bad code: $user->getOne('Profile')->get('Address');

The simple answer: the User or Profile object may have not been instantiated, and thereby has not inherited its attributes, associated values, or methods.

Listing 16.18: PHP array representation of a typical user's profile (ksorted)

- -

```
Array
(
    [address] => 1234 Main Street
    [blocked] =>
    [blockedafter] => 0
    [blockeduntil] => 0
    [city] => Daytona Beach
    [comment] => This is a comment: wish I had a Revo book ;)
    [country] => United States
    [dob] => -1293815439
    [email] => user@somedomain.com
    [extended] => Array
        (
            [College] => Array
                (
                    [Degree] => BAS Supervision And Management
                    [Secondary Degrees] => Array
                        (
                            [secDegree1] => AS Computer Programming
                        )
                )
        )
    [failedlogincount] => 0
    [fax] => 386 555 1212
    [fullname] => Default Admin User
    [gender] => 1
    [id] => 1
    [internalKey] => 1
    [lastlogin] => 1310675722
    [logincount] => 1745
    [mobilephone] => 386 555 3434
    [phone] => 386-555-9999
    [photo] =>
    [sessionid] => e0146b9df1f6f905835222ca8d791e4e
    [state] => FL
    [thislogin] => 1310730873
    [website] => shawnwilkerson.com
    [zip] => 32117
)
```

- -

getMany(): Accessing a 1:n Relationship

One user can have any number of settings associated with their account. The MODX Revolution API provides the basis to retrieve any data in a 1:n (one-to-many) database relationship, namely the getMany() function. To access all of the settings assigned to a user, simply utilize a user object with the getSettings() method to retrieve an array of all associated user settings.

Listing 16.19: PHP Snippet to access the settings of an instantiated user object

```
$user->getSettings();
```

An object represents a single row in a database table, in this case: a User. In situations where a group is returned, a collection is created - a group or an array of objects containing similar information, typically from a single table, depending on the implementation utilized to create the collection. Note: MODX Revolution can also easily retrieve collections across tables.

Excerpt 16.20: PHP excerpt from moduser.class.php demonstrating getMany()

```
public function getSettings() {
    $settings = array();
    $uss = $this->getMany('UserSettings');
    foreach ($uss as $us) {
        $settings[$us->get('key')] = $us->get('value');
    }
    $this->settings = $settings;
    return $settings;
}
```

In this implementation, a collection of user settings is retrieved, based on the user object which was previously instantiated. Each of the individual settings is actually an object ("a row in the database table") and thereby has direct API functionality.

In the getSettings() method found in moduser.class.php, a few lines make quick work out of accessing the database across a relation, retrieving the relevant information, and creating a simple array of only those values necessary to perform the given task.

This method illustrates an effective method of retrieving related objects and reducing them to a simple array. It can also serve as the basis to lower the load on a server, or to restrict available data by reducing the result set to only the data required.

Creating an Application Based on an API Implementation

When learning a new API, two practices used in conjunction can quickly help developers better understand the benefits and necessity of tight integration: duplicating logic used within the API itself, and repetitive usage.

In the *[[Snippets]] and Plug-ins: Adding PHP Dynamic Content* chapter, I demonstrated a very streamlined method to directly place values from an array into identically named placeholders in a Chunk used as a template for Snippet output.

In this example, I have taken the liberty to create a Chunk with placeholders directly representing the fields in the modx_site_content table, which contains all of the Resources within a given MODX Revolution project. Essentially, the API is simply going to act as a processor, utilizing the values stored in the table column to create output based on a Chunk template.

The following is all that is required to present a list of every Resource in the current Context created by the specified user. In its present rendition, this example will show all Resources, even those hidden from menus, unpublished, and/or deleted (and not purged) from the project.

Listing 16.21: Chunk to be used as an output template

```
[[+createdon:limit=`10`]] <a href="[[~[[+id]]]]" title="
[[+longtitle]]">[[+pagetitle]]</a>: [[+description]]<br/>
```

Listing 16.22 Snippet which processes a collection for a user

```
$user = (!empty($userId)) ? $modx->getObject('modUser', $userId) :
$modx->user;
$collection = $user->getMany('CreatedResources');
foreach ($collection as $obj) {
    $output .= $modx->getChunk('myChunk', $obj->toArray());
}
return $output;
```

Using the getSettings() method in the moduser.class.php as a "template", applications can be developed which greatly simplify the collection and presentation of information. The same foundation can be used to interact with any one-to-many relation in the database, just as getOne() can be used for one-to-one relationships, and get() can be used to retrieve a column value. Once the data is accessible, security and other considerations can be implemented.

Creating an Object Test Bed

When ever I begin working on a new facet of the MODX Revolution API, I like to read through the "Parent" class and go through each function, following it through other classes, finally landing at the xPDO Simple object. One of the tools I suggest developers implement, is a single simplified file which discloses as much information about an object as can be squeezed out. The following is only a small portion of functions contained in the user object.

Listing 16.23: PHP Snippet to display user related information

```php
<?php
/**
 * File testbedUser.php (requires MODx Revolution 2.1)
 * Created on: 7/19/11 at 12:07 PM
 * Project shawn_wilkerson
 * @author W. Shawn Wilkerson
 * @link http://www.shawnwilkerson.com
 * @license
 *
 */

/*
 * Instantiate a user object - defaults to current user
 */
$user = (!empty($userId)) ? $modx->getObject('modUser', $userId) :
$modx->user;

/*
 * If we have a user object
 */
if (is_object($user)) {
    /*
     * Output a JSON representation of the user
     */
    echo '<h2>Current User Object in JSON</h2>';
    echo $user->toJSON();

    /*
     * Output a PHP Array
     */
    echo '<h2>Current User Object in PHP Array</h2>';
    $u = $user->toArray();
    ksort($u);
```

```
print_r($u);

/*
 * Access specific user object attributes
 */
echo '<h2>Targeting Specific Fields</h2>';
echo $user->get('hash_class') . '<br/>';
echo $user->get('salt');
$fieldNamesArray = array('hash_class', 'salt');
print_r($user->get($fieldNamesArray));

/*
 * Instantiate a Profile Object of this User 1:1 relationship
 */
$profile = $user->getOne('Profile');

/*
 * If we have a profile object
 */
if (is_object($profile)) {

    /*
     * Output JSON representation of the user's profile
     */
    echo '<h2>Current User Profile as JSON</h2>';
    echo $profile->toJSON();

    /*
     * Output a PHP Array of the user's profile
     */
    echo '<h2>Current User Profile as a PHP Array</h2>';
    $u = $profile->toArray();
    ksort($u);
    print_r($u);

    /*
     * Access the singe table field to retrieve and display the
       user's extended field
     */
    echo '<h2>Current Extended Fields</h2>';
    $fields = $profile->get('extended');
    ksort($fields);
    print_r($fields);
}
```

```
/*
 * Output the user's settings
 */
echo '<h2>User Settings</h2>';
$userSettings = $user->getSettings();
print_r($userSettings);

/*
 * Simple method to switch PHP array to JSON array of objects
 */
echo '<h2>Create a JSON array of Objects</h2>';
$collection = $user->getMany('UserSettings');
$c = 0;
$output = '[';
foreach ($collection as $obj) {
    $output .= ($c > 0) ? ',' : '';
    $output .= $obj->toJSON();
    $c++;
}
$output .= ']';
echo $output;

/*
 * Get list of user names
 */
echo '<h2>User Group Names</h2>';
print_r($user->getUserGroupNames());

$output = '';
$collection = $user->getMany('CreatedResources');
foreach ($collection as $obj) {
    $output .= $modx->getChunk('createdByUserTemplate',
                                            $obj->toArray());
}
echo ($output) ? '<h2>Documents Created</h2>' . $output : '';

/*
 * Only process live active current user
 */
if ($user->get('id') === $modx->user->get('id')) {
    /*
     * Show waiting Message Count
     */
```

```
echo '<h2>Internal Mail System</h2>';
echo 'Unread Messages: ' . $user->countMessages('unread')
        . '/' . $user->countMessages() . '<br/>';

/*
 *  Send user Email
 */
$message = 'Please finish the revo book ASAP!';
echo 'Sent Email to User: ';
echo ($user->sendEmail($message, array(
            'subject' => 'Need Revo Book Now!!!',
                                        )
)) ? 'Success' : 'Failed';

/*
 * Displays the contexts of the user
 */
echo '<h2>Session Contexts</h2>';
print_r($user->getSessionContexts());

/*
 * Displays Current SESSION State
 */
echo '<h2>PHP $_SESSION</h2>';
$s = $_SESSION;
ksort($s);
print_r($s);
    }
}
```

This MODX Revolution Snippet demonstrates over a dozen simple methods for interacting with the user object. Many of the techniques demonstrated will perform functionally similar in many of the other MODX Revolution objects associated with its API.

I believe a good policy for learning any new API is to get a thorough understanding of each individual function, as well as programming practices - such as checking for the existence of an object to work on. Note: the use of echo and print_r() in a MODX Revolution Snippet is discouraged, but utilized here to directly attach output to a particular method for learning the API.

To begin, it is probably a good idea to test the application on an anonymous user. This will allow a baseline to be established. It should also demonstrates the need to uncache the Snippet call, so a previously logged in user will not have their information "leaked" onto another user's screen.

Listing 16.24: Output from running testbedUser on an Anonymous User

```
Current User Object in JSON{"id":null,"username":"(anonymous)",
"password":"","cachepwd":"","class_key":"modUser","active":tru
e,"remote_key":null,"remote_data":null,"hash_class":"hashing.
modPBKDF2","salt":""}
Current User Object in PHP Array
Array
(
    [active] => 1
    [cachepwd] =>
    [class_key] => modUser
    [hash_class] => hashing.modPBKDF2
    [id] =>
    [password] =>
    [remote_data] =>
    [remote_key] =>
    [salt] =>
    [username] => (anonymous)
)
Targeting Specific Fieldshashing.modPBKDF2Array
(
    [hash_class] => hashing.modPBKDF2
    [salt] =>
)
User SettingsArray
()
Create a JSON array of Objects[]User Group NamesArray
()
Internal Mail SystemUnread Messages: 0/0Sent Email to User:
FailedSession ContextsArray
()
PHP $_SESSIONArray
(
    [modx.user.0.userGroupNames] => Array
        ()

    [modx.user.contextTokens] => Array
        ()

)
```

Creating a Resource Programmatically

Until this point, I have only demonstrated functionality associated with "reading" the data in a MODX Revolution object. For many applications, data retrieval is the only requirement, but sooner or later a project will need the site users to actually place data within a database. The rest of this chapter will focus on updating the MODX Revolution database, in the areas of Resources, Elements, and Users using the API extensively to accomplish those tasks.

During the days of MODX Revolution 2.0.0-beta-5, I created a database linked application which created either 33,108 or an excess of 80,000 Resources in a matter of moments - depending on which mode I ran it in. I did this little experiment to ascertain the viability of building a major Social Networking application on top of MODX Revolution.

Both time and MODX Revolution have changed since mid 2009. I became more familiar with the API and thereby allowed to freely explore simpler methods, without the overhead associated with such a large number of dynamic pages. This application now utilizes a total of 4 Resources to represent all 80,000+ documents. Essentially, the MODX Revolution API handles the bulk of the dynamic workload, while other technologies transparently handle the translations.

Establish a Baseline

To begin, lets get a look at the database fields associated with the attributes of a Resource, as it is possible for them to change from time to time as development moves forward on the MODX Revolution project. Some of these changes are shown on my site: http://www.shawnwilkerson. com/modx-revolution/2012/02/25/compare-modx-revolution-objects/.

Examples of newly added fields: privateweb, privatemgr, content_dispo, url, uri_override, and others, which by the sound of them may lead to an implementation of a Manager user being restricted to a specific container or subset of Resources, similar to the feature request: http:// bugs.modx.com/issues/4926.

Simply stated: don't assume things stay the same between versions.

Listing 16.25: PHP Snippet to return a Resource in a PHP array format

```php
<?php
/* Discover Resource attributes directly from the API */
$newResourceObj = $modx->newObject('modResource');
print_r($newResourceObj->toArray());
```

Listing 16.26: PHP array representation of a 2.2.4 MODX Revolution Resource

```
[id] =>                          [deleted] => 0
[type] => document              [deletedon] => 0
[contentType] => text/html      [deletedby] => 0
[pagetitle] =>                   [publishedon] => 0
[longtitle] =>                   [publishedby] => 0
[description] =>                 [menutitle] =>
[alias] =>                       [donthit] => 0
[link_attributes] =>            [privateweb] => 0
[published] => 0                 [privatemgr] => 0
[pub_date] => 0                  [content_dispo] => 0
[unpub_date] => 0               [hidemenu] => 0
[parent] => 0                    [class_key] => modDocument
[isfolder] => 0                  [context_key] => web
[introtext] =>                   [content_type] => 1
[content] =>                     [uri] =>
[richtext] => 1                  [uri_override] => 0
[template] => 0                  [hide_children_in_tree] => 0
[menuindex] -> 0                 [show_in_tree] => 1
[searchable] => 1                [properties] ->
[cacheable] => 1
[crcatcdby] => 0
[createdon] => 0
[editedby] => 0
[editedon] => 0
```

Building an Implementation

I took the liberty to ksort() the Resource object array, as my experience has found users typically make fewer mistakes when a logical presentation of variables are utilized, and an alphabetical list is the simplest recognizable method to implement. Many of the values already associated with the new Resource object are fine for our example, but your mileage may vary.

Listing 16.27: PHP Snippet to create children under a Parent with ID of 2

- -

```php
<?php
$userId = $modx->user->get('id');
$mySettings = Array
(
    'alias' => '',
    'cacheable' => 1,
    'class_key' => modDocument,
    'content' => 'This could be some extravagant string',
    'contentType' => text / html,
    'content_dispo' => 0,
    'content_type' => 1,
    'context_key' => web,
    'createdby' => $userId,
    'createdon' => 0,
    'deleted' => '',
    'deletedby' => 0,
    'deletedon' => 0,
    'description' => 'Resource Created via Snippet',
    'donthit' => '', /* deprecated in the API */
    'editedby' => 0,
    'editedon' => 0,
    'hidemenu' => '',
    'id' => '',
    'introtext' => '<p>An open paragraph used by some Packages</p>',
    'isfolder' => '',
    'link_attributes' => '',
    'longtitle' => 'This is a detailed title for the page',
    'menuindex' => 0,
    'menutitle' => 'My Menu Text',
    'pagetitle' => 'Abbreviated Page Title',
    'parent' => 2,
    'privatemgr' => '',
    'privateweb' => '',
    'pub_date' => 0,
```

```
            'published' => '1',
            'publishedby' => $userId,
            'publishedon' => time(),
            'richtext' => 0,
            'searchable' => 1,
            'template' => 0,
            'type' => document,
            'unpub_date' => 0,
            'uri' => '',
            'uri_override' => 0,
    );
    $newResourceObj = $modx->newObject('modResource');
    $newResourceObj->fromArray($mySettings, '', true, true);
    $newResourceObj->save();
    echo 'Resource ' . $newResourceObj->get('id') . ' created';
```

- -

Listing 16.28: Shorter PHP array providing identical functionally to full version

- -

```
    $mySettings = Array
    (
        'content' => 'This could be some extravagant string',
        'createdby' => $userId,
        'description' => 'Resource Created via Snippet',
        'introtext' => '<p>An open paragraph used by some Packages</p>',
        'longtitle' => 'This is a detailed title for the page',
        'menutitle' => 'My Menu Text',
        'pagetitle' => 'Abbreviated Page Title',
        'parent' => 2,
        'published' => '1',
        'publishedby' => $userId,
        'publishedon' => time(),
        'richtext' => 0,
    );
```

- -

I opted to remove those "attributes" from the array which will be handled by the API via default settings located in the xPDO schema. For example, if Manager users have previously set the automatic_alias System Setting to a true value, the Resource alias will be automatically generated without any interaction on our part. The same holds true for many of the associated values. I also chose to assign the newly created Resources to the individual running the Snippet.

Updating the User On-The-Fly

Assuming I have a client which has created content targeted to gender or age group, it would be beneficial to "force" users to select the appropriate values before the content is actually displayed. For users who have authenticated with the site, this is a simple update to their profile. When the user is Anonymous, we must have a solution which will equally serve to present the correct content to them.

Listing 16.29: PHP Snippet to quickly allow users to select their gender

- -

```php
<?php
/**
 * File profileUpdate.php (requires MODx Revolution 2.1+)
 * Created on: 7/21/11 at 6:45 AM
 */

$user = $modx->user;
if (is_object($user)) {
    $uid = intval($user->get('id'));
    $u_session = 'modx.user.' . $uid;
    $gender = '';
    if ($uid > 0) {

        /* Authenticated User */
        $profile = $user->getOne('Profile');
        $gender = $profile->get('gender');
    } else {

        /* Anonymous User */

        $gender = $_SESSION[$u_session . '.gender'];
    }
    if (empty($gender)) {
        $setgender = $_GET['setgender'];
        if (!$setgender) {
            $value = '<form action="[[~[[*id]]]]" method="get">
                    <input type="radio" name="setgender" value="1"
                        /> Male<br />
                    <input type="radio" name="setgender" value="2"
                        /> Female<br />
                    <input type="submit" name accept="Male or
                        Female" />
                    </form>';
```

```
                    // send placeholder form
                    $modx->setPlaceholder('gender.form', $value);
            } else {
                if ($uid > 0 && is_numeric($setgender)
                            && $setgender > 0 && $setgender < 3) {

                    /* Save Gender to Authenticated User Profile*/
                    $gender = $profile->set('gender', $setgender);
                    $profile->save();
                } else {

                    /* Set in current Anonymous User $_SESSION*/
                    $u = 'modx.user.{' . $uid . '}';
                    $gender = $_SESSION[$u_session . '.gender'] =
                            $setgender;
                }
            }
        }
        if ($gender > 0) {
            $gender = ($gender == 1) ? 'male' : 'female';
        }
    }

    /*
     * Use an uncached placeholder to complete Elements for targeting
     * [[!$chunk[[+gender]]]]
     * $modx->setPlaceholder('gender', $gender);
     */

    return ($gender) ? $gender : false;
```

- -

This example represents a "down and dirty" method of quickly establishing the gender of the current user, and will make the selection a permanent part of their profile if they are logged into the site. Anonymous users can also benefit, by a temporary setting being sent to their $_SESSION to accomplish similar functionality during their current session on the project.

I also "violated" the acceptable coding practices by including (X)HTML source code in the Snippet. To avoid this situation, I could have simply retrieved and subsequently populated a MODX Revolution Chunk as a template. Additionally, two possible "endings" are shown, while I could have also simply set an empty attribute in a logged in users profile, which is required by the organization or project goals and ignored Anonymous users altogether.

Mastering the Elements

The actual implementation for creating and manipulating MODX Revolution Elements remains similar enough between the various types, they can be discussed in conjunction. This is largely due to the fact all of them extend either modElement (modTemplate, modChunk, modTemplateVars) or modSnippet (modPlugin, modSnippet).

Listing 16.30: PHP Snippet a single function to create 5 types of MODX Objects

- -

```php
if (!function_exists(createObject)) {
    function createObject($objType, $settings)
    {
        global $modx;
        $success = false;
        $obj = $modx->newObject('mod' . $objType);
        if (is_object($obj) && !empty($settings['name'])
                        && !empty($settings['content'])) {

            /* allow for naming differences in various Elements */

            $settings['templatename'] = $settings['name'];
            $settings['pagetitle'] = $settings['name'];
            $settings['plugincode'] = $settings['content'];
            $settings['snippet'] = $settings['content'];

            /* apply attributes based on settings */

            $obj->fromArray($settings);

            /* persist the changes, saving to database */
            $success = $obj->save();
            if ($settings['debug']) {
                /* retrieve the new object and display it */
                $newObj = $modx->getObject('mod'
                        . $objType, $obj->get('id'));
                print_r($newObj->toArray());
            }
        }
        return $success;
    }
}
$type = ($scriptProperties['type']) ?
            ucfirst(strtolower($scriptProperties['type'])) : '';
```

```
/*
 * Create an Element from Snippet Call
 */
$output = createObject($type, $scriptProperties);
$output .= createObject('Chunk', array_merge(array(
                          'name' => 'Test1',
                          'content' => 'Content1',
                          'debug' => 'true',
                       ), $scriptProperties));
$output .= createObject('Plugin', array_merge(array(
                          'name' => 'Test2',
                          'content' => 'Content2'
                       ), $scriptProperties));
$output .= createObject('Resource', array_merge(array(
                          'name' => 'Test3',
                          'content' => 'Content3',
                          'createdby' => $modx->user->get('id'),
                       ), $scriptProperties));
$output .= createObject('Snippet', array(
                          'name' => 'Test4',
                          'content' => 'Content4'
                       ));
$output .= createObject('Template', array(
                          'name' => 'Test5',
                          'content' => 'Content5'
                       ));
return ($output) ? $output : false;
```

- -

To demonstrate the simplicity by which a Chunk, Plugin, Resource, Snippet, and Template could be created, I decided to create a single Snippet facilitating five types of MODX Objects. Some "translation" was required between the respective types for similar properties, such as the name and content of the respective object. Also, an Event would still need to be assigned to the Plugin.

One of the advantages of having the object directly represent a table row, is the functionality of the MODX Revolution API to clean the input for each object by discarding those parameters which are not utilized or represented within the database.

Techniques like this, can be used to illustrate the value of building data directly for the database table from the onset, rather than "converting" or otherwise manipulating it just before entry. For many developers, developing applications with the intention of getting the data to the database in as few steps as possible, could provide exponential increased productivity.

The Small Print

The following items should be understood concerning how MODX Revolution views and interacts with the various Elements.

All Snippets are treated as functions

Listing 16.31: Original PHP Snippet

```php
<?php
$resourceObj = (!empty($resourceId)) ?
    $modx->getObject('modResource', $resourceId) : $modx->resource;
print_r($resourceObj->toArray());
```

Listing 16.32: Same Snippet from the MODX Revolution core/cache/snippets

```php
<?php  return 'function elements_modsnippet_3($scriptProperties =
array())
{
    global $modx;
    if (is_array($scriptProperties)) {
        extract($scriptProperties, EXTR_SKIP);
    }
$resourceObj = (!empty($resourceId)) ?
    $modx->getobject(\'modResource\', $resourceId) : $modx->resource;
print_r($resourceObj->toArray());
}
';
```

Understanding how MODX Revolution views Snippets, should help developers avoid scope issues and target production to "act" like a function with the same methodology, restrictions, and capabilities. It could also allow the inclusion of actual functions to be placed in the page before a Snippet utilizes it, to provide additional functionality, such as returning columns of formatted data, instead of the default output of a PHP array.

Developers simply need to understand Snippets will eventually operate as a PHP function(), whether they are cached or not. This should also explain why the input parameters of one Snippet are not always accessible to other Snippets unless they are deliberately passed in some way.

Resources are Cached as Arrays of Elements

Listing 16.33: Cache Representation of a Resource in MODX 2.2.1

- -

```php
<?php return array (
  'resourceClass' => 'modDocument',
  'resource' =>
  array (
    'id' => 1,
    'type' => 'document',
    'contentType' => 'text/html',
    'pagetitle' => 'Home',
    'longtitle' => 'Test page for book',
    'description' => 'description to test against ',
    'alias' => '',
    'link_attributes' => '',
    'published' => 1,
    'pub_date' => 0,
    'unpub_date' => 0,
    'parent' => 0,
    'isfolder' => 0,
    'introtext' => '',
    'content' => '<pre>[[showResource]]</pre>',
    'richtext' => 1,
    'template' => 1,
    'menuindex' => 0,
    'searchable' => 1,
    'cacheable' => 1,
    'createdby' => 1,
    'createdon' => 1309434142,
    'editedby' => 1,
    'editedon' => 1311508423,
    'deleted' => 0,
    'deletedon' => 0,
    'deletedby' => 0,
    'publishedon' => 0,
    'publishedby' => 0,
    'menutitle' => '',
    'donthit' => 0,
    'privateweb' => 0,
    'privatemgr' => 0,
    'content_dispo' => 0,
    'hidemenu' => 0,
```

```
          'class_key' => 'modDocument',
          'context_key' => 'web',
          'content_type' => 1,
          'uri' => '',
          'uri_override' => 0,
          '_content' => '<html>
<head>
<title>MODX Revolution - Home</title>
<base href="http://shawnwilkerson.com/" />
</head>
<body>
<pre>Array
(
    [id] => 1
    [type] => document
    [contentType] => text/html
    [pagetitle] => Home
    [longtitle] => Test page for book
    [description] => description to test against
    [alias] =>
    [link_attributes] =>
    [published] => 1
    [pub_date] => 0
    [unpub_date] => 0
    [parent] => 0
    [isfolder] =>
    [introtext] =>
    [content] => <pre></pre>
    [richtext] => 1
    [template] => 1
    [menuindex] => 0
    [searchable] => 1
    [cacheable] => 1
    [createdby] => 1
    [createdon] => 2011-06-30 06:42:22
    [editedby] => 1
    [editedon] => 2011-07-24 06:53:43
    [deleted] =>
    [deletedon] => 0
    [deletedby] => 0
    [publishedon] => 0
    [publishedby] => 0
    [menutitle] =>
    [donthit] =>
```

```
            [privateweb] =>
            [privatemgr] =>
            [content_dispo] => 0
            [hidemenu] =>
            [class_key] => modDocument
            [context_key] => web
            [content_type] => 1
            [uri] =>
            [uri_override] => 0
        )
        </pre>
        </body>
        </html>',
            '_isForward' => false,
        ),
        'contentType' =>
        array (
            'id' => 1,
            'name' => 'HTML',
            'description' => 'HTML content',
            'mime_type' => 'text/html',
            'file_extensions' => '.html',
            'headers' => NULL,
            'binary' => 0,
        ),
        'policyCache' =>
        array (
        ),
        'elementCache' =>
        array (
            '[[*pagetitle]]' => 'Home',
            '[[showResource]]' => 'Array
(
    [id] => 1
    [type] => document
    [contentType] => text/html
    [pagetitle] => Home
    [longtitle] => Test page for book
    [description] => description to test against
    [alias] =>
    [link_attributes] =>
    [published] => 1
    [pub_date] => 0
    [unpub_date] => 0
```

```
            [parent] => 0
            [isfolder] =>
            [introtext] =>
            [content] => <pre></pre>
            [richtext] => 1
            [template] => 1
            [menuindex] => 0
            [searchable] => 1
            [cacheable] => 1
            [createdby] => 1
            [createdon] => 2011-06-30 06:42:22
            [editedby] => 1
            [editedon] => 2011-07-24 06:53:43
            [deleted] =>
            [deletedon] => 0
            [deletedby] => 0
            [publishedon] => 0
            [publishedby] => 0
            [menutitle] =>
            [donthit] =>
            [privateweb] =>
            [privatemgr] =>
            [content_dispo] => 0
            [hidemenu] =>
            [class_key] => modDocument
            [context_key] => web
            [content_type] => 1
            [uri] =>
            [uri_override] => 0
    )
',
  ),
  'sourceCache' =>
  array (
    'modChunk' =>
    array (
    ),
    'modSnippet' =>
    array (
      'showResource' =>
      array (
        'fields' =>
        array (
          'id' => 3,
```

```
            'name' => 'showResource',
            'description' => 'Testbed for Resources',
            'editor_type' => 0,
            'category' => 0,
            'cache_type' => 0,
            'snippet' => '$resourceObj = (!empty($resourceId)) ?
$modx->getObject(\'modResource\', $resourceId) : $modx->resource;
print_r($resourceObj->toArray());',
            'locked' => false,
            'properties' =>
            array (
            ),
            'moduleguid' => '',
          ),
          'policies' =>
          array (
            'web' =>
            array (
            ),
          ),
        ),
      ),
    ),
    'modTemplateVar' =>
    array (
    ),
  ),
);
```

- -

Spending a couple of minutes perusing the "structure" of a Resource after it has been processed into the cache, should help developers get a better understanding of what is actually happening. *The Document Parser And Cache Mechanism* Appendix explains how this process effectively works in more detail. Please feel free to take time to read it.

Developers can greatly benefit from taking time to discover the actual "work flow" MODX Revolution utilizes to parse, examine, process, cache, and finally present content on the project. Scope issues can be prevented by simply understanding how the various rules of PHP arrays and functions apply throughout the application.

Astute developers can learn techniques to use this construction to their benefit, and also understand how the cache is working on Snippet Calls from one Resource to another. For many bug squashing sessions, simply allowing everything in a Resource to be cached, and then looking at the result in the /core/cache/[CONTEXT NAME] to help ascertain simple mistakes.

The Difference Between Cached and Non Cached Elements

Listing 16.34: excerpt demonstrating non cached content in Revolution 2.1.3

```
        'elementCache' =>
        array(
            '[[*pagetitle]]' => 'Home',
        ),
        'sourceCache' =>
        array(
            'modChunk' =>
            array(
                'youtube350x193' =>
                array(
                    'fields' =>
                    array(
                        'id' => 11,
                        'name' => 'youtube350x193',
                        'description' => 'requires ?videoID=',
                        'editor_type' => 0,
                        'category' => 0,
                        'cache_type' => 0,
                        'snippet' => '<br />
<object width="350" height="193"><param name="movie" value="http://
www.youtube.com/v/[[+videoID]]&hl=en_US&fs=1&rel=0&color1=0x2b4
05b&color2=0x6b8ab6&hd=1"></param><param name="allowFullScreen"
value="true"></param><param name="allowscriptaccess"
value="always"></param><embed src="http://www.youtube.com/v/
[[+videoID]]&hl=en_US&fs=1&rel=0&color1=0x2b405b&color2=0x6b8ab6&h
d=1" type="application/x-shockwave-flash" allowscriptaccess="always"
allowfullscreen="true" width="350" height="193"></embed></object>
<br />
',
                        'locked' => false,
                        'properties' =>
                        array(
                        ),
                ),
```

All Elements are stored by type in the sourceCache without their respective output being cached, whereas elementCache stores the output of any Element as it is presented in that Resource. There is a cache for Elements themselves located at /core/cache/[CONTEXT NAME].

Snippets Can Serve as Functions

Years before Shaun McCormick released RowBoat, I had a need which kept presenting itself: present an array of information in a table format - without using the same code in every Snippet requiring that functionality. The most important requirement - it had to be simple to implement.

Listing 16.35: PHP Function Snippet - function_displayColumns

```php
<?php
if (!function_exists('displayColumns'))
{ /* Creates (multiple) vertical columns of a single return field */
  function displayColumns($arry, $numberOfColumns)
  {
        $x= 0;
        $num_rows= count($arry);
        if ($num_rows < 15)
        {
            $numberOfColumns= 1;
        }
        $o= '<table><tbody><tr><td>';
        foreach ($arry as $row)
        {
            $o .= $row.'<br />';
            $x++;
            if ($x == ceil($num_rows / $numberOfColumns))
            {
                $o .= '       </td><td>';
                $x= 0;
            }
        }
        $o .= '</td></tr></tbody></table>';
        return $o;
  }
}
```

Listing 16.36: excerpt from another PHP Snippet returning an array

```php
return (function_exists('displayColumns')) ? displayColumns($o, 4)
                        : '<pre>'.print_r($o, true).'</pre>';
```

Summary

This chapter discussed many aspects of the MODX Revolution API and is intended to familiarize the reader with the primary concepts and common functionality. By no means, have I attempted to replace or extensively discuss all aspects of the extensive MODX Revolution API. I simply endeavored to demonstrate the ease at which developers can interact and manipulate the various MODX Revolution objects - which is the primary purpose of the API.

I have demonstrated, various techniques to retrieve the individual attributes of an object using: get() which provides a simple means to retrieve multiple data types while returning expected ones. I have also shown how objects can simply be converted to arrays with toArray() and into a JSON formatted string using toJSON(), providing a seamless transition to other PHP code, or to JavaScript and other internet technologies.

I then moved on to demonstrate how simple it is to work with Collections of objects in one-to-one relationships using getOne(), and one-to-many relationships with getMany(). Key to these topics was an explanation of when to utilize these functions and the requirement of database tables.

Open-ended examples were then presented to begin writing data back to the tables, as well as programmatically creating MODX Revolution objects, using a very detailed and exacting method, and then a brief array changing only those values necessary. A Snippet demonstrating the simplicity of creating a unified single implementation to interact with many objects was also presented, which also allowed a brief or extensive set of attributes, and the ability to create MODX Objects directly via a Snippet Call using its parameters.

The intent of this chapter, is to provide answer to some of the "hows" and "whys" of the MODX Revolution API, not necessarily replace the actual documentation. Hopefully, this chapter should encourage developers to simplify their projects, by strongly leaning on the API. It should also provide the basis to begin looking for answers as new projects are being taken on.

The single best way to learn any API is by imitation. I would suggest developers visit the Package Manager or the various github repositories to access MODX Revolution Packages, implementing an aspect of the API they are wanting to learn. For example, Login, Personalize, and other Packages demonstrate quite a bit of user related functionality, whereas getResources, getPage, Taglister, Wayfinder, Crumbz, and quite few others, implement many aspects concerning Resources.

The items discussed in this chapter combined with many of the MODX Revolution Packages, should quickly facilitate developers using very efficient and streamlined code greatly increasing their productivity and profitability.

The MODX Revolution Community is strongly encouraged to contribute to the project by sharing their implementations. The simplest method, is to get a free account on Github for development, while formal releases could utilize Packman to quickly create official Packages.

17

xPDO: Foundations For Development

Like many developers, I spent years working from one Content Management System to another. Until MODX Revolution, I felt all of them to have one thing in common: they never seemed to provide everything I needed. Whether the list of complaints was short or long, I found many others feeling the same, as product forums were dominated by posts by end-users asking how to hack, bypass, or kludge functionality which should have been included from the beginning.

The same frustration appears to have been a significant influence on the original purpose of MODX as it was originally a modification to provide functionality to a project which took the historic approach of making the majority of decisions for the users. The lead developer moved his efforts into a commercial application, while the originators of MODX sought to begin building the Content Management Platform *they* would like to use and give to others.

This is a bit ironic, because my experience has shown the largest "learning curve" for people moving their development platform to MODX Revolution, is the removal of the concept of being confined to predetermined work flows and implementation possibilities. Essentially, the hardest lesson to learn with MODX Revolution is that it was designed for developers by developers.

In this chapter, I am going to present the concepts necessary to build third-party applications beyond the objects contained within MODX Revolution. To begin with, I will be looking at a simple application centered around a third-party table in the MODX database. I will then move into defining relationships between database tables.

I am using a clean install of MODX Revolution to create the examples contained within this chapter. I would strongly suggest the use of a development server and clean installation to explore and learn these concepts, so easy backups and restores of the database can be utilized if necessary.

xPDO Overview

OpenExpedio (xPDO), developed by Jason Coward, is an open extension to PHP Data Objects (PDO), operating as a light-weight Object-relational bridge (ORB) library that takes advantage of the standard for database persistence in PHP 5.1+.

In laymen's terms, xPDO uses Active Record Pattern to handle all of the relationships found in the data, database access, and data manipulation. In essence, it does much of the work for developers, leaving them to focus on accomplishing project goals. xPDO effectively functions as a foundation to interact with multiple database management systems (DBMS) using the same code, while simultaneously abstracting data into objects providing streamlined interaction without unnecessary code.

Suffice it to say, the xPDO class can act as standalone wrapper for projects not built for use in MODX Revolution, or as the foundation of an entire web project - like the MODX Revolution project itself. For the purpose of this chapter, I will be presenting content as it relates to providing database connectivity, data abstraction, and relationship - based applications.

On one hand, xPDO handles all of the database functions of our data, while also providing the basis for PHP developers to directly manipulate values and develop platforms without necessarily being require to directly handle database system specific queries. Essentially, it allows developers to create a single version of code, relying on xPDO to handle the database end of it. If developers need to implement direct queries they can, but typically it is not necessary.

On the other hand, xPDO handles all of the relationships of data between tables, and even within the object itself. This allows developers to focus on logic and flow of data, instead of database connections, queries, and extensive variable definition and subsequent translation / casting.

I choose to describe xPDO to my clients as the method I am using to interact with their data and their databases. If they ask about the benefits, I can quickly point to MODX Revolution and say, "they were able to develop an entire Content Management System, including Access Control Lists, User Groups, and Document Groups on xPDO."

Additional information concerning xPDO can be found at the following locations:

The project web site	http://xpdo.org
API	http://www.xpdo.org/api/
Bug Tracker	http://bugs.modx.com/projects/xpdo
Documentation	http://rtfm.modx.com/display/xPDO20
Github	https://github.com/modxcms/xpdo
MODX Revolution	/core/xpdo

The examples in this chapter will guide the reader through the various components of xPDO, as my goal is to demonstrate functionality, leaving the fine tuning to the developer to expand into a complete application. To establish a baseline, the following summaries should clarify the basic purpose for each of the primary xPDO classes discussed in the remainder of this chapter.

xPDODriver

Provides database system specific declarations. Essentially, all sql languages have some similarity. The xPDODriver allows xPDO to understand the nuances of a specific database system. Currently, xPDO speaks MySQL, SQLite, and SQLSVR. The examples in this chapter will focus on the dominant MySQL variety as the majority of readers will probably be using it.

xPDOGenerator

Creates the various PHP Class files for use with xPDO and provides functionality to reverse engineer a preexisting database to a schema file. I recommend new xPDO users to reverse engineer their database at least once, to get an understanding on how the xPDO Schema file is laid out versus a UML or MySQL Workbench representation on a familiar structure.

> ☞ *TIP: MAKE A HABIT OUT OF BUILDING YOUR SCHEMA FILES BY HAND*
>
> *When I first started using xPDO, I made the mistake of trying to build a MySQL Schema by going through the process of laying it out with MySQL Workbench and then reverse engineering it. It actually ended up taking quite a bit more time using Workbench than simply building it by hand.*
>
> *I still had to go back and define the composite and aggregate relationships between tables. Somewhere around the third cut-and-paste it dawned on me: building the schema by hand was much faster than the way I had been doing it for years.*

xPDOManager

The easiest way to describe xPDOManager, is it provides much of the same functionality as the MySQL ALTER and CREATE commands. Similar to the MySQL variety, this class is seldom used, as changes to data bases structures are typically rare or frowned upon - unless necessary.

Project leaders should be aware of who is allowed to utilize this class, as it has the ability to drop tables and their associated data - without warning or second chances. Developers will have to create a mechanism to interface with users requiring them to indicate they are aware of their actions, effectively putting a block in front of the class in the User Interface.

xPDOObject

An abstract layer, which may or may not be directly attached to a database table, but used to define much of the functionality which is inherited by each xPDO object. Typically, this is used to define abstract relationships, such as those surrounding the modPluginEvents, which are not entirely comprised of data located in the database. In the event, an object is instantiated as an xPDOObject with a table attached, developers will usually indirectly access the object through a relationship, such as a accessing `modx_member_groups` or other many-to-many relationships.

xPDOSimpleObject

Extends xPDOObject, adding a integer field to be utilized as a primary key in a database table. The vast majority of implementations will at some point, extend this class, thereby benefitting from a direct map of application data to the database table which serves it.

MODX Revolution implements modUser, modResource, and many other objects by extending xPDOSimpleObject, vastly reducing code and greatly increasing productivity, as the same basic methods can be utilized regardless of which object is being interacted with.

This directly correlates to a lower learning curve, as developers only need to learn the basic methods and any additional object specific declarations as is needed. This was demonstrated extensively during the MODx Revolution API Concepts chapter, when the same methods were used to accomplish similar tasks with a variety of MODX objects.

MODX Revolution Rule #17: **The single best way to learn xPDO is to simply use it.**

Abbreviated explanations of xPDO can be remembered as follows:

♦ xPDO operates at the class / relationship level

♦ xPODriver defines which database management system is being accessed

♦ xPDOGenerator creates the base xPDO class files for each class in the scheama

♦ xPDOManager provides administrative functionality: ALTER, CREATE, and DROP

♦ xPDOObject allows abstract classes to be derived

♦ xPDOSimpleObject maps a database row to a PHP Object

Schemata

xPDO uses an Extensible Markup Language (XML) file to map data to the database and its associated PHP representation, typically implemented as an object or relationship. While simple to create and utilize, it does have a few components which should be understood before beginning to build any application extending or utilizing xPDO.

> ₸ *TIP: ACCESS YOUR OWN FLAVOR OF THE MODX SCHEMA*
>
> *The concepts presented here, will remain consistent regardless of the database system being used. Feel free to study and utilize the syntax of the various schema types for your installation of MODX Revolution in the* /core/model/schema/ *directory.*

Hierarchy Structure

Developers should consider using an xPDO schema on a single application and proceed with development from that perspective. It is quite common to build multiple faces of an application which utilizes a single schema, while building multiple applications from a single schema may need to be discouraged depending on the actual implementation. In other words, keep it simple.

Listing 17.01: /core/model/schema/modx.mysql.schema.xml base structure

```xml
<?xml version="1.0" encoding="UTF-8"?>
<model>
    <object>
        <field/>
    </object>
</model>
```

The significance of utilizing xPDO is straightforward simplicity and is created in "well-formed" XML files. Essentially this requires all tags to have an open and a close, utilizing one of the two types demonstrated above, in the <model></model> and <field/> examples. Additionally, each declaration is typically enclosed with double quotes as illustrated in the <?xml> line.

<model> serves as the root container for the entire application

<object> represents each aspect of the application which will be represented as an abstract object or a direct representation of a single row in the database

<field> represents each attribute of the object and/or a table row

The Model

Listing 17.02: model declaration excerpt from modx.mysql.schema.xml

```
<model package="modx"
       baseClass="xPDOObject"
       platform="mysql"
       defaultEngine="MyISAM"
       phpdoc-package="modx"
       phpdoc-subpackage=""
       version="1.1"
       tablePrefix="pre_" >
```

xPDO accomplishes quite a bit with the model declaration (tablePrefix added):

package, is what xPDO calls an application, and is used to create the base class utilized by xPDO for the entire application. This name is also used to define the working directory, in this example, xPDO will utilize the "modx" directory under /core/model/ to build its class files. Developers will typically implement their own model directory under their Snippet folder.

baseClass is typically an abstract class which will not be directly represented by an individual table in the database, but will instead inherit basic object and xPDO functionality for the Package to implement.

platform simply defines which database management system will be used with a schema. Developers can choose to support any, or all, of the DBMS serviced by xPDO. As of MODX Revolution 2.1.3, the primary database systems supported are MySQL, SQLSRV and SQLite., with the first two having the most attention in the majority of MODX Revolution Packages.

It is my hope, PostgreSQL and other database management systems will eventually be added.

defaultEngine designates which DBMS engine to use for database functionality. MODX developers recommend using MyISAM for MySQL DBMS, though InnoDB is also available. A separate schema needs to be created for each DBMS and engine combination used.

phpdoc-package, phpdoc-subpackage, and tablePrefix each represent additional attributes not required or currently utilized by xPDO itself. These can be added to the model declaration to facilitate additional functionality, such as the creation of documentation or as simple reminders - like the table prefix used in the names when xPDO created them.

version xPDO meta information designating which parser it is to use to process the schema.

The Object

Listing 17.03: excerpt of assorted object declarations

- -

```
<object class="modStaticResource" extends="modResource" />
<object class="modResource" table="site_content"
        extends="modAccessibleSimpleObject"></object>
<object class="modAccessibleSimpleObject"
        extends="modAccessibleObject"></object>
<object class="modAccessibleObject" extends="xPDOObject"/>
```

- -

xPDO "interprets" each <object> line as an object of a class extending some class:

object declarations will each become an object to be directly interacted with or an object based on a defined relationship. Only a single object attached to a given class should exist within the model with a given name. Base Objects should be extended whenever possible, instead of simply duplicating definitions, as is seen in the declaration of modResource and modDocument.

class designates the name of the file which will be created in the model directory of the Package being defined in the schema. These files represent the PHP side of the data map and may serve database tables or relationships. modUserGroupMember is a relationship implementation.

table defines the database table which will be created, utilized, and otherwise interacted with by xPDO. As shown in this example, not every object will be represented in the database. Also, take note that two classes can utilizing the same table, as shown in modStaticResource and modResource (as well as others not shown here). A table name itself, should typically be designated only a single time within a model.

extends denotes the object inheritance. In this example, the entire inheritance tree is illustrated. As with all xPDO objects, at some point they should eventually inherit xPDOObject, and thereby xPDO. Listing 17.03 shows modStaticResource extending modResource and thereby utilizes its database table and attributes.

It should also be noted, even though an object, such as modResource, has quite a large number of attributes assigned to it, xPDO will not be able to implement the database side of the map, until the object has extended either modAccessibleSimpleObject or modSimpleObject at some point in the inheritance tree.

The object declaration is what provides xPDO functionality to each of the objects. It could be said, that it is the doorway from a class extending xPDO to the actual object itself. All database functionality is simply inherited to the class and then passed to the objects.

The field

Listing 17.04: a single field from the modResource Object

```
<field key="pagetitle"
        dbtype="varchar"
        precision="255"
        phptype="string"
        null="false"
        default=""
        index="fulltext"
        indexgrp="content_ft_idx" />
```

----

key represents the name of the object's attribute and the table column. This field is not to be confused with the DBMS Primary Key, which is established automatically by xPDO for any object extended from modSimpleObject or modAccessibleSimpleObject.

dbtype declares the type of field being used to store the data in the database table and can be defined by many of the types understood by the specific DBMS. I, personally, tend to hover close to the most generic forms of text and integer fields for the widest compatibility.

precision defines the maximum number of characters to use for the database column. I do not believe this has any real-world relevance to PHP types, other than informing developers of the amount of possible information being returned or requested when an object is saved.

phptype tells xPDO what sort of data type to "translate" the field to and from, when interacting with the PHP aspect of the data map.

null declares whether or not the database field is allowed to be null

default establishes the default database value to use when a new object is being saved to the table. Quite often a default of "0" (zero) is used for User and Resource relationships.

index establishes the type of index being established for this field, if any

indexgrp the name of a multi-column index this field belongs to, if any. This can be used for a variety of reasons, with Full Text Searches being one of the most common.

attributes allows additional definition on fields which accept further definition, such as making an integer unsigned. As a rule of thumb, I will typically store integers as text, unless there is a possibility of the DBMS eventually needing to perform mathematical operations.

Relationships

xPDO offers three primary types of relationships: typical Object Oriented Programming inheritance, Aggregate, and Composite. Understanding the nuances of each of these can greatly simplify construction of a successful schema and quickly streamline your project.

Inheritance

modResource establishes the necessary attributes to create project Content which is displayed as users click on links or interact with the web project. It is extended to also handle modDocument, modStaticResource, modSymLink, modWebLink, and modXMLRPCResource requests. Each of these PHP classes utilize the modResource table and extend the object. MODX Revolution 2.2.2-pl added a properties field which Articles and other Packages can also use to extend modResources.

Aggregate: typically cardinality of one

An individual record can be deleted without any consideration regarding the cascading effects of the deletion, as it is autonomously removed. For example, if a Resource is created by a user and their account is removed, the Resources will remain. If a Resource is deleted the user is not.

Excerpt 17.05: of a mutual aggregate one-to-many relation (User to Resource)

```
<aggregate alias="CreatedBy" class="modUser" local="createdby"
           foreign="id" cardinality="one" owner="foreign" />
<aggregate alias="CreatedResources" class="modResource" local="id"
           foreign="createdby" cardinality="many" owner="local" />
```

Composite: typically cardinality of many

If a record is removed, xPDO will subsequently also remove composite records. Care should be given when establishing a composite relation to ensure deletions happen in the correct direction - secondary tables should not typically be able to cause a primary record to be deleted.

Excerpt 17.06: of a composite relation which will be deleted with the user

```
<composite alias="Profile" class="modUserProfile" local="id"
           foreign="internalKey" cardinality="one" owner="local" />
```

Quick Start: Creating a Single Database Lookup Table

Much of the available documentation demonstrates using a build script or a PHP native script to create an xPDO model. I am going to demonstrate the process utilizing MODX Revolution Snippets to accomplish the same tasks, as it should simplify the learning curve while also serving the majority of implementations.

₮ TIP: FOLLOW THE EXAMPLE SHOWN BY MODX DEVELOPERS

The process presented here, has been simplified to enable rapid learning in the implementation of xPDO based applications with MODX Revolution. Seasoned MODX Revolution Developers, will typically create their whole application outside of the directory structure and utilize a build script to facilitate the creation of all of the Elements and Components. For example, visit https://github.com/opengeek to get an idea of this technique, as well as seeing how his development process is tied directly into Github.

Step 1: Create a Simple xPDO Schema

The first time through this process, I would recommend keeping things very simple. This is not due to any significant level of difficulty, but rather due to the simplicity of it. More often than not, I have found people way over complicating this process. In an effort to help readers avoid making this mistake, I am simply building a three column lookup table comprised of the names and abbreviations of US States.

Listing 17.07: statelookup xPDO schema file

```xml
<?xml version="1.0" encoding="UTF-8"?>
<model package="statelookup" baseClass="xPDOObject" platform="mysql"
        defaultEngine="MyISAM" tablePrefix="eg">
    <object class="State" table="states" extends="xPDOSimpleObject">
        <field key="statename" dbtype="varchar" precision="40"
                phptype="string" null="true" />
        <field key="stateabbrv" dbtype="varchar" precision="2"
                phptype="string" null="true" />
    </object>
</model>
```

Note: In a fully functional geographical application I would use something like 'geo' to indicate a geographical application. In this case, I utilized 'eg' for example given.

Step 2: Create a Working Directory

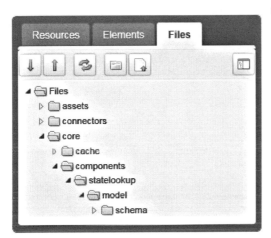

Create a directory named identically to the Package name under the /core/components directory. **This name should entirely in lowercase.** For this example, I will be building a statelookup Package.

Next create a model directory under the package named directory.

Finally create a schema within the model directory, which should resemble the one shown.

Note: in the future developers should actually have a concept in mind and develop accordingly - reversing the first two steps.

Step 3: Upload the Schema to the model/schema directory

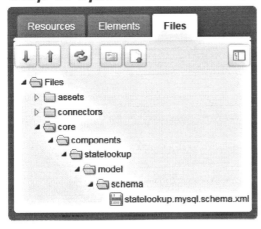

Once the schema file has been completed, upload it to the project and place it in the model/schema folder underneath the component directory bearing the same name as the Package declaration in the model.

For those individuals desiring to support MySQL, SQLSRV, and any other DBMS added in the future, I would suggest using search and replace to change between the query language dialects.

For those not wanting to learn, an entire new language, feel free to use the respective MODX Revolution schema to aide in the process.

☰ *TIP: USE LOWER CASE NAMES FOR PACKAGES, DIRECTORIES, AND DATABASE TABLES*

By keeping all of the names in lowercase, it provides a consistent naming convention and helps delineate the xPDO derived classes from the Package and Object Names. Additionally, I believe xPDO expects for these names to be lowercase.

I believe it is also recommended to avoid the use of camel-case in database table names.

Step 4: Build the xPDO Model

The purpose of the Schema file is to provide the basis for xPDO to create PHP Class files directly mapping the data in the database to PHP data types. Listing 17.08 contains a Snippet to create the MySQL files which only needs the name of the package to be supplied during the Snippet Call.

Listing 17.08: PHP Snippet to create xPDO Models - requires $packageName

```php
<?php
/**
 * @param string $packageName The name of the xPDO Package.
 */

// MODX Revolution standard is to use all lowercase for package name
$packageName = strtolower($packageName);

// Using a semi-hardcoded value for the Package path for consistency
$workingDirectory = 'core/components/' . $packageName . '/';
$model = MODX_BASE_PATH . $workingDirectory . 'model/';

// MODX Revolution standard places schema under the model directory
$schema = $model . 'schema/' . $packageName . '.mysql.schema.xml';

// Model Creation
$modx->setLogLevel(xPDO::LOG_LEVEL_INFO);
$modx->setLogTarget(XPDO_CLI_MODE ? 'ECHO' : 'HTML');
$manager = $modx->getManager();
$generator = $manager->getGenerator();
$res = $generator->parseSchema($schema, $model);
return ($res) ? 'Model Created at ' . $model . $packageName : false;
```

Snippet call: `[[!createModel?packageName=`statelookup`]]`

Note: make sure to run this uncached as shown.

Successful completion of Listing 17.08 should return a message similar to: Model Created at /home/user/public_html/core/components/statelookup/model/statelookup. Otherwise, xPDO will report any errors to the screen. Additionally, the class files should now be visible in the MODX Browser tree, as well as any other appropriate method utilized to view them.

Step 5: Creating Database Table(s) using the xPDO Model

Once the xPDO Model has successfully been created, it is a very simple process to create the associated database. For this purpose, I have created a Snippet to handle the creation process, which requires the same parameter used to create the model. **Caution, each Model should designate a table prefix to avoid the newly created table from having the same prefix as the installation of MODX Revolution and hopefully other Packages.**

Listing 17.09: PHP Snippet to create Database tables from xPDO Model

```php
<?php
// @param string $packageName The lowercase name of the xPDO Package
$packageName = strtolower($packageName);

// check system settings or use the default system core path setting
$modelPath = $modx->getOption($packageName . '.core_path', null,
            $modx->getOption('core_path') . 'components/'
                                          . $packageName . '/')
        . 'model/';

// @param string $prefix The name placed before each table name
$modx->addPackage($packageName, $modelPath, $prefix);
$manager = $modx->getManager();
$manager->createObjectContainer('State');
```

Snippet Call: `[[!createTablesFromModel?packageName=`statelookup`&prefix=`eg_`]]`

$modelPath uses `getOption($key, $options = null, $default = null)`, to select between runtime, a possible system setting, and a default value, which happens to also be a system setting in this case - with 'model/' being appended to which ever value is used.

$modx->addPackage() adds the package from the `modelpackage="statelookup"` schema declaration and assigns the appropriate table prefix so we can differentiate our model from the one used by MODX Revolution, while providing direct access to the classes and maps.

$manager->createObjectContainer('State') creates a table based on the field definitions of the 'State' object. Each object listed in the Schema, which inherits either `modAccessibleSimpleObject` or `modSimpleObject` would have to also be declared on subsequent lines for the associated table to be created. Note: this requires a connection to the database and defaults to the one utilized by MODX Revolution.

Listing 17.10: Success response from $manager->createObjectContainer()

```
Created table `eg_states`
SQL: CREATE TABLE `eg_states`
(`id` INTEGER unsigned NOT NULL AUTO_INCREMENT,
`statename` VARCHAR(40) NULL,
`stateabbrv` VARCHAR(2) NULL,
 PRIMARY KEY (`id`)) ENGINE=MyISAM
```

If there were any issues, error messages should be displayed on the screen and possibly in an error_log close to the site root - depending on your configuration. Common mistakes typically take one of three forms:

Syntactical issues usually related to character case utilized to declare the individual objects, or the class itself. Try to correct these issues manually, but do not spend more than a fair amount of time on it. When all else fails, copy comparative sections from a schema file targeted to the same DBMS from the /core/model/schema directory and use modified versions.

The idea is simply learning to find and correct the mistakes on your own. It typically takes only two or three schema constructions to establish a relatively firm grasp on the skill set. The key is to start the application with a minimal structure until it is functioning correctly, adding as necessary.

File collisions occurs when previous versions of PHP Class files which were derived from $generator->parseSchema($schema, $model) remain in the directory structure. The map files are updated with each subsequent run, but the Class files remain undisturbed. This is the expected behavior as developers can simply utilize the derived Class file extending xPDO as a basis to expand the class. Many applications simply use the same file, including MODX Revolution to create associated methods and functions. The following error is usually given, in collision issues:

Skipping /home/user/public_html/core/components/statelookup/model/statelookup/state.class.php; file already exists.
Move existing class files to regenerate them.

Table mismatch occurs when updates have been made to the model and have not been applied to the associated tabled in the database. If the table is empty, simply remove the offending table with removeObjectContainer() in place of the createObjectClassname() in step 5.

To fine tune database corrections, refer to the following functions: addField(), addIndex( ), alterField(), removeField(), and removeIndex() located in the /core/xpdo/xpdomanager. class.php file. You can also view utilization examples by looking at the related code contained in / setup/includes/upgrades/[mysql or sqlsrv]/ 2.2.0-rc-1.php of any current MODX Revo download.

Step 6: Instantiate an Object of the Package

Once a successful response is returned from Step 5's database creation, it is a simple matter to instantiate an object. There is a single issue to consider at this point: the database is empty, so we can't retrieve anything, but we can "establish a baseline" and verify the Class derived from xPDO is properly functioning by "looking" at the object.

Listing 17.11: statelookup.snippet.php

```
// establish the path to the model
$modelPath = $modx->getOption('statelookup.core_path', null,
        $modx->getOption('core_path') . 'components/statelookup/')
        . 'model/';

// Add a package so the $modx object can interact with it
$modx->addPackage('statelookup', $modelPath, 'eg_');

// instantiate and test our object
$obj = $modx->newObject('State');
print_r($obj->toArray());
```

$obj = $modx->newObject('State') instructs MODX to create a new instance of an object which has been defined in a xPDO Package at some point. In our statelookup.mysql. schema.xml file we declared State as an object in the line:

Listing 17.12: excerpt from statelookup xPDO schema file

```
<object class="State" table="states" extends="xPDOSimpleObject">
```

At this point, we are simply attempting to ascertain we actually have an object to be implemented in some way. After calling the Snippet with [[!statelookup]], there will be one of two responses returned by xPDO:

Success:	Failure:
Array ([id] => [statename] => [stateabbrv] =>)	Fatal error: Call to a member function toArray() on a non-object in

Step 7: Populate the Table

Once the object has been verified to work, there are a number of ways to populate the table: direct insertion via the DBMS, the result of a query, or simply utilizing a PHP array. I will be demonstrating two variations of the latter option.

Listing 17.13: populateStateTable by specifying object attribute = array value

- -

```php
<?php
$states = array(
  array('statename'=>'Alabama','stateabbrv'=>'AL'),
  array('statename'=>'Alaska','stateabbrv'=>'AK'),
  array('statename'=>'American Samoa','stateabbrv'=>'AS'),
  array('statename'=>'Arizona','stateabbrv'=>'AZ'),
  array('statename'=>'Arkansas','stateabbrv'=>'AR'),
  array('statename'=>'Armed Forces - Americas','stateabbrv'=>'AA'),
  array('statename'=>'Armed Forces - Europe','stateabbrv'=>'AE'),
  array('statename'=>'Armed Forces - Pacific','stateabbrv'=>'AP'),
  array('statename'=>'California','stateabbrv'=>'CA'),
  array('statename'=>'Colorado','stateabbrv'=>'CO'),
  array('statename'=>'Connecticut','stateabbrv'=>'CT'),
  array('statename'=>'Delaware','stateabbrv'=>'DE'),
// the rest of the states were removed for brevity
  );

$componentPath = $modx->getOption('statelookup.core_path', null,
                $modx->getOption('core_path')
                . 'components/statelookup/') . 'model/';
$modx->addPackage('statelookup', $componentPath, 'eg_');
foreach ($states as $state) {
    $obj = $modx->newObject('State');
    $obj->set('statestatename', $state['statename']);
    $obj->set('statestateabbrv', $state['stateabbrv']);
    $obj->save();
}
```

- -

$obj->set('statestateabbrv', $state['stateabbrv']) can be used in situations where the data does not line up with the database table: array key names, number of columns, data types, current expectations, structure changes, or whatever. It can also, simply be used out of personal preference. If the data is made to match the receiving table, a much simpler form can be used:

Listing 17.14: populateStateTable with array keys matching table names

```
// multi-dimensional $state array would be here

$componentPath = $modx->getOption('statelookup.core_path', null,
                $modx->getOption('core_path')
                . 'components/statelookup/') . 'model/';
$modx->addPackage('statelookup', $componentPath, 'eg_');
foreach ($states as $state) {
    $obj = $modx->newObject('State', $state);
    $obj->save();
}
```

In the MODx Revolution API Introduction chapter, I discussed some of the advantages to this method. Most notably, is its ability to cleanly place data within the table with column names directly matching the input array allowing "extra" data to simply be ignored.

Each of these methods should produce the desired result of having the entire list of states represented in the table, which can now simply be retrieved with $modx->getObject('State', $criteria). At this point we should have a "generically" functional application to build upon.

Step 8: Assign a Category (Optional)

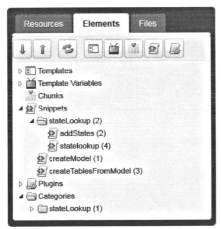

I believe the majority of Packages released for MODX Revolution, should probably be released with Categories assigned to them, making it much easier to associate related Elements. In the case of single file Packages, this would probably be excessive and possibly considered unnecessary.

Developers can implement Categories to distinguish one application from another, as well as delineate various development stages within the application itself.

On my primary MODX Revolution development server, I have hundreds of Snippets and Chunks - which is not uncommon for any company building projects for any length of time.

For those just starting out with MODX Revolution, consider the number of JavaScript, XML, JSON, PHP, and (X)HTML files comprised in a typical project. It doesn't take long for the Resource and Element trees to become unwieldy.

Packaging Components via Packman

As an author and contributor for MODX Revolution, I have to admit I have an ulterior motive: I want people to feel very comfortable developing, and thereby contributing Packages to the community. The easiest way for people to get involved is to simply find a need in the community and get to work.

In the previous section, I laid out the eight most common steps utilized to build most xPDO Snippets. Not all Snippets developed for MODX Revolution, will utilize or even require all of the steps presented. Hopefully, the content will quickly get you moving forward. As the chapter progresses the examples will become more complex.

For those who have taken time to develop their own Snippet, and who feel they are ready to Package it, the process for utilizing the Packman Component is laid out below. Packman is located under the Component menu in the Manger, once it has been installed via Package Management and is great for those not creating Custom Manager Pages.

For this example, I am going to Package a randomImage Snippet I wrote in 2009, which is available at `https://github.com/wshawn/`. This Snippet does not implement database access, or xPDO Schemas. Essentially, it is a single-file Package, which I was asked to add some working examples to, which I did in the form of Chunks.

Once the display for Packman loads in the browser, enter the Package name, a version number, and the type of release: beta, rc (release candidate), or PL (public launch). The Readme, License, and Changelog are all optional, though they should be included to facilitate communication.

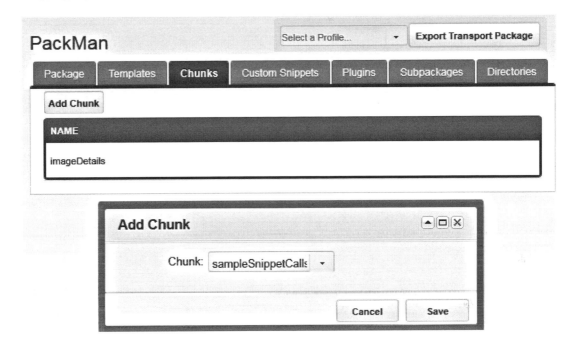

I will not be adding any Templates to the Package, so I can skip directly to the Chunks Tab.

I have already added the first Chunk and subsequently clicked the Add Chunk button to add the next one: sampleSnippetCalls.

Packman provides a very convenient drop-down box, allowing each Chunk to be very quickly added.

𝓕 *TIP:* *KEEP DEVELOPMENT SERVERS AS CLEAN AS POSSIBLE*

Screen real estate is limited. Though the drop-down box makes short work of adding Chunks to a Package, Manager Users may find the interface a bit impractical on development servers with dozens or hundreds of Elements.

I would recommend a clean server to develop and create packages on, and another to store the individual Packages. Developers may also choose to utilize Github and contribute to the MODX Revolution Repository to "share the load."

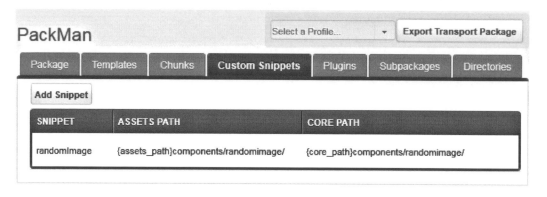

On the Custom Snippets Page, I add the associative paths for my Snippet.

Notice the Assets Path. I could have actually used that in my Snippet, but left the path as a run time configuration in the Snippet Call.

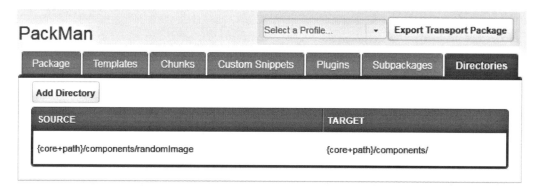

For my Snippet, I could have simply used Packman to include the Snippet and Chunks directly into MODX Revolution Elements. I also decided place the files in the Component/package_name directory.

Note: the target folder will be auto completed with the Package Name.

Finally, click the Export Transport Package to have the transport package sent to the browser for downloading. I took the liberty to unzip the file on my computer to make sure it contained the structure I was looking for. I typically leave Packman open until the Package has been successfully created. Optionally, feel free to create a profile so future updates will be greatly simplified, as it can be loaded to update the Package for new versions.

Contribute the Transport Package to http://modx.com/extras/ or place them in your own repo.

Creating a Multi-Table Schema

To begin this process, I will start with the schema. During the many applications I have developed I have learned to spend plenty of time thinking though the schema and the relationships contained therein. More often than not, I will have a very solid understanding of the logic associated with the application before I even get beyond the schema creation.

Solutions Diversify As Complexity Increases

I typically build each xPDO schema from the perspective of the most familiar object or the most centric to the application. There are times when the simplest method, is to simply replicate an established work flow from a client into a web application. Every developer has their own methods for working through the various stages of schema design,

For larger projects with various skill sets and disciplines involved, multiple individuals may be called on to develop a portion of an xPDO schema. This would be comparable to an individual building out the User object and all its associated objects, while another may be tasked with developing the Resource object and its associations.

A small group may be tasked with joining each of the various components together into a seamless application. It is even possible for an individual to make final decisions on the actual implementation and to ensure site security, data integrity, and goal completion. Each person should clearly understand the needs of client, the goals of the project, and their individual tasks.

Over the next few pages, I have provided a multi-table application - sophisticated enough to demonstrate a wide array of techniques, while simple enough for the real world examples to facilitate a quick understanding of the concepts. This schema should provide a solid foundation to begin building much larger applications.

Specific explanations will be discussed after the code has been presented. For now, I will explain the methodology behind the application, which originated from two sources: my position as head of technology at my church, and my youngest daughter's sweet sixteen birthday party.

At the Church, it would be very beneficial to see which worship lists were recently used, as well as which songs tend to be used the most (or least). It might also be helpful to go back and critique the overall effectiveness of a given list - though this typically has more to do with the people.

My daughter, Kymberli, wanted to have her party around a "night club" theme, which was pretty daring considering the very wide range of ages and preferences in attendance. Throughout the night, there were multiple issues, which could have easily been avoided.

I decided to build an application which could handle both environments. The following schema signifies the beginning of that effort. Keep in mind, this schema is a very early base, upon which a much larger application is to be built, as such much of the fine tuning is expected to occur later.

Listing 17.15: discjockey primary object schema - building a foundation

```xml
<?xml version="1.0" encoding="UTF-8"?>


<model package="discjockey" baseClass="xPDOObject" platform="mysql"
    defaultEngine="MyISAM" tablePrefix="dj_" phpdoc-package="playlist"
    phpdoc-subpackage="" version="1.1">


  <object class="djEvent" table="events" extends="xPDOSimpleObject">
    <field key="name" dbtype="varchar" precision="100" phptype="string"
        null="false" default="" index="index"/>
    <field key="createdon" dbtype="datetime" phptype="datetime"/>
    <field key="createdby" dbtype="integer" precision="10" phptype="integer"
        attributes="unsigned" null="false" default="0"/>
    <field key="createdfor" dbtype="integer" precision="10" phptype="integer"
        attributes="unsigned" null="false" default="0"/>
    <field key="resource" dbtype="int" precision="10" phptype="integer"
        attributes="unsigned" null="false" default="0"/>
    <field key="comment" dbtype="varchar" precision="300" phptype="string"
        null="false" default=""/>
  </object>


  <object class="djPlayList" table="playlists" extends="xPDOSimpleObject">
    <field key="eventid" dbtype="varchar" precision="10" phptype="string"
        null="false" default=""/>
    <field key="title" dbtype="varchar" precision="100" phptype="string"
        null="false" default=""/>
    <field key="playdate" dbtype="datetime" phptype="datetime"/>
  </object>
```

```
<object class="djSong" table="songs" extends="xPDOSimpleObject">
    <field key="album" dbtype="varchar" precision="100" phptype="string"
        null="false" default=""/>
    <field key="track" dbtype="varchar" precision="4" phptype="string"
        null="false" default=""/>
    <field key="title" dbtype="varchar" precision="100" phptype="string"
        null="false" default="" index="index"/>
    <field key="artist" dbtype="varchar" precision="100" phptype="string"
        null="false" default=""/>
    <field key="duration" dbtype="varchar" precision="6" phptype="string"
        null="false" default=""/>
    <field key="leadin" dbtype="varchar" precision="4" phptype="string"
        null="false" default=""/>
    <field key="deleted" dbtype="tinyint" precision="1" phptype="string"
        null="false" default="0"/>
    <field key="inactive" dbtype="tinyint" precision="1" phptype="string"
        null="false" default="0"/>
    <field key="restricted" dbtype="tinyint" precision="1" phptype="string"
        null="false" default="0"/>
    <field key="seasonal" dbtype="tinyint" precision="1" phptype="string"
        null="false" default="0"/>
</object>

</model>
```

Lay the Primary Tables Out First

The application represents a very straightforward work flow. An event is scheduled, and at least one list of songs is created. For events divided into sections or multiple days, the ability to establish multiple lists for each event would be necessary.

At this point, it should be clear that the Event table would need a one to many relationship. It is better to insert a temporary comment to remind the developer where they suspect the project is heading, than to begin jumping around prematurely.

Once the Event table was laid out, I began creating the Playlist, and Song tables. I next went back to the Event table and started thinking about the end user working with the application, and began filling in missing fields in those tables.

Table Normalization

I assume the majority of people delving into this topic are quite familiar with normalization. For the rest of you, it simply means: the removal of redundant and unnecessary data, each table is to serve only a single purpose, and removing any columns holding static data which could better be presented by a query - like the number of times a song is played.

Normalization is an art form, in and of itself, and the web contains plenty of information regarding the topic. But keep in mind, most database applications have some violation of at least one of the three normalization forms. The idea is to keep the tables as clean as possible, but not over complicate the segmentation of the data to the point the queries themselves become a larger issue than having redundant data to sift through.

A perfect example of "acceptable" poor database design, is the United States method of structuring addresses. Across the country there are cities which are not "recognized" by the Post Office and even situations where Zip Codes cross city lines - more often than not, into these "unofficial" cites. We even have situations where the same city name is used in multiple states. In Florida, Jacksonville is so large it actually exists in two counties. Is it then two cities?

These are just a few of the anomalies, in our addressing system. Rather than deal with this cacophony of data, most developers simply let each record reflect an entire address, thereby populating the DBMS with massive quantities of duplicate data. Very few database designers have gone to the trouble to build a matrix which only requires the street number, street name, and a key pointing the rest of the address information. I undertook this process a few years ago to learn xPDO, I would suggest building simpler applications first.

In this "discjockey" application, one of the first choices I made in the normalization process, was to affix a play date to the playlist, rather than moving in the direction of an "event scheduling" application - though it could be extended in that direction quite easily.

Using Names and Variables to Establish Consistency

After a few additional optimizations, I began looking at column and Class names, and noticed I had "shortcut" the object names, leaving them very ambiguous. Earlier in the chapter, I defined a "State" object, which is making a huge assumption: no other Package, Class, or Snippet installed in the project would not also have the name of "State."

I am sure someone is thinking about namespaces and how they will resolve any possible variable collisions. While this is indeed true, they do nothing for the end users attempting to implement our wonderful creation. How are they supposed to know which "State" object is being worked on, or even better how do developers keep from getting them confused? It is best to remove as much of the ambiguous nature of our applications as possible, while still clearly communicating purpose.

A MODX Revolution rule of thumb, is to add the initials of the Package to the beginning of the Class Names and variable names - especially those serving as parameters. If database tables are implemented, it is also a common practice to use those initials to serve as the table prefix. This directly places a very logical connection between the implementation and the individual tables in the respective DBMS holding the various aspects of the data. At the very minimum, this should communicate a set of tables belonging together.

⟲ TIP: THE PREFIX MUST BE DEFINED WHEN THE TABLE IS CREATED

Though I referenced the tablePrefix in the schema, this is for "my" information and is not read or interpreted by xPDO. In effect, it is nothing more than a comment:
```
<model package="discjockey"  .... tablePrefix="dj_" .... >
```

The table prefix must be defined when the package is added, or it may fail to function:
```
$modx->addPackage('discjockey', $modelPath, 'dj_');
```

Developers should create each field in the schema with the focus of it being an attribute of an object, thereby selecting short and definitive names. By changing the perspective to declaring attributes in the schema instead of defining table fields project streamlining can began at its earliest stages - in the schema and in guidelines established for the project: use lowercase, etc.

Traditionally, database engineers would have to concern themselves with possible ambiguity issues, especially when multiple tables had identically named columns, for example: `city.name` and `state.name`. It just became easier to utilize `city.cityname` and `state.statename`. Though this has not been completely eradicated, it has become much more efficient to plan the column names to be treated as attributes. By thinking through to the implementation, the simplicity of `$cityObj=>get('name')`, may become the standard for application development.

Use the Schema Structure to Clearly Represent Function

Consider carefully, how the schema is laid out. On complex schemata, like the one used for MODX Revolution, an alphabetical approach is best - especially if the names are used to indicate relationships. For example, the structure of the Revolution schema utilizes modResource as the basis of the primary and subsequent classes: modResource, modResourceGroup, etc.

Take time to look through the main project schema, location in /core/model/schema, as it can greatly help developers construct very effective xPDO schemas. For example, the main Project is "MODX " so each of the objects are defined with a prefix of mod. Progressively the names take on the name of each of the primary objects, such as modUser, which eventually is used as the basename of the objects which depend on the previous one: modUserGroup, modUserProfile, etc. This helps delineate each of these as belonging first to MODX and then to the modUser class and so on. Each capital letter designates a class or subclass - this same technique is used throughout the schema and is an excellent concept to replicate.

For smaller schema constructions, like discjockey, it could prove beneficial to simply indicate the order of precedence, or directly represent the business workflow. I opted to use a descending structure which indicates relationship, dependence, and relevance.

Listing 17.16: typical xPDO object declaration

```
<model ......>
  <object class="djEvent" table="events" extends="xPDOSimpleObject">
  </object>

  <object class="djPlayList" table="playlists"
          extends="xPDOSimpleObject">
  </object>

  <object class="djListSong" table="playlistsongs"
          extends="xPDOSimpleObject">
   </object>

  <object class="djSong" table="songs" extends="xPDOSimpleObject">
  </object>

  <object class="djVendor" table="resources"
          extends="xPDOSimpleObject">
  </object>
</model>
```

Establishing The Ground Rules For Relationships

Once the structure has been defined for each of the primary tables, it is time to establish the relationships between them. There are a wide array of methods utilized for this process. Personally, I will select the largest relationship stream and work from the top of it - what the user will be interacting with, following each to the bottom.

If the schema is flawed in some way or does not represent the primary component of the work flow process in a clear and concise manner, it should become very apparent within the next few minutes.

It has been my experience, the level of complexity in the implementation is directly proportionate to the simplicity utilized in the schema definition.

As for as discjockey is concerned, the primary workflow is as follows:

An event is created

A playlist is attached optionally attached

Songs are selected for the playlist

These basic rules should apply:

Rule	Relationship
♦ One event can have multiple playlists ♦ a playlist can occur once per event ♦ a playlist can only be assigned to one event	**One-to-many**
♦ events need to store modUser ID of the person creating the event record ♦ events must also store a modUser ID for the client - when applicable	**One-to-one** (Not one-to-many, but could be)
♦ Each playlists can have multiple songs ♦ and the same song can appear in multiple positions of the same list	**Many-to-many**
♦ A playlist can not be duplicated ♦ Songs can be added to new playlists	**One-to-many**
♦ Songs need to be linked to vendors much like a user has a profile	**One-to-one**

Composite Relationships: Planning Cascading Deletions

Once the application needs have been established, I will typically define the rules for row deletion. Composite relationships are usually the simplest method to quickly target deletions across database tables, due to their symbiotic existence. In the case of discjockey, this is relatively straight forward, but in some projects developers will need to consider the ramifications from the top down, and then from the bottom up.

Rules for record deletion:

Rule	Relationship Effects
◆ Event can be deleted	◆ Deletion will cascade to include associated playlists ◆ Individual songs will not be deleted ◆ modUser accounts will not be deleted
◆ Playlists can be autonomously deleted	◆ Will not effect songs, or events
◆ Songs can be autonomously deleted	◆ Should only happen if the song is not attached to any playlists ◆ Deletion will cascade to include associated Resource ◆ Will not effect Playlists

Listing 17.17: xPDO composite cascading relationship of an Event object

- -

```
<composite alias="Playlists" class="djPlayList" local="id"
        foreign="eventid" cardinality="many" owner="local"/>
```

- -

Aggregate: Establishing Non-deleting Relationships

The vast majority of database relationships are aggregate in nature, due to their being loosely related. In the case of discjockey, it is possible to create an event and it not require any playlists, which in turn can be devoid of songs. Though this would be counter productive to a "discjockey", it does demonstrate the looseness of the various relationships.

Once relationships surrounding deletions have been thoroughly thought out and established, the non-destructive relations should be defined.

Rules for non-destructive relations:

Rule	Relationship Effects
◆ Events	◆ Optionally have playlists attached ◆ creator is mandatory, but this must be done via the implementation via modUser ◆ createdfor is optional ◆ resource is an optional modResource ID
◆ Playlists can be created	◆ Optionally contain songs
◆ Songs can be added	◆ Can be optionally added to playlists ◆ Can optionally have various vendor related resources attached ◆ resource is an optional modResource ID

Listing 17.18: xPDO aggregate loose relationship

- -

```
<aggregate alias="Client" class="modUser" local="createdfor"
        foreign="id" cardinality="one" owner="foreign"/>
```

- -

Common Solutions to Simple Mistakes

A number of people making the switch from traditional structured query language queries to xPDO, wrestle with the object oriented nature of the schema. I suppose for many of them, the concept of a single representation being used to accomplish two very different things is the largest hurdle. Hopefully, I can help simplify things, making the process much easier.

Concepts to facilitate the implementation of xPDO:

♦ The Schema is not doing two distinct things. It is simply doing one - establishing a foundation of objects and relationships from which xPDO will work. Even though it can act as an abstraction layer for database queries, I believe the primary functionality of xPDO centers around its command and manipulation of objects within an object model.

♦ To a point, it is best to simply ignore the fact, the schema is being used to interface a web project with a database. It is better to simply focus on defining the attributes of each object and how their subsequent relationships will interact and cascade. xPDO will gladly handle the rest of it for you, with very little effort on your part.

♦ Focusing on queries and the possible means to optimize the result set, while attempting to design and create a schema may easily distract and eventually frustrate many developers. For most applications, query optimization should be an after thought, simply because xPDO handles the majority of them with very little effort from the developer.

♦ xPDO is intended to remove the workload from developers. Anyone attempting to second guess how to help it, may very well find themselves being counterproductive.

♦ Everything in a Schema is an object, meaning it is "one" of something. Quite often, when I have to correct a developers xPDO Schema, it became convoluted due to nothing more than the class declaration being plural which simply confused their understanding into thinking they were working with a group of items, rather than a single entity. Remember, groups are typically retrieved in database queries.

Listing 17.19: typical xPDO object declaration

- -

```
<object class="djEvent" table="events" extends="xPDOSimpleObject">
```

- -

♦ Database table names are typically plural as they designate holding a group of things. Listing 17.19 should be understood as, " the djEvent Object represents a single row stored in the events table of the database." Note how it is logical to name the table "events" as it will be storing multiple event objects (rows).

- Each alias should directly and clearly represent the relationship. A one to many, should have a plural alias on the "one" side and a singular alias on the "many side".

- Try and stay clear of utilizing object names which could be confused with those declared in the MODX Revolution Schema. Slipping into using Resource, ID, User or other objects similarly named can cause quite a problem. Below I am obviously linking to a MODX Revolution Resource, but it may be a good idea to establish a rule those names are reserved for MODX Revolution objects.

- Far more often than not, the owner of a relationship is the one locally connected to it via an "id" field. Typically ownership is closest to the top of the process: "djEvents" owns "djPlaylists" which owns "djSongs" which in turn owns "djVendor".

Excerpt 17.20: from discjockey schema - displaying relationship ownership

- -

```
<aggregate alias="Lists" class="djListSong" local="id"
          foreign="songid" cardinality="many" owner="local"/>
<aggregate alias="Resource" class="modResource" local="resource"
          foreign="id" cardinality="one" owner="foreign"/>
```

- -

- Many relationships can be graphically represented utilizing a linear sequence.

- "id" is automatically added to every table as the Primary key by xPDO for every object which extends modAccessibleSimpleObject or modSimpleObject. It is not necessary to include it yourself.

- Over thinking the process is a major temptation when implementing xPDO. Remember, it was designed to make application development rapid and streamlined, while leaving its raw strength in reserve for those needing to create their own procedures, and queries.

Best Examples: Learning from Project Schema

For many developers, the single best example to learn from, is the schemata included with MODX Revolution. For those just starting out it can be quite intimidating, especially since the introduction of direct support of multiple Database Management Systems, each of which requiring its own dialect of an application schema.

I would suggest starting on a very simple example, and slowly add concepts and complexity as your understanding grows. Over time, many developers establish their own base structure for a schema and extend it as necessary. Simplicity is always the key to a successful schema and its resulting application.

Summary

In this chapter I have covered quite a bit of territory. For some, it was "too wordy". For others, it was just enough to get each of the concept. In either case, a solid understanding of each of the topics presented herein is necessary to successfully and efficiently develop those third-part applications for which you can become "famous".

At the beginning, I discussed the main components of xPDO itself and discussed the function of each of them. Some of you may have noticed I neglected to actually show how to export a schema by hand. This was for two reasons: it will have to be corrected anyway and the freedom which comes with building it "manually" needs to be experienced sooner than later. There are plenty of examples online, including the one on my site: http://www.shawnwilkerson.com/xpdo.

We then moved into the structure of a typical xPDO model, where we discussed each aspect typically utilized within a schema. In short, xPDO models contain objects which are comprised of fields having some sort of relationship with each other and other tables. Eventually developers will implement xPDO validation into their skill set, but this is beyond the scope of introduction.

I then presented eight steps typically attributed to many xPDO applications. All applications will not require each of these steps to be completed, while others may very well require more - like unit testing! You are free to wield this tool in any fashion you so desire, using my workflow and/ or Shaun McCormick's modExtra as a foundation. You can also simply develop your own.

Utilizing PackMan to create a simple package was described through the entire process as I disclosed my ulterior motive: I want people to feel very comfortable developing and contributing Packages to the community. Share what you have learned, as the information you hold may very well unlock the door to a huge experience for someone else.

I spent the last section of this chapter discussing quite a few topics centered around developing a schema for use within a multi-tabled application. In the process I took the liberty to "skip rocks" across huge topics like the three normalization forms. Entire university courses or segments of classes are centered on this topic. I simply opted to "bottom-line" it to give a general understanding of the concept. For many of you, the learning will come after having to ask why something was done "the hard way" a few times.

I then discussed concepts of using the schema itself to make application development easier and even streamlined by establishing a simple and consistent naming scheme and very straight forward relationships. To do this, I presented a typical method to "flesh" out the construction and overall interrelation of each table by establishing which relations are so closely related if one if deleted then it should cascade through the relationships. The rest of the relations are generally aggregate.

Finally, we looked at common mistakes made by xPDO developers. The better those topics are understood, the more likely you will succeed. Now its time to move into building our application.

18

xPDO: Third-Party Applications

The Army Rangers have the Florida Phase. Paris Island Marines have the Crucible. The Navy Seals have the Land Warfare Phase. University Students have Commencement. Dating can evolve into marriage, the first child, and the moment when parents become proud grandparents. Each of these moments in time, are indicative of the capability and endurance it takes for an individual to pass from one phase of their lives to another. They either have the necessary skills or they do not. There are no more quizzes, lectures, or study guides. There is only the test, the right of passage, which is pivotal to the definition of an individual and the direction their life will begin to take.

For many of you, the last major section of this chapter is your "final exam" - it is a "self-test" which should clearly indicate, how well you have mastered the topics in this book. Your ability to recognize new techniques and integrate multiple technologies will become apparent.

Many of us remember our first crush, first kiss, and first date. Hopefully by now, your relationship with MODX Revolution has encountered each of these and is ready to move to the "next level". Through each of the chapters I have been laying foundations which were intentionally crafted to walk the reader through one level of understanding to the next, while constantly utilizing and referring to content previously discussed to keep it all fresh and relevant.

By design, this chapter will present the culmination of those topics and demonstrate many of the typical components utilized **to get an application to its initial testing and implementation phase**. The methods utilized in this chapter, were chosen to provide simple bridges between technologies which are readily available. The reader should focus on the interaction of these various bridges in order to benefit from their implementation.

To my knowledge, this chapter is the first time an entire MODX Revolution implementation will be presented in a single fluid stream. As a result, it is hoped readers will insist on using xPDO, and subsequently MODX Revolution, as their platform of choice for application development.

Development Considerations

It is essential for developers to understand the nuances and intricacies of each of the technologies being implemented in any given project. For many development teams, this should not be an issue, as members specializing in one field or another will simply focus on their discipline to accomplishing their allotment of the project goals.

For smaller companies, a single individual may find themselves wrestling with issues from each additional technology being implemented, for no other reason than their unfamiliarity. Personally, I program in almost a dozen languages, which comes in handy when I have the fortune of using my Linux box and want to change or add functionality to a program, thereby contributing back to the community.

In the process of writing this book and accomplishing my Bachelors in Supervision and Management, MODX Revolution underwent quite a few changes, resulting in versions 2.03 through 2.2.4, with 2.2.5 being feverishly worked on. I personally, submitted over a hundred bug reports and feature requests as a result of this work, many of which have been implemented.

Additionally, jQuery went from 1.4.3 to 1.7.2 with entire sections of it being streamlined, rethought, and then refactored. To say that things had changed during my "year off", would be an a complete understatement. Even xPDO went through upgrades and the caching mechanism had been rewritten. I really had to take it up a few notches to get my head back in the game.

The changes in each of these projects, caused me to place some hard boundaries over the contents of this chapter. I wanted to push the boundaries further than the rest of the book had, and even further than what I had seen on various web sites, but I wanted to do it in such a way it could be easily understood and assimilated into the skill-sets of the various readers.

Project goals, parameters, and baselines :

- ♦ jQuery AJAX / JSON have silent failures
- ♦ Create consistent and simple implementations for developers new to Revolution
- ♦ Rowboat does not perform IN queries at this time (limited to a single table)
- ♦ The goal is not to finish the application, but provide a working foundation (90%)
- ♦ Keep the Manager as clean as possible
- ♦ Utilize "best case" scenarios without exotic implementations
- ♦ Use the most popular features of the API and xPDO
- ♦ Keep the concept generic enough to be packaged for as many people as possible
- ♦ Define a specific functionality for the project to be "done" enough for print
- ♦ Stay true to the purpose of the book: translate Revolution to those just learning it or who are improving their skills

Choosing How To Load The Application

There is one more topic to be discussed before moving forward: the technique utilized to load the project's associated classes. In addition to inheritance and abstraction typically used by developers to develop their classes, MODX Revolution currently provides three primary methods to load PHP class-based applications.

This number may increase in future Media Source implementations and other technologies, but these primary methods will probably be somewhere in the equation regardless of the innovations being introduced to MODX Revolution. The choice is ultimately up to the developer, though I strongly encourage the utilization of the last two methods. Hopefully, I can shed some light on the nuances of each of these methods:

include(), include_once(), require(), and require_once() are the

traditional PHP methods used to import the contents of one file into another, and is typically treated as HTML, except for contents PHP finds within <?php ?> which eventually gets executed. Files using these methods have a scope limited to the context in which it is loaded. If the file is loaded into a function, it will only have scope within that function.

loadClass() is used to load classes from any Packages currently added to the xPDO instance.

It has the added benefit of also loading Object-Relational Maps to describe data structures, such as those created during the parsing of an xPDO schema file. I typically use this loading method for Packages not primarily responsible for providing the main source of content for a site.

Occasionally, as in this chapter, loadClass() is used to load a "parent" class, which in turn loads the package and Object-Relational Maps. The primary function of this implementation is to keep derivative Snippets from being top-heavy with repetitive class loading to complete simple tasks. The modx.class.php file also loads its primary classes with this method.

The significance of loadClass() is each PHP class being added to the xPDO instance and able to be accessed exactly the same as any other class in the instance, such as $modx->user. Once loadClass() successfully executes, the class can be seen and accessed via the $modx->classname object from any Snippet within the site.

getService() is typically used to load a "service" class which provides a large amount

of input and interaction with a given project. It accepts a reference to an xPDO instance as the first parameter and is useful for loading reusable classes which might be used by multiple components in a single request. Additionally, the service is accessible from the xPDO instance using the specified variable key. I have used it to create the foundation of a social network, which provides constant access to geographical data and user information. A recent addition to MODX Revolution, which also uses this functionality, is the modHashing class introduced in MODX 2.1, which provides access to a simple message hashing class which is used by the core user system for hashing user passwords for storage.

Laying the Foundation

By this stage, I hope you have developed, tested, and implemented enough xPDO schemata the process will have become somewhat repetitive. For many of us, the workflow is typically repeated from one project to the next, so we might as well get very good at it.

In Chapter 17, I spread this process across eight steps, to help those unfamiliar with the concepts to have a foundation to begin with. In this chapter I have reduced the process to less than half of those steps: create a structure and begin development, initialize the schema, and populate the tables. Though the last chapter detailed more steps, most seasoned developers will implement methods to automate and simplify them into fewer steps, as I have done here.

Create The Application Directory Tree(s)

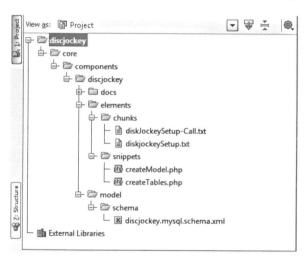

To begin I will be using my IDE to build my application to match the typical Package directory structure for MODX Revolution, allowing me to simply upload the entire tree to the server in a matter of a few seconds.

Note: it may be a good idea for developers to create a skeleton structure, allowing them to copy it as the starting point for each new application being assigned to them.

This is also the premise behind modExtra which can be forked, copied, and subsequently modified by visiting Shaun McCormick's Github: `https://github.com/splittingred/modExtra`.

Initialize An xPDO Schema

By this time, you should have a somewhat functional schema ready for xPDO to parse, create the package model and any associated database tables. Very few people get it perfect the first time. Even MODX Revolution itself, has undergone schemata changes during various version upgrades. They key is to begin development, by building a solid foundation to get a generally functional application, which can be further constrained or expanded as needed.

Many of my applications are conversions to xPDO, and this is the stage I create the Object-Relational Map and Package class files. Subsequently, I also convert the old data to objects in the Package and inject those into the newly created tables as was shown in Chapter 17.

Listing 18.01: initializeModel PHP Snippet

- -

```php
<?php
/**
 * File initializeModel.php (requires MODx Revolution 2.1)
 * Created on: 8/3/11 at 8:24 AM
 * Project shawn_wilkerson
 * @package discjockey
 */

$packageName = strtolower($package);
$modelPath = $modx->getOption($packageName . '.core_path', null,
$modx->getOption('core_path') . 'components/' . $packageName . '/')
                                . 'model/';
$schema = $modelPath . 'schema/' . $packageName
                        . '.mysql.schema.xml';
$modx->setLogLevel(xPDO::LOG_LEVEL_INFO);
$modx->setLogTarget(XPDO_CLI_MODE ? 'ECHO' : 'HTML');
$manager = $modx->getManager();
$generator = $manager->getGenerator();
$success = $generator->parseSchema($schema, $modelPath);
$modx->addPackage($packageName, $modelPath, $prefix);
$manager = $modx->getManager();
$tlist = explode(',', $tables);
foreach ($tlist as $t) {
    $success += $manager->createObjectContainer(trim($t));
}
return ($success > count($tlist)) ? '<h2>Success</h2><p>Model
Created at ' . $modelPath . $packageName . ' and all tables
successfully created.</p>' : '<h2>Operation Failed</h2>';
```

- -

Listing 18.02: initiateModel Snippet Call

- -

```
[[initializeModel?package=`discjockey`
                &prefix=`discjockey_`
                &tables=`djEvent,djPlaylist,djPlaylistSong,
                        djSong,djSongVendor,djSongGenre`]]
```

- -

Create a "Parent Class" For the Project

As this project will require additional functionality to that provided by xPDO, I will be utilizing a class to hold the various functions and methods. Additionally, the PHP class will load the discjockey Package for the various components to utilize and benefit from.

Listing 18.03: discjockey.class.php (in its earliest rendition)

```php
<?php
/**
 * Discjockey
 *
 * Copyright 2011 by Shawn Wilkerson <shawn@sanityllc.com>
 *
 */

/**
 * The base class for Discjockey.
 *
 * @package discjockey
 */
class Discjockey {
    /**
     * @var array An array of configuration options
     */
    public $config = array();
    /**
     * @var A reference to the djDebug object
     */
    public $debug = null;
    /**
     * @var modX A reference to the modX object.
     */
    public $modx = null;

    function __construct(modX &$modx, array $config = array()) {
        $this->modx =& $modx;
        $corePath = $this->modx->getOption(
                        'discjockey.core_path',
                        $config,
                        $this->modx->getOption('core_path')
                                . 'components/discjockey/');
        $assetsUrl = $this->modx->getOption(
```

```
                              'diskjockey.assets_url',
                              $config,
                              $this->modx->getOption('assets_url')
                                      . 'components/discjockey/');
          $this->config = array_merge(array(
                  'assetsUrl' => $assetsUrl,
                  'cssUrl' => $assetsUrl . 'css/',
                  'jsUrl' => $assetsUrl . 'js/',
                  'imagesUrl' => $assetsUrl . 'images/',
                  'corePath' => $corePath,
                  'modelPath' => $corePath . 'model/',
                  'chunksPath' => $corePath . 'elements/chunks/',
                  'snippetsPath' => $corePath . 'elements/snippets/',
                  'processorsPath' => $corePath . 'processors/',
                  'prefix' => 'discjockey_',
                  ), $config);
          $this->modx->addPackage('discjockey',
                  $this->config['modelPath'],
                  $this->config['prefix']);
      }
  }
```

- -

Listing 18.04: Simple discjockey instantiation test

- -

```
  $out = 'failed';
  $discjockey_base = $modx->getOption('discjockey.core_path',
          $scriptProperties,
          $modx->getOption('core_path') . 'components/discjockey/');
  if ($modx->loadClass('Discjockey', $discjockey_base
                              . 'model/discjockey/', true, true)) {
      $dj = new Discjockey($modx, $scriptProperties);
      $out = var_dump($dj->config);
  }
  return $out;
```

- -

At this point, either of two routes can be chosen. A slight detour involving data import, or we can simply "drive on" and begin developing on top of the newly derived Package and xPDO class files. As mentioned in the last chapter, I prefer to "play" with the objects before development.

Populate Tables With Data

My church has been compiling playlists and using an ever growing list of songs for years. The current work flow involves my having to directly access phpMyAdmin to add new songs to the lists, and to make any corrections. Initially, I built the application under versions of MODX predating Evolution, so very little thought was given to objects or creating a full blown application. Now, I need to get the data from a very limited and poorly designed structure to my new discjockey application. Fortunately, phpMyAdmin provides the facility to export the data into PHP arrays, allowing me to quickly format the data as needed.

Listing 18.04: importGenreCategories PHP Snippet - New Data

```php
<?php
/**
 * File importGenreCategories.php (requires MODx Revolution 2.1x)
 * Created on: 8/6/11 at 8:54 AM
 * Project shawn_wilkerson
 * @package discjockey
 *
 */

$genres = array(
    array(
        'amazon' => 'Alternative & Indie Rock',
        'gracenote' => 'Alternative & Punk',
    ),
    array(
        'amazon' => '',
        'gracenote' => 'Books & Spoken',
    ),
    array(
        'amazon' => 'Blues',
        'gracenote' => 'Blues',
    ),
    array(
        'amazon' => 'Broadway & Vocalists',
        'gracenote' => '',
    ),
    array(
        'amazon' => "Children's Music",
        'gracenote' => "Children's Music",
    ),
    array(
```

```
        'amazon' => 'Christian & Gospel',
        'gracenote' => 'Gospel & Religious',
),
array(
        'amazon' => 'Classical',
        'gracenote' => 'Classical',
),
array(
        'amazon' => 'Classic Rock',
        'gracenote' => '',
),
array(
        'amazon' => 'Comedy & Miscellaneous',
        'gracenote' -> '',
),
array(
        'amazon' => 'Country',
        'gracenote' => 'Country',
),
array(
        'amazon' => 'Dance & Electronic',
        'gracenote' => 'Electronica/Dance',
),
array(
        'amazon' => '',
        'gracenote' => 'Easy Listening',
),
array(
        'amazon' => 'Folk',
        'gracenote' => 'Folk',
),
array(
        'amazon' => 'Hard Rock & Metal',
        'gracenote' => 'Metal',
),
array(
        'amazon' => '',
        'gracenote' => 'Holiday',
),
array(
        'amazon' => '',
        'gracenote' => 'Industrial',
),
array(
```

```php
        'amazon' => 'Jazz',
        'gracenote' => 'Jazz',
    ),
    array(
        'amazon' => 'Latin Music',
        'gracenote' => 'Latin',
    ),
    array(
        'amazon' => 'New Age',
        'gracenote' => 'New Age',
    ),
    array(
        'amazon' => 'Opera & Vocal',
        'gracenote' => '',
    ),
    array(
        'amazon' => 'Pop',
        'gracenote' => 'Pop',
    ),
    array(
        'amazon' => 'R&B',
        'gracenote' => 'R&B',
    ),
    array(
        'amazon' => 'Rap & Hip-Hop',
        'gracenote' => 'Hip Hop/Rap',
    ),
    array(
        'amazon' => '',
        'gracenote' => 'Reggae',
    ),
    array(
        'amazon' => 'Rock',
        'gracenote' => 'Rock',
    ),
    array(
        'amazon' => 'Soundtracks',
        'gracenote' => 'Soundtrack',
    ),
    array(
        'amazon' => '',
        'gracenote' => 'Unclassifiable',
    ),
    array(
```

```
                'amazon' => 'World Music',
                'gracenote' => 'World',
            ),
    );

    $out = false;
    $discjockey_base = $modx->getOption('discjockey.core_path',
                $scriptProperties,
                $modx->getOption('core_path') . 'components/discjockey/');
    if ($modx->loadClass('Discjockey', $discjockey_base
                                    . 'model/discjockey/', true, true)) {
        $dj = new Discjockey($modx, $scriptProperties);
        foreach ($genres as $genre) {
            $g = $modx->newObject('djSongGenre', $genre);
            $out = $g->save();
        }
    }
    return ($out) ? 'Genres added' : $out;
```

I opted to utilize the two primary genre providers currently available to create the basis of a filter and grouping of the various songs. Gracenote reportedly supplies iTunes and Amazon is a world unto itself. It is my belief, the majority of people will purchase their tracks from these sources and will typically utilize the same provider, whenever possible.

As far as development is concerned, each subsequent "supporting" or "lookup" class should probably be populated at this time with any available data. This is for two primary reasons: to have the data available for implementation, and Unit Testing. It is better to begin thinking about testing early on in development, instead of an afterthought.

I believe the quicker developers begin to interact with their objects, the faster the project will be completed. It also helps foster the mentality of working with objects towards actual implementation, rather than the distraction of the traditional database queries, connections, data preparation, etc. This simply allows developers to get to work accomplishing project goals.

Essentially, an object is created, values are attached to its properties, and finally the resulting object is saved to the database associated database table represented in the xPDO class defined in the schema file. xPDO provides a variety of methods of getting formatted data to the database. Over the course of this project we will be interacting with JSON, PHP arrays, and other methods typically encountered when a developer has to take information stored in one system and import it into another. The rest of this section is optional, though the examples contained therein may prove illuminating to those creating their first, or subsequent, third-party application.

Listing 18.05 importSongs Snippet to import songs from a PHP array

----

```php
<?php
/**
 * File importSongs.php (requires MODx Revolution 2.1x)
 * Created on: 8/4/11 at 6:15 AM
 * Project shawn_wilkerson
 * @package discjockey
 */
$oldSongs = array(
    array('id' => '1', 'album' => 'Worship [Live]', 'track' => '0',
            'title' => 'Above All', 'artist' => 'Michael W. Smith',
            'duration' => '4:21', 'leadin' => '0:13', 'genre' => '6',
            'tempo' => '', 'deleted' => '0', 'inactive' => '0',
            'resource' => '0'),

    /***********    Many deleted For Brevity   *********/
);

$out = false;
$discjockey_base = $modx->getOption('discjockey.core_path',
            $scriptProperties,
            $modx->getOption('core_path') . 'components/discjockey/');
if ($modx->loadClass('Discjockey', $discjockey_base
                                . 'model/discjockey/', true, true)) {
    $dj = new Discjockey($modx, $scriptProperties);
    foreach ($oldSongs as $oldSong) {
        $song = $modx->newObject('djSong');
        $song->fromArray($oldSong, '', true, true);
        $song->set('track', 0);
        $song->set('genre', 6);

        /* Attach a 1:1 Vendor relation to the current song */
        $song->addOne($modx->newObject('djSongVendor'));
        $out += $song->save();
    }
}
return ($out) ? $out .' Songs Added' : false;
```

In listing 18.5, I simply loop through the array of songs and implement fromArray() to directly import each song Array into a djSong object. Additionally, I apply default settings to attach the Song to djGenre and create a one-to-one relation with djVendor.

Listing 18.06 importPlaylists Snippet to import old playlists from PHP array

```php
<?php
/**
 * File importPlaylists.php (requires MODx Revolution 2.1)
 * Created on: 8/4/11 at 6:53 AM
 * Project shawn_wilkerson
 * @package discjockey
 */
$worshipLists =
        array
        (
            array
            (
                'idworshipList' => '25',        'first' => '82',
                'second' => '40',               'third' => '69',
                'forth' => '93',                'fifth' => '0',
                'sixth' => '0',                 'seventh' => '0',
                'eighth' => '0',                'nineth' => '0',
                'tenth' => '0',                 'eleventh' => '0',
                'twelvth' => '0',               'thirteenth' => '0',
                'fourteenth' => '0',            'fifteenth' => '0',
                'sixteenth' => '0',             'seventeenth' => '0',
                'eighteenth' => '0',            'nineteenth' => '0',
                'twentieth' => '0',
                'eventType' => 'Sunday Celebration',
                'creatorID' => '11',
                'creationDate' => '1271552701',
                'title' => '',
                'playDate' => '0'
            ),
            /***********    Many deleted For Brevity   *********/
        );


$out = false;
$debug = $modx->getOption('debug', $scriptProperties, false);
if ($debug == true) {
    $modx->setLogLevel(xPDO::LOG_LEVEL_INFO);
    $modx->setLogTarget(XPDO_CLI_MODE ? 'ECHO' : 'HTML');
    $modx->setDebug(true);
}
```

```
$discjockey_base = $modx->getOption('discjockey.core_path',
$scriptProperties, $modx->getOption('core_path')
                    . 'components/discjockey/');

if ($modx->loadClass('Discjockey', $discjockey_base . 'model/
discjockey/', true, true)) {
    $dj = new Discjockey($modx, $scriptProperties);
    foreach ($worshipLists as $oldlist) {
        $event = $modx->getObject('djEvent', array(
                            'name' => $oldlist['eventType'],));
        if (!is_object($event)) {
            $event = $modx->newObject('djEvent');
            $event->set('name', $oldlist['eventType']);
            $event->set('createdon', date('Ymd His',
                                $oldlist['creationDate']));
            $event->set('createdby', $oldlist['creatorID']);
            $event->save();
        }
        $playdate = strtotime('Next Sunday 10:30:00',
                                $oldlist['creationDate']);

        /* Create a Playlist */
        $playlist = $modx->newObject('djPlaylist');
        $playlist->set('eventid', $event->get('id'));
        $playlist->set('playdate', date('Ymd His', $playdate));
        $playlist->set('title', date('l, M d Y', $playdate));
        $playlist->set('createdby', $oldlist['creatorID']);
        $playlist->set('createdon', date('Ymd His',
                                $oldlist['creationDate']));
        $songs = array (
                    $oldlist['first'],
                    $oldlist['second'],
                    $oldlist['third'],
                    $oldlist['forth'],
                    $oldlist['fifth'],
                    $oldlist['sixth'],
                    $oldlist['seventh'],
                    $oldlist['eighth'],
                    $oldlist['nineth'],
                    $oldlist['tenth'],
                    $oldlist['eleventh'],
                    $oldlist['twelvth'],
                    $oldlist['thirteenth'],
                    $oldlist['fourteenth'],
```

```
                        $oldlist['fifteenth'],
                        $oldlist['sixteenth'],
                        $oldlist['seventeenth'],
                        $oldlist['eighteenth'],
                        $oldlist['nineteenth'],
                        $oldlist['twentieth'],
                    );
            $position = 1;
            foreach ($songs as $s) {
                $song = $modx->getObject('djSong', $s);
                if (is_object($song)) {
                    $listSong = $modx->newObject('djPlaylistSong');
                    $listSong->set('songid', $song->get('id'));
                    $listSong->set('position', $position++);
                    $listsongs[] = $listSong;
                }
            }

            /* Add 1:n Playlist to Songs Relation */
            $playlist->addMany($listsongs);
            $out = $playlist->save();
            unset($event, $listSongs, $oldlist, $playlist, $song, $s);

        } // end foreach $worshipLists as $oldlist

    }  // end if modx->loadClass

    return ($out) ? 'Playlists added' : 'Discjockey Class Not Found';
```

This segment introduces the ability, provided by xPDO, to activate `$modx->setDebug(true)`, which will present associated feedback as xPDO processes through the tasks assigned to it. In this example, simply calling the Snippet with `[[importPlaylists?debug=`1`]]` should activate the extended output. Also, take notice of the `$playlist->addMany()` used to add all of the songs associated with a playlist in a single line, simply by passing an array of djPlaylistSong objects.

Some of you may be thinking, what a poorly thought out original implementation and I would have to agree. I should have utilized a one to many relationship, at the very least, not to mention actually learning xPDO in its 1.0 version.

Four years after throwing this quick little application together, I contemplated updating it by converting it to xPDO. I decided to intentionally use this redesign for the last chapter of this book, as it represents typical conditions, which many will face when porting projects to xPDO.

Once a developer has grown somewhat comfortable with xPDO, they could simply use a Snippet to export the current database table into a xPDO schema. Then the associated objects could be mapped directly together. If you were able to conceptualize this suggestion, you may very well be on your way to being a MODX Revolution Grandmaster!

Some of you may have noticed: I have never demonstrated how to build a xPDO schema from an existing database. There are two reasons for this: I wrote an article about this topic on my web site years ago and I also believe it to be a "last" resort or "teaching" scenario. The sooner developers are creating their schema from hand, the more comfortable they will become with the entire process. An example MySQL to XML example can be seen in its entirety by visiting: `https://github.com/wshawn/mysqlToXML`.

Small Beginnings

Now that I have my data safely tucked away in my discjockey application, I can begin hashing out how to best approach the presentation layer. In the last chapter, I mentioned the three primary "interfaces" or "viewports" which we be using for a typical discjockey workflow: djEvent, djPlaylist, and djSongs.

Remember, each of these objects have highly beneficial functionality, simply due to their extending, and thereby inheriting, the xPDO, xPDOObject, and xPDOSimpleObject classes. We will want to lean as heavily as possible on these ancestor classes to reduce production time.

I would suggest the use flowcharts and simplified user interface mock-ups to get everyone on the "same page." Many developers will have the tendency to think in a linear fashion - with the purpose of accomplishing the goals as quick as possible. I would suggest a momentary change of "hats" with their sketching out what they think would best be served based on the structure of the application or at the minimum a list of available attributes designers can draw from.

An alternative which can serve the developer in even a greater way, would be to have a front end designer to create a very simplified mock-up of what they are expecting, as far as functionality. For many applications this is a critical stage in the development process. Effective communication from each of the teams involved, can greatly facilitate production and expedite completion of project goals - especially in the early development stages.

Client sketches can also be utilized to target development towards specific implementations. The primary page is going to implement jQuery in numerous functions, such as hiding and showing page contents, filtering the list of available songs, replacing the event box with playlist content, and placing the songs in the selection box from the full list to the right for final processing.

Simple sketches, a project whiteboard, and flowcharts can quickly get everyone working in the same direction, while simultaneously keeping the client "in the loop". Graphical representations of projects can greatly reduce the level of confusion and the amount of scope creep.

Client Sketch Describing Basic Functionality

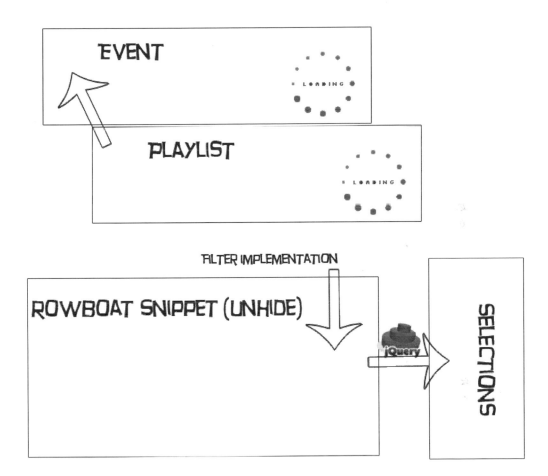

The final result will probably look different than this sketch, but it does communicate a simple explanation of what the client is looking for. Developers can begin working at filling in the various components an actual Professional Discjockey could use to run a company, or a Worship Leader at a church could use to select song lists. By design, our Package should be generic enough to allow users in either area to use it without having to "translate" it for their clients.

Once a general direction has been defined, attention may very well turn to establishing the basis of getting information from the database to the browser and eventually processing some sort of user input for specific actions, such as playlist notification and creation.

Retrieving Base Components

In the *[[Snippets]] and Plug-ins: Adding PHP Dynamic Content* chapter, I presented MODX Revolution Rule #6 => **"Only code when and what you have to"**. In keeping with this rule, a decision needs to be made: "Do we code a database retrieval and template system, or do we utilize a preexisting Package?"

To answer this question, simply reflect back to the "primary" discjockey objects: events, playlist, songs, and their relationships. The method utilized to store their data was generic enough a developer could use a vast number of methods to retrieve information for the site visitor. This flexibility is the number one reason to utilize xPDO, and by extension: MODX Revolution.

Logically, the next question would be based around the demands of the application: "Does the chosen JavaScript library, jQuery, have any considerations which are going to mandate a choice of implementation?" One of the primary reasons I use jQuery for basic User Interface /User Experience implementation is directly related to its overall effectiveness at working with (X) HTML tables and list items. For this application, there are no limiting JavaScript factors and so we can finally make a descision.

Respecting MODX Revolution Rule #6, I am going to install Shaun McCormick's Rowboat package and use it as the basis of retrieving and presenting various aspects of discjockey's information. We can also build our own solutions where Rowboat may not be effective.

Some of you might be asking, why create two solutions. I also have another motivation for using Rowboat - it is read only. I do not have to concern myself with Manager users overwriting or gaining access to data, when they simply need to create output.

The project will extensively use AJAX and jQuery to provide a workflow using Chunk templates for Rowboat. In essence, I plan on creating an AJAX wrapper for Rowboat, which should prove quite handy for many projects in the future. If I am building an application, I might as well create new tools and develop concepts which I can use to land future projects.

The image on the following page was my first attempt at building discjockey. I intentionally, built it without using any class files or anything of my own. I also relied mostly on traditional code to achieve the goals. A major issue became very apparent: a very high cost to screen real estate, when dozens of Elements, Templates, and Resources were stored in the Manager for a single application. To make matters worse, this was before a web site was even built.

For those who have not made the transition from procedural coding to object oriented programming, this is the quagmire of files necessary to get a somewhat functional application ready to present to the client. I hope the following pages will serve two purposes: encourage procedural coders to invest in making the move to OOP and also lay a complete foundation for developing a third party application.

From this point on, the code is yours to explore, and comments will be minimal.

A Procedural Programming Quagmire

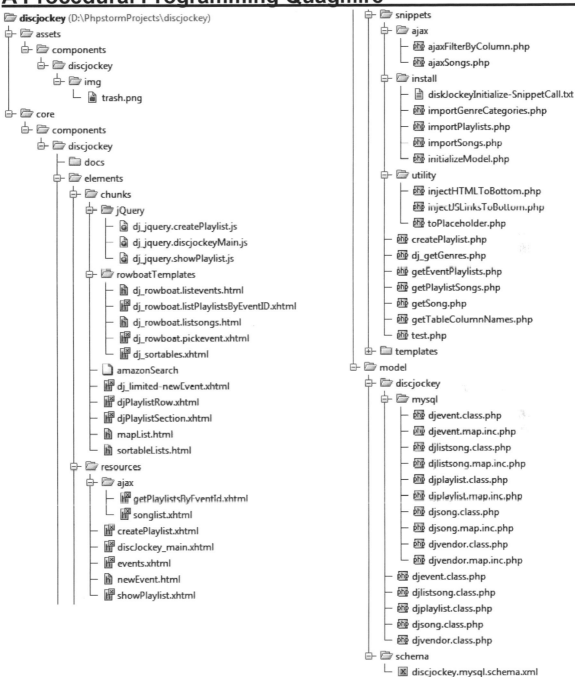

discjockey xPDO Schema

Listing 18:07 discjockey.mysql.schema.xml

```xml
<?xml version="1.0" encoding="UTF-8"?>
<model package="discjockey" baseClass="xPDOObject" platform="mysql"
    defaultEngine="MyISAM" tablePrefix="discjockey_"
    phpdoc-package="playlist" phpdoc-subpackage="" version="1.1">

  <object class="djEvent" table="events" extends="xPDOSimpleObject">
    <field key="name" dbtype="varchar" precision="100" phptype="string"
        null="false" default="" index="index"/>
    <field key="createdon" dbtype="datetime" phptype="datetime"/>
    <field key="createdby" dbtype="integer" precision="10" phptype="integer"
        attributes="unsigned" null="false" default="0"/>
    <field key="createdfor" dbtype="integer" precision="10" phptype="integer"
        attributes="unsigned" null="false" default="0"/>
    <field key="resource" dbtype="int" precision="10" phptype="integer"
        attributes="unsigned" null="false" default="0"/>
    <field key="comment" dbtype="varchar" precision="300" phptype="string"
        null="false" default=""  index="index"/>

    <aggregate alias="Client" class="modUser" local="createdfor"
        foreign="id" cardinality="one" owner="foreign"/>
    <aggregate alias="Creator" class="modUser" local="createdby"
        foreign="id" cardinality="one" owner="foreign"/>
    <aggregate alias="Resource" class="modResource"  local="resource"
        foreign="id" cardinality="one" owner="foreign"/>

    <composite alias="Playlists" class="djPlayList" local="id"
        foreign="eventid" cardinality="many" owner="local"/>
  </object>



  <object class="djPlaylist" table="playlists" extends="xPDOSimpleObject">
    <field key="eventid" dbtype="integer" precision="10" phptype="integer"
        attributes="unsigned" null="false"  default="0"/>
    <field key="title" dbtype="varchar" precision="100"
        phptype="string" null="false" default=""/>
```

```
        <field key="playdate" dbtype="datetime" phptype="datetime"/>
        <field key="createdby" dbtype="integer" precision="10"
                phptype="integer" attributes="unsigned" null="false" default="0"/>
        <field key="createdon" dbtype="datetime" phptype="datetime"/>

        <aggregate alias="Creator" class="modUser" local="createdby" foreign="id"
            cardinality="one" owner="foreign"/>
        <aggregate alias="Event" class="djEvent" local="eventid" foreign="id"
            cardinality="one" owner="foreign"/>
        <aggregate alias="Songs" class="djPlaylistSong" local="id" foreign="listid"
            cardinality="many" owner="local"/>
</object>


<object class="djPlaylistSong" table="playlist_songs" extends="xPDOObject">
    <field key="listid" dbtype="integer" precision="10" phptype="integer"
            attributes="unsigned" null="false" default="0" index="pk"/>
    <field key="position" dbtype="integer" precision="10" phptype="integer"
            attributes="unsigned" null="false" default="0" index="pk"/>
    <field key="songid" dbtype="integer" precision="10" phptype="integer"
            null="false" default="0"/>
    <field key="skipped" dbtype="tinyint" precision="1" phptype="boolean"
            null="false" default="0"/>
    <field key="note" dbtype="varchar" precision="100" phptype="string"
            null="false" default=""/>
    <index alias="PRIMARY" name="PRIMARY" primary="true" unique="true"
            type="BTREE">
        <column kcy="listid" length="" collation="A" null="false"/>
        <column key="position" length="" collation="A"  null="false"/>
     </index>

    <aggregate alias="List" class="djPlayList" local="listid"  foreign="id"
            cardinality="one" owner="foreign"/>
    <aggregate alias="Song" class="djSong" local="songid" foreign="id"
            cardinality="one" owner="foreign"/>
</object>
```

```xml
<object class="djSong" table="songs" extends="xPDOSimpleObject">
    <field key="track" dbtype="varchar" precision="4"
        phptype="string" null="false" default=""/>
    <field key="title" dbtype="varchar" precision="100"
        phptype="string" null="false" default="" index="index"/>
    <field key="artist" dbtype="varchar" precision="100"
        phptype="string" null="false" default="" index="index"/>
    <field key="duration" dbtype="varchar" precision="6"
        phptype="string" null="false" default=""/>
    <field key="leadin" dbtype="varchar" precision="4"
        phptype="string" null="false" default=""/>
    <field key="genre" dbtype="int" precision="10" phptype="integer"
        attributes="unsigned" null="false" default="0" index="index"/>
    <field key="tempo" dbtype="varchar" precision="3"
        phptype="string" null="false" default=""/>
    <field key="exclusiveto" dbtype="integer" precision="10" phptype="integer"
        attributes="unsigned" null="false" default="0"/>
    <field key="addedon" dbtype="datetime" phptype="datetime"/>
    <field key="addedby" dbtype="integer" precision="10" phptype="integer"
        attributes="unsigned" null="false" default="0"/>
    <field key="suggestedon" dbtype="datetime" phptype="datetime"/>
    <field key="suggestedby" dbtype="integer" precision="10" phptype="integer"
        attributes="unsigned" null="false" default="0"/>
    <field key="deleted" dbtype="tinyint" precision="1" phptype="boolean"
        null="false" default="0"/>
    <field key="inactive" dbtype="tinyint" precision="1" phptype="boolean"
        null="false" default="1"/>
    <field key="resource" dbtype="int" precision="10" phptype="integer"
        attributes="unsigned" null="false" default="0"/>
    <field key="suggested" dbtype="tinyint" precision="1"
        phptype="boolean" null="false" default="0"/>
```

```xml
    <aggregate alias="Addedby" class="modUser" local="addedby"
        foreign="id" cardinality="one" owner="foreign"/>
    <aggregate alias="Exclusiveto" class="modUser"
        local="addedby" foreign="id" cardinality="one" owner="foreign"/>
    <aggregate alias="Genre" class="djSongGenre" local="genre"
        foreign="id" cardinality="one" owner="foreign"/>
    <aggregate alias="Lists" class="djPlaylistSong" local="id" foreign="songid"
        cardinality="many" owner="local"/>
    <aggregate alias="Resource" class="modResource"
        local="resource" foreign="id" cardinality="one" owner="foreign"/>
    <aggregate alias="Suggestedby" class="modUser"
        local="addedby" foreign="id" cardinality="one" owner="foreign"/>
    <composite alias="Vendor" class="djSongVendor" local="id"
        foreign="songid" cardinality="one" owner="local"/>
</object>




<object class="djSongGenre" table="song_genre"
        extends="xPDOSimpleObject">
    <field key="amazon" dbtype="varchar" precision="50"
        phptype="string" null="false" default="n/a"/>
    <field key="gracenote" dbtype="varchar" precision="50"
        phptype="string" null="false" default="n/a"/>
</object>
```

```
<object class="djSongVendor" table="song_vendors"
                  extends="xPDOSimpleObject">
  <field key="songid" dbtype="int" precision="10"
      phptype="integer" null="false" index="unique"/>
  <field key="album" dbtype="varchar" precision="20"
      phptype="string" null="false" default=""/>
  <field key="albumart" dbtype="varchar" precision="20"
      phptype="string" null="false" default=""/>
  <field key="amazon" dbtype="varchar" precision="20"
      phptype="string" null="false" default=""/>
  <field key="ccli" dbtype="varchar" precision="40" phptype="string"
      null="false" default=""/>
  <field key="freedb" dbtype="varchar" precision="20"
      phptype="string" null="false" default=""/>
  <field key="googlemusic" dbtype="varchar" precision="50"
      phptype="string" null="false" default=""/>
  <field key="gracenote" dbtype="varchar" precision="20"
      phptype="string" null="false" default=""/>
  <field key="itunes" dbtype="varchar" precision="20"
      phptype="string" null="false" default=""/>
  <field key="lyrics" dbtype="varchar" precision="20"
      phptype="string" null="false" default=""/>
  <field key="musicbrainz" dbtype="varchar" precision="50"
      phptype="string" null="false" default=""/>
  <field key="metacafe" dbtype="varchar" precision="40"
      phptype="string" null="false" default=""/>
  <field key="recordlabel" dbtype="varchar" precision="40"
      phptype="string" null="false" default=""/>
  <field key="vevo" dbtype="varchar" precision="20"
      phptype="string" null="false" default=""/>
  <field key="vimeo" dbtype="varchar" precision="20"
      phptype="string" null="false" default=""/>
  <field key="yahoo" dbtype="varchar" precision="20"
      phptype="string" null="false" default=""/>
  <field key="youtube" dbtype="varchar" precision="20"
      phptype="string" null="false" default=""/>
  <aggregate alias="Song" class="djSong" local="songid"
      foreign="id" cardinality="one" owner="foreign"/>
</object>
</model>
```

Discjockey Main Class

Listing 18.08 discjockey.class.php

```php
<?php
/**
 * Discjockey
 * The base class for Discjockey.
 *
 * @package discjockey
 */
class Discjockey {

    /**
     * @var array An array of configuration options
     */
    public $config = array();

    /**
     * @var djDebug A reference to the djDebug object
     */
    public $debug = null;

    /**
     * @var modX A reference to the modX object.
     */
    public $modx = null;

    /**
     * @param modX $modx import reference to MODX Object
     * @param array $conflg Runtime configuration overrides
     */
    function __construct(modX &$modx, array $config = array()) {
        $this->modx =& $modx;
        $corePath = $this->modx->getOption('discjockey.core_path',
                    $config, $this->modx->getOption('core_path')
                . 'components/discjockey/');
        $assetsUrl = $this->modx->getOption('diskjockey.assets_url',
                    $config, $this->modx->getOption('assets_url')
                . 'components/discjockey/');
```

```
$assetsPath = $_SERVER["DOCUMENT_ROOT"] . $assetsUrl;


$this->config = array_merge(
    array(
        'assetsUrl' => $assetsUrl,
        'cssUrl' => $assetsUrl . 'css/',
        'jsUrl' => $assetsUrl . 'js/',
        'imagesUrl' => $assetsUrl . 'images/',
        'jsPath' => $assetsPath . 'js/',
        'cssPath' => $assetsPath . 'css/',
        'corePath' => $corePath,
        'modelPath' => $corePath . 'model/',
        'chunksPath' => $corePath . 'elements/chunks/',
        'snippetsPath' => $corePath . 'elements/snippets/',
        'processorsPath' => $corePath . 'processors/',

        'chunkSuffix' => '.chunk.tpl',
        'prefix' => 'discjockey_',

        'excludeFieldsPlaylist' => strtolower($this->modx->
                        getOption('discjockey.excludeFromFilter.playlist'
                                    , '', 'eventid')),
        'excludeFieldsSong' => strtolower($this->modx->
                        getOption('discjockey.excludeFromFilter.song', ''
                                    , 'deleted,exclusiveto,genre,inactive,leadin
                                    ,resource, suggested,title')),
        'excludeFieldsSongVendor' => strtolower($this->modx->
                        getOption('discjockey.excludeFromFilter.songVendor',
                                    '', 'songid')),
        'filterByTpl' => strtolower($this->modx->
                        getOption('discjockey.filterTemplate', '', 'dj_filterby')),
        'genreList' => strtolower($this->modx->
                        getOption('discjockey.usegenrelist', '', 'amazon')),
        'playlistRowTpl' => strtolower($this->modx->
                        getOption('disckockey.playlistRowTemplate',
                                    '', 'dj_playlistrow')),
        'playlistSectionTpl' => strtolower($this->modx->
                        getOption('discjockey.playlistSectionTemplate', ''
                                    , 'dj_playlistsection')),
```

```
                'songPlaylistTpl' => strtolower($this->modx->
                            getOption('discjockey.songPlaylistTemplate',
                                    '', 'dj_showsongplaylist')),
            'songTpl' => strtolower($this->modx->
                    getOption('discjockey.songTemplate', '', 'dj_showsong')),
            'showstats' => intval($this->modx-> getOption('showstats', '', 1)),
            'useMinify' => $this->modx->getOption('diskjockey.use_minify', '', false),
            ), $config);

        /* System Settings which need to be converted to URLs */
        $this->makeURLs = array('discjockey.parent_id', 'discjockey.ajax_id');
        /* Process any Placeholder Requests */
        $this->modx->toPlaceholder($config['ph'], $config['src'], '');
        $this->modx->addPackage('discjockey', $this->config['modelPath'],
            $this->config['prefix']);
    }


    /**
     * @param $collection array of objects
     * @return array
     */
    private function _collectionToArray($collection) {
        $array = array();
        foreach ($collection as $object) {
            if (is_object($object)) {
                $array[] = $object->toArray();
            }
        }
        return $array;
    }


    /**
     * @param  int  $limit Number of records to limit search to
     * @param  string  $direction ASC or DESC, defaults to (DESC)
     * @return array  Associative Array of Database records
     */
    private function _getPopularSongs($limit = 10, $direction = 'DESC') {
        $r = array();
        $q = $this->modx->newQuery('djPlaylistSong', '', false);
        $q->select('songid, COUNT("songid") AS count');
```

```
        $q->groupby('songid');
        $q->sortby('count', $direction);
        $q->limit((int)$limit);
        if ($q->prepare() && $q->stmt->execute()) {
            $r = $q->stmt->fetchAll(PDO::FETCH_ASSOC);
        }
        return $r;
    }

    /**
     * Returns a modChunk object from a template file.
     *
     * @access private
     * @param string $name of the Chunk: "name"
     * @param string $suffix of chunk filename, default: .chunk.tpl
     * @see  Shaun McCormick helper functions
     * @return  modChunk/boolean modChunk object, otherwise false.
     */
    private function _getTplChunk($name, $suffix = '.chunk.tpl') {
        $chunk = false;
        $f = $this->config['chunksPath'] . strtolower($name).$suffix;
        if (file_exists($f)) {
            $o = file_get_contents($f);
            $chunk = $this->modx->newObject('modChunk');
            $chunk->set('name', $name);
            $chunk->setContent($o);
        }
        return $chunk;
    }

    /**
     * @param string $contents The Contents of a file
     * @return string Parsed content, with system settings replaced
     */
    private function _parseFile($contents = '') {
        if (!empty($contents)) {
            $settings = array_merge($this->modx->_systemConfig, $this->config);
            foreach ($settings as $key => $val) {
                $val = htmlspecialchars($val);
                /* check makeURL Discjockey System Settings */
```

```php
        if (in_array($key, $this->makeURLs)) {
            $val = $this->modx->makeUrl($val);
        }
        $contents = str_replace('[[++' . $key . ']]', $val, $contents);
      }
   }
   return $contents;
}




/**
 * Transforms a jQuery Serialized String to a PHP Array
 * @param string $str Receives a Serialized jQuery String
 * @return array|bool
 */
public function _strToArray($str) {
   $out = array();
   parse_str($str, $arry);
   foreach ($arry as $nested) {
      foreach ($nested as $item => $song) {
         if (is_numeric($song)) {
            $out[] = $song;
         }
      }
   }
   return (!empty($out)) ? $out : false;
}




/**
 * @param string $xpdoClass Class to limit search to
 * @param string $filterOnField Class Field to limit search to
 * @param string $genre Limit to a specific genre in djSong
 * @return array
 */
public function createFilter($xpdoClass = 'djSong', $filterOnField = '',
                                                    $genre = '') {

   $arry = '';
   if (!empty($filterOnField)) {
```

```
$query = $this->modx->newQuery($xpdoClass);
$query->select(array($filterOnField));
if ($filterOnField != "genre" && (!empty($genre))) {
   $query->where(array('genre' => $genre,));
}

$query->groupby($filterOnField, 'ASC');
$iterator = $this->modx->getIterator($xpdoClass, $query);
$arry = array();
foreach ($iterator as $obj) {
   if ($filterOnField != 'genre') {
      $display = $obj->get($filterOnField);
      if ($xpdoClass == 'djSong' && $filterOnField == 'tempo') {
         $display = $obj->setTempoText($display);
      }
   } else {
      $g = $this->modx->getObject('djSongGenre', $obj->get($filterOnField));
      $display = $g->get($this->config['genreList']);
      if (empty($display)) {
         if ($this->config['genreList'] == 'amazon') {
            $display = $g->get('gracenote');
         } else {
            $display = $g->get('amazon');
         }
      }
   }

   $arry[] = array(
      'optionValue' => $obj->get($filterOnField),
      'optionDisplay' => $display,
   );
}
}
return $arry;
}
/**
 * @param string $classname The xPDO Class of a Database table
 * @param string $runtimeExcludes Additional fields to add to the exclude set
 * @param bool $useConfigSettings Toggles inclusion of $this->config excludes
 * @return string From Template Content
```

```php
    */
    public function createFilterFields($classname = 'djSong', $runtimeExcludes = '',
                    $useConfigSettings = true) {
        $out = '';
        $arry = array();
        $fields = array_keys($this->modx->getFields($classname));
        asort($fields);
        if (count($fields) > 0) {
            $exclude = 'id,' . $runtimeExcludes;
            if ($useConfigSettings == true) {
                $classname = str_replace('dj', 'excludeFields', $classname);
                $exclude .= ',' . $this->config[$classname];
            }
            $excludedFields = explode(',', $exclude);
            foreach ($fields as $field) {
                if (!in_array($field, $excludedFields)) {
                    $out .= $this->getChunk($this->config['filterByTpl'], array(
                            'optionDisplay' => ucfirst($field),
                            'optionValue' => $field,
                        ));
                }
            }
        }
        return $out;
    }


    /**
     * Operates directly from $_POST  - xPDO schema to lockdown vars
     * @return array of djPlaylistSong Objects
     */
    public function createPlaylistSongs() {
        $position = 1;
        $songs = array();
        for ($i = 1; $i < 5; $i++) {
            foreach ($this->_strToArray($_POST['set' . $i]) as $selection) {
                $listsong = $this->modx->newObject('djPlaylistSong');
                $listsong->set('songid', $selection);
                $listsong->set('position', $position++);
                $listsong->set('note', $_POST['section' . $i]);
                $listsongs[] = $listsong;
```

```
      }
   }
   return $listsongs;
}

/**
 * Operates directly from $_POST - xPDO schema to lockdown vars
 * @return int Playlist ID number
 */
public function createPlaylist() {
   $playlist = $this->modx->newObject('djPlaylist', $_POST);
   $playlist->set('createdby', $this->modx->user->get('id'));
   $playlist->set('createdon', strftime('%Y-%m-%d %H:%M:%S'));
   $listsongs = $this->createPlaylistSongs();
   $playlist->addMany($listsongs);
   $playlist->save();
   return $playlist->get('id');
}


/**
 * Gets and caches a Chunk, falls back to file-based templates
 *
 * @access  public
 * @param   string  $name The name of the Chunk
 * @param   array   $properties The properties for the Chunk
 * @see     Shaun McCormick helper functions
 * @return  string  The processed content of the Chunk
 */
public function getChunk($name, array $properties = array()) {
   $chunk = null;
   if (!isset($this->chunks[$name])) {
      $chunk = $this->modx->getObject('modChunk', array(
                        'name' => $name), true);
      if (empty($chunk)) {
         $chunk = $this->->_getTplChunk($name, $this->config['chunkSuffix']);
         if ($chunk == false) return false;
      }
      $this->chunks[$name] = $chunk->getContent();
   } else {
      $o = $this->chunks[$name];
```

```
        $chunk = $this->modx->newObject('modChunk');
        $chunk->setContent($o);
    }
    $chunk->setCacheable(false);
    return $chunk->process($properties);
}


/**
 * Can be used to create templated CSS files
 *
 * @param $name The filename without the extension
 * @return string The parsed contents of a CSS File
 */
public function getCssFile($name) {
    if ($this->config['useMinify'] == true) {
        $f = $this->modx->getOption('site  url');
        $f .= 'min/f=' . $this->config['cssUrl'];
    } else {
        $f = $this->config['cssPath'];
    }
    $f .= strtolower($name) . '.css';
    $contents = file_get_contents($f);
    $contents = '<style type="text/css" charset="'
        . $this->modx->getOption('modx_charset')
        . '">' . $this->_parseFile($contents) . '</style>';
    return $contents;
}


/**
 * Can be used to create templated Js files
 *
 * @param $name The filename without the extension
 * @return string The parsed contents of a Javascript File
 */
public function getJavaScriptFile($name) {
    if ($this->config['useMinify'] == true) {
        $f = $this->modx->getOption('site_url');
        $f .= 'min/f=' . $this->config['jsUrl'];
    } else {
        $f = $this->config['jsPath'];
```

```
      }
      $f .= strtolower($name) . '.js';
      $contents = file_get_contents($f);
      $contents = '<script type="text/javascript" charset="'
              . $this->modx->getOption('modx_charset') . '">'
              . $this->_parseFile($contents) . '</script>';
    return $contents;
  }


  /**
   * Finds the least popular song(s)
   * @param int $limit The number of rows to fetch
   * @return array songid, number of times used
   */
  public function getLeastPopularSongs($limit = 1) {
    return $this->_getPopularSongs($limit, 'ASC');
  }


  /**
   * Finds the most popular song(s)
   * @param int $limit The number of rows to fetch
   * @return array songid, number of times used
   */
  public function getMostPopularSongs($limit = 1) {
    return $this->_getPopularSongs($limit);
  }


  /**
   * @param int $startId Playlist id - typically a songs first run
   * @param string $endId Playlist id - defaults to last playlist
   * @return int
   */
  public function getNumberOfListsBetween($startId = 1, $endId = '') {
    $endId = (int)(!empty($endId)) ? $endId : $this->getPlaylistCount();
    $q = $this->modx->newQuery('djPlaylist');
    $q->select(array('id'));
    $q->where(array('id:>' => $startId,));
    $q->andCondition(array('id:<=' => $endId,));
    return $this->modx->getCount('djPlaylist', $q);
  }
```

```
/**
 * @return int The total number of playlists
 */
public function getPlaylistCount() {
    return $this->modx->getCount('djPlaylist');
}

/**
 * Finds the song(s) which have never been placed in a playlist.
 * @return array os unused song ids
 */
public function getUnusedSongs($limit = 1) {
    $usedSongsId = array();
    $q = $this->modx->newQuery('djPlaylistSong', '', false);
    $q->select('songid');
    $q->groupby('songid');
    if ($q->prepare() && $q->stmt->execute()) {
        $usedSongsId = $q->stmt->fetchAll(PDO::FETCH_COLUMN);
    }

    $songIds = array();
    $q = $this->modx->newQuery('djSong', '', false);
    $q->select('id');
    $object = $this->modx->getIterator('djSong', $q);
    foreach ($object as $song) {
        $id = $song->get('id');
        if (!in_array($id, $usedSongsId)) {
            $songIds[]['songid'] = $id;
        }
    }
    return array_slice($songIds, 0, $limit);
}

/**
 * @param $urlfile The relative URL for the file.
 *           Example: 'assets/js/overlay/overlay.css'
 * @return void
 */
```

```
public function setCssLink($urlfile) {
    if (substr($urlfile, -4) == '.css') {
        if ($this->config['useMinify'] == true) {
            $f = $this->modx->getOption('site_url');
            $f .= 'min/f=' . $urlfile;
        } else {
            $f = $urlfile;
        }
        $this->modx->regClientCSS($f);
        return $urlfile;
    }
}

/**
 * Formats the display of playlists using templates
 * @param array $array An array of a djPlaylist Object
 * @param string $rowTpl Template to use for each song
 * @param string $sectionTpl Template for a section of songs
 * @return string of Templated output
 */
public function showPlaylist($playlist, $rowTpl = '', $sectionTpl = '') {
    $out = '';
    $rowTpl = (!empty($rowTpl)) ? $rowTpl : $this->config['playlistRowTpl'];
    $sectionTpl = (!empty($sectionTpl)) ? $sectionTpl
                                        : $this->config['playlistSectionTpl'];
    $duration = array();
    $oldnote = false;
    $songRow = '';
    $c = 0;
    foreach ($playlist->Songs as $playlistsongs) {
        $note = $playlistsongs->get('note');
        $playlistsongs->Song = $this->modx->getObject('djSong',
                    $playlistsongs->get('songid'));
        $row = $this->getChunk($rowTpl, $playlistsongs->Song->toArray());
        $dur = $playlistsongs->Song->get('duration');

        /* still in current section */
        if ($oldnote !== $note) {
            $playlistsongs->set('entries', $songRow);
            $playlistsongs->set('note', $oldnote);
```

```php
        $playlistsongs->set('sectionDuration',
                                      $playlist->showDuration($duration));

        /* skip first run as it will always be true */
        if ($c++ > 0) {
            $out .= $this->getChunk($sectionTpl, $playlistsongs->toArray());
        }

        /* replace oldnote with new version once a section was created */
        $oldnote = $note;
        /* reset values to begin new section */
        unset ($songRow, $duration);
    }

    /* cumulative variables */
    $songRow .= $row;
    $duration[] = $dur;
}

/* catch any stragglers at the end of the playlist */
if (!empty($songRow)) {
    $playlistsongs->set('entries', $songRow);
    $playlistsongs->set('note', $oldnote);
    $playlistsongs->set('sectionDuration', $playlist->showDuration($duration));
    $out .= $this->getChunk($sectionTpl, $playlistsongs->toArray());
}
return $out;
}


/**
 * @param int $djplaylistId Playlist id number
 * @param string $rowTpl Template to use for each song
 * @param string $sectionTpl Template to use for a section
 * @return bool|string False or String if out is created
 */
public function showPlaylistFromTable($djplaylistId = 0,
                 $rowTpl = '', $sectionTpl = '') {
    $out = false;
    $playlistId = (!empty($playlistId)) ? (int)$djplaylistId : (int)$_GET['djplaylistId'];
```

```
    if (!empty($playlistId) && is_integer($playlistId)) {
      $rowTpl = (!empty($rowTpl)) ? $rowTpl : $this->config['playlistRowTpl'];
      $sectionTpl = (!empty($sectionTpl)) ? $sectionTpl
                                          : $this->config['playlistSectionTpl'];

      $duration = array();
      $oldnote = false;
      $songRow = '';
      $totalTime = array();
      $c = 0;

/* used a collectionGraph for demonstration and possible future */
$collection = $this->modx->getCollectionGraph('djPlaylist',
                                    '{"Event":{}, "Songs":{}}', $playlistId);
      foreach ($collection as $playlist) {
        $out .= $this->showPlaylist($playlist);
      }
    }
    return $out;
  }
}
```

Extended xPDO Derived Classes

Listing 18.09 djplaylist.class.php

```php
<?php
class djPlaylist extends xPDOSimpleObject {

  /**
   * @param Array $durations of playlist songs to be accumulated
   * @return string Formatted to Hours:Minutes:Seconds
   */
  public function showDuration($durations) {
    $total = '';
    foreach ($durations as $duration) {
      $duration = explode(':', $duration);
      if (substr_count($duration, ':') == 3) {
        $total += ($duration[0] * 3600) + ($duration[1] *60) + $duration[2];
      } else {
```

```php
            $total += ($duration[0] * 60) + $duration[1];
        }
    }
    return gmdate("H:i:s", $total);
}

/**
 * @return string output of the accumulated array of durations
 */
public function getTotalDuration() {
    $durations = array();
    foreach ($this->getSongs() as $song) {
        $durations[] = $song->get('duration');
    }
    return $this->showDuration($durations);
}

/**
 * @return array of djSong Objects
 */
public function getSongs() {
    $songs = array();
    $this->getMany('Songs');
    $playlistsongs =& $this->Songs;
    foreach ($playlistsongs as $listsong) {
        $songs[] = $this->xpdo->getObject('djSong', $listsong->get('songid'));
    }
    return $songs;
}

/* consider overriding the save() function to ensure user is
   authenticated and allowed to create lists.  Already protected
   on creation page with buttons and associated JavaScript files only
   injected to users with permission for them */

}
```

Listing 18.10 djsong.class.php implemented to provide helper functions

```php
<?php
class djSong extends xPDOSimpleObject {

  /**
   * @param string $direction The sort direction
   * @return int The listid attached to the songid
   */
  protected function _getPlaylistId($direction = 'ASC') {
    $q = $this->xpdo->newQuery('djPlaylistSong');
    $q->select(array(
                      'listid',
          ));
    $q->where(array(
                      'songid' => $this->get('id'),
          ));
    $q->sortby('listid', $direction);
    $q->limit(1);
    $playlist = $this->xpdo->getObject('djPlaylistSong', $q);
    return is_object($playlist) ? $playlist->get('listid') : false;
  }


  /**
   * @return int The ID of the first playlist a song appears in
   */
  public function getFirstListId() {
    return $this->_getPlaylistId();
  }

  /**
   * @return int The ID of the last playlist a song appears in
   */
  public function getLastListId() {
    return $this->_getPlaylistId('DESC');
  }
```

```
/**
 * @return int The number of times a song is added to playlists
 */
public function getListingCount() {
    return $this->xpdo->getCount('djPlaylistSong', array(
                                        'songid' => $this->get('id')));
}

/**
 * @return int The number of times a song is actually played
 */
public function getPlayCount() {
    return $this->xpdo->getCount('djPlaylistSong',
        array('songid' => $this->get('id'), 'skipped' => '0'));
}

/**
 * @return float Percentage of times a song is skipped if listed
 */
public function getPlayPercentage() {
    if ($this->getListingCount() > 0) {
        return round($this->getPlayCount() / $this->getListingCount(), 2) * 100;
    }
}

/**
 * @return int The number of times a song is skipped
 */
public function getSkippedCount() {
    return $this->xpdo->getCount('djPlaylistSong',
        array(
                'songid' => $this->get('id'),
                'skipped' => '1')
                );
}
```

```php
/**
 * @return float The percentage of times a song is played
 */
public function getSkippedPercentage() {
    if ($this->getListingCount() > 0) {
        return round($this->getSkippedCount() / $this->getListingCount(), 2) * 100;
    }
}

/**
 * @return string Text matched to tempo value
 */
public function setTempoText() {
    switch ($this->get('tempo')) {
        case 3:
            $t = 'Fast';
            break;
        case 2:
            $t = 'Moderate';
            break;
        case 1:
            $t = 'Slow';
            break;
        default :
            $t = 'Not set';
    }
    return $t;
}
}
```

MODX Revolution Snippets

Listing 18.11 discjockey.ajax.php

```php
<?php
/**
 * File discjockey.ajax.php (requires MODx Revolution 2.1)
 * Created on: 9/7/11 at 6:17 AM
 * Project shawn_wilkerson
 * @package discjockey
 *
 */
$out = false;
$discjockey_base = $modx->getOption('discjockey.core_path',
      $scriptProperties,
      $modx->getOption('core_path') . 'components/discjockey/');
if ($modx->loadClass('Discjockey', $discjockey_base
                  . 'model/discjockey/', true, true)) {
  $dj = new Discjockey($modx, $scriptProperties);
  $context = $modx->context->key;

/**
 * next line unnecessary due to MODX Revolution sanitizing
 * superglobals - could have been $action = strtolower($_REQUEST);
 */
  $action = strtolower($modx->request->getParameters('djaction', 'REQUEST'));
  switch ($action) {
    case 'geteventplaylists':
      $w = (isset($_GET['eventid'])) ? '{"eventid" : "' . $_GET['eventid'] . '"}' : '';
      $rowBoatProperties = array(
        'table' => 'discjockey_playlists',
        'tpl' => 'dj_rowboat.listPlaylistsByEventId',
        'chunksPath' => $dj->config['chunksPath'],
        'cacheResults' => '0',
        'limit' => '104',
        'sortBy' => 'id',
        'sortDir' => 'DESC',
        'where' => (!empty($w)) ? $w : ''
      );
      $out = $modx->runSnippet('Rowboat', $rowBoatProperties);
```

```
      break;

  case 'showplaylistsongs':
    $out = $dj->showPlaylistFromTable();
    break;

  case 'showsongs':
    $rowBoatProperties = array(
            'table' => 'discjockey_songs',
            'tpl' => 'dj_rowboat.listsongs',
            'chunksPath' => $dj->config['chunksPath'],
            'cacheResults' => 0,
            'limit' => 0,
            'sortBy' => 'title',
    );
    $w = array(
       'deleted' => false,
       'inactive' => false,
    );
    if ($_GET['filter'] && $_GET['value']) {
       $w[$_GET['filter']] = $_GET['value'];
    }
    if ($_GET['genre']) {
       $w['genre'] = $_GET['genre'];
    }
    $rowBoatProperties['where'] = json_encode($w);
    $out = $modx->runSnippet('Rowboat', $rowBoatProperties);
    break;

  case 'getsong':
    $songid = (int)$modx->getOption('songid',
                                         $scriptProperties, $_GET['songid']);
    if (!empty($songid) && is_integer($songid)) {
       /* merge arrays and merge into chunk template */
       $song = $modx->getObject('djSong', $songid);
       $song->set('tempo', $song->setTempoText());
       $vendor = $song->getOne('Vendor');
       $genre = $song->getOne('Genre');
       $songArry = array_merge($vendor->toArray(), $song->toArray());
       $songArry['genre.name'] = $genre->get($dj->config['genreList']);
```

```
/* handle playlists */
$playlists = $song->getMany('Lists', array(
                    'skipped' => 0,));
$c = 0;
$p = '';
foreach ($playlists as $lst) {
   $p .= $dj->getChunk($dj->config['songPlaylistTpl'], $lst->toArray());
}
$songlisted = $song->getListingCount();
$songplayed = $song->getPlayCount();
$songskipped = $song->getSkippedCount();
$totalnumberlists = $dj->getPlaylistCount();
$stats = 'Added on: ' . substr($songArry['addedon'], 0, 9) . '<br/>';
$stats .= 'Added by: ' . $song->getOne('Addedby')->get('username')
                    . '<br/>';
$stats .= 'Selection Rate: (' . round($songplayed /
       $dj->getNumberOfListsBetween($song->getFirstListId()), 2) * 100
          . '%) since being added<br/>';
$stats .= 'Overall: In ' . $songplayed . ' of '
                    . $totalnumberlists . ' playlists ('
                    . $song->getPlayPercentage() . '%)<br/>';
$stats .= 'Skipped : ' . $songskipped . ' ('
                    . $song->getSkippedPercentage() . '%) times<br/>';
$out = $dj->getChunk($dj->config['songTpl'], $songArry);
$out = str_replace('[[+dj_songInPlaylists]]', $p, $out);
$out = str_replace('[[+dj_songStatistics]]', $stats, $out);
unset($c, $p, $songid);
   }
   break;

case 'createfilter':
   $out = json_encode($dj->createFilter('djSong',
                            $_GET['filter'], $_GET['genre']));
   break;

/* handle various playlist creation options */

case 'playlist_emailonly':
   $playlist = $dj->createPlaylist();
   echo $msg = $dj->showPlaylist($playlist);
```

```
            $modx->user->sendEmail($msg, array(
                        'subject' => 'Playlist ' . $playlist->get('title'),
                    ));
        break;


    case 'playlist_savepersonallist':
        break;


    case 'playlist_saveemailgroup':
        break;


    case 'playlist_saveforclient':
        break;


    case 'playlist_printonly':
      /*
       * should never get here - in page JavaScript should
       * grab it.  This is simply a blocker
       */
      break;


    default: // intentionally do nothing - except during testing
        break;
  }
}
return $out;
```

Listing 18.12 createPlaylist.php (presumably a Manager user creation)

```php
<?php
/**
 * File createPlaylist.php (requires MODx Revolution 2.1)
 * Created on: 9/9/11 at 6:13 PM
 * Project shawn_wilkerson
 * @package
 *
 * Completely works for Stats and playlist viewing, actual
 * implementation left up to individual developer
 */

$out = false;
$discjockey_base = $modx->getOption('discjockey.core_path',
      $scriptProperties,
      $modx->getOption('core_path') . 'components/discjockey/');
if ($modx->loadClass('Discjockey', $discjockey_base
                  . 'model/discjockey/', true, true)) {
  $dj = new Discjockey($modx, $scriptProperties);

  foreach ($dj->createFilter('djSong', 'genre') as $arry) {
    $genre .= $dj->getChunk($dj->config['filterByTpl'], $arry);
  }

  /**
   * The following represents ideas to implement and are left to
   *  you to discover - should be considered pseudo code
   */

  /* only create buttons for users allowed to see them and only
   * inject javascript when a button is created
   */
  if ($modx->user->isAuthenticated($context)) {


    /* create buttons which will be attached to jquery ajax
     * functions with djaction named the same as the button id
     */
    if (!empty($dj->config['dj_MemberGroups'])) {
```

```
/* check for membership in a group allowed access*/
if ($modx->user->isMember($dj->config['dj_MemberGroups'])) {

    /* at this point check the user against the minimum
     * role required to save playlist and email to
     * group(s)
     */
    $buttons .= '<button type="button"
              id="playlist_saveemailgroup">
              Save and E-mail the group</button>';
} else {
    /* possibly allow them to save personal playlists to
     * their "own" event"
     */
    $buttons .= '<button type="button"
              id="playlist_savepersonallist">
              Save Personal List</button>';
} // end if mod->user->isMember
} else {
    /* email a list to themselves only without saving it  */
    $buttons = '<button type="button" id="playlist_
            emailonly">E-mail Me This List</button>';
}

if ($dj->config['dj_useDiscjockeyForClients'] == true) {
    if (in_array($dj->config['djClientHome'],
                     $modx->getParentIds($modx->resource->get('id')))) {
        $buttons .= '<button type="button"
                          id="playlist_saveforclient">Save For Client</button>';
        $modx->regClientScript($dj->
                          getJavaScriptFile('dj_jquery.playlist.saveforclient'));
    }
}
}
/* anyone can only print a playlist */
$buttons = '<button type="button" id="playlist_printonly">Print Playlist</
button>';
$modx->regClientScript($dj->getJavaScriptFile('dj_jquery.playlist.print'));
```

```php
/**
 * end of pseudo code
 */

$dj->setCssLink('assets/js/jquery.overlay/overlay.css');
$dj->setCssLink('assets/components/discjockey/css/discjockey.css');
$modx->regClientScript($dj->getJavaScriptFile('dj_jquery.createplaylist'));
$modx->toPlaceholder('dj_chunkpath', $dj->config['chunksPath']);
$modx->toPlaceholder('dj_createFilterFields', $dj->createFilterFields());
$modx->toPlaceholder('dj_filterGenre', $genre);
$modx->toPlaceholder('dj_savebuttons', $buttons);
}
return $out;
```

Listing 18.13 discjockey.snippet.php

```php
<?php
/**
 * File discjockey.snippet.php (requires MODx Revolution 2.1)
 * Created on: 9/2/11 at 4:17 PM
 * Project shawn_wilkerson
 * @package
 */
if (!function_exists('makeList')) {
   function makelist($array, $dj) {
      global $modx;
      $out = '';

      foreach ($array as $song) {
         $s = $modx->getObject('djSong', array('id' =>$song['songid']));
         if ($song['count'] > 0) {
            $s->set('count', $song['count']);
         }
         $out .= $dj->getChunk('dj_showsongpopularity', $s->toArray());
      }
```

```
      return $out;
   }
}
   /* Actual Page Control Happens here with injections */

$out = false;
$discjockey_base = $modx->getOption('discjockey.core_path',
      $scriptProperties,
      $modx->getOption('core_path') . 'components/discjockey/');
if ($modx->loadClass('Discjockey', $discjockey_base
                                    . 'model/discjockey/', true, true)) {
   $dj = new Discjockey($modx, $scriptProperties);

   if ($dj->config['showstats'] == false) {
      $w = (isset($_GET['eventid'])) ? '{"eventid" : "' . $_GET['eventid'] . '"}' : '';
      $modx->toPlaceholder('chunkPath', $dj->config['chunksPath)']);
      $modx->toPlaceholder('where', '&where=`' . $w . '`');
   } else {
      $modx->regClientCSS($dj->setCssLink('assets/js/jquery.overlay/overlay.
                                                            css'));
      $modx->regClientScript('/assets/js/jquery.paginator.js');
      $modx->regClientScript($dj->getJavaScriptFile('dj_jquery.main'));
      $modx->toPlaceholder('dj_mostplayed',
               makelist($dj->getMostPopularSongs(5), $dj));
      $modx->toPlaceholder('dj_leastplayed',
               makelist($dj->getLeastPopularSongs(5), $dj));
      $modx->toPlaceholder('dj_notplayed',
                  makelist($dj->getUnusedSongs(3), $dj));
   }
}
```

jQuery Javascript Files

Listing 18.14 dj_jquery.main.js

```
$(function() {
  $("a[rel]").overlay({
    mask: 'darkblue',
    effect: 'apple',
    onBeforeLoad: function() {
      var wrap = this.getOverlay().find(".contentWrap");
      wrap.load(this.getTrigger().attr("href"));
    }
  }).button();
});


$("#dj_listevents button").click(
  function() {
    $("#dj_songs").hide("slow");
    var event = "<h1>" + $(this).text() + "</h1>";
    $.get("[[++discjockey.ajax_id]]", {"eventid": $(this).val(),
               "djaction": "geteventplaylists" },
               function(data) {
      $("#dj_playlistsByEventId").html(event);
      $("#dj_playlistsByEventId").append('<table
            id="pageEvents">' + data + '</table>');
      $("#pageEvents").paginate(5, 300);
      $("#dj_playlistsByEventId button").click(
        function() {
          $("#dj_songs").html("<h2>" + $(this).text() + "</h1>");
          $.get("[[++discjockey.ajax_id]]", {
            "djplaylistId": $(this).val() , "djaction": "showplaylistsongs" },
              function(data) {
                $("#dj_songs").append(data).show();
                $("#dj_songs button").button();
                $("#dj_songs a[rel]").overlay({
                  mask: 'darkblue',
                  effect: 'apple',
                  onBeforeLoad: function() {
                    var wrap = this.getOverlay()
```

```
                        .find(".contentWrap");
                wrap.load(this.getTrigger()
                    .attr("href"));
            }
        });
    });
    }).button();
    $("#dj_playlistStatistics").hide();
    });
}).button();

var modal_triggers = $(".modalNewEvent").overlay({
    mask: {
        color: '#ebecff',
        loadSpeed: 200,
        opacity: 0.9
    },
    closeOnClick: false
});
```

Listing 18.15 dj_jquery.createplaylist.js

```
function getSongs() {
    $.get("[[++discjockey.ajax_id]]", { "filter": $("#filterby option:selected").val(),
        "value": $("#filters option:selected").val(),
        "genre": $("#genre option:selected").val(),
        "djaction": "showsongs"}
    , function(data) {
        if (data && data.length > 11) {
            $("#selectable").html(data);
        } else {
            $("#selectable").html("Please change Genre, no data
                        found...");
        }
    });

    /* reattach class if in playlist*/
    $("#dj_songs").ajaxComplete(function() {
        var id = '';
        $("#dj_playlist li").each(function() {
```

```
         id = $(this).attr("id");
         $("#dj_songs li#" + id).addClass("insortable");
      });
      return false;
   });
   return false;
}

function saveList(action, event) {
   var playdate = ($("#datepick").val().length == 10)
      ? $("#datepick").val() + " " + $("#dj_hours").val() + ":"
                                    + $("#dj_ minutes").val() + ":00"
      : "0000-00-00 00:00:00";
   var title = ($("#dj_playtitle").val().length > 1)
      ? $("#dj_playtitle").val()
      : event.text() + " " + playdate;
   $.post("[[++discjockey.ajax_id]]", {
         eventid: event.val(),
         djaction:  action,
         title: title,
         playdate: playdate,
         section1: $("#dj_section1").val(),
         section2: $("#dj_section2").val(),
         section3: $("#dj_section3").val(),
         section4: $("#dj_section4").val(),
         set1: $("#sortable1").sortable('serialize'),
         set2: $("#sortable2").sortable('serialize'),
         set3: $("#sortable3").sortable('serialize'),
         set4: $("#sortable4").sortable('serialize')
      },
      function(data) {
         alert("Data Loaded: " + data);
      });
}

$(function() {
      getSongs();
      $("select#genre").change(function() {
         $("select#filters").find('option').remove().end();
         $("select#filterby").val("");
```

```
      getSongs();
});


$("select#filters").change(getSongs);

$("select#filterby").change(function() {
    $.getJSON("[[++discjockey.ajax_id]]&" + new Date().getTime(),
      {"filter": $(this).val(),
       "genre": $("#genre option:selected").val(),
       "djaction": "createfilter"}, function(j) {
          var options = '<option value="">Choose...
                                  </option>';
        for (var i = 0; i < j.length; i++) {
          options += '<option value="'
                + j[i].optionValue + '">'
                + j[i].optionDisplay + '</option>';
        }
        $("select#filters").html(options);
    });
    if ($("#filters option").length) {
        $("#filteritems").show("slow");
    }
    return false;
});


$("#selectable").selectable({
    filter: 'li', stop: function() {
       var result = $("#sortable2");
       $(".ui-selected", this).each(function(index) {
          var songid = $(this).attr("id");
          var songtext = $(this).text();
          result.append('<li class="playlistsong" id="'
                + songid + '">' + songtext + '</li>');
          $(this).addClass("insortable");
       });
       if ($("#dj_playlist li").length
          && $('#dj_playlist').is(':hidden')) {
             $("#dj_playlist").show("slide", {
                direction: "right" }, 1000);
       }
```

```
    }
});

$(".droptrue").sortable({
   connectWith: '.droptrue',
   dropOnEmpty: true,
   update: function(event, ui) {
     if (this.id == 'sortable-delete') {
       var id = ui.item.attr('id');
       $("#dj_songs li#" + id).removeClass("insortable");
       if ($("#dj_songs li#" + id).hasClass('ui-selected')) {
           $("#dj_songs li#" + id).removeClass("ui-selected");
        }
         $("#sortable-delete li").remove();
     }
   }
}).disableSelection();

$("button#dj_reset").click(function() {
   $(':input', '#dj_filter')
     .not(':button, :submit, :reset, :hidden')
     .val('')
     .removeAttr('checked')
     .removeAttr('selected');
   $("select#filters").find('option').remove().end()
   $("#filteritems").hide("slow");
   getSongs();
   return false;
});

$("#dj_showSave").click(function() {
   $("#dj_filter").hide("slide", { direction: "left" }, 200);
   $("#dj_playlist").hide("slide", { direction: "left" }, 200);
   $("#dj_songs").hide("slide", { direction: "left" }, 200);
   $("#dj_playlist h2").text("Check List and Order");
   $("#dj_showSave").hide();
   $("#dj_playlist").show("slide", { direction: "left" }, 300);
     $("#dj_save").show("slide", { direction: "left" }, 500);
   }
);
```

```
    $("#datepick").click(function() {
            $("#dj_pickevent").show("slide", {direction: "left" }, 300);
      }).dateinput({format : "yyyy-mm-dd"});

    $("#dj_pickevent button").button().click(function() {
      var event = $(this);
      $("#dj_savebuttons").show("slide", { direction: "left"}, 300);
      $("#dj_savebuttons button").button().click(function() {
        saveList($(this).attr('id'), event);
      });
    });

    /* apply additional jQuery ui styling */
    $("#dj_reset, #dj_saveonly, #dj_emailsave, #dj_clientsave").button();
    $("#dj_hours").rangeinput({ progress: true, max: 23 });
    $("#dj_minutes").rangeinput({ progress: true, max: 60, step: 5 });
  }
);
```

Page Template

Listing 18.16 discjockey.template.xhtml

```
<!DOCTYPE html PUBLIC "-//W3C//DTD XHTML 1.0 Strict//EN" "http://
www.w3.org/TR/xhtml1/DTD/xhtml1-strict.dtd">
<html xmlns="http://www.w3.org/1999/xhtml" xml:lang="en-GB">
<head>
<title>Some Title</title>
    <link rel="stylesheet" type="text/css"
        href="//ajax.googleapis.com/ajax/libs/jqueryui/1.8.14/
                    themes/flick/jquery-ui.css" media="screen"/>
    <link rel="stylesheet" type="text/css" href="style.css"
media="screen"/>
</head>
<body>
[[!injectJSLinksToBottom?src= [[$jsLibraries]],min/g=js&amp;1`]]
<div id="header">
</div>
<div class="colmask leftmenu">
    <div class="colleft">
        <div class="col1">
            [[*content]]
        </div>
        <div class="col2">
            [[+filterForm]]
            [[+playlist]]
        </div>
    </div>
</div>
<div id="footer">
</div>
</body>
</html>
```

Note: It is also possible to inject the JavaScipt links via filters with:

```
[[$jsLibraries:jsToBottom]]
```

Resources

Listing 18.17 mainpage-events.xhtml

- -

```
[[!discjockey?ph=`filterForm`&src=`
<h2>Menu</h2>
[[Wayfinder?]]
<h2 id="dj_eventButtons">Select event:</h2>
<div id="dj_listevents">
    [[!rowboat?
    &table=`discjockey_events`
    &chunksPath=`[[++core_path]]components/discjockey/elements/
chunks`
    &tpl=`dj_rowboat.listevents`
    &cacheResults=`0`
    &limit=`15`
    &sortBy=`id`
    &sortDir =`DESC`
    ]]
</div>
`]]
<div id="dj_playlistStatistics">
    <div>
        <h2>Most Played</h2>
        <table class="dj_playlistStats">[[+dj_mostplayed]]</table>
    </div>
    <div>
        <h2>Least Played</h2>
        <table class="dj_playlistStats">[[+dj_leastplayed]]</table>
    </div>
    <div>
        <h2>Not Played</h2>
        <table class="dj_playlistStats">[[+dj_notplayed]]</table>
    </div>
</div>
<div id="dj_playlistsByEventId"></div>
<div id="dj_songs"></div>
<div class="apple_overlay" id="overlay">
    <div class="contentWrap"></div>
</div>
<div id="dj_createEvent"></div>
```

- -

Listing 18.18 createPlaylists.xhtml

- -

```
[[!createPlaylist]]
[[toPlaceholder?ph=`filterForm`&src=`
<form id="dj_filter" action="#">
    <h2>Step 1: Filter List (Optional)</h2>
    <fieldset>
        <div id="dj_genres"><label for="genre">Select Genre</label>
            <select name="name" id="genre">
                <option value=""></option>
                [[+dj_filterGenre]]
            </select>
        </div>
        <label for="filterby" accesskey="f">Filter by</label>
        <select name="name" id="filterby">
            <option value=""></option>
            [[+dj_createFilterFields]]
        </select>
        <div id="filteritems">
            <label for="filters">Show Only:</label>
            <select name="choices" id="filters">
                <option value=""></option>
            </select>
        </div>

        <div><label for="dj_reset">Clear All Filters</label>
            <button type="button" id="dj_reset"
                    name="clearfilters">Clear Filters</button>
        </div>
    </fieldset>
</form>`]]
[[toPlaceholder?ph=`genre`&src=`[[dj_getGenres]]`]]
[[toPlaceholder?ph=`playlist`&src=`
<div id="dj_playlist">
    <h2>Step 2: Select &amp; Sort Songs</h2>


    <form id="dj_sections" action="#">
        <fieldset>
            <legend>Optionally, name each block for this playlist
            </legend>
            <label for="dj_section1">First:</label>
            <input id="dj_section1" name="section_1" type="text"/>
```

```
                <ul class="droptrue" id="sortable1"></ul>

                <label for="dj_section2">Second:</label>
                <input id="dj_section2" name="section_2" type="text"/>

                <ul class="droptrue" id="sortable2"></ul>
                <label for="dj_section3">Third:</label>
                <input id="dj_section3" name="section_3" type="text"/>

                <ul class="droptrue" id="sortable3"></ul>
                <label for="dj_section4">Forth:</label>
                <input id="dj_section4" name="section_4" type="text"/>

                <ul class="droptrue" id="sortable4"></ul>
                <ul class="droptrue" id="sortable-delete"></ul>
                <button type="button" id="dj_showSave">Save Playlist
                </button>
            </fieldset>
        </form>
</div>`]]
<span class="tooltip"> </span>

<div id="dj_songs">
    <ul id="selectable"></ul>
</div>

<div id="dj_save">

    <form action="#">
        <fieldset>
            <legend>Playlist details:</legend>
            <p>
                <label for="dj_playtitle">Name:</label>
                <input id="dj_playtitle" name="title"
                        type="text"/><br/>
            </p>

            <p>
                <label for="datepick">Select play date:</label>
                <input id="datepick" type="text"
                                    name="playdate"/><br/>
            </p>

            <p><strong>Select Start Time (add 12 to hours for PM):</
```

```
strong></p>
                <input id="dj_hours" name="hour" type="range" min="0"
                        max="23" value="10"/><br/>
                <input id="dj_minutes" name="minutes" type="range"
                        min="0" max="60" value="30" step="5"/><br/>

                <div id="dj_pickevent">
                    <br/>

                    <h2><strong>Choose Event for this List:</strong></h2>
                    [[!rowboat?
                    &table=`discjockey_events`
                    &chunksPath=`[[+dj_chunkpath]]`
                    &tpl=`dj rowboat.pickevent`
                    &cacheResults=`0`
                    &limit=`10`
                    &sortBy=`id`
                    &sortDir =`DESC`
                    ]]
                </div>
                <div id="dj_savebuttons">
                    <br/>

                    <h2><strong>Finalize Playlist:</strong></h2>
                    [[+dj_savebuttons]]
                </div>
            </fieldset>
        </form>
    </div>
```

Chunk Templates

Listing 18.19 dj_filterby.chunk.tpl

```
<option value="[[+optionValue]]">[[+optionDisplay]]</option>
```

Listing 18.20 dj_playlistrow.chunk.tpl

```
<tr>
    <td><a href="[[~[[++discjockey.ajax_id]]]]&songid=[[+id]]&djacti
on=getsong" rel="#overlay" style="text-decoration:none">
    <button type="button" value="[[+id]]">[[+title]]</button>
        </a>
    </td>
    <td>[[+artist]]</td>
    <td>[[+leadin]]</td>
    <td>[[+duration]]</td>
</tr>
```

Listing 18.21 dj_playlistsection.chunk.tpl

```
<table>
    <thead>
    <tr><th>[[+note]]</th></tr>
    </thead>
    <tfoot>
    <tr>
        <td colspan="25" style="text-align: right;">
            <strong>(Runtime: [[+sectionDuration]])</strong></td>
    </tr>
    </tfoot>
    <tbody>[[+entries]]</tbody>
</table>
```

Listing 18.22 dj_rowboat.listevents.chunk.tpl

```
<button type="button" value="[[+id]]">[[+name]]</button><br />
```

Listing 18.23 dj_rowboat.listplaylistsbyeventid.chunk.tpl

```
<tr>
    <td><button type="button" value="[[+id]]">[[+title]]</button>
    </td>
    <td>[[+playdate]]</td>
    <td>[[+createdby]]</td>
</tr>
```

Listing 18.24 dj_rowboat.listsongs.chunk.tpl

```
<li id="songid-[[+id]]" class="dj_song row[[_alt]]"
    title="Artist: [[+artist]] Album:[[+album]] Duration:
    [[+duration]] Leadin:[[+leadin]]">[[+title]]
</li>
```

Listing 18.25 dj_rowboat.pickevent.chunk.tpl

```
<button type="button" id="event[[+id]]" name="eventid"
value="[[+id]]">[[+name]]</button><br/>
```

Listing 18.26 dj_showsong.chunk.tpl

```
<h1 style="border-bottom-style:double;">[[+title]]</h1>
<table style="width:500px; vertical-align:top; margin: 0 50px;">
    <tr>
        <td><h3>Details:</h3>
            Album: [[+album]]<br/>
            Artist: [[+artist]]<br/>
            Duration : [[+duration]]<br/>
            Leadin: [[+leadin]]<br/>
            Genre: [[+genre.name]]<br/>
            Tempo: [[+tempo]]
            <h3>Statistics:</h3>
            [[+dj_songStatistics]]
        </td>
        <td><h3>Appears in Playlist:</h3>
            <ul>[[+dj_songInPlaylists]]</ul>
        </td>
    </tr>
</table>
```

Listing 18.27 dj_showsongplaylist.chunk.tpl

```
<li>[[+listid]] in position [[+position]]. Note: [[+note]]</li>
```

Listing 18.28 dj_showsongpopularity.chunk.tpl

```
<tr>
    <td><a href="[[~[[++discjockey.ajax_id]]]]&songid=[[+id]]&djacti
on=getsong" rel="#overlay" style="text-decoration:none">
        <button type="button" value="[[+id]]">[[+title]]</button>
    </a></td>
    <td>[[+artist]]</td>
    <td>[[+album]]</td>
    <td>[[+count]]</td>
</tr>
```

Primary Cascading Style Sheet

Listing 18.29 discjockey.css

- -

```css
/* jQuery UI - Selectable */

#feedback {
    font-size: 1.4em;
}

#selectable .ui-selecting {
    background: #FECA40;
}

#selectable .ui-selected {
    background: #F39814;
    color: white;
}

#selectable {
    list-style-type: none;
    margin: 0;
    padding: 0;
    width: 400px;
}

#selectable li {
    list-style-type: none;
    margin: 3px;
    padding: 0.4em;
    font-size: 1.2em;
    height: 22px;
    border: 1px solid #000;
}

.insortable {
    background: #E3E3E3;
    color: #c7c7c7;
}
```

```css
.songdetails span {
    padding: 0 12px;
    margin-top: -5px;
    font-size: 70%;
    color: #0000ff
}

/* jQuery UI Sortable */

#sortable1, #sortable2, #sortable3, #sortable4 {
    list-style-type: none;
    margin: 0;
    margin-right: 10px;
    background: #00688B;
    padding: 5px;
    width: 335px;
}

#sortable1 li, #sortable2 li, #sortable3 li, #sortable4 li {
    margin: 5px;
    padding: 5px;
    font-size: 1.2em;
    width: 315px;
    border: 1px solid #000;
    background: #67C8FF;
}

#sortable-delete {
    height: 64px;
    overflow: hidden;
    background: url('../images/trash.png') 0 50% no-repeat;
}

#sortable-delete li {
    height: 0;
    width: 0;
    overflow: hidden;
}

#dj_playlist, #dj_save, #dj_savebuttons, #dj_savelist,
#dj_pickevent, .songdetails {
    display: none;
}
```

```css
li.playlistsong:hover {
    cursor: move;
}

/* filter form */
#dj_filter {
    display: block;
    width: 225px;
    text-align: left;
    border: none;
}

#dj_filter fieldset {
    border: none;
}

#dj_filter input, #dj_save input {
    border: 1px solid #006;
    background: #ffc;
}

#dj_filter input:hover, #dj_save input:hover {
    border: 1px solid #f00;
    background: #ff6;
}

#dj_filter label, #dj_save label {
    display: block;
    width: 200px;
    float: left;
    margin: 2px 4px 6px 4px;
    text-align: left;
    font-size: 1.4em;
}

#dj_save lebel {
    width: 400px;
}

#dj_filter select {
    position: relative;
    color: #0000FF;
    left: 10px;
}
```

```css
#dj_save {
    width: 500px;
}

/* calendar */
.date {
    border: 1px solid #ccc;
    font-size: 18px;
    padding: 4px;
    text-align: center;
    width: 194px;
    -moz-box-shadow: 0 0 10px #eee inset;
    -webkit-box-shadow: 0 0 10px #eee inset;
}

#calroot {
    z-index: 10000;
    margin-top: -1px;
    width: 198px;
    padding: 2px;
    background-color: #fff;
    font-size: 11px;
    border: 1px solid #ccc;
    -moz-border-radius: 5px;
    -webkit-border-radius: 5px;
    -moz-box-shadow: 0 0 15px #666;
    -webkit-box-shadow: 0 0 15px #666;
}

#calhead {
    padding: 2px 0;
    height: 22px;
}

#caltitle {
    font-size: 14px;
    color: #0150D1;
    float: left;
    text-align: center;
    width: 155px;
    line-height: 20px;
    text-shadow: 0 1px 0 #ddd;
}
```

```css
#calnext, #calprev {
    display: block;
    width: 20px;
    height: 20px;
    background: transparent url('../images/prev.gif') no-repeat
                                        scroll center center;
    float: left;
    cursor: pointer;
}

#calnext {
    background-image: url('../images/next.gif');
    float: right;
}

#calprev.caldisabled, #calnext.caldisabled {
    visibility: hidden;
}

#caltitle select {
    font-size: 10px;
}

#caldays {
    height: 14px;
    border-bottom: 1px solid #ddd;
}

#caldays span {
    display: block;
    float: left;
    width: 28px;
    text-align: center;
}

#calweeks {
    background-color: #fff;
    margin-top: 4px;
}

.calweek {
    clear: left;
    height: 22px;
}
```

```css
.calweek a {
    display: block;
    float: left;
    width: 27px;
    height: 20px;
    text-decoration: none;
    font-size: 11px;
    margin-left: 1px;
    text-align: center;
    line-height: 20px;
    color: #666;
    -moz-border-radius: 3px;
    -webkit-border-radius: 3px;
}

.calweek a:hover, .calfocus {
    background-color: #ddd;
}

a.calsun {
    color: red;
}

a.caloff {
    color: #ccc;
}

a.caloff:hover {
    background-color: rgb(245, 245, 250);
}

a.caldisabled {
    background-color: #efefef !important;
    color: #ccc !important;
    cursor: default;
}

#calcurrent {
    background-color: #498CE2;
    color: #fff;
}

#caltoday {
    background-color: #333;
```

```css
    color: #fff;
}

/* slider */
/* slider root element */
.slider {
    background: #3C72E6 url('../images/h30.png') repeat-x 0 0;
    height: 9px;
    position: relative;
    cursor: pointer;
    border: 1px solid #333;
    width: 675px;
    float: left;
    clear: right;
    margin-top: 10px;
    -moz-border-radius: 5px;
    -webkit-border-radius: 5px;
    -moz-box-shadow: inset 0 0 8px #000;
}

/* progress bar (enabled with progress: true) */
.progress {
    height: 9px;
    background-color: #C5FF00;
    display: none;
    opacity: 0.6;
}

/* drag handle */
.handle {
    background: #fff url('../images/h30.png') repeat-x 0 0;
    height: 28px;
    width: 28px;
    top: -12px;
    position: absolute;
    display: block;
    margin-top: 1px;
    border: 1px solid #000;
    cursor: move;
    -moz-box-shadow: 0 0 6px #000;
    -webkit-box-shadow: 0 0 6px #000;
    -moz-border-radius: 14px;
    -webkit-border-radius: 14px;
}
```

```css
/* the input field */
.range {
    border: 1px inset #ddd;
    float: left;
    font-size: 20px;
    margin: 0 0 0 15px;
    padding: 3px 0;
    text-align: center;
    width: 50px;
    -moz-border-radius: 5px;
    -webkit-border-radius: 5px;
}

.slider {
    height: 9px;
    width: 300px;
    margin: 0 0 0 60px;
}

.handle {
    top: 0;
    left: -10px;
}

.progress {
    width: 9px;
    position: absolute;
    bottom: 0;
}
```

Screen Shots From discjockey Created For This Chapter

Menu

- test
- create

Select event:

Jenkins

Alter Ministry

Sunday Celebration

Most Played

One Desire	Hillsong	This Is Our God	13
Revelation Song	Darlene Zschech	Integrity's iWorship 24:7	13
In Christ Alone	Adrienne Liesching & Geoff Moore	Secrets of the Vine: Music	12
None But Jesus	Hillsong United	United We Stand	11
Faithful God	Thibodaux Family Church	Thibodaux Family Church	10

Least Played

He Reigns (w/ Easter opener)	Newsboys	Adoration	1
Beautiful Savior	Casting Crowns	Live in Atlanta	1
Hallelujahs	Chris Rice	Hallelujahs - A Rocketown Worship Collection	1
I Have A Friend	Clint Brown	Night of Destiny	1
Come Now Is The Time To Worship	Brain Doerksen	Open The Eyes of My Heart	1

Not Played

Days of Elijah	Robin Mark	Revival In Belfast
Give Thanks	Don Moen	25 Best Worship Songs Hosanna Music
Let It Rain	Michael W. Smith	Worship

Discjockey's Front Optional Statistics Page

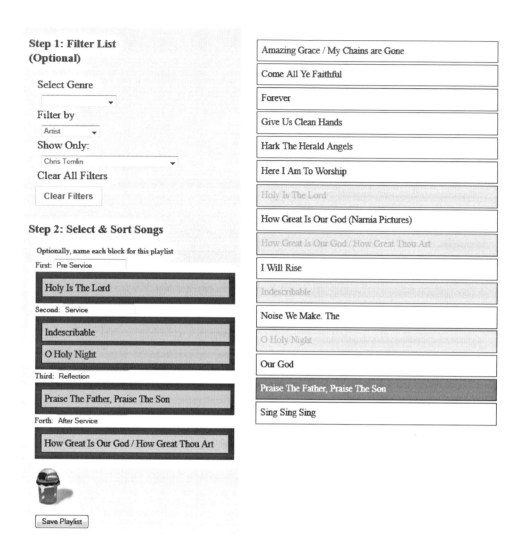

Step 1: Filter List (Optional)

Select Genre
[▼]

Filter by
[Artist ▼]

Show Only:
[Chris Tomlin ▼]

Clear All Filters
[Clear Filters]

Step 2: Select & Sort Songs

Optionally, name each block for this playlist

First: Pre Service
[Holy Is The Lord]

Second: Service
[Indescribable]
[O Holy Night]

Third: Reflection
[Praise The Father, Praise The Son]

Forth: After Service
[How Great Is Our God / How Great Thou Art]

[Save Playlist]

Amazing Grace / My Chains are Gone

Come All Ye Faithful

Forever

Give Us Clean Hands

Hark The Herald Angels

Here I Am To Worship

Holy Is The Lord

How Great Is Our God (Narnia Pictures)

How Great Is Our God / How Great Thou Art

I Will Rise

Indescribable

Noise We Make. The

O Holy Night

Our God

Praise The Father, Praise The Son

Sing Sing Sing

Discjockey's AJAX Create Playlist Page utilizes jQueryUI

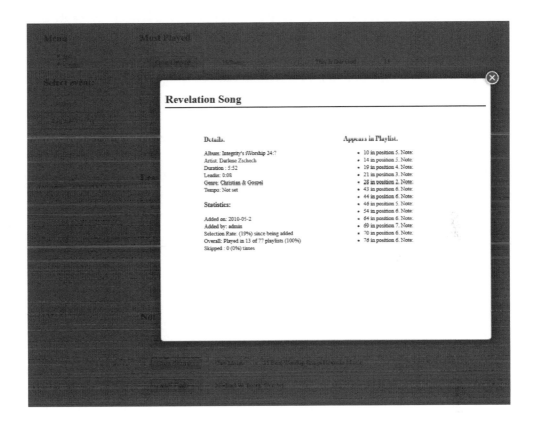

Song information using Overlay from jQuery Tools

MODX Revolution Rule #18: **Target the largest possible audience with your application.**

Summary

If you were able to follow along without looking in the previous chapters more than a few times - you may be able to think of yourself as a MODX Revolution expert. At the very least you should be ready for certification through MODX U and recognition throughout the MODX community, as you begin contributing and Packaging applications.

The methods demonstrated in this chapter were a mixture of commonly available products, and were selected in an effort to combine functionality across a wide array of skill-sets which participate in the development of a typical web project.

In some situations, I could have done things much easier, but desired to demonstrate "how" specific functionality could be introduced into a typical third-party application. For example, one of the first things I will be "undoing" is the inclusion of Rowboat to process template chunks. For demonstration purposes, it performs exactly as the doctor ordered, and is an excellent tool for quick presentation of tabled information.

When one considers the overhead of another class being used to simply spit out table contents, when the information is readily available it doesn't make much sense. I had actually acquired the base helper functions used by Shaun McCormick in a number of his packages, which I then extended to provide a pseudo-parser allowing me to template external Cascading Style Sheets and JavaScript files with MODX Revolution System Settings and Placeholders.

Also hidden away in the main class file was the ability to utilize Minify on the fly - even on the files which required various placeholders to be "permanently" set. Once the settings have been changed out for the url links, colors or whatever else I choose to template, Minify could create a more permanent copy or at least make the code much less readable. In this implementation. In its present state, Minify is "asked" to recreate the file each time, leaving it to its own devices on how it chooses to do so. If nothing else, the code will be compressed and gzipped. I will probably extend this functionality further into a MODX Revolution Plugin or a full blown application.

This chapter is not intended to demonstrate how well I can code in multiple technologies, nor was it to provide a 100% working application, though it is working above 90%, with only two things needing any real work: which can typically only done on an individual basis. It simply provides a platform for people to discover the integration of techniques or new capabilities previously not experienced by the reader.

Minimal styling was utilized, in order to simplify the reproduction of the process and its associated code. The purpose of this chapter was to present a real-world implementation in its entirety, rather than presenting components with the assumption the reader is familiar enough with the content. I simply chose to take the opportunity to present content which would usually be spread across multiple Blog articles, forum posts, API documention, and other forms of media.

I hope you found the concepts in this chapter worth digging through.

Some of the things hidden in the code:

◆ Extending the Class files created by xPDOGenerator rather than utilize new ones

◆ Creating a helper class, for the purpose of dealing with groups of objects and associated functions.

◆ Directly passing instantiated objects from one function to another - even between classes, to reduce code and simply development

◆ Practical usage of xPDO's getcount()

◆ getCollectionGraph was utilized in one of the Playlist functions,, where I actually removed the subclass Song from Songs, as it was redundant - it went from {"Event":{}, "Songs":{"Song":{}}}' to {"Event":{}, "Songs":{}}'

◆ Parsing external files, using them as templates, but also passing them along to Minify

◆ Multiple methods of AJAX functionality: $_POST, $_GET, and .load() all pointed to the same MODX Revolution Resource

◆ Third-party libraries from multiple vendors, with the examples left very close to those presented on the providers web site - to lower the expectations on coding

◆ On-the-fly content injection from the PHP Snippets, class files, and even the Resources themselves, which prompted a feature request which was introduced in the MODX Revolution 2.2 release

◆ Reliance on MODX Revolution to Sanitize the PHP Globals on each page request, providing a straightforward level of security, easily built upon

◆ Allowing xPDO to deal with individual values being assigned to object properties, as it provides additional Sanity in the process, which can even be further enhanced by creating validation for the various objects in the schema

◆ Implementing a runtime method to interact with Minify for JavaScript and CSS files

◆ Using external files as a potential template platform - regardless of the technology

◆ Running the Rowboat Package via an AJAX interface, which we also did to getResources in the Power Blogging Chapter

◆ The use of xPDO's getIterator() rather than getCollection() to speed up results and reduce overhead whenever applicable

◆ Working with 1:1 and 1:m relationships with getOne() and getMany()

◆ using PHP's array_merge($secondaryObject, $secondaryObject, $primaryObject) to parse the results directly into a Chunk template in a single step

◆ Demonstrated the ability to selectively add preemptive "security" planning to site content, by simply not providing any of the functionality or scripts involved unless they are needed, by intentionally injecting only what a specific user needs

19
Now What?

Finally, we come to the end of all things - well at least the end of what I felt needed to be placed in a book on MODX Revolution. For some of you, the tone and examples could have been more "professional", but after three decades in this industry I have come to realize how easy it is for us "techie" people to hide behind our many words and never really say anything.

I have satisfied my goal for this book, which was to introduce and thoroughly discuss MODX Revolution in a way the majority of people could actually benefit from - even those having limited web programming experience. I also did not want to ignore the developing arm of the community by endless and extensive lists of data which would only serve to bury functionality and effectively neuter the concepts.

This book has a single purpose: to bridge the brilliance found within the foundation of the MODX Revolution Platform and the rest of the world. By now, many of you should have surmised, it is not a thing to be conquered, but a world to be explored. MODX Revolution is unique in its ability to allow its users to explore it in almost any way they find themselves comfortable - hence the subtitle on this book: *A Journey Through a Content Management Framework*. Hopefully, this journey will enable readers to continue on their own quests through MODX 3, upon its release.

Where I am headed now? I am moving all of my design focus into HTML5, and have already began noticing the overcomplicated mess being thrown at the feet of people in this area. Much of this will eventually be found unnecessary, as people learn each aspect of this technology family and begin to simplify it.

I have been asked to begin construction on a major new web project, which is intended to grow into a niche social network over the coming months. I expect to greatly enjoy this project for two reasons: I can actually get back to "using" MODX Revolution instead of dissecting it and get back into developing xPDO applications which I enjoy - and of course there is the money.

I recently formalized my Limited Liability Corporation and filed all of the necessary papers with the state. The process usually takes three to five business days to complete, and mine took less than two hours - which has to be considered a miracle considering this included filling out the paperwork and waiting on the turn around.

In June 2012, I began my own publishing company, as a direct result of two publishers being unable to successfully publish this book due to their own internal issues. Sanity Press can work with authors to publish additional MODX materials, or other works as they are introduced.

While writing this book I also managed to graduate with a Bachelors in Supervision and Management, which offers me a perspective and a competitive edge over most of my competition. I am now qualified to run major corporations and also see business, and even non-profits, from a new perspective - though those two worlds are entirely different and can't be entirely boxed in together. In just two semesters I took over 30 semester hours of classes - and managed to write much of the first half of this work, which was rewritten when the original requester of this book dropped the project as their concept was not providing the book sales utilizing the same focus. This freed me to write the book I felt was needed - which ended up being around the length I thought it would, which was twice what they were wanting to be written.

Some of you may be thinking, "Wow!," while others are thinking, "How in the world were you able to run your company?" The fact is, I essentially shut my business down to write this book and complete my BAS, as I understood there was no way I could do three full-time "jobs" at once. Money has been tight and this decision cost my family quite a bit, but we agreed on this direction and have walked through it together.

Will there be books in the future from me? Most definitely, though some of them will be focused on Christian topics or even non fiction. The goal for my company is to grow it to where it is self-sustaining with a planned growth path, so I can be free to "explore the things I must" which is how I operate. I have no choice but to do this - it is who I am: I have to explore and love to show people what I find.

The book is a result of a few of those journeys, as I have "taken trips" throughout different aspects of MODX Revolution, hence the subtitle: *A Journey Through A Content Management Framework.* What you now hold in your hands, is literally an entire year of my life. For me, it was time well spent. Not only have I learned much about this amazing framework, I have also endeavored to make it better with hundreds of requests at `http://tracker.modx.com/users/11` and even more pages dedicated to the topic. It also allowed me to ask in IRC why the parser was hitting each of the Element tags twice, which I discovered when I laid out a flowchart of its processes to better understand the topic.

Additionally, the MODX Revolution documentation has come grown significantly over the last two years, but it still needs quite a bit of help. What most of you may not realize, *MODX Revolution: Building The Web Your Way* was largely written by an author who had to take multiple laps through thousands of lines of source code and as a result of quite a bit of "trial and error". Most of the content on the web and in the documentation did not exist when this project was started, though this is turning around nicely.

With multiple books now released into the hands of the community, many of you can begin contributing to the documentation, in the forums, and by developing Packages. From this point forward, I believe the community should thrive and begin to grow exponentially - simply because we have had authors pioneer and define some of the major highways which can quickly facilitate people in maximizing their skill sets, instead of wandering through back country roads aimlessly testing and hacking other software, when they should simply be using MODX Revolution.

As many of you may know, I have nine computer degrees and certificates, which continuously are combined with three decades of experience - perhaps, in far too many areas. There comes a time, when each of us has to decide which direction to primarily or exclusively pursue and I believe I have finally decided to boil it all down to writing books and building xPDO based applications.

To further establish my credentials in these areas, I am currently working my way through obtaining a Masters of Arts in Information Technology Management. I should graduate Fall 2014. from a university accredited in multiple countries and recognized by organizations and various state and national government agencies throughout the United States.

It, has been a joy and an honor to present this work to you. Hopefully, *MODX Revolution: Building The Web Your Way* proves to be helpful and an invaluable resource. Primarily, I would like to see this work equip people with the information they need to expand their individual potential, thereby unleashing the raw power of MODX Revolution - and building the web their way.

MODX Revolution Rule #19: **Anything that matters has a cost - invest wisely.**

P.S. I would like to give a shout-out to Sunrise Foursquare Church for being a home away from home and "Hotlead" and "MaxE<3" for running a clean clan and keeping *America's Army 3* fun - even for a "Hammer". Last of all, I owe a word of thanks to my readers, I hope this book helps you along your MODX journeys - I believe there will be more books to come.

Appendices

The appendices contain lists, quick reference materials, and instructional information which should assist the reader in various aspects of MODX Revolution.

Terminology

Resource/System Settings

MODX Object Cheat Sheets

Parser Function

Caching Technologies

MODX "Rules"

Appendix A
MODX Revolution Terminology

As with many forms of technology, MODX Revolutions has its own terminology. In the interest of clear and open communication, I would like to introduce the various terms associated with the MODX Revolution Application Platform.

These terms are used:

- Throughout this book
- The MODX forums
- The official MODX Revolution Documentation (http://rtfm.modx.com/)
- The associated IRC channels (#xpdo, #modx)
- The bug tracker (http://tracker.modx.com/)
- Community and fan web sites

I have taken the liberty to reduce the full list of MODX Revolution terminology to those which are the most commonly used across all levels of users and also to paraphrase the definitions.

Revolution Term	Description
Add-on	Provides extra functionality but does not modify the Core or extend any of its classes.
Asset	Any type of file resource, including images, css, JavaScript, classes, etc.
Bugs	`http://bugs.modx.com/` OR `http://tracker.modx.com/`
Cached	Calling an element without the exclamation point (!) which would designate it being uncached.
Category	An optional classifying name that can be attached to any Element and PropertySet indicating functional grouping
Chunk Tags	Tags in the form [[$ChunkName]] that can be used in reference to (X)HTML Chunks in the Element Tree
Component	Usually provides extra functionality in the form of an Add-on, Core Extension, Manager function, or Template
Content Type	Found on the Setting tab and defines the extension, mime-type and binary setting for any Resource within the site. Additional types can be added in the System Menu
Context	Typically attached to a domain name or the Manager.
Docs	`http://rtfm.modx.com`
Document	A specific type of Resource, usually a web page.
Element	A unique Template, Template Variable, Chunk, Snippet, Plugin, Category, or Property Set.
Evo	Community nickname for MODX Evolution
Extra	Synonymous with Addon
Link Tags	Tags in the form [[~ResourceId]] that reference the URL of a particular Resource populated by MODX Revo
Manager	The "back-end" of the MODX interface.
Media Sources	A tool used to incorporate internet technologies and services into a native MODX Revolution "File System"

Revolution Term	Description
Placeholder Tags	Tags in the form [[+PlaceholderName]] usually with the value set within a Snippet or Plugin.
Property	A single variable / parameter for an Element.
Property Set	A group of properties used with an Element.
Resource	A type of container that is interpreted by the Parser to fetch content: mostly accessed as a Document or Page.
Resource Field	Any of the database fields of the site_content table accessible via the documentObject.
Resource Identifier	The number that uniquely identifies the Resource specified, which can be found in Resource Tree.
Resource Tags	Tags in the form [[*ResourceField/TV]], used to refer to Resource Fields, or Template Variables.
Revo	Community nickname for MODX Revolution
Setting Tags	Tags in the form [[++SettingName]] that reference MODX System, Context, and / or User Settings.
Snippet Tags	Tags in the form [[SnippetName]], also referred to as Snippet Calls which execute PHP code.
Static Resource	A Resource that exists on the file system on the MODX site such as a pdf file or image.
Symlink	A type of Resource which will effectively place the content of one Resource inside the other
System Setting	A project-wide variable accessible to each Context.
Template Variables	Custom Resource Fields created and defined by Manager users, typically attached to a given Template using Resource Tags.
Transport Package	A packaged collection of Transport Vehicles, which can be created via PackMan or by building a project.
User Setting	A unique user-specific setting able to override similar Context and / or System Setting.

Appendix B
Resource and System Settings

Resource Settings	[[*alias]]	web-site-hosting
	[[*cacheable]]	1
	[[*class_key]]	modDocument
	[[*content]]	** May cause infinite loop use: `resource->getContent()`
	[[*content_dispo]]	0
	[[*context_key]]	web
	[[*content_type]]	1
	[[*contentType]]	text/html
	[[*createdby]]	1
	[[*createdon]]	2011-07-03 08:06:56
	[[*description]]	We offer 8-core Xeon Servers for hosting
	[[*donthit]]	
	[[*editedby]]	1
	[[*editedon]]	2011-07-04 09:28:29
	[[*deleted]]	
	[[*deletedby]]	0
	[[*deletedon]]	0
	[[*hide_children_in_tree]]	0
	[[*hidemenu]]	
	[[*id]]	31

Resource Settings	[[*introtext]]	This could summarize the page
	[[*isfolder]]	
	[[*link_attributes]]	
	[[*longtitle]]	Rock Solid Web Site Hosting
	[[*menuindex]]	6
	[[*menutitle]]	web hosting
	[[*pagetitle]]	Web Site Hosting
	[[*parent]]	0
	[[*privateweb]]	
	[[*privatemgr]]	
	[[*properties]]	
	[[*pub_date]]	0
	[[*published]]	1
	[[*publishedon]]	2011-07-03 08:13:00
	[[*publishedby]]	1
	[[*richtext]]	1
	[[*searchable]]	1
	[[*show_in_tree]]	1
	[[*template]]	1
	[[*type]]	document
	[[*unpub_date]]	0
	[[*uri]]	web-site-hosting.html
	[[*uri_override]]	0

┳ *EXAMPLE VALUES PROVIDED FROM MODX REVOLUTION 2.2.4-PL*

Many of the values demonstrated in this appendix, were intentionally left as close to "default" as possible, and are provided here solely for information.

┳ *MODX REVOLUTION COMMENTS INTRODUCED IN 2.2.0*

Sometimes it would be a great thing to leave comments in our Templates and Chunks without needing to worry about their presence on the front end. We can now do this with:
[[- put some comment text here]]

	[[+modx.user.id]]	0
	[[+modx.user.username]]	(anonymous)
	[[++access_category_enabled]]	1
	[[++access_context_enabled]]	1
	[[++access_policies_version]]	1.0
	[[++access_resource_group_enabled]]	1
	[[++allow_forward_across_contexts]]	**null**
	[[++ allow_manager_login_forgot_password]]	1
	[[++allow_multiple_emails]]	1
	[[++allow_tags_in_post]]	1
	[[++archive_with]]	**null**
	[[++assets_path]]	/home/user/public_html/assets/
	[[++assets_url]]	/assets/
	[[++auto_check_pkg_updates]]	1
	[[++auto_check_pkg_updates_cache_expire]]	15
	[[++auto_menuindex]]	1
	[[++automatic_alias]]	**null**
	[[++base_help_url]]	http://rtfm.modx.com/display/ revolution20/
	[[++base_path]]	/home/user/public_html/
	[[++base_url]]	/
	[[++blocked_minutes]]	60
	[[++cache_action_map]]	1
	[[++cache_context_settings]]	1
System Settings	[[++cache_db]]	**null**
	[[++cache_db_expires]]	**null**
	[[++cache_db_session]]	**null**
	[[++cache_db_session_lifetime]]	**null**
	[[++cache_default]]	1
	[[++cache_disabled]]	**null**
	[[++cache_expires]]	**null**
	[[++cache_format]]	**null**
	[[++cache_handler]]	xPDOFileCache

<table>
<tr><td rowspan="33" style="writing-mode: vertical-lr">System Settings</td><td>[[++ cache_lang_js]]</td><td>1</td></tr>
</table>

	[[++ cache_lang_js]]	1
	[[++cache_key]]	default
	[[++cache_lang_js]]	1
	[[++cache_lexicon_topics]]	1
	[[++cache_noncore_lexicon_topics]]	1
	[[++cache_path]]	/home/user/public_html/core/cache/
	[[++cache_resource]]	1
	[[++cache_resource_expires]]	**null**
	[[++cache_scripts]]	1
	[[++cache_system_settings]]	1
	[[++cache_system_settings_key]]	system_settings
	[[++charset]]	utf8
	[[++clear_cache_refresh_trees]]	**null**
	[[++compress_css]]	1
	[[++compress_js]]	1
	[[++compress_js_max_files]]	10
	[[++ compress_js_groups]]	**null**
	[[++concat_js]]	1
	[[++connectors_path]]	/home/user/public_html/connectors/
	[[++connectors_url]]	/connectors/
	[[++container_suffix]]	/
	[[++context_tree_sort]]	**null**
	[[++context_tree_sortby]]	rank
	[[++context_tree_sortdir]]	ASC
	[[++core_path]]	/home/user/public_html/core/
	[[++cultureKey]]	en
	[[++date_timezone]]	**null**
	[[++debug]]	**null**
	[[++dbtype]]	mysql
	[[++default_context]]	web
	[[++default_duplicate_publish_option]]	preserve
	[[++default_media_source]]	1
	[[++default_per_page]]	20

	[[++default_template]]	1
	[[++default_content_type]]	1
	[[++dsn]]	mysql:host=localhost;dbname=user _revobook;charset=utf8
	[[++editor_css_path]]	**null**
	[[++editor_css_selectors]]	**null**
	[[++emailsender]]	somename@domain.com
	[[++emailsubject]]	Your login details
	[[++enable_dragdrop]]	1
	[[++error_handler_class]]	error.modErrorHandler
	[[++error_page]]	1
	[[++failed_login_attempts]]	5
System Settings	[[++fe_editor_lang]]	en
	[[++feed_modx_news]]	http://feeds.feedburner.com/modx announce
	[[++feed_modx_news_enabled]]	1
	[[++feed_modx_security]]	http://feeds.feedburner.com/ modxsecurity
	[[++feed_modx_security_enabled]]	1
	[[++forgot_login_email]]	Hello , A request for a password reset has been issued for your MODX user. If you sent this, you may follow this link and use this password to login. If you did not send this request, please ignore this email. Activation Link: ?modahsh= Username: Password: After you log into the MODX Manager, you can change your password again, if you wish. Regards, Site Administrator

<table>
<tr><td>[[++form_customization_use_all_groups]]</td><td>**null**</td></tr>
<tr><td>[[++forward_merge_excludes]]</td><td>type,published,class_key,context_key</td></tr>
<tr><td>[[++friendly_alias_lowercase_only]]</td><td>1</td></tr>
<tr><td>[[++friendly_alias_max_length]]</td><td>0</td></tr>
<tr><td>[[++friendly_alias_restrict_chars]]</td><td>pattern</td></tr>
<tr><td>[[++friendly_alias_restrict_chars_pattern]]</td><td>/[\0\x0B\t\n\r\f\a&=+%#<>"~:`@\?\[\]\{\}\/\|\^'\\]/</td></tr>
<tr><td>[[++friendly_alias_strip_element_tags]]</td><td>1</td></tr>
<tr><td>[[++friendly_alias_translit]]</td><td>none</td></tr>
<tr><td>[[++friendly_alias_translit_class]]</td><td>translit.modTransliterate</td></tr>
<tr><td>[[++friendly_alias_translit_class_path]]</td><td>{core_path}components/</td></tr>
<tr><td>[[++friendly_alias_trim_chars]]</td><td>/.-_</td></tr>
<tr><td>[[++friendly_alias_word_delimiter]]</td><td>-</td></tr>
<tr><td>[[++friendly_alias_word_delimiters]]</td><td>-_</td></tr>
<tr><td>[[++friendly_urls]]</td><td>**null**</td></tr>
<tr><td>[[++friendly_urls_strict]]</td><td>**null**</td></tr>
<tr><td>[[++global_duplicate_uri_check]]</td><td>**null**</td></tr>
<tr><td>[[++hidemenu_default]]</td><td>**null**</td></tr>
<tr><td>[[++http_host]]</td><td>www.domain.com</td></tr>
<tr><td>[[++https_port]]</td><td>443</td></tr>
<tr><td>[[++hydrate_adhoc_fields]]</td><td>1</td></tr>
<tr><td>[[++hydrate_fields]]</td><td>1</td></tr>
<tr><td>[[++hydrate_related_objects]]</td><td>1</td></tr>
<tr><td>[[++inline_help]]</td><td>1</td></tr>
<tr><td>[[++link_tag_scheme]]</td><td>-1</td></tr>
<tr><td>[[++locale]]</td><td>**null**</td></tr>
<tr><td>[[++lock_ttl]]</td><td>360</td></tr>
<tr><td>[[++log_level]]</td><td>1</td></tr>
<tr><td>[[++log_target]]</td><td>FILE</td></tr>
<tr><td>[[++mail_charset]]</td><td>UTF-8</td></tr>
<tr><td>[[++mail_encoding]]</td><td>8bit</td></tr>
<tr><td>[[++mail_smtp_auth]]</td><td>**null**</td></tr>
<tr><td>[[++mail_smtp_helo]]</td><td>**null**</td></tr>
</table>

System Settings

[[++mail_smtp_hosts]]	localhost
[[++mail_smtp_keepalive]]	**null**
[[++mail_smtp_pass]]	**null**
[[++mail_smtp_port]]	587
[[++mail_smtp_prefix]]	**null**
[[++mail_smtp_single_to]]	**null**
[[++mail_smtp_timeout]]	10
[[++mail_smtp_user]]	**null**
[[++mail_use_smtp]]	**null**
[[++manager_date_format]]	Y-m-d
[[++manager_direction]]	ltr
[[++manager_favicon_url]]	**null**
[[++manager_html5_cache]]	0
[[++manager_js_cache_file_locking]]	1
[[++manager_js_cache_max_age]]	3600
[[++manager_js_document_root]]	**null**
[[++manager_js_zlib_output_compression]]	0
[[++manager_lang_attribute]]	en
[[++manager_language]]	en
[[++manager_login_url_alternate]]	**null**
[[++manager_path]]	/home/user/public_html/manager/
[[++manager_theme]]	default
[[++manager_time_format]]	g:i a
[[++manager_url]]	/manager/
[[++manager_week_start]]	0
[[++modx_browser_default_sort]]	name
[[++modx_charset]]	UTF-8
[[++password]]	1truth
[[++password_generated_length]]	8
[[++password_min_length]]	8
[[++phpthumb_allow_src_above_docroot]]	**null**
[[++phpthumb_cache_maxage]]	30
[[++phpthumb_cache_maxfiles]]	10000

System Settings

	[[++phpthumb_cache_maxsize]]	100
	[[++phpthumb_cache_source_enabled]]	**null**
	[[++phpthumb_document_root]]	**null**
	[[++phpthumb_error_bgcolor]]	CCCCFF
	[[++phpthumb_error_fontsize]]	1
	[[++phpthumb_error_textcolor]]	FF0000
	[[++phpthumb_far]]	C
	[[++phpthumb_imagemagick_path]]	**null**
	[[++phpthumb_nohotlink_enabled]]	1
	[[++phpthumb_nohotlink_erase_image]]	1
	[[++phpthumb_nohotlink_text_message]]	Off-server thumbnailing is not allowed
	[[++phpthumb_nohotlink_valid_domains]]	{http_host}
	[[++phpthumb_nooffsitelink_enabled]]	**null**
	[[++phpthumb_nooffsitelink_erase_image]]	1
	[[++phpthumb_nooffsitelink_require_refer]]	**null**
	[[++phpthumb_nooffsitelink_text_message]]	Off-server linking is not allowed
	[[++phpthumb_nooffsitelink_valid_domains]]	{http_host}
	[[++phpthumb_nooffsitelink_watermark_src]]	**null**
	[[++phpthumb_zoomcrop]]	**null**
	[[++principal_targets]]	modAccessContext,modAccessResourceGroup,modAccessCategory, sources.modAccessMediaSource
	[[++processors_path]]	/home/user/public_html/core/model/modx/processors/
System Settings	[[++proxy_auth_type]]	BASIC
	[[++proxy_host]]	**null**
	[[++proxy_password]]	**null**
	[[++proxy_port]]	**null**
	[[++proxy_username]]	**null**
	[[++publish_default]]	**null**
	[[++rb_base_dir]]	**null**
	[[++rb_base_url]]	**null**
	[[++request_controller]]	index.php

[[++request_method_strict]]	0
[[++request_param_alias]]	q
[[++request_param_id]]	id
[[++resolve_hostnames]]	0
[[++resource_tree_node_name]]	pagetitle
[[++resource_tree_node_tooltip]]	**null**
[[++richtext_default]]	1
[[++search_default]]	1
[[++server_offset_time]]	0
[[++server_protocol]]	http
[[++session_cookie_domain]]	**null**
[[++session_cookie_lifetime]]	604800
[[++session_cookie_path]]	/
[[++session_cookie_secure]]	**null**
[[++session_gc_maxlifetime]]	**null**
[[++session_handler_class]]	modSessionHandler
[[++session_name]]	**null**
[[++set_header]]	1
[[++settings_distro]]	traditional
[[++settings_version]]	2.2.4-pl
[[++show_tv_categories_heade]]	1
[[++signupemail_message]]	Hello , Here are your login details for the MODX Manager: Username: Password: Once you log into the MODX Manager at , you can change your password. Regards, Site Administrator
[[++site_name]]	MODX Revolution

System Settings

	[[++site_start]]	1
	[[++site_status]]	1
	[[++site_unavailable_message]]	The site is currently unavailable
	[[++site_unavailable_page]]	**null**
	[[++site_url]]	http://shawnwilkerson.com/
	[[++strip_image_paths]]	1
	[[++symlink_merge_fields]]	1
	[[++table_prefix]]	modx_
	[[++topmenu_show_descriptions]]	1
	[[++tree_default_sort]]	menuindex
	[[++tree_root_id]]	**null**
	[[++tvs_below_content]]	0
	[[++udperms_allowroot]]	**null**
	[[++unauthorized_page]]	1
	[[++upload_files]]	txt,html,htm,xml,js,css,zip,gz,rar,z,tgz,tar,htaccess,mp3,mp4,aac,wav,au,wmv,avi,mpg,mpeg,pdf,doc,xls,txt,ppt,pptx,docx,xlsx,jpg,jpeg,png,gif,psd,ico,bmp,odt,ods,odp,odb,odg,odf,docx,pptx,xlsx
	[[++upload_flash]]	swf,fla
	[[++upload_images]]	jpg,jpeg,png,gif,psd,ico,bmp
	[[++upload_maxsize]]	1048576
	[[++upload_media]]	mp3,wav,au,wmv,avi,mpg,mpeg
	[[++url_scheme]]	http://
System Settings	[[++use_alias_path]]	**null**
	[[++use_browser]]	1
	[[++use_editor]]	1
	[[++use_multibyte]]	1
	[[++use_weblink_target]]	**null**
	[[++validate_on_save]]	1
	[[++validator_class]]	validation.modValidator

System Settings	Hello , To activate your new password click the following link: If successful you can use the following password to login: Password: If you did not request this email then please ignore it. Regards, Site Administrator	
	[[++websignupemail_message]]	Hello , Here are your login details for : Username: Password: Once you log into at , you can change your password. Regards, Site Administrator
	[[++welcome_screen]]	**null**
	[[++welcome_screen_url]]	http://misc.modx.com/revolution/welcome.22.html
	[[++which_editor]]	**null**
	[[++which_element_editor]]	**null**
	[[++xhtml_urls]]	1

☞ *TIP: THESE SETTINGS AND THEIR VALUES ARE SUBJECT TO CHANGE*

I attempted to include every System Setting I knew of. Some were intentionally left off, like those for the filemanager, which should give deference to Media Sources.

These settings were valid on July 10, 2012 for MODX Revolution 2.2.4-pl Traditional.

null denotes fields without value or possibly set to zero by default.

Appendix C
Primary Object Cheat Sheets

In this section, I created a few cheat sheets on some of the primary MODX Revolution objects typically utilized or implemented during third-party application development. I hope you find these helpful, as each of them provide a rapid lookup for a specific object, its schematic definition and its direct relationships - typically within a single page pair.

Also, take note of any default values which are supplied in the respective schema, but shown in the Table Fields section of each object. These values do not have to be defined at object instantiation as xPDO will provide the basis of any value required.

This appendix was updated to version 2.2.4-pl of MODX Revolution, which should serve as a solid foundation for future releases - at least for the next few versions. I also included the changes introduced to modResource via the Articles Package, which focus mostly on the Container attribute.

Wherever possible, I attempted to keep all the information for a given object on two facing pages to provide a quick reference for those wishing to implement or extend these MODX Revolution objects.

modChunk

Table Fields

[id] =>
[source] => 0
[property_preprocess] => 0
[name] =>
[description] => Chunk
[editor_type] => 0
[category] => 0
[cache_type] => 0
[snippet] =>
[locked] => 0
[properties] =>
[static] => 0
[static_file] =>

Ancestors

[0] => modChunk
[1] => modElement
[2] => modAccessibleSimpleObject
[3] => modAccessibleObject
[4] => xPDOObject

Aggregate Relations

[CategoryAcls] =>
   [class] => modAccessCategory
   [local] => category
   [foreign] => target
   [owner] => local
   [cardinality] => many

[Source] =>
   [class] => sources.modMediaSource
   [local] => source
   [foreign] => id
   [owner] => foreign
   [cardinality] => one

[Category] =>
   [class] => modCategory
   [key] => id
   [local] => category
   [foreign] => id
   [cardinality] => one
   [owner] => foreign

Composite Relations

[Acls] =>
   [class] => modAccessElement
   [local] => id
   [foreign] => target
   [owner] => local
   [cardinality] => many

[PropertySets] =>
   [class] => modElementPropertySet
   [local] => id
   [foreign] => element
   [owner] => local
   [cardinality] => many
   [criteria] =>
      [foreign] =>
         [element_class] =>modChunk

Schema Definition

[id] =>
  [dbtype] => int
  [precision] => 10
  [attributes] => unsigned
  [phptype] => integer
  [null] =>
  [index] => pk
  [gencrated] => native

[source] =>
  [dbtype] => int
  [attributes] => unsigned
  [phptype] => integer
  [null] ->
  [default] => 0
  [index] => fk

[property_preprocess] =>
  [dbtype] => tinyint
  [precision] => 1
  [attributes] => unsigned
  [phptype] => boolean
  [null] =>
  [default] => 0

[name] =>
  [dbtype] => varchar
  [precision] => 50
  [phptype] => string
  [null] =>
  [default] =>
  [index] => unique

[description] =>
  [dbtype] => varchar
  [precision] => 255
  [phptype] => string
  [null] =>
  [default] => Chunk

[editor_type] =>
  [dbtype] => int
  [precision] => 11
  [phptype] => integer
  [null] ->
  [default] => 0

[category] =>
  [dbtype] => int
  [precision] => 11
  [phptype] => integer
  [null] =>
  [default] => 0
  [index] => fk

[cache_type] =>
  [dbtype] => tinyint
  [precision] => 1
  [phptype] => integer
  [null] =>
  [default] => 0

[snippet] =>
  [dbtype] => mediumtext
  [phptype] => string

[locked] =>
  [dbtype] => tinyint
  [precision] => 1
  [attributes] => unsigned
  [phptype] => boolean
  [null] =>
  [default] => 0
  [index] => index

[properties] =>
  [dbtype] => text
  [phptype] => array
  [null] => 1

[static] =>
  [dbtype] => tinyint
  [precision] => 1
  [attributes] => unsigned
  [phptype] => boolean
  [null] =>
  [dcfault] => 0
  [index] => index

[static_file] =>
  [dbtype] => varchar
  [precision] => 255
  [phptypc] -> string
  [null] =>
  [default] =>

modPlugin

Table Fields
[id] =>
[source] => 0
[property_preprocess] => 0
[name] =>
[description] =>
[editor_type] => 0
[category] => 0
[cache_type] => 0
[plugincode] =>
[locked] => 0
[properties] =>
[disabled] => 0
[moduleguid] =>
[static] => 0
[static_file] =>

Ancestors
[0] => modPlugin
[1] => modScript
[2] => modElement
[3] => modAccessibleSimpleObject
[4] => modAccessibleObject
[5] => xPDOObject

Aggregate Relations
[CategoryAcls] =>
   [class] => modAccessCategory
   [local] => category
   [foreign] => target
   [owner] => local
   [cardinality] => many

[Source] =>
   [class] => sources.modMediaSource
   [local] => source
   [foreign] => id
   [owner] => foreign
   [cardinality] => one

[Category] =>
   [class] => modCategory
   [key] => id
   [local] => category
   [foreign] => id
   [cardinality] => one
   [owner] => foreign

Composite Relations
[Acls] =>
   [class] => modAccessElement
   [local] => id
   [foreign] => target
   [owner] => local
   [cardinality] => many

[PropertySets] =>
   [class] => modElementPropertySet
   [local] => id
   [foreign] => element
   [owner] => local
   [cardinality] => many
   [criteria] =>
      [foreign] =>
         [element_class] =>modPlugin

[PluginEvents] =>
   [class] => modPluginEvent
   [local] => id
   [foreign] => pluginid
   [cardinality] => many
   [owner] => local

Schema Definition

[id] =>
  [dbtype] => int
  [precision] => 10
  [attributes] => unsigned
  [phptype] => integer
  [null] =>
  [index] => pk
  [generated] => native

[source] =>
  [dbtype] => int
  [attributes] => unsigned
  [phptype] => integer
  [null] =>
  [default] => 0
  [index] => fk

[property_preprocess] =>
  [dbtype] => tinyint
  [precision] => 1
  [attributes] => unsigned
  [phptype] => boolean
  [null] =>
  [default] => 0

[name] =>
  [dbtype] => varchar
  [precision] => 50
  [phptype] => string
  [null] =>
  [default] =>
  [index] => unique

[description] =>
  [dbtype] => varchar
  [precision] => 255
  [phptype] => string
  [null] =>
  [default] =>

[editor_type] =>
  [dbtype] => int
  [precision] => 11
  [phptype] => integer
  [null] =>
  [default] => 0

[category] =>
  [dbtype] => int
  [precision] => 11
  [phptype] => integer
  [null] =>
  [default] => 0
  [index] => fk

[cache_type] =>
  [dbtype] => tinyint
  [precision] => 1
  [phptype] => integer
  [null] =>
  [default] => 0

[plugincode] =>
  [dbtype] => mediumtext
  [phptype] => string
  [null] =>
  [default] =>

[locked] =>
  [dbtype] => tinyint
  [precision] => 1
  [attributes] => unsigned
  [phptype] => boolean
  [null] =>
  [default] => 0
  [index] => index

[properties] =>
  [dbtype] => text
  [phptype] => array
  [null] => 1

[disabled] =>
  [dbtype] => tinyint
  [precision] => 1
  [attributes] => unsigned
  [phptype] => boolean
  [null] =>
  [default] => 0
  [index] => index

[moduleguid] =>
  [dbtype] => varchar
  [precision] => 32
  [phptype] => string
  [null] =>
  [default] =>
  [index] => fk

[static] =>
  [dbtype] => tinyint
  [precision] => 1
  [attributes] => unsigned
  [phptype] => boolean
  [null] =>
  [default] => 0
  [index] => index

[static_file] =>
  [dbtype] => varchar
  [precision] => 255
  [phptype] => string
  [null] =>
  [default] =>

modSnippet

Table Fields
[id] =>
[source] => 0
[property_preprocess] => 0
[name] =>
[description] =>
[editor_type] => 0
[category] => 0
[cache_type] => 0
[snippet] =>
[locked] => 0
[properties] =>
[moduleguid] =>
[static] => 0
[static_file] =>

Ancestors
[0] => modSnippet
[1] => modScript
[2] => modElement
[3] => modAccessibleSimpleObject
[4] => modAccessibleObject
[5] => xPDOObject

Aggregate Relations
[CategoryAcls] =>
    [class] => modAccessCategory
    [local] => category
    [foreign] => target
    [owner] => local
    [cardinality] => many

[Source] =>
    [class] => sources.modMediaSource
    [local] => source
    [foreign] => id
    [owner] => foreign
    [cardinality] => one

[Category] =>
    [class] => modCategory
    [key] => id
    [local] => category
    [foreign] => id
    [cardinality] => one
    [owner] => foreign

Composite Relations
[Acls] =>
    [class] => modAccessElement
    [local] => id
    [foreign] => target
    [owner] => local
    [cardinality] => many

[PropertySets] =>
    [class] => modElementPropertySet
    [local] => id
    [foreign] => element
    [owner] => local
    [cardinality] => many
    [criteria] =>
        [foreign] =>
            [element_class] => modSnippet

Schema Definition

[id] =>
   [dbtype] => int
   [precision] => 10
   [attributes] => unsigned
   [phptype] => integer
   [null] =>
   [index] => pk
   [generated] => native

[source] =>
   [dbtype] => int
   [attributes] => unsigned
   [phptype] => integer
   [null] =>
   [default] => 0
   [index] => fk

[property_preprocess] =>
   [dbtype] => tinyint
   [precision] => 1
   [attributes] => unsigned
   [phptype] => boolean
   [null] =>
   [default] => 0

[name] =>
   [dbtype] => varchar
   [precision] => 50
   [phptype] => string
   [null] =>
   [default] =>
   [index] => unique

[description] =>
   [dbtype] => varchar
   [precision] => 255
   [phptype] => string
   [null] =>
   [default] =>

[editor_type] =>
   [dbtype] => int
   [precision] => 11
   [phptype] => integer
   [null] =>
   [default] => 0

[category] =>
   [dbtype] => int
   [precision] => 11
   [phptype] => integer
   [null] =>
   [default] => 0
   [index] => fk

[cache_type] =>
   [dbtype] => tinyint
   [precision] => 1
   [phptype] => integer
   [null] =>
   [default] => 0

[snippet] =>
   [dbtype] => mediumtext
   [phptype] => string

[locked] =>
   [dbtype] => tinyint
   [precision] => 1
   [attributes] => unsigned
   [phptype] => boolean
   [null] =>
   [default] => 0
   [index] => index

[properties] =>
   [dbtype] => text
   [phptype] => array
   [null] => 1

[moduleguid] =>
   [dbtype] => varchar
   [precision] => 32
   [phptype] => string
   [null] =>
   [default] =>
   [index] => fk

[static] =>
   [dbtype] => tinyint
   [precision] => 1
   [attributes] => unsigned
   [phptype] => boolean
   [null] =>
   [default] => 0
   [index] => index

[static_file] =>
   [dbtype] => varchar
   [precision] => 255
   [phptype] => string
   [null] =>
   [default] =>

modUser

Table Fields
[id] =>
[username] =>
[password] =>
[cachepwd] =>
[class_key] => modUser
[active] => 1
[remote_key] =>
[remote_data] =>
[hash_class] => hashing.modPBKDF2
[salt] =>
[primary_group] => 0
[session_stale] =>
[sudo] => 0

Ancestors
[0] => modUser
[1] => modPrincipal
[2] => xPDOSimpleObject
[3] => xPDOObject

Aggregate Relations
[CreatedResources] =>
    [class] => modResource
    [local] => id
    [foreign] => createdby
    [cardinality] => many
    [owner] => local

[EditedResources] =>
    [class] => modResource
    [local] => id
    [foreign] => editedby
    [cardinality] => many
    [owner] => local

[DeletedResources] =>
    [class] => modResource

[local] => id
[foreign] => deletedby
[cardinality] => many
[owner] => local

[PublishedResources] =>
    [class] => modResource
    [local] => id
    [foreign] => publishedby
    [cardinality] => many
    [owner] => local

[SentMessages] =>
    [class] => modUserMessage
    [local] => id
    [foreign] => sender
    [cardinality] => many
    [owner] => local

[ReceivedMessages] =>
    [class] => modUserMessage
    [local] => id
    [foreign] => recipient
    [cardinality] => many
    [owner] => local

[PrimaryGroup] =>
    [class] => modUserGroup
    [local] => primary_group
    [foreign] => id
    [cardinality] => one
    [owner] => foreign

Composite Relations
[Acls] =>
    [class] => modAccess
    [local] => id
    [foreign] => principal

[cardinality] => many
[owner] => local

[Profile] =>
   [class] => modUserProfile
   [local] => id
   [foreign] => internalKey
   [cardinality] => one
   [owner] => local

[UserSettings] =>
   [class] => modUserSetting
   [local] => id
   [foreign] => user
   [cardinality] => many
   [owner] => local

[UserGroupMembers] =>
   [class] =>
      modUserGroupMember
   [local] => id
   [foreign] => member
   [cardinality] => many
   [owner] => local

Schema Definition

[id] =>
   [dbtype] => INTEGER
   [phptype] => integer
   [null] =>
   [index] => pk
   [generated] => native
   [attributes] => unsigned

[username] =>
   [dbtype] => varchar
   [precision] => 100
   [phptype] => string
   [null] =>

[default] =>
[index] => unique

[password] =>
   [dbtype] => varchar
   [precision] => 100
   [phptype] => string
   [null] =>
   [default] =>

[cachepwd] =>
   [dbtype] => varchar
   [precision] => 100
   [phptype] => string
   [null] =>
   [default] =>

[class_key] =>
   [dbtype] => varchar
   [precision] => 100
   [phptype] => string
   [null] =>
   [default] => modUser
   [index] => index

[active] =>
   [dbtype] => tinyint
   [precision] => 1
   [phptype] => boolean
   [attributes] => unsigned
   [null] =>
   [default] => 1

[remote_key] =>
   [dbtype] => varchar
   [precision] => 255
   [phptype] => string
   [null] => 1
   [index] => index

[remote_data] =>
   [dbtype] => text
   [phptype] => json
   [null] => 1

[hash_class] =>
   [dbtype] => varchar
   [precision] => 100
   [phptype] => string
   [null] =>
   [default] =>
      hashing.modPBKDF2

[salt] =>
   [dbtype] => varchar
   [precision] => 100
   [phptype] => string
   [null] =>
   [default] =>

[primary_group] =>
   [dbtype] => int
   [precision] => 10
   [phptype] => integer
   [attributes] => unsigned
   [null] =>
   [default] => 0
   [index] => index

[session_stale] =>
   [dbtype] => text
   [phptype] => array
   [null] => 1

[sudo] =>
   [dbtype] => tinyint
   [precision] => 1
   [phptype] => boolean
   [attributes] => unsigned
   [null] =>
   [default] => 0

modResource

Table Fields

[id] =>
[type] => document
[contentType] => text/html
[pagetitle] =>
[longtitle] =>
[description] =>
[alias] =>
[link_attributes] =>
[published] => 0
[pub_date] => 0
[unpub_date] => 0
[parent] => 0
[isfolder] => 0
[introtext] =>
[content] =>
[richtext] => 1
[template] => 0
[menuindex] => 0
[searchable] => 1
[cacheable] => 1
[createdby] => 0
[createdon] => 0
[editedby] => 0
[editedon] => 0
[deleted] => 0
[deletedon] => 0
[deletedby] => 0
[publishedon] => 0
[publishedby] => 0
[menutitle] =>
[donthit] => 0
[privateweb] => 0
[privatemgr] => 0
[content_dispo] => 0
[hidemenu] => 0
[class_key] => modDocument
[context_key] => web

[content_type] => 1
[uri] =>
[uri_override] => 0
[hide_children_in_tree] => 0
[show_in_tree] => 1
[properties] =>

Ancestors

[0] => modResource
[1] => modAccessibleSimpleObject
[2] => modAccessibleObject
[3] => xPDOObject

Composite Relations

[TemplateVarResources] =>
   [class] => modTemplateVarResource
   [local] => id
   [foreign] => contentid
   [cardinality] => many
   [owner] => local

[ResourceGroupResources] =>
   [class] => modResourceGroupResource
   [local] => id
   [foreign] => document
   [cardinality] => many
   [owner] => local

[Acls] =>
   [class] => modAccessResource
   [local] => id
   [foreign] => target
   [owner] => local
   [cardinality] => many

[ContextResources] =>
  [class] => modContextResource
  [local] => id
  [foreign] => resource
  [cardinality] => many
  [owner] => local

[Articles] (via Articles Package) =>
  [class] => Article
  [local] => id
  [foreign] => parent
  [cardinality] => many
  [owner] => local

Aggregate Relations

[Parent] =>
  [class] => modResource
  [local] => parent
  [foreign] => id
  [cardinality] => one
  [owner] => foreign

[Children] =>
  [class] => modResource
  [local] => id
  [foreign] => parent
  [cardinality] => many
  [owner] => local

[CreatedBy] =>
  [class] => modUser
  [local] => createdby
  [foreign] => id
  [cardinality] => one
  [owner] => foreign

[EditedBy] =>
  [class] => modUser
  [local] => editedby

  [foreign] => id
  [cardinality] => one
  [owner] => foreign

[DeletedBy] =>
  [class] => modUser
  [local] => deletedby
  [foreign] => id
  [cardinality] => one
  [owner] => foreign

[PublishedBy] =>
  [class] => modUser
  [local] => publishedby
  [foreign] => id
  [cardinality] => one
  [owner] => foreign

[Template] =>
  [class] => modTemplate
  [local] => template
  [foreign] => id
  [cardinality] => one
  [owner] => foreign

[TemplateVars] =>
  [class] => modTemplateVar
  [local] => id:template
  [foreign] => contentid:templateid
  [cardinality] => many
  [owner] => local

[TemplateVarTemplates] =>
  [class] => modTemplateVarTemplate
  [local] => template
  [foreign] => templateid
  [cardinality] => many
  [owner] => local

```
[ContentType] =>
    [class] => modContentType
    [local] => content_type
    [foreign] => id
    [owner] => foreign
    [cardinality] => one


[Context] =>
    [class] => modContext
    [local] => context_key
    [foreign] => key
    [owner] => foreign
    [cardinality] => one


[Container] (via Articles Package) =>
    [class] => ArticlesContainer
    [local] => parent
    [foreign] => id
    [cardinality] => one
    [owner] => foreign
```

Schema Definition

```
[id] =>
    [dbtype] => int
    [precision] => 10
    [attributes] => unsigned
    [phptype] => integer
    [null] =>
    [index] => pk
    [generated] => native


[type] =>
    [dbtype] => varchar
    [precision] => 20
    [phptype] => string
    [null] =>
    [default] => document


[contentType] =>
```

```
    [dbtype] => varchar
    [precision] => 50
    [phptype] => string
    [null] =>
    [default] => text/html


[pagetitle] =>
    [dbtype] => varchar
    [precision] => 255
    [phptype] => string
    [null] =>
    [default] =>
    [index] => fulltext
    [indexgrp] => content_ft_idx


[longtitle] =>
    [dbtype] => varchar
    [precision] => 255
    [phptype] => string
    [null] =>
    [default] =>
    [index] => fulltext
    [indexgrp] => content_ft_idx


[description] =>
    [dbtype] => varchar
    [precision] => 255
    [phptype] => string
    [null] =>
    [default] =>
    [index] => fulltext
    [indexgrp] => content_ft_idx


[alias] =>
    [dbtype] => varchar
    [precision] => 255
    [phptype] => string
    [null] => 1
    [default] =>
    [index] => index
```

[link_attributes] =>
   [dbtype] => varchar
   [precision] => 255
   [phptype] => string
   [null] =>
   [default] =>

[published] =>
   [dbtype] => tinyint
   [precision] => 1
   [attributes] => unsigned
   [phptype] => boolean
   [null] =>
   [default] => 0
   [index] => index

[pub_date] =>
   [dbtype] => int
   [precision] => 20
   [phptype] => timestamp
   [null] =>
   [default] => 0
   [index] => index

[unpub_date] =>
   [dbtype] => int
   [precision] => 20
   [phptype] => timestamp
   [null] =>
   [default] => 0
   [index] => index

[parent] =>
   [dbtype] => int
   [precision] => 10
   [phptype] => integer
   [null] =>
   [default] => 0
   [index] => index

[isfolder] =>
   [dbtype] => tinyint
   [precision] => 1
   [attributes] => unsigned
   [phptype] => boolean
   [null] =>
   [default] => 0
   [index] => index

[introtext] =>
   [dbtype] => text
   [phptype] => string
   [index] => fulltext
   [indexgrp] => content_ft_idx

[content] =>
   [dbtype] => mediumtext
   [phptype] => string
   [index] => fulltext
   [indexgrp] => content_ft_idx

[richtext] =>
   [dbtype] => tinyint
   [precision] => 1
   [attributes] => unsigned
   [phptype] => boolean
   [null] =>
   [default] => 1

[template] =>
   [dbtype] => int
   [precision] => 10
   [phptype] => integer
   [null] =>
   [default] => 0
   [index] => index

```
[menuindex] =>
    [dbtype] => int
    [precision] => 10
    [phptype] => integer
    [null] =>
    [default] => 0
    [index] => index

[searchable] =>
    [dbtype] => tinyint
    [precision] => 1
    [attributes] => unsigned
    [phptype] => boolean
    [null] =>
    [default] => 1
    [index] => index

[cacheable] =>
    [dbtype] => tinyint
    [precision] => 1
    [attributes] => unsigned
    [phptype] => boolean
    [null] =>
    [default] => 1
    [index] => index

[createdby] =>
    [dbtype] => int
    [precision] => 10
    [phptype] => integer
    [null] =>
    [default] => 0

[createdon] =>
    [dbtype] => int
    [precision] => 20
    [phptype] => timestamp
    [null] =>
    [default] => 0

[editedby] =>
    [dbtype] => int
    [precision] => 10
    [phptype] => integer
    [null] =>
    [default] => 0

[editedon] =>
    [dbtype] => int
    [precision] => 20
    [phptype] => timestamp
    [null] =>
    [default] => 0

[deleted] =>
    [dbtype] => tinyint
    [precision] => 1
    [attributes] => unsigned
    [phptype] => boolean
    [null] =>
    [default] => 0

[deletedon] =>
    [dbtype] => int
    [precision] => 20
    [phptype] => timestamp
    [null] =>
    [default] => 0

[deletedby] =>
    [dbtype] => int
    [precision] => 10
    [phptype] => integer
    [null] =>
    [default] => 0
```

[publishedon] =>
  [dbtype] => int
  [precision] => 20
  [phptype] => timestamp
  [null] =>
  [default] => 0

[publishedby] =>
  [dbtype] => int
  [precision] => 10
  [phptype] => integer
  [null] =>
  [default] => 0

[menutitle] =>
  [dbtype] => varchar
  [precision] => 255
  [phptype] => string
  [null] =>
  [default] =>

[donthit] =>
  [dbtype] => tinyint
  [precision] => 1
  [attributes] => unsigned
  [phptype] => boolean
  [null] =>
  [default] => 0

[privateweb] =>
  [dbtype] => tinyint
  [precision] => 1
  [attributes] => unsigned
  [phptype] => boolean
  [null] =>
  [default] => 0

[privatemgr] =>
  [dbtype] => tinyint
  [precision] => 1
  [attributes] => unsigned
  [phptype] => boolean
  [null] =>
  [default] => 0

[content_dispo] =>
  [dbtype] => tinyint
  [precision] => 1
  [phptype] => integer
  [null] =>
  [default] => 0

[hidemenu] =>
  [dbtype] => tinyint
  [precision] => 1
  [attributes] => unsigned
  [phptype] => boolean
  [null] =>
  [default] => 0
  [index] => index

[class_key] =>
  [dbtype] => varchar
  [precision] => 100
  [phptype] => string
  [null] =>
  [default] => modDocument
  [index] => index

[context_key] =>
  [dbtype] => varchar
  [precision] => 100
  [phptype] => string
  [null] =>
  [default] => web
  [index] => index

[content_type] =>
  [dbtype] => int
  [precision] => 11
  [attributes] => unsigned
  [phptype] => integer
  [null] =>
  [default] => 1

[uri] =>
  [dbtype] => text
  [phptype] => string
  [null] => 1
  [index] => index

[uri_override] =>
  [dbtype] => tinyint
  [precision] => 1
  [phptype] => integer
  [null] =>
  [default] => 0
  [index] => index

[hide_children_in_tree] =>
  [dbtype] => tinyint
  [precision] => 1
  [phptype] => integer
  [null] =>
  [default] => 0
  [index] => index

[show_in_tree] =>
  [dbtype] => tinyint
  [precision] => 1
  [phptype] => integer
  [null] =>
  [default] => 1
  [index] => index

[properties] =>
  [dbtype] => mediumtext
  [phptype] => json
  [null] => 1

Note: For newer releases of MODX Revolution, please visit http://www.shawnwilkerson.com **to view changes to these and other MODX Revolution objects.**

Hint: click on the "cheatsheet" tag in the MODX Revolution and MODX3 folders, as they are made available.

Appendix D
The Document Parser
And Cache Mechanism

I have seen plenty of theories on the web on how the MODX Revolution document parser performs its tasks. After taking an hour reading over the associated classes in MODX Revolution version 2.2.4pl, I believe this description to be fairly accurate to the core code. When in doubt, it is always best to look to the code, this content is subject to change.

Understanding the "flow" of the Parser can prove invaluable on many levels, especially a reduction in hours spent troubleshooting mysterious implementation quirks, which appear to have no bearing in reality. In other words: the code is "flawless" and MODX Revolution appears to completely ignore the expectations placed on it.

Hundreds of times over the years, many of us have simply needed to tell people to "clear the cache" to get something working on the project. I began to wonder how many of us actually understood why that appeared to work. Before beginning that next big web production, and moments before we place the **Element** tag in the page with the hope of getting a **Snippet**, **Chunk**, **Template Variable**, etcetera working the way we want it to, we should understand the MODX Revolution environment we are working in - especially the parser.

To begin, let us take a brief look at the influence of cache of the Parser. If an **Element** is set to be cached, the Document Parser will first attempt to load the content from the project's cache - if it finds non-expired Element information. Otherwise, the cache simply returns null and the Element tag will be processed directly from its source and then added to the cache at that time.

The following pages should break this into more discernible components and steps.

Simplified Parser Sequence of Default Operation

If we understand the sequence of events, it may help us understand how to avoid **Resource** errors:

1. Site visitor requests a Resource (page)
2. Start up
3. Retrieve and process the Resource Template
4. Retrieve and process the Resource Content
5. MODX OnParseDocument Event is invoked
6. An array of Element Tags is created
7. Works through the Resource, beginning with the Template and then its Elements
8. Every Element Type has its own process(), which in turn requests the parser to processElementTags on its own content
9. Excluding Placeholders, each Element is requested from the cache
10. If a cacheable Element is not found in the cache, the raw source is retrieved and the Element content is flagged as ready for caching
11. Each nested layer has the cached content parsed
12. This process repeats through each nested layer upwards towards the parent Element
13. All cached content is merged into the completed Resource
14. Process body scripts
15. Process scripts placed in page head
16. Uncached items appear to be Parsed just before Resource is returned
17. Remaining tags which could not be parsed are removed from content
18. Page is sent to visitors browser

Becoming familiar with these stages should greatly help any Manager user tasked with combining various Elements into a single Resource. More often than not, when a user is asking for help when something isn't working quite the way they suppose it should, they are told to make sure to check the order each item is placed in the Content. This is only "mostly" correct. They should also check the placement of cached versus uncached items. If a nested uncached item is required to finish before a specific cached item, things can go awry.

When a Resource is being looked at in its entirety, Manager users should keep in mind **all of the cached content will be parsed from each nested layer first**. For example, if a Manager user implements an uncached Snippet to build an xPDO model and inadvertently calls cached Snippet calls afterwards pulling from objects in the model - only the build script will successfully complete. The cached Snippet calls will process first and be referencing non existent Objects.

Straight From The Core - with additional comments added

Listing Appendix D01: Excerpt from modResponse from MODX Revolution 2.2.4

```
/* Handles the cacheable content in the Resource */
$this->modx->resource->_output= $this->modx->resource->process();


/* Additional JavaScript is added to the page */
$this->modx->resource->_jscripts= $this->modx->jscripts;
$this->modx->resource->_sjscripts= $this->modx->sjscripts;


/* Registered CSS and JavaScript is injected in the page */
$this->modx->resource->_loadedjscripts= $this->modx->loadedjscripts;


/* collect any uncached element tags in the content and process them
 */
$this->modx->getParser();
$maxIterations = intval($this->modx->getOption('parser_max_
                        iterations', $options, 10));

/* Process uncached Elements - notice you can make your own tags */
$this->modx->parser->processElementTags('', $this->modx->resource->_
        output, true, false, '[[', ']]', array(), $maxIterations);

/* Remove any remaining Tags after one last attempt to process */
$this->modx->parser->processElementTags('', $this->modx->resource->_
        output, true, true, '[[', ']]', array(), $maxIterations);
```

This excerpt of code taken from modResponse prepares the "final response" from the parser. The Resource is processed, and subsequently each of its cached Elements are processed before the JavaScript and CSS is added to the page. From then on, the parser is placed in "working with uncached items mode", essentially dealing with raw output of each remaining item, with the final pass removing any tags it is not able to process, as the tags may not have existing Elements.

The salient point to keep in mind, is that **the Resource, and each its subsequent Elements each have a process() function which can call the parser.** Essentially, the Resource, informs the Parser to process the Template, and the Template hands off its Elements to the Parser, and each Element in turn hands off its "content" to the Parser, beginning with nested Elements.

Cache Mechanism

MODX Revolution provides a highly functional caching mechanism, which can be implemented from the Resource down to the level of an individual Element. Most of this caching is automatic and simply works without any additional interaction required. This can cause quite a bit of contention when dynamic content is inadvertently cached.

Static content seldom changes and, as such, should be cached. Examples of this might include global navigation, site footers, and blocks of JavaScript code. These items should probably be cached as they are typically "written in stone" once sites reach a live status. If any of these items are edited in the Manager, they are usually cleared from the cache. A new copy is written back to the cache, once the specific item is requested by a site visitor.

Dynamic content may change often an should not be cached. Examples of this might include counters, some implementations of Google Analytics, IP address trackers, news feeds, weather feeds, user-specific content, etc. Arguably some of these could be moderately cached, but the vast majority of these should be updated on every page load. Forgetting to turn the cache off in these instances can produce very undesirable consequences. Quite a few complaints have been registered via the various MODX support venues which ended in a caching issue. To turn caching off within any MODX Revolution Element, simply include an exclamation point ("!") before its name: `[[!$notCachedChunk]]`. As can be imagined, this step can be easily overlooked.

MODX Revolution has a wonderful caching mechanism, designed to expedite the merging of the various pieces of content into the Resource currently being requested by the site visitors. For static content this can be a huge benefit in reducing the server load and page delivery time, while the individual **Elements** are processed and placed within each Resource.

Many web sites contain content which rarely changes and as such, it makes little sense to have it recreated upon every page request. Items which display the current date, global navigation, and the page footer probably change very little, and even more importantly -- many of these items appear on multiple pages which could benefit from the cache.

With approximately two dozen references to "cache" within the system settings, the significance of caching becomes very apparent - where even result sets from database queries can be cached. For many sites under initial development, it may prove beneficial to begin with each Element being uncached. At a later time, project leaders should reevaluate the caching choice on each Element and by a per-use basis.

This is where the MODX Revolution cache comes in, as all Elements and Resources should automatically become cached upon their first request, due to the **cache_default** system setting. For those who do not want this behavior, this setting can be overridden by setting **cache_disabled** to Yes in the System Settings Menu in the Manager, but this is highly discouraged due to the possible impact on the server and the over all responsiveness of the web site in general.

Cached Versus Uncached Snippet Calls

It has been my experience, very few Snippets should actually be called in such a way as to where their output is actually cached. An example of a cached Snippet call would look something like [[snippetCall?var=`parameter`]]. But how often will a PHP coded Snippet provide unchanging content? Due to the dynamic nature of data and database tables, I would typically alter the initial Snippet call to: [[!snippetCall?var=`parameter`]]. The simple addition of an exclamation point before the name of the Snippet is all that is needed to bypass the MODX cache when this particular instance is parsed and merged into the current page.

If it feels as if I am pushing against the notion of caching Snippets and their subsequent output, then the message is coming across as intended. One of the most avoidable issues associated with MODX Revolution is simply those dealing with the misuse of the cache, or simply not understanding how the cache affects the site content.

Things can become very interesting, when a single Element can be called multiple times within a given resource, each with their own cache configurations, parameters, and implementation. In Wayfinder discussions in this book, I had as many as three calls of the Snippet in a given page. The Global navigation menu rarely changes, so I chose to cache that particular Snippet call. The same holds true for the top level category pages, those are also cached. Once the project is at a level to where the content changes more readily, I may began implementing uncached Wayfinder calls to ensure updates to the page are being made as needed.

Suffice it to say, many of our Snippet calls begin uncached until we understand exactly how the output is being effected by the MODX Cache and Parser. The question might be asked, "Why does it matter?" That depends. On many web sites, simply call all of the Snippets uncached and keep moving. On larger sites, where hardware resource utilization is a factor, correctly implementing the cache can benefit the entire site - with exponential returns.

Placeholder Considerations

For some reason, there are those who seem to have issues with Placeholders, and not because they are overly difficult to use. These problems can arise, when the syntax used in the Placeholder name does not match what the Snippet is targeting. Using cut and paste on those names can work wonders in this area, but don't forget about any prefixes being declared in the Snippet. Another culprit may very well take the crown: simply being unaware of how the MODX Revolution Document Parser operates.

Pay close attention to the placement of the Snippet serving the output and the Placeholders which will eventually display that output. If the Parser reaches the Placeholder before it has a chance to process the Snippet, it will have no way of going backwards in the page to insert the Snippet output into the Placeholder - not to mention it may have already been replaced with nothing.

In some situations we have found it beneficial to place a Snippet at the beginning of a Template, or inside of a Chunk which is going to be parsed before the actual content which is entered into the Resource in the Manager. In other words, we remove the ability for our Manager Users to interact with the placement of the Snippet, while allowing them to utilize the associated Placeholders any way they choose, as the output will be ready for them.

Common Errors to Avoid

Understanding the actual order of events, should help developers and designers avoid unpleasant bug hunts which can be solved with simple Element call corrections. This troubleshooting list should help minimize common errors:

Errors	Solution
Placeholders remain empty	◆ Place all Snippet calls before the Placeholders they provide content for ◆ Double check the syntax of the Placeholder name
Content never changes	◆ Initially, call the Placeholders and the Snippets uncached by inserting an exclamation point after the initial brackets: [[! instead of [[. I do not believe Placeholders are "cacheable", but they can get processed before the Snippet.
Snippet does not return anything	◆ Make sure the Snippet ends with a return statement ◆ Validate the output to ensure it is not a JSON or PHP array. Additional steps may be necessary in those situations
Still nothing happens	◆ Check the case of the name and parameters-- [[Snippet]] does not necessarily equal [[snippet]] ◆ Concerning run time parameters, developers may want to use strtolower on all incoming parameters to reduce the possibility for this issue
I still need help	◆ Take a break and get a fresh look at it ◆ Get another set of eyes involved ◆ Try using sample Snippet calls provided by the documentation ◆ Try adding only one Parameter at a time ◆ Use pastie.org or pastebin.com to paste the code and ask in #MODX IRC channel or forums

Appendix E
Internet Caching Technologies

Should we cache or not? The issue of caching can become quite complex with regards to MODX Revolution Elements. This holds even more significance when considering Snippets, simply due to the vast number of caching mechanisms available for PHP, combined with various server technologies.

When we consider that many of these caching mechanisms have little or nothing to do with the MODX Revolution cache, it is not very difficult to fathom the frustration, confusion, and precious time lost on project, when an unknown cache is transparently at work behind a web project or between the visitor and the site.

Understanding how some of these caching technologies operate may help alleviate some of issues associated with caching.

JavaScript and CSS Caching

On many of our sites we utilize minify (`http://code.google.com/p/minify/`) to compress and consolidate our Cascading Style Sheets and JavaScript code. This is an amazing application which we strongly encourage every site to take advantage of. The only issue with this product, is it does its job very well -- sometimes too well.

Fortunately, the included documentation references methods to break or reset minify's cache on a local site. By following the author's suggestions when making updates to the site's CSS and JavaScript, further frustration and confusion can be avoided. We also suggest a simple removal of all the files in the cache directory when updates are being made to related content within the project. See configuration settings for the location of the file, if minify has been implemented on a site.

HTTP Protocol Caching

One of the simplest methods used for quite a while to cache web content, is to simply manipulate the headers of our web page. There are quite a few methods to accomplish this and can even be forced with the web server software itself, though this is not a typical configuration. To illustrate how these headers may be manipulated, we will first see how to make a page never cached:

Listing Appendix E01: Forcing a page to never be cached using HTTP meta tags

- -

```
<meta http-equiv="expires" content="Sat, 01 Jan 1970 05:00:00 GMT"/>
<meta http-equiv="pragma" content="no-cache" />
```

- -

This simply informs the web browser that the current page is always going to be out of date. If we were to tell MODX Revolution to cache our content, but the meta tags tell the browser not to, we would have to assume the server content will remain cached, but the web browser will not be caching it. This could be seen as defeating part of the benefits of caching because new copies of the page would still be requested upon every landing. If the date was in the future, browsers could be manipulated into thinking they have the current content even if the web site is showing new information. We could not guarantee the content is actually being received by clients, which could lead to some intense phone conversations with clients. We would probably want to Google for an online tool to check our http headers, especially if we are using a new hosting company or a new server -- just to be on the safe side. Some hosting companies adjust HTTP headers on the fly through the server software, which can also increase our consternation.

Assuming our headers are clear of caching manipulations, the next place we may want to look is directly under our nose. Many of the individuals reading this chapter have backgrounds in PHP, but sometimes the easiest solution is the one directly in front of us. PHP provides very convenient and simple methods to manipulate the HTTP headers of any given page or an entire project, very easily. Sometimes, we may forget how simple PHP can make administrative functions:

Listing Appendix E02: Forcing a page to never be cached using PHP

- -

```
<?php
 header('Expires: Sat, 01 Jan 1970 05:00:00 GMT');
 header('Cache-Control: no-store, no-cache, must-revalidate');
 header('Cache-Control: post-check=0, pre-check=0', FALSE);
 header('Pragma: no-cache');
```

- -

Granted, your code may not even touch the headers, but what about the PHP class or the other Snippets and PHP code which has been included into the page. Additionally, did someone on the web project decide they needed to edit the main MODX Revolution index.php file to force the headers they needed? It should also be noted JavaScript, ActionScript and plenty of other technologies also provide methodology to manipulate HTTP headers.

We would suggest that a senior developer create Snippets and other tests to make sure the MODX Revolution caching mechanism is not being directly interfered with by Elements being placed into the project. It may also prove beneficial to have someone, or a group of senior developers go through and verify each implementation on the project, including the Templates.

PHP Caching

Outside of the MODX Revolution installation, there can be any number of other caching mechanisms involved with content delivery from the site. It would probably be a good idea to visit the System Info link locating in the Reports Menu of the Manager and look for any signs of caching in the phpinfo() link provided. In some situations multiple caching mechanisms will be present in the server configurations. Typically, Zend Optimizer is part of default PHP install.

Additional PHP caching mechanisms have been made available, including eAccelerator, PHP accelerator, Turck MMCache, and others. Many of these can be configured in such a way as to work nicely with MODX Revolution, but they can also become quite a nuisance. If your cached content is not functioning the way you feel it should be, the server configurations may need to be checked. The easiest method to find a server cache culprit is to

1. Turn all of the caching software off, usually in the php.ini file
2. Retest content and check the results
3. If results have not changed fix the Snippet, or Snippet call
4. If desired results have been obtained, turn one caching software on at a time
5. Verify results after each startup, until the offending application is discovered
6. Adjust settings in the offending application or leave it disabled

Internet Proxies

It took us quite a few months, multiple e-mails and pulling slick little tricks out of thin air to finally unmask this type of culprit. If the following story seems to relate to the issues being experienced, it may prove beneficial to trace packets from the client to the server and to duplicate that operation in the reverse direction.

For over five years we worked with the largest manufacturer of (notebook) Ring Metals in the world, providing them a web site which dominated Google and all other search engines. Our contact in the United States would send us updates, press releases, and product information which we would immediately begin work on. Once we were finished we would send a link back for his approval.

There was a small problem with this sequence of events: our contact utilized AOL for their internet provider, who in turn used proxies to provide content to their customers. We had to create methods for this client to see what the rest of the world was able to see immediately outside of AOL. Even simple changes to Adobe Flash content would take days or even weeks to show natively to the client.

The problem with Internet proxy servers, is web project administrators seldom have the ability to adjust their settings or interact with the server administrators. Occasionally, a very large ISP will have a method set in place which will allow communication with the department operating the proxy and a request can be submitted to remove a site from their proxy.

Organizations using Squid or another proxy server in house, may very well need to create an ACL which will cause the proxy to not cache a specific site. As far as Squid goes this is a very straightforward process. Simply edit the squid.conf file and add a line similar to the following:

Listing Appendix E03: removing a site from a Squid Proxie Server

----

```
acl Local dst 10.0.1.0/24
no_cache deny Local
```

Closing Thoughts on Internet Caching Technologies

We have covered a few of the prevailing technologies and methods utilized to cache web content. Hopefully, I have provided enough insight to get the creative juices heading in the correct directions if cache troubleshooting needs to pursued.

Fortunately, most web hosting companies and server administrators understand how to implement these technologies mutually beneficial to the hosting company and their clients. Many web hosts look for simple unobtrusive methods to lower server usage and to free up the very finite amount of bandwidth available to their networks. Clients on the other hand, typically don't begin to think about caching until they get their first bill for excessive bandwidth usage.

As a project leader, or web site owner we should postulate a guess on the number of people which will potentially visit a site based on the relevance, content, and audience. Once we have guessed a number of visits, multiply that number by 10 or even 100 and attempt to view the site in the light of those numbers. This may very well cause a site to be better streamlined during its initial development stages. At the very least, this should help pinpoint bottlenecks and heavy pages, which may be implemented using a "cleaner" method.

Caching is a very low cost and effective technology when used correctly. It can also become a nightmare if developers blindly push through a project without the first thought as to double check the environment in which they are building.

The significance of these areas of caching in regards to MODX Revolution becomes very apparent once we understand that its caching operates before many of these other technologies. Does it matter to us, if we are seeing the results of MODX Revolution's cache, or the result of multiple optimizers which in-turn have fed MODX Revolution's cache? Or are we looking at the result of MODX Revolution's cache after it has been cached externally using another technology?

When all else fails, strip the page content down to only the Snippet in question, placed in a predominately empty Template, with only the [[*content]] or [[*#content]] tag. All other content should be removed. Many developers find this combined with Unit Testing to be the most effective testing mechanism.

Additionally, there is always the option of placing our content onto another server or web site to see if we can replicate the issue. On shared hosting servers, the same configuration can be used as the basis for each site, while control panels and accounts may individually allow each site to override and change the server wide settings. It has been our experience the people setting up web servers typically know what they are doing. Change only what is needed and leave the rest alone. When in doubt, try posting a request in the MODX forums or create a trouble ticket with the web host.

Hopefully, we have enough information to move forward into actually using our own Snippets. Though many of the issues mention in this section have been known to create issues in certain configurations, more often than not we can simply use the caching software with very little thought or adjustments. Every site is different, so your mileage may very well be different.

Appendix F:
MODX Revolution "Rules"

#1: Focus on utilizing and maximizing your strengths.
#2: Add all you want, but keep only what you need.
#3: Choose names indicating function and purpose.
#4: All Element parameters require the use of the backtick `.
#5: Do not over think the task. Take the simplest route.
#6: Only code when and what you have to.
#7: Use the simplest Element output for the greatest flexibility.
#8: Continually build your tool-set and use it generously.
#9: A web project only has one purpose: the visitor.
#10: Future-proof web projects as much as possible.
#11: Web browsers only see the results of MODX Elements.
#12: Presentation should be clean, simple, and intuitive.
#13: Only duplicates of the MODX Policies should be edited.
#14: Site Administrators have to be manually added to groups.
#15: Contexts focus on content - users are secondary.
#16: Be very careful of who has access to the project.
#17: The single best way to learn xPDO is to simply use it.
#18: Target the largest possible audience with your application.
#19: Anything that matters has a cost - invest wisely.

Index Of Code Listings

Dynamic JavaScript, CSS, and jQuery Essentials   268

MODX Revolution API Concepts   380

Note: All chapters are intentionally listed whether or not they contain code listings.

Index

X

Made in the USA
San Bernardino, CA
11 September 2013